WHITEHALL HISTORIES: NAVAL STAFF HISTORIES
Series Editor: Capt. Christopher Page
ISSN: 1471-0757

THE ROYAL NAVY AND THE MEDITERRANEAN
VOLUME I: September 1939–October 1940

NAVAL STAFF HISTORIES
Series Editor: Capt. Christopher Page
ISSN: 1471-0757

Naval Staff Histories were produced after the Second World War in order to provide as full an account of the various actions and operations as was possible at the time. In some cases the Histories were based on earlier Battle Summaries written much sooner after the event, and designed to provide more immediate assessments. The target audience for these Naval Staff Histories was largely serving officers; some of the volumes were originally classified, not to restrict their distribution but to allow the writers to be as candid as possible. These histories have been in the Public Record Office for some time, and some have already been published.

The Evacuation from Dunkirk: Operation 'Dynamo', 26 May–4 June 1940
With a preface by W. J. R. Gardner

Naval Operations of the Campaign in Norway, April–June 1940
With a preface by David Brown

The Royal Navy and the Mediterranean, Volume I: September 1939–October 1940
With an introduction by David Brown

The Royal Navy and the Mediterranean, Volume II: November 1940–December 1941
With an introduction by David Brown

German Capital Ships and Raiders in World War II:
Vol. I: From Graf Spee to Bismarck, 1939–1941
Vol. II: From Scharnhorst to Tirpitz, 1942–1944
With an introduction by Eric Grove

The Royal Navy and the Palestine Patrol
With a preface by Ninian Stewart

THE ROYAL NAVY AND THE MEDITERRANEAN

VOLUME I: September 1939–October 1940

With an Introduction by
DAVID BROWN
Former Head of the Naval Historical Branch, Ministry of Defence

WHITEHALL HISTORY PUBLISHING
in association with
FRANK CASS
LONDON • PORTLAND, OR

First published in 2002 in Great Britain by
FRANK CASS PUBLISHERS
Crown House, 47 Chase Side, Southgate
London N14 5BP

and in the United States of America by
FRANK CASS PUBLISHERS
c/o ISBS, 5824 N.E. Hassalo Street
Portland, Oregon, 97213-3644

Website: www.frankcass.com

© Crown Copyright 2002

British Library Cataloguing in Publication Data

The Royal Navy and the Mediterranean. – New ed.
  Vol. 1: September 1939–October 1940 – (Whitehall histories.
  Naval staff histories)
  1. Great Britain. Royal Navy – History 2. World War,
  1939–1945 – Campaigns – Mediterranean Region
  940.5'421

ISBN 0-7146-5179-6 (cloth)
ISSN 1471-0757

Library of Congress Cataloging-in-Publication Data

The Royal Navy and the Mediterranean / [G.A. Titterton]; with a preface by David Brown.
  p. cm. – (Whitehall histories. Naval Staff histories, ISSN 1471-0757)
  Originally appeared as a classified document in 1952 prepared by
G.A. Titterton for the Historical Section of the Admiralty.
  Includes bibliographical references and index.
  ISBN 0-7146-5179-6
  1. World War, 1939–1945 – Campaigns – Mediterranean Region. 2. World
War, 1939–1945 – Naval operations, British.   I. Titterton, G.A.   II.
Great Britain. Admiralty. Historical Section.   III. Series.
  D771 .M38 2001
  940.54'5941–dc21

2001047640

Published on behalf of the Whitehall History Publishing Consortium. Applications to reproduce Crown copyright protected material in this publication should be submitted in writing to: HMSO, Copyright Unit, St Clements House, 2–16 Colegate, Norwich NR3 1BQ. Fax: 01603 723000. E-mail: copyright@hmso.gov.uk

Production co-ordination by Mike Moran

Printed in Great Britain by
Bookcraft Ltd, Midsomer Norton, Somerset

During the production of this Naval Staff History, it was learned with great regret that David Brown, OBE FRHistS, the author of the new Introduction to this volume, died on 11 August 2001. He had dedicated his life to naval history and was Head of the Naval Historical Branch of the Ministry of Defence for more than a quarter of a century.

CONTENTS

Foreword by Admiral Sir Nigel Essenhigh KCB ADC, First Sea Lord	ix
Introduction to the new edition by David Brown	xi
Mediterranean Volume I:	[i]
Preface	[iii]
Contents	[iv]
Appendices	[v]
Illustrations	[vi]
Plans	[vii]
Abbreviations	[viii]
Chapter 1: Introduction	1
Chapter 2: Uneasy Calm	6
Chapter 3: Challenge to 'Mare Nostrum'	15
Chapter 4: Sighting Shots	31
Chapter 5: Reinforcements, Air and Submarine Activities	50
Chapter 6: British Command of the Sea Established	63
Appendices (A–K)	82
Bibliography	168
Index	171
Plans (1–16)	180

Republication of the Naval Staff History of the Second World War – The Mediterranean Volume I, September 1939 – October 1940

Foreword by Admiral Sir Nigel Essenhigh KCB ADC
First Sea Lord and Chief of the Naval Staff

This Naval Staff History was first produced in 1952 as a classified account for internal use by government and defence officials, incorporating information from German and Italian sources to amend the previously-prepared Battle Summary Reports which were written very soon after the relevant individual events. It provides a candid, dispassionate and sometimes critical view of some of the crucial moments of the Second World War, but one which, overall, reflects great credit on our ships and men of the time and their commanders.

The Mediterranean was a vital theatre in the Second World War, and this republished volume deals with the role of the Royal Navy during the early part of the conflict in that region. Rarely has a Commander-in-Chief been faced with so rapidly-changing a strategic situation as was Admiral Cunningham during this period. At the start there was a comfortable feeling that, with French naval support, command of the Mediterranean was assured, particularly as Italy was at first non-belligerent. But as we now know, after an early phase of uneasy calm, circumstances changed markedly in the middle of 1940 with the fall of France and the entry of Italy into the war on Germany's side. This history shows that Cunningham's judgements in reacting to each changing circumstance were prudent and sensible.

In addition to the measures taken against the Italians, the history covers the sensitive matter of our actions against the French Navy. Few episodes of the war have generated so much controversy as these latter engagements, undertaken at a time when Britain stood weak and alone, recovering from serious setbacks on land in France. But by such actions, and particularly after Taranto in November 1940, British command of the sea was established, command of the sea without which the timely supply of Wavell's forces in Egypt, the interdiction of Italian convoys to support their army in Libya, and the support of our Greek allies would not have been possible. The strategic situation was to change again when the Germans entered the theatre later in the war and when British sea control was once more seriously disputed, but this will be covered in another volume.

Unusually, nearly fifty per cent of the text in this edition is in the form of appendices of useful information which, in conjunction with the narrative and the sixteen plans, will be of value to the casual reader and dedicated naval historian alike. I see its re-publication as a small but worthy tribute to those who participated in these historic events.

Ministry of Defence
March 2001

INTRODUCTION TO THE NEW EDITION

This Admiralty Staff History, written by Commander G. A. Titterton RN, appeared in 1952. It was intended to provide a relatively small professional readership with a background to the more detailed accounts contained in a series of 'Battle Summaries' which covered, in the case of the Mediterranean, specific areas of activity such as shore bombardments, convoys and amphibious operations. The work did, however, include more details of plans and deliberations than were then in the public domain and, because the sources would remain confidential for many years, it was classified. The intention was that three volumes would cover the whole of the war in the Mediterranean, but two years later the first volumes of two Official Histories in the Cabinet Office Second World War series appeared: Captain Stephen Roskill's *The War at Sea* and General I. S. O. Playfair's *The Mediterranean and Middle East*. These works covered much the same ground as the Staff Histories and Battle Summaries together, and had the further advantage that though they, too, were based on papers which would not be opened to the public for many years, they were written for public consumption. The second volume of this Mediterranean Staff History, dealing with activities up to the end of 1941 (also to be published in this series), was at this time virtually complete and was released in 1957, but it was decided to abandon the intended third volume, reportedly on the grounds of economy.

Volume I outlines the events between 3 September 1939 and 31 October 1940 in just 94 pages, which contain much detail not included in the Official Histories; the 79 pages of appendices reproduce original documents and signals, summaries of events and activities (the latter including a résumé of the Royal Hellenic Navy's operations up to the end of 1944), as well as the orders of battle. Commander Titterton's approach to supplementary information is thus somewhat Catholic, but it results in much useful detail that is missing from more conventional histories.

The conduct of maritime operations in the Mediterranean during the Second World War has been neglected by English-language historians in recent years. The North Atlantic and Pacific have been the dominant theatres for regional studies and these have been supplemented (if not almost supplanted) by studies devoted to themes, broad and narrow. But the abiding interest in such individual topics as submarine warfare, carrier operations, amphibious assault and all forms of intelligence (in particular 'code-breaking') is at the expense of not just the description of routine activity and the explanation of administration and logistics, but even of surface action. This last, the oldest form of naval warfare, had its recorded origins in the Mediterranean and continued unabated during the Second World War – between the first sinking by gunfire on 28 June 1940 and the last by patrol forces' torpedo on 23 April 1945 more warships of minesweeper size and upwards were sunk in Mediterranean surface engagements than in any other single theatre.

Not only was historical experience repeated, every aspect of modern maritime warfare was featured and more than one was pioneered in the Middle Sea, ranging from major conceptual advances, such as amphibious undertakings and airborne assaults, through to the successful employment of naval special forces to neutralise a battlefleet, to the use of radar in fast-moving tactical settings. Embarked aviation confirmed the potential suggested during the spring 1940 Norwegian campaign[1] and rapidly came of age as an offensive force capable of upsetting a strategic balance. But of more day-to-day significance was the confidence that the Royal Navy possessed and the self-belief at every level that allowed the Commander-in-Chief, Mediterranean Fleet to use his out-numbered forces offensively from the outset, thereby securing a moral advantage that was never surrendered, even in the darkest months of 1941 and 1942.

Part of this confidence was innate – history itself bore witness to the success of the Royal Navy, but most of it was based on the more solid foundation of exceedingly hard peacetime training in the areas in which it expected to fight in wartime. Fleet exercises were used to evaluate tactics and doctrine, which evolved from the lessons gleaned to form the basis of the ever-changing and improving 'Fighting Instructions', whose latest forms were in their turn evaluated at sea. The necessity for such a process was fully understood by the politicians and the Admiralty's civil servants, and sea exercises were spared the more stringent of the economies to which the rest of the Service's activities were subject. Commanders and crews also had confidence in their equipment: the ships and weapons in service with the Mediterranean Fleet in 1939 did not represent the further bounds of technology – compared with their Italian counterparts, for example, the ships were much slower and their guns outranged – but they could be relied upon to keep going and to score hits.

Jointness and Alliance

A source of strength, if not necessarily of confidence, was the Mediterranean Fleet's relationships with 'outsiders'. The need for close (and genuine) co-operation with the Middle East Commands of the Army and Royal Air Force was fully appreciated and, although he habitually flew his flag in a ship based at Alexandria, the Commander-in-Chief and his staff conferred regularly at the military and air force headquarters in Cairo with their Service opposite numbers, and he was permanently represented at GHQ by a Commodore. This officer was also a member of the Joint Planning Staff, which was created in June 1939, together with a Joint Intelligence Centre; the Navy retained its own intelligence centre at Alexandria. At a lower level, an RAF Group, with headquarters at Alexandria, was dedicated to maritime co-operation, but its resources were slight and the Air Officer Commanding Middle East's authority had to be sought before enlisting the assistance of the Group supporting the Army in the Western Desert for operations in support of the Navy. There was little opportunity during the period between the outbreak of war in western Europe and Italy's joining hostilities for large-scale air–sea exercises, but the procedures for close co-operation were in place.

The Directives issued to the three Commanders-in-Chief,[2] besides laying stress on 'jointness', pointed out their responsibility for co-ordinating their operations with those of the French ally. There had been Mediterranean theatre inter-Staff talks during successive crises since 1935 and these had been resumed early in January 1939, when the international situation was once again deteriorating. Agreement was reached in the Mediterranean that naval operations in the western basin would be a French responsibility, the two would co-ordinate operations in the central sector under French direction, with light forces based on Bizerta and Malta in the event of war. Agreement was reached on joint operational control and the common use of facilities, to enable the Royal Navy to continue to operate in the likely event of the neutralisation of Malta by air attack. Arrangements were also made for the reinforcement of the island; if this could not be achieved before the outbreak of war, the French undertook to transport men and material overland from Algiers (or even Casablanca) to Tunisia for onward shipment.

The Royal Navy would look after most of the eastern basin, where the French had an interest, owing to the colony of Syria and, unbeknownst to the British until August 1939, the intention of turning the Aegean and eastern Balkans into an active theatre of war.[3] Despite differences arising from what the British saw as over-rigid centralisation on the part of the Commander-in-Chief of the French Navy, Admiral Darlan, who intended initially to pursue a defensive strategy in the western basin, the two local commanders further decided to co-ordinate their respective attacks on the Italian seaboard.[4] As elsewhere, liaison officers were appointed to the more important operational commanders.

INTRODUCTION TO THE NEW EDITION

There was thus a willingness to co-operate at the operational level, but on the French side politics prevailed above, with Darlan playing for position not only with his allies, but also against his fellow chiefs of staff and even within the French Navy, where he reshuffled senior commanders and reorganised fleet commands to further strengthen his primacy and absolute control over all aspects. All significant French operations in the Mediterranean during the period of Italian neutrality were undertaken on Darlan's instructions, but those that affected the British Mediterranean Fleet were generally undertaken for political motives and few had any practical value. When, on 12 April 1940, the Italian Fleet was mobilised and neutrality showed signs of ending, the Royal Navy was sufficiently committed in the North Atlantic and off Norway to be concerned that it might not be able to reinforce the Mediterranean Fleet should Italy declare war. On 16 April, therefore, the Admiralty asked whether, in the event of Italy's entering the war, the French Navy would be willing to take operational responsibility for the whole of the Mediterranean, with support from British forces. The *Amirauté* in Paris agreed without hesitation and immediately began a study into the command organisation in the Mediterranean, but a week later, on 23 April, the Allied Supreme Council declined to give its approval to the proposed single (French) command, preferring to maintain the existing structure of British command in the eastern basin and French in the west. The command arrangements were made more flexible than hitherto, with the rigid boundary in the central Mediterranean being abolished to enable the two navies to operate in one another's zones according to the local situation.

Bases and Host-Nation Support

Whether the French Navy's Mediterranean administrative and logistic infrastructure would have proved equal to the task is open to doubt, for the only major dockyard, at Toulon, was within easy reach of the Italian air force, as was the operating base at Bizerta, in Tunisia. The brand-new base at Mers-el-Kebir, near Oran in western Algeria, was at a more comfortable distance but lacked major repair facilities and stores depôts. The British had an excellent and well-stocked dockyard and base at Malta but in April 1937 the Cabinet, made fearful by the pipe-dreams of the proponents of air power for its own sake, decided to move the Mediterranean Fleet main base, docks, stocks and barrels, to Alexandria.[5] It would, of course, have been quicker and much cheaper to reinforce the air defences of Malta than to build from nothing a complete dockyard, but the arcana of juggling public finances and the inviolability of Service 'Votes' made such a long-term scheme attractive. A year later, attempting to find 'economies' to meet a substantial reduction in the War Office budget, the Secretary of War persuaded the Cabinet to accept savings on the fixed defences of Gibraltar, Hong Kong and Malta. The coastal defences of the last named were not to be weakened, they would 'remain as approved when we were not contemplating war with a Mediterranean Power'.[6] Only financial desperation could account for such a sacrifice of logic. The fleet was moved out of Malta at vast expense, precisely because 'war with a Mediterranean Power' *was* contemplated.

The development of the Alexandria base and its support facilities are adequately described in the Staff History and the opening volume of Playfair's *The Mediterranean and Middle East*.[7] The latter also explains the political background to the British presence in Egypt, which, unlike Malta and Gibraltar, was not a colony. Until 1936, Britain had maintained a military occupation, which ensured its control over the Suez Canal but effectively denied many of the sovereign rights of the Egyptian government. In December 1936, a treaty was signed which restored most of the functions of government and, although they would remain on a reduced scale, British forces would be withdrawn into 'the Canal Zone' by 1941, other than those in the Alexandria area, where they would remain until the end of 1944. In return for British equipment and training of the Egyptian armed forces, the Egyptian government would improve road and rail communications, prepare landing grounds in the Western Desert and improve the facilities at Alexandria, including the construction of a 1,000ft (305m) graving dock. By March 1939, it was evident that the dock would not be completed in the foreseeable future and a large floating dock had to be towed out from the

MEDITERRANEAN, SEPTEMBER 1939–OCTOBER 1940

United Kingdom, arriving in August 1939. The Army and RAF also lacked infrastructure facilities, which had been promised by the treaty, particularly the advanced airfields and communications and the 'Host Nation's' main support was to be the supply of unskilled labour.

The Other Side of the Hill

The Royal Navy, though not as well prepared in the Mediterranean as its commanders would have wished, was in far better condition for a defensive war than was the *Regia Marina*[8] for the offensive war which Mussolini's public ambitions demanded. Five years of grandiose exhortation, naval confrontation and plans for war with Britain, of quasi-war in Spain, and of naval building programmes had not produced an instrument capable of establishing Italian Mediterranean mastery. Germany had been courted from 1936, with Mussolini claiming in November that Rome and Berlin had established 'an axis round which all European states animated by the will to collaboration and peace can also collaborate'. In the autumn of 1937, Italy joined Germany and Japan in the Anti-Comintern Pact. Like the 'Axis', this pact was something short of an alliance, for although the signatories agreed 'that they will mutually keep each other informed concerning the activities of the Communist International, will confer upon the necessary measure of defence, and will carry out such measures in close co-operation', establishing a standing committee to consider measures to counter the activities of the Comintern, they took no steps to organise staff meetings until the spring of 1939. Despite this lack of co-ordination – and even of commitment – the Italian Naval Staff continued to base its long-term plans and concept of operations on the involvement of the German Navy in the Atlantic and of the Japanese Navy in the Far East, in expectation of the draw-down effect that these operations would have on the British Mediterranean Fleet.

Ships and Bases

In 1936, using this assumed co-operation to propose a much smaller fleet than would have been necessary for Italy to attempt a 'break-out' war, Admiral Domenico Cavagnari, the chief of staff and under-secretary of the navy, struck out the aircraft carriers proposed by his planners, considering them to be unnecessary, as land-based aircraft would provide the necessary support within the Mediterranean. Mussolini did not approve additional battleships and heavy cruisers, and the navy had to be content with larger numbers of destroyers and submarines than it had actually requested – 28 destroyers and torpedo-boats and 20 submarines.[9] These vessels were completed remarkably quickly, actually 'telescoping' with the previous, more modest, programme, so that between April 1937 and March 1939 34 destroyers and torpedo-boats and 28 submarines were actually completed. Impressive as this expansion may have been, the programme, which also included two new battleships and the reconstruction of four older battleships, was achieved only at a huge cost in raw materials, virtually all of which Italy had to import: between 1935 and 1939, the overall Italian military budget came to 89 per cent of Britain's, but this had to be found from an income that was only 25 per cent of Britain's.[10]

The expansion programme was also achieved at the cost of balance. The absence of aircraft carriers has already been noted; the assumption that the Italian air force, the *Regia Aeronautica*, would provide support was no more than that – an assumption without discussion as to what could be expected, other than that it would not be sufficient for continuous operations at the extremities of the Mediterranean. Even 'traditional' naval tasks were left to assumption. Thus, although the Italian Navy intended to depend heavily upon mine and submarine warfare, the mine stocks were not modernised or increased, no major provision was made for an anti-submarine escort force and none whatsoever was made for a purpose-built fleet (i.e. deep-sea) minesweeping capability. Instead, all torpedo-boats were fitted with high-speed minesweeping gear and they provided the backbone of the escort force, augmented by destroyers when the latter could be spared from fleet screening duties. A series of small craft, capable of coastal

INTRODUCTION TO THE NEW EDITION

minesweeping, local escort and patrol duties, existed, but only three of these had been added since 1926 and the Italian Navy, like its Axis and Allied contemporaries, would have to take fishing vessels up from trade to undertake these subsidiary but vital duties.

Base facilities constituted another inadequacy. None of the existing main Fleet dockyards, at Taranto, in the 'heel' of Italy, at La Spezia, high on the west coast, or at Venice, was adequately defended against air attack or, indeed, against attack from the sea. The same was true of the operating bases at Naples, Augusta, in Sicily, and Cagliari, on the south coast of Sardinia. In 1935–36 the naval staff recommended the building of a completely new base on the Gulf of Gaeta, between Naples and Rome, but this was rejected by the navy ministry, as was a recommendation to build a new base at Milazzo,[11] near the northeast corner of Sicily. None of the navy's arsenals could dock the new 'Littorio'-class battleships: although the first pair was laid down in 1934, it was not until 1937 that the navy ministry approved the upgrading of Taranto to support these ships and the project was not completed until 1942.[12] In the meantime, only the commercial dry dock at Genoa was capable of taking the new ships.

The Italian naval authorities were as well aware of this fragile material state as they were that the political leadership was bent on confrontation with the world's leading naval power, but, other than establishing the outlines, little was done to implement a coherent strategy that would maximise the country's advantages. These were not negligible, and the December 1935 decision that the main strength of the fleet would be concentrated in the central Mediterranean (to the west of Crete and east of Sardinia) to secure Italian communications with North Africa[13] should have enabled the navy to make good use of the slender resources. This was subsequently extended to cutting British and French communications to and from the Middle East, but, unfortunately for the Italian war effort, insufficient attention was devoted to the practicalities of even this limited strategy. Not until June 1938 was a naval staff study undertaken into the means of creating a barrier across the Sicilian Channel and only after the Czechoslovakian crisis had subsided, in November 1938, did the staff consider how it would transport and support the expeditionary corps that the Italian Army intended would invade Egypt from Cyrenaïca.[14] It was immediately apparent to those involved in this study that forces based on Malta presented such a threat to Italian communications and that the island had to be neutralised; simultaneously, the naval high command came to the same conclusion, and in December the staff was ordered to plan for the capture of Malta.[15]

The theory was now in place, but the practicalities were sadly lacking. The Italian Navy had acknowledged during the Abyssinian crisis that it had no night-fighting capability, and this had scarcely improved during the following four years, principally as a result of lack of exercises and training, owing to the constant need for economy in the use of fuel oil, and partly because no flashless propellant was ever procured for the guns of the heaviest calibres in service up to May 1940.[16] Lack of practice at sea resulted in the stultification of doctrine, and the rigid direction of operations by shore-based commanders provided little scope for the development of initiative on the part of those at sea, who were further handicapped by their notoriously unreliable naval communications equipment. Even the Italian contribution to the Nationalist cause in the Spanish Civil War did not benefit the navy to any noticeable extent, although the efficiency of the submarine arm, which had a very poor record of success during the opening phase, did improve somewhat.

Italian Inter-Service Co-operation

The *Regia Aeronautica*, on the other hand, did learn from the war in Spain, and as a result of these lessons it was prepared to make a significant contribution to Italian maritime operations. From the outset of the Italian involvement in Spain, bomber units based in the Balearic Islands had assisted in the blockade of the Mediterranean ports occupied by the Republican forces, inflicting considerable damage on shipping in harbour. This was, of course, noted by the future Allies, who recognised the threat to their own merchant ports and naval bases. Less obvious to the French and British but apparent to the Italians was the bombers' lack of success against ships at sea. Measures were already in hand to remedy this, however, and parallel development of air-dropped torpedoes and a dive-bombing aircraft was accelerated during the late 1930s.

The common understanding that the Italian air force authorities were largely responsible for the lack of co-operation with the navy[17] should perhaps be questioned. Although the naval command was correct in its assumption that the air force certainly intended to take part in maritime operations, there was no attempt on the part of the senior officers, let alone the staffs, to discuss how operations could be co-ordinated. Written exchanges between the navy and air force chiefs of staff in May 1939 were little more than demands for co-operation on the part of the former and statements of intent by the latter. In the words of one naval staff officer, there was 'an almost total absence of any clear and rational doctrine' for aeronaval warfare.[18]

In fact, the *Regia Aeronautica* was making a serious commitment to maritime operations and by June 1940 over 250 aircraft were dedicated to such tasks, under naval tactical direction, ashore and in the air. Furthermore, it is difficult to sustain the claim that the Italian Navy was worse served than the Mediterranean Fleet, for the reconnaissance units had mixed crews, the floatplanes carried by the battleships and cruisers for scouting and spotting duties being flown by air force pilots with navy observers while the crew of the long-range flying boats,[19] of which just over 200 were in service at the outbreak of war, operating under naval 'opcon' (operational control), included a coastguard (*guardiamarina*) officer as navigator and 'mission commander'. It is not always appreciated that only as recently as May 1939 had the Royal Navy regained control of its shipboard aircraft and personnel, and the Commander-in-Chief Mediterranean Fleet could call upon no more than a dozen RAF Sunderlands, with entirely air force crews and no specialised Coastal Command staff, such as there was in the UK, for all his long-range reconnaissance and patrol requirements. Four dozen modern 'maritime bombers'[20] were available for attacks on ports, bases and ships at sea. More significant than this last was the formation in the autumn of 1939 of a torpedo-bomber trials-and-training unit: from October 1939 all Savoia-Marchetti SM.79 aircraft were completed with the necessary fittings to enable them to carry and release torpedoes. The *Regia Aeronautica* also pressed on with training a dive-bombing unit, which practised on a full-scale outline of a battleship hull and then undertook some mutual training with naval units. The chosen mount, the Savoia-Marchetti SM.85, was a total failure in front-line service,[21] and it was fortunate, therefore, that relations between the new Italian air force commander and the *Luftwaffe* hierarchy were much better than that of the Italian naval and army chiefs with their German opposites, and he was able to procure the Junkers Ju87 *Stuka* – which under the right circumstances was deadly against shipping. It was not entirely a 'one-way street', however, for the Italian air torpedo, steadily developed at the air force's insistence to be released at greater heights and speeds than its Western equivalents, was so successful that in September 1939 the Germans ordered the manufacturer's entire output, and it was not until some months later that the *Regia Aeronautica* was able to negotiate the supply of four torpedoes per month from the Italian Navy's quota from another factory.[22]

Relations with the Italian Army were, if anything, even less satisfactory. The naval staff produced their study on the reinforcement of North Africa, which involved the neutralisation of the French base at Bizerta, the capture of Malta and the transport of as much material as possible before the outbreak of hostilities. The army did no more than provide the number of men and the amount of material that needed to be transported, with no details of where these were to be embarked or landed. Furthermore, there was no joint discussion of the problems involved in the invasion of Malta and thus no plans were made for this essential operation. Only in East Africa, where the governor was also the overall commander-in-chief, were coherent and integrated plans for joint operations drawn up by the three services to provide an offensive strategy, which envisaged the seizure of French and British colonies in the Horn of Africa.[23]

Throughout this period, and indeed since 1925, there had been a 'central' military staff in Rome, the *Stato Maggiore Generale*, commonly known as the *Comando Supremo*, led throughout by Marshal Pietro Badoglio. Although charged with co-ordinating the plans of the services, Badoglio and his small secretariat were hamstrung by Mussolini's organisation of military affairs and his methods of retaining control.

INTRODUCTION TO THE NEW EDITION

Resisting the creation of a 'defence' ministry, *Il Duce* appointed himself head of each of the three service ministries, with the chiefs of staff as under-ministers; he thus felt free to discuss 'service business' individually with these deputies without involving Badoglio, who often found out about major decisions affecting across-the-board capabilities or budgetary provisions after they had been cast in stone by the dictator's agreement. A cautious man, Badoglio opposed Mussolini's more grandiose plans and, recognising Italy's profound weaknesses, used what influence he was allowed to promote a defensive strategy.

Axis Staff Talks

Although the probability of an alliance between Italy and Germany had existed since the proclamation of the Rome–Berlin Axis in late 1936, it was not until April 1939 that the first official inter-army staff conversations occurred, followed in late June by a conference in Friedrichshafen between Cavagnari and Raeder and their staffs. Both sides brought reservations to the meetings; the Germans were forbidden by Hitler to discuss questions of strategy or operational co-operation arising from recent crises (Czechoslovakia) or future German ambitions (Poland), while the Italians were ordered to make no mention of the plans to attack Djibouti and British Somaliland. The Italian delegation was also influenced by a recent (27 May) memorandum from Mussolini to the service chiefs, informing the latter that although war with the Western powers was inevitable, the Italy armed forces would not be in a fit state to undertake it before 1942 and planning should therefore not envisage an outbreak of war before 1943.[24]

The formal agenda for the naval conference, held on 20 and 21 June 1939, was entirely procedural and technical but the naval commanders exceeded their remit by exchanging thoughts on strategy. Raeder's readiness to consider undertaking ocean warfare in the Atlantic pleased Cavagnari, though not to the extent that he would accept German pressure to abandon the central Mediterranean defensive strategy in favour of attacking and defeating the French in the western basin; Hitler continued to believe that war with Britain was not imminent, but the Italians were not convinced.[25] The Friedrichshafen conference could not be regarded as a success – all that was decided was that the two parties would operate independently in separate major spheres of operations and, should operations be conducted in other theatres, such as the Indian or Pacific Ocean, then these would take place in separate, mutually agreed zones.

This was the only meeting between the Axis naval chiefs and their staffs prior to the Italian declaration of war, nearly a year later. Neither side requested nor showed any desire for a follow-up and the naval attachés complained of their hosts' lack of interest in co-operation. Instead of the alliance working towards a common objective or even a workable compromise, mutual distrust grew the longer that Italy remained out of the war.

The Final Months of Peace

During the seven months between the outbreak of war and Mussolini's order to mobilise the Italian Fleet on 12 April 1940, *Il Duce* replaced his army and air force chiefs but retained Cavagnari, who unlike his *confrères* had never made extravagant boasts on behalf of his service,[26] and Badoglio, who in late August 1939 had issued a thoroughly defensive strategic directive for the Italian forces. Indeed, Cavagnari had become increasingly pessimistic about the prospects of success in a war with Britain, sharing his fears with Badoglio, and did not shrink from cautioning Mussolini, who believed that Italy could (and should) take part in a brief successful war, which would earn it a victor's place at the peace conference.[27]

Certainly, the naval war plans office believed, the Italian Navy could not sustain a long war. No major expansion programme would be possible and ship losses would be for all practical purposes irreplaceable, owing to the shortage of raw materials which would accompany a blockade and the basic lack of industrial capacity – three light cruisers, together with five destroyers, one torpedo-boat and 15 fast escorts were completed before Italy's surrender in September 1943, but none of these units entered service before February 1942. The Italian merchant shipbuilding industry was in an equally parlous state, for, although it was capable of producing 300,000grt of vessels a year in peacetime, because of shortages and disruption, only 12 ships of 74,000grt were to be completed in Italian yards during 1940 and 1941, against losses through war causes of 172 ships of 650,000grt during the same period.[28] Operations would be greatly hampered by oil fuel shortage, for even after the completion of additional bulk-storage facilities no more than seven months' war consumption could be stocked. There was also a general shortage of ammunition, particularly for the shore anti-aircraft batteries defending the inadequately protected arsenals and naval bases, and there were no more than 25,000 mines for all defensive and offensive purposes. Shortages of resources, and funds to pay for them, meant that urgently needed anti-torpedo defences could not be provided at the major fleet bases and, faced with a budgetary crisis in November 1939, the naval high command had to suspend all training activities for the rest of that month and was not able to resume fleet exercises until the New Year. The lack of any realistic live exercise to justify the planners' suppositions and hopes or to underpin a half-hearted doctrine which took counsel of their fears was perhaps the most significant omission on the part of the Italian Navy.

Mussolini, watching impatiently on the sidelines of a war which would decide the destinies of the totalitarian states, believed in the latter days of May 1940 that the disintegration of the French Army offered the opportunity for the short war that Italy could sustain and instructed his service chiefs to be ready to commence hostilities on 5 June. In the event, a request from Hitler for a postponement delayed the declaration of war until 10 June.

War

A week later, on 17 June 1940, the French government sued for an armistice and a week after that, on 24 June, a ceasefire came into effect. Italian Navy hopes for reinforcement by acquisition were dashed by Hitler's remarkably lenient treatment of the French Navy, and any questions Mussolini may have had as to the intention of Britain to fight on were swiftly answered by Churchill's attack on the erstwhile ally. Admiral Darlan, the French Chief of Naval Staff and Commander-in-Chief of the Navy, had concentrated four of the five operational capital ships at Mers-el-Kebir beyond the reach of Axis air attack at the end of May and had sent a barely complete battleship to Dakar shortly before the collapse; a sixth, incomplete and ill-armed ship had escaped to Casablanca. The Royal Navy's attacks on Mers-el-Kebir on 3 and 6 July and on Dakar on 8 July destroyed one of these ships and crippled three others, leaving the French with only one operational capital ship under their control, the Strasbourg at Toulon.[29] On the 9th, during the Battle of Punta Stilo, as the Italians preferred to name what the Royal Navy referred to as the 'Action off Calabria', one of the older Italian battleships was hit at long range by a 15in (380mm) shell, bringing the Royal Navy's score of capital ships sunk and damaged to seven in a month,[30] five in the previous six days.

The object lesson in unhesitating ruthlessness given by the attack on the French Fleet, undertaken ostensibly to prevent the battleships from falling into German hands, gave notice to all that Britain intended to fight on alone and that it would not be a short war. This was not lost on the important neutrals, the friendly United States and fascist Spain, or on Italy, whose navy was now committed to a war that it could not sustain and, because it had believed until 12 April that it would not have to fight before 1943, for which it had not adequately planned. Worse, the German surface fleet on which Italian hopes lay for drawing off the Royal Navy, had been effectively crippled during the Norwegian campaign, so that little assistance could be looked for from that direction.

British Priorities

The Mediterranean Fleet, stripped from September 1939 to provide ships for more active theatres, had been brought back up to strength during May 1940. The British War Cabinet showed no hesitation, at a time when the Norwegian campaign was at its height and the Allied collapse in northern France and the

INTRODUCTION TO THE NEW EDITION

Low Countries was introducing the real threat of invasion, in transferring two flotillas of modern fleet destroyers and four anti-aircraft ships from the Home Fleet to Alexandria; a month later, Force 'H' had to be formed and despatched to Gibraltar. Not surprisingly, after these diversions and the heavy destroyer casualties of Dunkirk, when it was decided in August to send further reinforcements – the navy's newest aircraft carrier, the *Illustrious*, a battleship, two A/A (anti-aircraft) cruisers and two 'conventional' cruisers – no destroyers were available for redeployment.

The RAF, too, sent scarce resources to Egypt, the first being a detachment of three 'DWI' Wellington bombers converted by the addition of a large 'hoop' and a magnetic field generator to serve as mine-countermeasures aircraft. There was an acute need for such aircraft in UK waters, but there were few minesweeping vessels available in the Mediterranean and the Suez Canal could not be defended against aerial minelaying along its full length; the Wellingtons left the UK at the end of May and, flying across France, were operational by the outbreak of war.[31] France had fallen by the time that the next significant aerial reinforcement was attempted, in mid-July, so the Hawker Hurricane fighters had to be ferried by aircraft carrier to within flying-off distance of Malta and then forwarded via Greek islands to Egypt. As Fighter Command was girding itself for the Battle of Britain, having suffered heavy material losses in the Battle of France, it was decided to send 72 Hurricanes and their pilots to the Middle East during the coming months; this figure was actually doubled and no fewer than 60 fighters were sent out in September 1940 alone, at the height of the Battle of Britain.[32] Equally important in the longer term were the Wellingtons, which began to arrive in September, providing Middle East Air Force (MEAF) with the only truly strategic bombing force in a theatre where the only truly strategic targets were ports.

Before the Mediterranean Fleet reinforcements sailed, it was decided, on 12 August, to accompany the force with a substantial military reinforcement, including three armoured regiments, anti-tank guns and mines and modern field artillery. Between sailing on 21 August and reaching the latitude of Gibraltar a week later it was decided not to risk this valuable cargo by passing the freighters through the Mediterranean, but to send them round the Cape of Good Hope, accompanied by the two cruisers as escort against raiders; the warships arrived at Alexandria on 6 September and the freighters reached Suez on the 23rd. The decision to send the men and material when the risk of invasion of Britain was regarded as high showed the high priority accorded to the defence of Egypt and the Suez Canal, but also the confidence and courage of a very high order on the part of the Chiefs of Staff and Cabinet.

The second decision, to tie them up in the safer but longer passage round Africa, stemmed from the firm belief on the part of the Middle East Intelligence staffs that no Italian offensive could be mounted against Egypt 'for several weeks', unless the preparations had been concealed 'with remarkable skill'.[33] Why this belief should have been so confidently held is not explained. Regular MEAF reconnaissance of Tobruk and Derna had for several weeks reported large numbers of ships at the former – 20 merchant vessels on 5 July and 24 on 19 July, for example – and although successful attacks had been made on shipping in harbour by RAF and Royal Navy aircraft, they had made no great impression on the Italian build-up in Cyrenaïca. During the month of August alone there were 134 arrivals at Tripoli from Italy or ports further to the east from Tripoli: three of these ships were sunk on passage or after arrival, just one in the second half of the month, when the Italian activity was at its height, with 87 arrivals in 54 convoys, none of which had been sighted. Naval signals intelligence had been available during the first month of the war with Italy but changes to the main naval book cyphers thereafter defeated the government Code and Cypher School's cryptanalysts,[34] and not until after the period covered by this Staff History did 'Sigint' (signals intelligence) and the wider reconnaissance web made possible by an increase in the number of patrol aircraft reveal that the convoys bound for North Africa were routed to the west of Malta, and not to the east, as had been assumed. By default, and much to its surprise, the Italian Navy was attaining one of its prime strategic objectives, at virtually no cost.

The Italian invasion of Egypt began on 13 September, the day after GHQ Middle East had informed London that a major offensive was not expected in the next few days. The Italian Army had limited

MEDITERRANEAN, SEPTEMBER 1939–OCTOBER 1940

objectives, but their capture did include the advanced airfields from which MEAF fighters had operated to protect warship movements and which the naval Swordfish had used in successful attacks on Tobruk and Derna. On 17 September, however, aircraft flew from the *Illustrious* to mine the more westerly port of Benghazi and attack shipping with bombs: two destroyers and two merchant vessels were sunk that night and a third merchant ship was lost on a mine several days later. Welcome as these successes were, as with the four submarine sinkings which followed during the next four weeks, they were insufficient to support the claim made by the title of the final chapter of this Staff History: 'British Command of the Sea Established: October 1940'. That would have to wait until the following month, where Volume II takes up the story and relates how the Royal Navy endeavoured to maintain the 'command of the sea' established by the attack on the Italian Fleet base at Taranto.

DAVID BROWN
Former Head of Naval Historical Branch,
Ministry of Defence, London
April 2001

Notes

1. See Naval Historical Branch, *Naval Operations of the Campaign in Norway, April–June 1940*, Whitehall Histories Series (Cass, London, 2000).
2. I. S. O. Playfair, *The Mediterranean and Middle East*, Vol. I (HMSO, London, 1954), Appendices.
3. M. A. Reussner, *Les conversations franco-britanniques d'Etat-Major 1935–39* (Service Historique de la Marine, Vincennes, 1969), pp. 284–6.
4. Admiral Sir Andrew Cunningham and Vice-amiral d'escadre Emmanuel Ollive. Reussner, op. cit.; Cunningham, *A Sailor's Odyssey* (Hutchinson, London, 1957), pp. 211–12.
5. Playfair, op. cit., pp. 9–10.
6. Ibid., p. 482.
7. Ibid., pp. 75–8.
8. That is, 'Royal Navy' – Italy was a kingdom, under Victor Emmanuel III, who abdicated under pressure in 1946 to allow the foundation of a democratic republic.
9. R. Mallett, *The Italian Navy and Fascist Expansionism, 1935–40* (Cass, London, 1998), pp. 54, 59 and fn. The torpedo-boats should not be confused with 'motor torpedo-boats'; these were sea-going light destroyers of up to 1,000 tons; the escort destroyers were 1,200-ton vessels comparable with the later British 'Hunt'-class.
10. Ibid., p. 48.
11. Ibid., pp. 105–6.
12. Ibid., p. 107.
13. M. Gabriele, *La Battaglia dei Convogli – Le Premesse* (Ufficio Storico della Marina Militare, Rome, 1994), p. 105.
14. Ibid., pp. 107–9.
15. Mallett, op. cit., p. 133.
16. The 12.6in (320mm) guns of the 'Cavour' and 'Doria'-class battleships and the 8in (203mm) guns of the heavy cruisers. A. Fraccaroli, *The Cruiser Zara* (Profile Publications, Windsor, 1973).
17. Mallett, op. cit., *passim*; Staff History, Section 22.
18. Mallett, op. cit., p. 147.
19. CRDA Cant. Z.501 flying boat.
20. CRDA Cant. Z.506 floatplane.
21. E. Brotzu, M. Caso and G. Cosolo, *Dimensione Cielo* (Bizzari, Rome, 1972), Vol. IV, p. 62. A. Borgiotti and C. Gori, *Gli Stuka della Regia Aeronautica* (STEM Mucchi, Modena, 1976), p. 8.
22. Brotzu *et al.*, op. cit.
23. Mallett, op. cit., pp. 144–5.
24. Ibid., pp. 151–2.
25. Ibid., pp. 149–50; E. Weichold, *Axis Naval Policy and Operations in the Mediterranean, 1939 to May 1943* (Admiralty, London, 1951), p. 1.

INTRODUCTION TO THE NEW EDITION

26 Alberto Pariani, the late CoS of the army, had in August 1939 stated – against all the evidence – that the army was ready to join Germany in a general war, while Giuseppe Valle of the air force had assured Mussolini that there were 2,300 front-line aircraft when in fact only 640 were ready for combat. Mallett, op. cit., pp. 158 and 166.
27 Ibid., p. 166, *passim*.
28 G. Fioravanzo, *Dati Statistici*, Tables VIIIa and b, XC (Ufficio Storico della Marina Militare, Rome, 1972).
29 The incomplete *Jean Bart*, at Casablanca, was not attacked.
30 The *Scharnhorst* on 8 June, *Gneisenau* on 20 June, *Bretagne*, *Provence* and *Dunkerque* at Mers-el-Kebir, *Richelieu* at Dakar and the *Guilio Cesare* on 9 July.
31 The Italians possessed no air-laid magnetic mines and these weapons were not laid in the Canal until early in 1941, by the *Luftwaffe*.
32 Air Historical Branch Narrative, *The Middle East Campaigns, Vol. I. Operations in Libya and the Western Desert September 1939–June 1941*, Appendix 24.
33 Playfair, op. cit., p. 192.
34 F. H. Hinsley *et al.*, *British Intelligence in the Second World War* (HMSO, London, 1979), Vol. I, p. 210.

Table 1: Warship Losses in the Mediterranean, June–October 1940: Italian Navy

Date	Cruisers	Destroyers	T/Bs	Submarines	Cause	Agent	Area
15-Jun-40				*Macallè*	accident	stranded	Red Sea
17-Jun-40				*Provana*	depth-charge	French *La Curieuse*	north of Oran
19-Jun-40				*Galilei*	captured	HMS *Moonstone*	off Aden
20-Jun-40				*Diamante*	torpedo	HM/SM *Parthian*	off Tobruk
23-Jun-40				*Torricelli*	gunfire	HMS *Kandahar, Kingston, Shoreham*	north of Perim, Red Sea
24-Jun-40				*Galvani*	depth-charge	HMS *Falmouth*	Gulf of Oman
27-Jun-40				*Liuzzi*	depth-charge	HMS *Dainty & Defender*	south of Crete
28-Jun-40				*Argonauta*	depth-charge	230 Sqdn RAF	central Med.
28-Jun-40		*Espero*			gunfire	HMS *Orion* + 7th Cruiser Sqdn	south of Crete
29-Jun-40				*Uebi Scebeli*	depth-charge	HMS *Dainty & Ilex*	west of Crete
29-Jun-40				*Rubino*	depth-charge	230 Sqdn RAF	Ionian Sea
05-Jul-40		*Zeffiro*			torpedo	813 Sqdn (ex-*Eagle*)	Tobruk
10-Jul-40		*Pancaldo*			torpedo	813 Sqdn	Augusta
19-Jul-40	*Colleoni*				gunfire	HMAS *Sydney*	west of Crete
20-Jul-40		*Ostro*			torpedo	824 Sqdn (ex-*Eagle*)	Tobruk
20-Jul-40		*Nembo*			torpedo	824 Sqdn (ex-*Eagle*)	Tobruk
22-Aug-40				*Iride*	torpedo	824 Sqdn (ex-*Eagle*)	Bomba
17-Sep-40		*Borea*			bomb	815 Sqdn (*Illustrious*)	Benghazi
17-Sep-40		*Aquilone*			mine	819 Sqdn (*Illustrious*)	Benghazi
22-Sep-40			*Palestro*		torpedo	HM/SM *Osiris*	Otranto Straits
30-Sep-40				*Gondar*	depth-charge	HMAS *Stuart* & 230 Sqdn RAF	off Alexandria
02-Oct-40				*Berillo*	depth-charge	HMS *Havoc & Hasty*	off Sidi Barrani
08-Oct-40				*Gemma*	torpedo	own goal – S/M *Tricheco*	off Scarpanto
12-Oct-40		*Artigliere*			gunfire	HMS *Ajax*	east of Malta
12-Oct-40			*Airone*		gunfire	HMS *Ajax*	east of Malta
12-Oct-40			*Ariel*		gunfire	HMS *Ajax*	east of Malta
18-Oct-40				*Durbo*	depth-charge	HMS *Firedrake, Wrestler* & 202 Sqdn RAF	east of Gibraltar
20-Oct-40				*Lafolè*	depth-charge	HMS *Gallant, Griffin, Holspur*	east of Gibraltar
21-Oct-40		*Nullo*			gunfire	HMS *Kimberley*	NE of Massawa
Totals	1	9	3	16			

Table 2: Warship Losses in the Mediterranean, June–October 1940: Royal Navy

Date	Cruisers	Destroyers	Sloop	Submarines	Cause	Agent	Area
12-Jun-40	*Calypso*				torpedo	S/M *Bagnolini*	south of Crete
13-Jun-40					torpedo/gunfire	*Strale*	Gulf of Taranto
16-Jun-40				*Odin*	depth-charge	*Circe, Clio*	off Syracuse
16-Jun-40				*Grampus*	depth-charge	*Turbine*	off Tobruk
22-Jun-40				*Orpheus*	accident	explosion (torpedo air vessel)	off Perim, Red Sea
23-Jun-40		*Khartoum*			torpedo	S/M *Galvani*	off Bombay
11-Jul-40			*Pathan*		torpedo	S/M *Marconi*	north of Algiers
16-Jul-40		*Escort*		*Phoenix*	depth-charge	*Albatros*	off Augusta
01-Aug-40				*Oswald*	rammed	*Vivaldi*	south of C Spartivento
23-Aug-40		*Hostile*			mine		SE of C Bon
01-Oct-40				*Rainbow*	collision	merchant vessel	Otranto Straits
15-Oct-40				*Triad*	gunfire	S/M *Toti*	off Gulf of Taranto
Totals	1	3	1	7			

Copy No 21

~~CONFIDENTIAL~~   B.R.1736(4Q)(I).
~~C.B. 3302 (1)~~

Attention is called to the penalties attaching to any infraction of the Official Secrets Acts.

NAVAL STAFF HISTORY
SECOND WORLD WAR

Mediterranean
Volume I
September 1939-October 1940

HISTORICAL SECTION
ADMIRALTY
S.W.1

"The Best of Prophets of the Future is the Past."

Lord Byron, 1821.

PREFACE

THE NAVAL Staff History of Naval Operations in the Mediterranean during the Second World War is being written in four volumes.

This volume is designed to give the reader a broad outline of events from the outbreak of war to October 1940, when Italy attacked Greece. For a more detailed study of certain important operations the text refers to the appropriate Battle Summary;[1] for example, the operations against the French fleet at Oran and the attack on the *Richelieu* at Dakar. Such Battle Summaries form an integral part of the Naval Staff History. They are being revised as necessary, or completely rewritten, to include information obtained from German and Italian sources since the war ended.

The Appendices, which reproduce memoranda dealing with Admiralty policy, the views of the Commander-in-Chief, important signals and dispositions, are for the student an important part of the volume. Also, full use should be made of the comprehensive index if it is desired to obtain information on any particular matter; for example, Malta and its defences.

To Follow

VOLUME II
November 1940 to December 1941

Air and Sea Power (November 1940 to June 1941).
Support to the Army (July 1941 to December 1941).

VOLUME III

The Vital Struggle for Supplies (January 1942 to June 1942).
Threat to Egypt Met and Overcome (July 1942 to December 1942).

VOLUME IV
January 1943 to May 1945

Our Offensive Develops (January to December 1943).
Line Cleared from Gibraltar to Suez (January to October 1944).
Mopping Up (November 1944 to May 1945).

---

[1] References to serial numbers of B.R. 1736 in this issue should be disregarded as these documents are being revised, and the new B.R. 1736 serial number may be different. The numbers of the Battle Summaries themselves will remain as at present.

CONTENTS

Chapter 1   INTRODUCTION   Sections 1 to 7

Comparison with former times – Balance of power – Situation in the summer, 1939 – The Commander-in-Chief – Bases – Strategic objectives – Final preliminaries, July–August 1939.

Chapter 2   UNEASY CALM   Sections 8 to 21
(September 1939 to May 1940)

Germany hostile, Italy non-belligerent – Precautionary measures and War Plans, August–September 1939 – Strength and Disposition of Fleets in the Mediterranean, September 1939 – Contraband control and Allied shipping – U-boats – The British Fleet leaves the Mediterranean, November 1939 – Eve of total war – British Fleet returns to the Mediterranean, April–May, 1940.

Chapter 3   CHALLENGE TO 'MARE NOSTRUM'   Sections 22 to 45
(June 1940)

Clearing for action – Choice of plans – Italy enters the War – Operations begin – Fleet cruise, 11th to 14th June, 1940 – Air activities – Action between Seventh Cruiser Squadron and enemy destroyers – Operation MA.3 – Submarine activities – Bombardment of Bardia – The French collapse; British Fleet in Mediterranean reinforced with Force H.

Chapter 4   SIGHTING SHOTS   Sections 46 to 63
(July, August 1940)

Operations against the French Fleet at Casablanca, Dakar and Oran – Enemy supply routes – Fleet Air Arm attacks on Catania and Tobruk – Third Cruiser Squadron bombard Bardia – Operation MA.5, 7th to 15th July – Fleet Air attacks, enemy and British – Action off Calabria, 9th July – Support by Force H in the Western Mediterranean – Loss of H.M.S. *Escort* – Attacks on shipping – Action with Italian cruisers off Crete, 19th July.

Chapter 5   REINFORCEMENTS, AIR AND SUBMARINE ACTIVITIES   Sections 64 to 78
(September 1940)

Reinforcements for the Fleet and Malta – Fleet cruise 27th to 29th July – Fighters for Malta, Operation Hurry – Enemy movements – Operation Hats, 30th August to 5th September – Attacks on enemy air bases in the Dodecanese – Force H, activities in Western Mediterranean – Attacks on airfield at Cagliari – Enemy air attacks – Defence of Malta, Alexandria and Haifa – F.A.A. and R.A.F. operations – Submarine patrols.

Chapter 6   BRITISH COMMAND OF THE SEA ESTABLISHED   Sections 79 to 101
(October 1940)

Operations off Cyrenaica – Italian advance into Egypt, 13th to 17th September – Fleet cruises, September to October – Enemy convoys to Libya – Operation MB. 6, night action, H.M.S. *Ajax* and enemy destroyers – Italy attacks Greece, 28th October 1940 – British base at Suda Bay.

APPENDICES

		Page
A.	Precautionary measures, August–September 1939	82
B.	Contraband Control areas, September 1939 to June 1940	84
C.	Plans and Policy	85
D.	Command and Staff	
	(a) Mediterranean Fleet	106
	(b) Force 'H'	113
	(c) Sea Transport Service, Middle East 1940	116
E.	Summary of Signals	118
F.	Disposition of Fleets of the Mediterranean Powers	
	(a) September 1939	136
	(b) June 1940	
	Part I. Ships, including seaborne aircraft	144
	Part II. Shore-based aircraft	152
G.	Summary of activities of the Greek Fleet	
	(1) Before collapse of Greece, October 1940 to April 1941	154
	(2) After collapse of Greece, May 1941 to April 1944	154
	(3) Greek warships' services during the war	155
H.	Monthly report for September 1940 of the Sea Transport Officer, Port Sudan	159
J.	Royal Naval Armament Supply – Eastern Mediterranean, 1939–40	163
K.	Royal Naval Medical arrangements – Eastern Mediterranean	166
	Bibliography	168

ILLUSTRATIONS

Between pages 32 and 33.

1. Admiral Sir Andrew B. Cunningham, G.C.B., D.S.O.
2. Cairo, showing vicinity of G.H.Q., Middle East
3. H.M.S. *Warspite*
4. H.M.S. *Malaya*
5. H.M.S. *Resource*
6. H.M.S. *Royal Sovereign*
7. Italian battleship *Vittorio Veneto*
8. French submarine *Narval*
9. Italian 6-inch cruiser *Giuseppe Garibaldi*
10. H.M.S. *Calypso*
11. Italian submarine *Diamante*
12. Italian destroyer *Ostro*
13. The submarine base at Malta
14. Gibraltar
15. Vice-Admiral Sir James F. Somerville, K.C.G., D.S.O.
16. Battleship *Richelieu*
17. French 6-inch cruisers *Georges Leygues* and *Emile Bertin*

FRENCH SQUADRON AT ALEXANDRIA:

18. Battleship *Lorraine*
19. 6-inch cruiser *Duguay-Trouin*
20. 8-inch cruiser *Duquesne*

BOMBARDMENT OF ORAN:

21. Fort on the hill of Mers-el-Kebir, west of Oran
22. The *Strasbourg* and the *Dunkerque*
23. Aerial torpedo hitting the *Dunkerque*
24. French battlecruiser *Dunkerque*
25. First bombs falling on the jetty and round the squadron
26. The *Provence* with her after-deck ablaze
27. French destroyer *Vauban*

Between pages 112 and 113.

28. Walrus

TYPES OF FLEET AIR ARM AIRCRAFT, 1940:

29. Swordfish
30. Hurricanes
31. Italian battleship *Conte di Cavour*
32. Italian battleship *Giulio Cesare*
33. H.M.S. *Faulknor*
34. H.M.S. *Escort*
35. H.M.A.S. *Sydney*
36. H.M.S. *Eagle*
37. H.M.S. *Ark Royal*

38. H.M.S. *Renown*
39. Malta – food supplies
40. H.M. submarine *Rorqual*
41. H.M. submarine *Osiris*
42. H.M.S. *Kent*
43. H.M.S. *Jervis*
44. H.M.S. *Aphis*
45. H.M.S. *Greyhound* and *Ladybird*
46. H.M.A.S. *Stuart*
47. H.M.S. *Ajax*
48. Italian destroyer *Artigliere*
49. Italian destroyer *Camicia Nera*
50. H.M.S. *Liverpool*
51. Greek light cruiser H.H.M.S. *Helle*
52. H.M.S. *Protector*

(Photographs supplied by Chief of Naval Information)

	Page
View of Alexandria Harbour, May 1940	12
Third Cruiser Squadron off Bardia, 6th July, 1940	39
Italian high-level bomb attack on H.M.S. *Malaya*	41
The *Bartolomeo Colleoni* under fire	47

PLANS

(*at back of book*)

1 Mediterranean and Black Sea, Political Map

2 Diagram of Fleet and Air dispositions, June 1940

3 Action between Seventh Cruiser Squadron and three Italian destroyers, 28th June, 1940

4 Aegean convoy operation (MA.3), 27th June to 2nd July, 1940

5 to 8 Attack on French battleship *Richelieu* at Dakar, 8th July, 1940

9, 10 Operations against French Fleet at Oran, 3rd and 6th July, 1940

11 to 13 Action with Italian Fleet off Calabria, 9th July, 1940

14 Action with Italian cruisers off Cape Spada, Crete, 19th July, 1940

15 Fleet Air Arm strike in Bomba Bay, 22nd August, 1940

16 Military position, Cyrenaica and Egypt, autumn 1940

NOTE. – *Distances are given here in nautical miles of 6,080 feet.*

ABBREVIATIONS

A/A	Anti-aircraft.		of A.M.C.s. is given the figures refer to displacement.)
A.B.R.	Amphibious Boat Reconnaissance.		
A.B.V.	Armed Boarding Vessel.	H/A.	High-angle gun.
A/C.	Aircraft.	H.E.	High explosive.
A.M.C.	Armed Merchant Cruiser.		
A.N.A.	Assistant Naval Attaché.	I.E.	Initial equipment, aircraft.
A.O.C.	Air Officer Commanding.	I.P.C.	Iraq Petroleum Company.
A.P.	Armour-piercing.	I.R.	Initial equipment, aircraft (reserve).
A.S.	Anti-submarine.		
A/S (prefix to a vessel)	Fitted with asdics.	L/A	Low-angle gun.
A.S.I.S.	Armament Store Issuing Ship.	L.L.	Anti-magnetic minesweeping apparatus.
A/T	Anti-torpedo.	L.R.	Light Reconnaissance aircraft.
B.N.L.O.	British Naval Liaison Officer.	M.A.S.	Italian motor anti-submarine boat.
		M/L.	Motor Launch.
C.Bs.	Confidential books.	M/S	Minesweeper.
C.I.D.	Committee or Imperial Defence.	M.T.	Mechanical transport (vehicles).
C.I.G.S.	Chief of Imperial General Staff.	M.T.B.	Motor torpedo boat.
C.O.S.	Chief of Staff.	M/V.	Merchant vessel.
C.R.H.	Calibre radius head (e.g. 15-inch four or six C.R.H.).	M.W.T.	Ministry of War Transport.
C.T.	Contre-torpilleur (treated here as Fleet Destroyer).	N.A.	Naval Attaché.
		N.C.S.O.	Naval Control Service Officer.
		N.O.I.C.	Naval Officer-in-Charge.
D/C.	Depth charge.		
D.G.	Degaussing gear.	p.v.	Paravane.
D.E.W.D.	Director of Economic Warfare Department.	pom-pom	Short-range anti-aircraft gun.
D/F.	Direction-finding.	P.S.T.O.	Principal Sea Transport Officer.
D.S.T.O.	Divisional Sea Transport Officer.	P.S.T.O. (E)	Principal Sea Transport Officer, Egypt.
D.W.I.	Directional Wireless Installation. (Name given to Wellington aircraft specially fitted for magnetic minesweeping.)	R.A. (L)	Rear-Admiral, Alexandria.
		R.D/F.	Radar (formerly Radio Direction Finding).
		R.F.A.	Royal Fleet Auxiliary.
E-boats	Enemy boats, normally torpedo-boats.	R.U.S.I.	Royal United Service Institution.
F.A.A.	Fleet Air Arm.	S.A.P.	Semi armour-piercing.
F.B.	Flying Boat.	S.B.N.O.S.C.A.	Senior British Naval Officer, Suez Canal area.
F.L.O.	French Liaison Officer.	S/M.	Submarine.
F O.C.N.A.	Flag Officer Commanding, North Africa.	S.N.O.L.A.	Senior Naval Officer, Levant area.
FO.I.C.	Flag Officer-in-Charge.	S.Ps.	Signal publications.
F.O.R.S.C.A.	Flag Officer, Red Sea and Canal area.	S.S.	Steamship.
F.P.B.	French floatplane, bomber.	S.T.O.	Sea Transport Officer-in-Charge.
F.P.R.	French floatplane, reconnaissance.		
F.R.	Italian fighter-reconnaissance aircraft.	T.B.	Torpedo-boat.
		T.B.R.	Torpedo-bomber-reconnaissance aircraft.
G.H.Q.	General Headquarters.	T.S.D.S.	Two speed destroyer sweep.
G.I.C.	Gunnery, individual ship control.	T.S.R.	Torpedo-spotting-reconnaissance aircraft.
G.R.T.	Gross registered tonnage. (When tonnage of M/V's. is given the figures refer to G.R.T. When tonnage of warships is given the figures refer to displacement. When tonnage	W/T	Wireless telegraphy.
		Y.M.S.	'Yard'-type minesweeper.

CHAPTER 1

INTRODUCTION

1

THE BRITISH supremacy of the Mediterranean Sea established by Lord Nelson between 1798 and 1805 was not seriously threatened until shortly before the Second World War (1939–45). The nineteenth century witnessed several wars and 'incidents', for example: the Greek War of Independence against Turkey, 1821–30; the Crimean War, 1854–56; the formation of the kingdom of Italy, 1860–61; the Austro-Prussian War of 1866, when Italy seized the chance to attack Austria and, though defeated, secured Venice at the resultant Peace Treaty; the Egyptian campaigns, 1882–85; the Fashoda incident of 1898, which for a short time caused strained relations with France; the Cretan insurrection 1897–98, which led to the expulsion of the Turks from Crete. Early in the twentieth century, in 1911–12, Italy and Turkey were at war for the suzerainty of Libya, and in 1911 there was considerable tension for a time over the Agadir incident, where the German gunboat *Panther* had been sent ostensibly to guard German interests, following the occupation of Fez by French troops.[1] With all of these affairs we were concerned and in some of them directly involved, but none of them caused deep uneasiness over the question of our supremacy. In the First World War, 1914–18, German U-boats hampered, but offered no major threat to our Mediterranean communications; it was not until 1935, after a lapse of 130 years, that signs of a major threat arose. In that year the Italians began a short war of conquest of Abyssinia, and followed up their success in 1936–37 by sending 40,000 troops to Spain to assist General Franco in his civil war against the Republicans. The expedition was a violation of a specific Treaty not to send arms to either side in Spain, and it was supported at sea by a surreptitious submarine campaign when both neutral and Spanish ships were sunk. At the same time the Germans sent strong Air Forces to Spain, and it looked indeed as if the Axis powers, Germany and Italy, were preparing to challenge our control of the Western Mediterranean area.

When considering how this challenge developed, and how it was met, it is interesting to note that some of the scenes of action in ancient days, before English ships appeared in the Mediterranean, were once again to witness the clash of fleets and armies, totally different in appearance and weapons but inspired with the same purpose of deciding who should control the Middle Sea. The Battle of Spartivento in November 1940, for instance, was fought on almost the same stretch of water as the Battle off Cape Trapani, in 241 B.C., when the Romans defeated the Carthaginians and ended the First Punic War. The action off Calabria in July 1940, was not far from the scene of Actium where, in 31 B.C., Octavius Caesar defeated the Egyptians under Antony and Cleopatra. Once more Greece and the Aegean were to see bitter fighting; this time it was New Zealanders instead of Spartans at the Pass of Thermopylae, fighting just as determinedly and refusing to withdraw 'according to plan'.

Finally Crete, which must surely hold the record for more fighting to the square mile than any place on earth, again became, though only for a short while, the centre of fierce combat. Lying at the corner of

---

1 See Hazel's Annual 1919, pp. 217 to 222. 'On 1st July, 1911 the *Panther* went to Agadir and this demonstration of international ruthlessness seems to have awakened grave anxiety in Italy as to the security of her interests in Tripoli.'

1

Europe and Asia, its possession has been fought for and won by Greeks, Romans, Byzantines, Saracens, Venetians, Turks, then again by the Greeks and finally by Germans and British. It is in Crete, also, that we see an outstanding example of how the tempo of warfare has been speeded up. What, in olden days, took years to effect is now accomplished in about the same number of days. For instance, Candia on the north coast was held in the seventeenth century by the Venetians for over 20 years against the Turkish army and navy,[1] and after its capitulation in 1669 the Turks sent General Francesco Morosini and his garrison back to Italy as free men. In 1941 the island fell after less than three weeks' intensive siege; not all the valour of British and Dominion troops under General Freyberg, V.C., backed by Greeks and Cretans, could hold out against overwhelming German air attacks. Yet it should be noted that the island was never wholly conquered, for Greek guerillas under Colonel Mandakas, supported by 1,000 or so survivors of the siege, kept up resistance and harassed the Germans to the end.

The German campaign in the Balkans and Crete will be described in more detail in Volume 2; here it will be sufficient to say that, although their immediate objectives, the occupation of Yugoslavia, Greece and Crete were attained, yet in its overall effect on the German chances of winning the war the result was negative. Mr. Churchill describes the German conquest of Crete as a Pyrrhic victory, as indeed it was. Accounts of German losses differ, but in all probability their total casualties in Crete did not exceed 12,000. This was not a large figure; but it included the whole of the 7th Airborne Division, and this loss had a disastrous effect on their plans for extending operations into Syria and Iraq. According to Directive No. 31, issued by Hitler from Fuhrer Headquarters on 9th June, 1941 ...

'Crete ... will be the operational base from which to carry on the air war in the Eastern Mediterranean, in co-ordination with the situation in North Africa.' The intention was there, but the weapon had been blunted. By the end of May 1941, simultaneous with the fall of Crete, we had occupied Iraq, and early in June 1941 we advanced into Syria. A further adverse effect of the five weeks' delay in German plans caused by the Balkan campaign and the Battle of Crete was not felt until December 1941, when the German advance into Russia was halted in front of Moscow. Marshal Zhukov had time to assemble his Siberian reserves, and General Frost was operating at a temperature below zero on the attackers' long line of communications.[2]

2

The balance of power in the Mediterranean during the nineteenth century witnessed at least one major change when, in the 1820s, Britain helped Greece to attain independence after 400 years of Turkish domination. The twentieth century was to witness considerably greater changes. In 1912, Italy, seeking overseas bases, took Libya from the Turks and in 1924 the Dodecanese were ceded by Turkey to Italy at the Treaty of Lausanne. The First World War (1914–19) left France, Italy, Spain, Greece and ourselves as the principal Mediterranean powers. France was never seriously considered as a potential enemy. Greece was friendly; but Italy, in the months immediately before the Second World War, began to seize 'points d'appui' and prepare them as bases, whilst Spain showed distinctly friendly feelings towards both Germany and Italy. In April 1939, on Good Friday, Italy invaded Albania, thus gaining a foothold in the Balkan Peninsula as well as the control of both shores of the entrance to the Adriatic. In May 1939, a German squadron visited Spanish ports, and in view of German and Italian help given to Spain in the civil war of 1936–38, and the obvious advantage to Germany of Italian naval assistance in the Mediterranean, this visit pointed to the possibilities of further anti-British collaboration. In July 1939, the Italian Fleet carried out large-scale manoeuvres, when their main fleet operating from home ports intercepted and brought to action an 'attacking force' coming from the Eastern Mediterranean. This looked remarkably like a rehearsal of operations against the British Fleet coming from Alexandria.

---

1 Accounts of the length of the siege vary. In B.R.516A, Greece, Volume II, the period is stated as three years, but Haydn's Dictionary of Dates gives 24 years, while the Encyclopaedia Britannica and Cambridge Modern History favour the longer period with the inference that Francesco Morosini was in command during the last three years of close investment.

2 Cf. Volume III, p. 268, Mr. Churchill's 'The Second World War', also Appendix E one to this volume, and Remarks by Admiral Doenitz, Appendix C.2(b).

3

During the six months immediately preceding the outbreak of the Second World War on 3rd September, 1939, the Commander-in-Chief, Mediterranean, was confronted with a situation of considerable complexity. Metaphorically speaking, his problem was not so much that of one cat waiting to jump off one fence in one of two directions, rather was it a case of several cats on separate fences with various directions to choose from. Probably Germany would set the ball rolling in Europe; that was clear enough. Her policy of 'Drang nach Osten' which led up to the First World War in 1914 was still operative, and all her actions pointed to an early repetition of an attempt to gain the wealth of the Middle East, for which attempt to succeed she or an ally must control the Mediterranean. Italy, as already mentioned, had for years been extending her power by seizing and occupying territory in North Africa, the Aegean and, early in 1939, Albania.

If the U.S.S.R. stayed neutral, and especially if, as in fact happened, she signed a pact of non-aggression with Germany, then the possibility of Germany establishing herself in the Eastern Mediterranean and disputing our control of the Eastern Mediterranean bases became the more threatening. Further, a real danger to our position in the Mediterranean was the possibility of Japan joining the Axis Powers at the outset, since this would mean leaving the Eastern as well as the Western Basin to the care of the French;[1] but fortunately this contingency did not arise. The Cabinet Defence Requirements Committee had consistently urged from 1935 onwards the undesirability of our having to face a Three-Power enemy until our defences were in better shape, and our Foreign Policy was directed accordingly. In 1939, in their European Appreciation 1939–40, the Chiefs of Staff stressed the priority of our naval disposition in the order Germany, Italy, Japan, instead of the previous order Germany, Japan, Italy. In the report of the Defence Plans (Policy) Committee (61 and 62/1937) the Chiefs of Staff had appreciated that sending all our capital ships to the Far East would lead to the loss of control of the Eastern Mediterranean, and this was considered unacceptable having regard to our commitments in the Middle East.[2]

Apart from Japan, Russia and Italy, how would Spain, France, Greece and the Balkans, Turkey, Egypt react to Germany's next step? If friendly to us, how much reliance could be placed on their assistance? In the case of France, who was to take over the Western Basin, would the French Fleet be active, or would they repeat their relative inactivity of the First World War?

These were some of the questions prevalent in the summer of 1939, and it was fortunate that when the storm in Europe burst, in September 1939, two of the key posts of the Royal Navy, the First Sea Lord and the Commander-in-Chief, Mediterranean, were held by Admirals who knew the Station from end to end.

4

From March 1936, till June 1939, Admiral Sir Dudley Pound, G.C.B., G.C.V.O., had been C.-in-C. Mediterranean, having succeeded Admiral Sir W. W. Fisher, K.C.B., after serving as his Chief of Staff during the Italo-Abyssinian War (1935–36). For the first two years of his command the Spanish Civil War was in progress, in which Italian warships played a prominent part. He had also served as Chief of Staff from 1925 to 1927 to Admiral Sir Roger Keyes, who was then C.-in-C., Mediterranean. In June 1939, when Admiral Pound went to the Admiralty as First Sea Lord, he was succeeded in the Mediterranean by Admiral Sir Andrew B. Cunningham, K.C.B., D.S.O., with Rear-Admiral A. U. Willis as Chief of Staff.[3] Admiral Cunningham had served many years on the Station, including 1935–36 as Rear-Admiral Commanding Mediterranean destroyers; and in 1936–37 as Vice-Admiral, Second in Command, with his flag in H.M.S. *Hood*. During 1938–39 he was at the Admiralty as Deputy Chief of the Naval Staff.

---

1 See Appendix D for Command and Staff.

2 In July 1939 a battleship floating dock was installed in Alexandria, and during the autumn some 800 men were employed there, increasing later to 22,500. Gibraltar was reinforced from 1,500 men to 2,000 by December 1940, and later to 3,000.

3 See F.N.—Section 3. A more detailed account of the development of Alexandria naval dockyard will be given as an appendix to Volume 2.

SEC. 6 MEDITERRANEAN, SEPTEMBER 1939–OCTOBER 1940

5

Mention has been made (Section 3) of the questions prevalent in the summer of 1939, on the correct answer to which depended the Commander-in-Chief's disposition of his fleet. So long as Italy remained quiescent it would he safe to keep the main part of the fleet at Malta, but this would obviously become impracticable if there were any likelihood of heavy air attack.

Air action against Malta in fact eventually denied to us the use of its valuable dockyard which employed some 8,000 men as a routine repair base, and correspondingly increased the strain on Gibraltar and Alexandria, where, although both bases were manned to the limit of their capacity, the lack of repair facilities, available only in a main dockyard, was keenly felt.[1]

In the event of war breaking out with Italy and Germany, the French Fleet would take over the Western Basin and the British Fleet would move to Alexandria, where preparations were already being made to turn that port from a merchant shipping port of call into a main naval base.[2]

Alexandria had already acted as our main naval base in 1935–36 during the Italian-Abyssinian campaign and its capabilities were therefore known, though it was hardly possible to foresee the extent to which those capabilities would be tried. Up to June 1942 much of the work was done by a repair ship, H.M.S. *Resource*, assisted by the commercial repair yards. In 1942 various Admiralty workshops came into being. Additional assistance was provided by opening minor repair yards at Port Said, Haifa and Beirut. The story of the supply, repair and maintenance, and medical work at Alexandria, Port Said and Haifa from 1940 to 1944, bearing in mind that battleships, aircraft carriers, cruisers, destroyers and all kinds of small craft were concerned and units of each class dealt with in varying stages of damage from torpedo, mine, bomb and gunfire, is one of magnificent achievement that cannot be fully dealt with here. Some details of the armament supply and medical arrangements are given in Appendices J and K, but for the remainder it must be sufficient to say that without the skill and remarkable powers of improvisation displayed by the constructors, engineers, victualling and naval store, and medical officers concerned, the British Fleet in the Mediterranean would have been hamstrung.[3] The same may be said of the work of the Sea Transport Service, a brief description of which is given in Appendix D (c). In order to illustrate the problems confronting a Sea Transport Officer a verbatim copy of the monthly report of the S.T.O. Port Sudan, for September 1940, is given in Appendix H.

6

The strategic objectives which governed the Commander-in-Chief's dispositions may be classified as follows:–

(*a*) The destruction of the Italian Fleet and merchant vessels, and German ships (if they appeared);

(*b*) Support of the Army in North Africa or for any expedition they might undertake;

(*c*) The safe conduct of British and Allied merchant ships through the Mediterranean and Red Sea;

(*d*) The prevention of enemy attack by sea on Gibraltar, Malta, Cyprus, Egypt or the Levant coast.

Close co-operation with the Army and R.A.F. would be required. G.H.Q. of the Middle East was in Cairo, and this made the presence of the naval Commander-in-Chief in Egypt desirable. Direct telephonic communications from Cairo G.H.Q. to the flagship at Alexandria enabled the Staffs to keep in touch, and the Naval Intelligence Centre established on the Ras el Tin Peninsula of Alexandria harbour, in direct communication at all times with Cairo, passed information to the Commander-in-Chief when he was at sea.

---

1 C.I.D. Papers, Volume II. D P(p) 5b, 1439, report of Anglo-French Staff Conversations, 1938 and 1939:– 'French Forces will control the Western Basin of the Mediterranean, the British being responsible for the East' (A.F.C.25, Annex. II). See also Admiral Doenitz's remarks on German hopes of joining hands with Japan through the Red Sea, Appendix C.2 (b).

2 See section 23, 'choice of plans'.

3 See Cabinet Official Military History, Middle East section, chapter on the maintenance of large forces in the Middle East. The remarks on dockyard work are based on information supplied by the Director of Dockyards from material provided by Engineer Rear-Admiral Dunlop.

The sphere of command of the Army of the Middle East was no small one; for it included Egypt, Sudan, Syria, Palestine, Transjordan, Iraq and Iran, and Italian East Africa.

Occupation of Iraq, Syria, Iran and Italian East Africa was necessary in order to safeguard the Suez Canal and the Nile Valley. Supplies from Britain, the Empire and the United States through the Red Sea had also to be ensured. Middle East oil supplies had to be prevented from falling into German hands, and from mid-1941 it was necessary to maintain a route for British and American supplies to the U.S.S.R. through the Persian Gulf, the Caspian Sea and the Caucasus. Until that time the U.S.S.R. was a pseudo-ally of Germany. The area had, however, to be watched in the meantime so that German intrigues in the Middle East could be checked.

Since there was so much detail arising from the large areas and issues concerned which involved consultation between the Commanders-in-Chief of the three Services, an additional Naval Chief of Staff was appointed to work in Cairo, where an R.N. G.H.Q. was set up. This meant that the Commander-in-Chief would only have to be present in person in Cairo when discussions on major issues of policy were required.

7

In addition to the Commander-in-Chief and his two Chiefs of Staff (one at sea and one on shore in Cairo), Flag Officers at Gibraltar, Malta, Alexandria were responsible for their respective areas; the Red Sea south of Suez was under the C.-in-C., East Indies until October 1941, while the Canal area was in charge of a Vice-Admiral at Ismailia (short title S.B.N.O.S.C.A., Senior British Naval Officer, Suez Canal Area), and a Captain at Haifa (short title N.O.I.C. Haifa). Later on this latter post was expanded to Senior Naval Officer, Levant Area (short title S.N.O.L.A.), and was held by a Commodore with headquarters at Beirut.[1]

In July 1939 a French squadron under the command of Admiral Ollive visited Malta, and details were completed for French action in the Western Basin if the British Fleet had to move to Alexandria.

In August 1939 full Staffs for the Flag and Senior Officers concerned were sent out, and at the end of that month the Commander-in-Chief, flying his flag in H.M.S. *Warspite*, left Malta with the fleet for Alexandria.

By 1st September, 1939, when Germany launched her attack on Poland, the British and French navies were ready so far as circumstances permitted, in case Italy declared war. The British Navy could not be regarded as satisfactorily prepared for war in the Mediterranean unless it could use Malta as an offensive base, and its power to do this was dependent on that island's ability to provide protection against air attack. For some years before 1939 efforts were made to obtain authority to build submarine rock shelters, also to provide adequate air defence including four squadrons of fighter aircraft, the cost of which with necessary ground organisation would have been three million pounds. These efforts, however, proved unsuccessful.[2] Up to 1935 it was held by the Cabinet that 'no expenditure need be incurred on measures of defence required exclusively against attack by Italy.' Another difficulty was the doubt felt by the Air Ministry of ensuring the use of the island by the fleet even with the maximum supply of fighter aircraft. The Italian air striking forces available to attack Malta late in 1939 consisted of 276 bombers, 54 ground attack fighters and 54 escort fighters. Of these, all the fighters and one-third of the bombers could operate from Sicily, only 60 miles away, and the rest from Naples. As a counter measure to reduce the weight of attack on Malta it was hoped to establish a powerful air striking force in Tunisia. Owing, however, to demands from other areas and a hesitancy to believe in Italian hostility, the various plans for increasing Malta's ability to resist air attack were not undertaken until after the war with Italy had broken out. Consequently, the C.-in-C., Mediterranean, was obliged to forgo the use of his main naval base for offensive operations until nearly a year had elapsed. Later on, when provision of fighter protection enabled surface and submarine forces to operate from the island, the effect on the enemy's communications to Libya was prominent. This development will be seen as the story unfolds.

---

1 A nominal list of the Mediterranean Fleet and Force H and Sea Transport Service, Middle East, in the autumn of 1940 is given in Appendix D.
2 Joint Defence Committee papers, J.D.C. 261, 280, 297, 317, 319, 467, 497, 513; also Plans Division, Admiralty, P.D. 07500/39.

CHAPTER 2

UNEASY CALM

(SEPTEMBER 1939 TO MAY 1940)

8

IN THE latter part of August 1939, events moved rapidly to a climax. On 23rd August Germany signed a pact of non-aggression with the U.S.S.R. This was taken as a warning signal by Great Britain who had already begun preliminary mobilisation, and the Admiralty at once assumed control of all merchant shipping. Great Britain re-affirmed her pledge to Poland on 28th August, having on the previous day stopped the passage of shipping through the Mediterranean until Italy's attitude became clear. On 29th August the Admiralty ordered the fleet to mobilise. Germany invaded Poland at 0445, 1st September, 1939,[1] and a few hours later the Admiralty sent out the warning telegram ordering the 'precautionary period.'

Great Britain declared war on Germany at 1100, 3rd September, 1939, and on that day the Right Honourable Winston S. Churchill assumed the office of First Lord of the Admiralty, the same post he had occupied 25 years previously at the outbreak of the First World War. Japan announced her neutrality and Italy declared that she would be non-belligerent, the difference in the two terms being indistinguishable for practical purposes. Tension in the Mediterranean consequently subsided, and for two months the Mediterranean Fleet held a watching brief, after which ships were dispersed temporarily to other stations. (S.16.) Poland was overwhelmed before the end of September; but her collapse did not affect the general strategic situation in the Mediterranean. (Admiralty message, 1442/26/9/39 (Appendix E.2).)

9

The Naval War Memorandum (European), which was based on the Chiefs of Staff appreciation of the European situation, 1939, had been issued to all Commanders-in-Chief and Flag Officers in January 1939 (M.00697/1939). The details of precautionary measures taken in the Mediterranean (Appendix A) during the few days prior to the outbreak of war with Germany were based on this memorandum, which assumed the British Commonwealth to be at war against a combination of Germany and Italy with France as our ally. Included in these measures were the arming of merchant ships, particularly tankers; bringing A/A and coast defences to short notice; initiating the war W/T organisation; closure of the Mediterranean to outside shipping; patrolling the Great Pass at Alexandria by destroyers; requisitioning British ships; censorship; laying minefields and indicator nets; the institution of examination services, and of contraband control services at Haifa, Gibraltar, Suez and Port Said. Italian ships were exempted from examination. (C.-in-C.'s, Mediterranean, War Diary, 3rd September.)

As the Suez Canal Convention provided that no belligerent rights should be exercised in the Canal Zone, special measures were necessary for the Suez Canal Area. The principal one was the offer of

---

[1] The German executive order for zero hour was given p.m. 31st August. A copy signed by Hitler is on view in the Maritime Museum at Greenwich.

voluntary examination to northbound vessels at Port Said, thus obviating the need of diversion to Haifa (para. 100 of M.00697/1939). The duty of stopping vessels outside the three-mile limit off Port Said was performed at first by destroyers, and later by armed boarding vessels.

In the case of vessels southward bound, it was pointed out that the necessity for examining them would cease in the event of a close blockade of both coasts of Italian East Africa being established, as all vessels attempting to approach these coasts would then be stopped by the blockading forces.

10

The main functions of our fleet in the Mediterranean were given in paragraph 15 of the Naval War Memorandum as follows:–

(a) To bring enemy naval forces to action wherever they can be met.
(b) To ensure the safe passage of reinforcements to our fleet and garrisons in the Mediterranean, which will, if possible, be sent out before the outbreak of war.
(c) To obtain command of the sea in the Eastern Basin of the Mediterranean, thereby denying any opportunity of seaborne Italian attack on Egypt, Palestine or Cyprus.
(d) Interruption of Italian sea communications with Libya.
(e) Interruption of Italian trade with the Black Sea.

The plan also included steps to be taken in the event of war with Japan at the same time as a war in Europe. These steps would have denuded the Mediterranean of British naval forces other than those essential for the local defence of Malta, Egypt and the Suez Canal, and would have left us dependent on French naval action for any restraint to be placed on Italian operations. In view of the actual course of events in June 1940, when the French Fleet was immobilised after the capitulation of France, it was well for us that Japan kept neutral until December 1941. By that time we had taken the measure of the Italian Fleet.

11

COUNTRY	BATTLE-SHIPS	BATTLE CRUISERS	AIRCRAFT CARRIERS	CRUISERS 8-inch	CRUISERS 6-inch	DESTROYERS & T.B.S.	S/MS	ESCORT VESSELS
MEDITERRANEAN								
Great Britain	3	–	1	3	3	44	9	4
France	3	–	1	6	4	37	55	8
Italy	4	–	1[1]	7	12	111	101	10
Spain	–	–	–	1	5	29	5	42
Greece	–	–	–	1	1	23	6	–
Turkey	–	1	–	–	2	4	6	–
Yugoslavia	–	–	1 (small)	–	–	8	4	–
BLACK SEA								
Bulgaria	–	–	–	–	–	6	–	–
Rumania	–	–	–	–	–	7	1	–
U.S.S.R.	1	–	–	–	4	25	25	–
RED SEA (C.-in-C., East Indies)								
Great Britain	–	–	–	–	–	3	–	–
Italy	–	–	–	–	–	9	4	4

---

1 This was the *Miraglia,* whose main function was to carry aircraft from one port to another; there is no record of her taking part in Fleet operations.

The preceding table shows the comparative strength of the fleets of the Mediterranean Powers in September 1939. The disposition of forces is shown in Appendix F(a).

12

With Italy non-belligerent, the principal tasks of the Mediterranean Fleet consisted in the interception of German shipping and cargoes, and the protection of Allied shipping.

On 5th September the Admiralty ordered the release of shipping and the formation of east- and west-bound convoys in the Mediterranean, except for ships of over 15 knots, which were to proceed independently and zigzag during daylight. The first east-bound convoy (GREEN 1) (speed 8 knots) left Gibraltar at 2000/7th September and consisted of 25 ships, five of which were for North African ports. The Vice-Admiral, Bizerta, was asked to provide air reconnaissance along the North African coast. With regard to routeing, the Commander-in-Chief instructed the Rear-Admiral, Gibraltar, and the Senior British Naval Officer, Canal Area, that convoys should be routed well clear of each other, should pass in daylight except in the Cape Bon–Marsala area, and should go well south of Malta.

The Commander-in-Chief informed the Admiralty (2241/8th September) that shipping at ports other than Gibraltar and Port Said, for which convoy could not be arranged, would be sailed independently; all ships to be evasively routed, to zigzag and to darken at night. Similar advice was given to French, Egyptian and Polish shipping. The first west-bound convoy, BLUE 1, escorted by Captain D.2 in H.M.S. *Hardy* with the 3rd Division of destroyers and H.M.S. *Aberdeen*, left Port Said on 9th September and was joined by ships from Alexandria. This commenced an eight day cycle of east-bound and west-bound convoys. Allied and neutral ships were admitted to convoy on 22nd September. Meanwhile enemy merchant ships, immobilised by the presence of the French Fleet in the Western Basin, and of the British in the Eastern, took shelter in Spanish, Italian, Adriatic, Greek and Black Sea ports. By 24th September 45 German ships were lying confined in neutral ports, mainly Italian and Spanish.

13

The Admiralty general directive for action against enemy seaborne trade, as given in paragraphs 80 to 85 of M.00697/1939, will be found in Appendix C.1, though it should be noted that Italian ships were at first exempted from examination. (S.9.) Since all the coastline of the Mediterranean was either Allied or neutral, a close blockade of Germany was not feasible and instructions were given that neutral ships were only to be boarded if this was necessary for identification, and for no other purpose. This policy, however, obviously rendered the capture of contraband in neutral vessels impracticable, and accordingly on 8th September the Commander-in-Chief, by direction of the Admiralty, ordered contraband control to be applied without discrimination to all neutral flags. The importance, however, of avoiding 'incidents' with Italian ships was stressed and only 'obvious cases' were to be sent in for examination (C.-in-C., Mediterranean, 0209/8th September). This task of contraband control at sea was carried out by a Detached Squadron consisting of cruisers, armed merchant cruisers, armed boarding vessels and destroyers, under the command of Vice-Admiral J. C. Tovey. Patrols for this purpose were instituted in the Aegean, in the approaches to the Adriatic, and in the area south of the Straits of Messina. German cargoes were searched for and seized under the recognised belligerent right of visit and search on the high seas, but leakages inevitably occurred. For instance, on 14th September, the Admiralty reported that the Italian S.S. *Bosforo* would leave Salonika on 15th September for Trieste with 100 tons of tobacco for Germany (A.T.1942/14th September). A glance at the map will show that she could make the whole voyage in territorial waters, so that even if we had possessed a spare ship to intercept her she could still have passed unmolested. A complete story of contraband control in the Mediterranean would constitute a separate study; here only such references to it will be made as will emphasise the considerable demands made by it on the fleet's slender resources.

Cotton as a cargo, and particularly Egyptian cotton, was a matter of obvious concern to the Commander-in-Chief, and on 21st September, as a result of meetings with the Embassy staff and the Consul-General, he raised the question with the Admiralty (C.-in-C., Mediterranean, 1216/21st September). He pointed out that cotton was being exported in neutral ships to countries adjacent to Germany, and that the Egyptian Customs were not controlling this trade satisfactorily. He concluded by saying that he intended to intercept and divert any cargoes which were known to be suspicious.

To assist in the contraband control system the S.O. (1) Alexandria collected and issued a weekly summary of information regarding ships carrying contraband.

14

Our own shipping quickly got into its convoy stride, and by 22nd September all our light forces that were not employed on contraband control were absorbed in escort work. The Commander-in-Chief took the fleet to sea west of Crete between 12th and 16th September, as he thought the mass of shipping passing through the area at that period needed support. A dividing line for east-bound and west-bound convoys was established on 13th September. It passed 30 miles north of the Algerian coast, 20 miles N.E. of Cape Bon, between Malta and Sicily, to a point 6.5 miles N.W. of Port Said. This proved to be unsatisfactory as it 'jammed' traffic too much together and resulted in a head-on collision (causing serious damage to four ships) on 21st September between two French convoys, when 80 miles west of Gozo. The C.-in-C.'s Staff Officer (Operations) went to Toulon and arranged for modifications to be made both in the general convoy arrangements and in the routeing. As a result the British were made responsible for Gibraltar–Port Said convoys; the French for Algiers–Marseilles, and new boundary lines came into force on 15th October as follows:–

(1) A through line from Gibraltar–Malta–Beirut (ZZ).
(2) A lane (YY–XX) 10 miles wide along the north African coast, eastbound traffic to keep to the southern half, and west-bound to the northern.
(3) Lines between Marseilles and Oran (WW), between Marseilles and Algiers (UU), between Marseilles and Galita Island (XX), northbound traffic to keep east of these lines. Regulations were introduced which governed the time of crossing between the E.–W. and N.–S. lines; also, ships within 15 miles of UU, VV, WW and ZZ were to burn dimmed navigation lights if on a course of 40 degrees or more different. from the direction of these lines and also when crossing the lane XX–YY.

15

No serious threat from U-boats to our shipping in the Mediterranean developed during the months September 1939 to May 1940; there were a number of reports of sightings by aircraft, and contacts by A/S vessels. These, if genuine, were probably Italian U-boats carrying out reconnaissance patrols. The Commander-in-Chief issued instructions on 4th September that, while existing relations with Italy persisted, a submerged submarine was only to be attacked if:–

(a) she committed a hostile act;
(b) she was inside British or Allied territorial waters;
(c) if she was in, or would shortly be in, a position to deliver an attack on British or Allied warships other than light craft, fleet auxiliaries or merchant vessels.

On 9th September, H.M.S. *Grenville* reported a contact and aircraft were sent from Alexandria to search, but there were no developments. In view of this and other similar reports the Admiralty were asked urgently for a ruling on our anti-submarine precautions; meanwhile the Naval Attaché in Rome reported that the Italians had readily agreed that their submarines should proceed on the surface and under escort outside exercise areas. A final agreement on these lines was signed in Rome on 21st September, 1939, and the Fleet was informed of the Italian submarine exercise areas in Part 1, Article 41 of Mediterranean War Memoranda.[1]

---
1 In a reply to a similar query from Commander-in-Chief, East Indies (0649/16/9) the Admiralty stated that the existence and details of any agreement about S/M. areas between ourselves and the Italian should be kept strictly secret (1708/21/9/39).

As time passed without any evidence of German U-boat activity in the Mediterranean,[1] independent sailings for through voyages except for troop transports were resumed on 16th October, but the sailing of ships in convoy inside the Mediterranean and bound only for other Mediterranean ports continued until 17th November. Ships bound for the United Kingdom from Port Said, however, were formed into convoys at that port until 2nd December, after which date Gibraltar became their assembly port for convoy.

16

As the situation in the Mediterranean by early November only called for contraband control work and local defence activities it was decided to utilise the battleships and modern cruisers elsewhere. Accordingly, the battleships *Barham* and *Warspite* returned to the United Kingdom for service in the North Sea and North Atlantic; the *Malaya* (later relieved by the *Ramillies*), with the aircraft carrier *Glorious* passed through the Suez Canal and operated from Aden, hunting raiders in the Indian Ocean. The First Cruiser Squadron *(Devonshire, Suffolk* and *Norfolk*[2]) joined the Home Fleet. The only destroyer flotilla left was the 21st, with Captain (D) in H.M.S. *Duncan*. It remained at Malta until relieved by a division of Australian destroyers in mid-December, then returning to the United Kingdom. Other departures during November consisted of the hospital ship *Atlantis*, the submarine depôt ship *Maidstone* (for Freetown), and the destroyer depôt ship *Woolwich* (for the United Kingdom). The 12 M.T.Bs. based at Malta together with their depôt ship, H.M.S. *Vulcan*, also returned home, the M.T.Bs. sailing by way of Ajaccio, Marseilles and the French canals to Le Havre and Portsmouth.

The Mediterranean Fleet was thus reduced to skeleton form; four light cruisers *(Arethusa, Penelope, Galatea* and *Capetown)*, one flotilla leader (H.M.A.S. *Stuart*) and four destroyers (H.M.A.S. *Vampire, Vendetta, Voyager* and *Waterhen*), three submarines for A/S training (H.M.S. *Oswald, Osiris, Otway*), an aircraft carrier for deck landing training (H.M.S. *Argus*), four armed boarding vessels (H.M. ships *Chakla, Fiona, Juna, Rosaura*), two armed merchant cruisers H.M.S. *Antenor* and *Ranpura* (later relieved by the *Voltaire*) and a number of A/S trawlers and minesweepers. The Commander-in-Chief transferred his flag ashore at Malta on 1st November, and after a quick docking H.M.S. *Warspite* sailed for the United Kingdom. The whole of the Operational Intelligence Centre and the main sections of the Staff Office (Intelligence), Mediterranean, returned to Malta from Alexandria on 13th November and worked in Lascaris Barracks, close to the Commander-in-Chief's offices in the Castille. For the six months, November 1939 to May 1940, Malta acted as the Mediterranean Fleet base, while at Alexandria preparations to complete dockyard workshops and to build up stores were continued.

The contraband control work continued as already outlined; our ships kept a strict surveillance, and obtained a certain amount of results for their labours (see Appendix B). Occasional difficulties arose with the Italians, who claimed a six-mile limit for territorial waters. On 11th November the Commander-in-Chief pointed out to the Admiralty (1413/11th November) that grounds for Italian complaints were not understood, unless it was accepted that the Italian territorial waters extended to six miles, in which case the interception of neutral vessels carrying contraband would be extremely difficult. The occasion of this signal was a complaint that H.M.S. *Sikh* had boarded a ship just over five miles from the Italian coast.

On one occasion in December, the French cruisers *Tourville* and *Colbert*, assisted by their sloop *D'Iberville*, conducted a sweep of the contraband control area west of Greece, then through the Dodecanese and the Gulf of Adalia to Beirut. The results were disappointing and the Commander-in-Chief reported to the Admiralty (1901/12th December) that, while reinforcement of actual patrols was welcome, sporadic efforts by ships outside his command were not of value. The *Tourville* and French destroyers carried out sweeps in Greek waters on several occasions later.

---

1 From German documents we now know that U.26 paid a short visit to the Western Mediterranean in November 1939. She claimed to have sunk a ship off Alboran Island on 13th November, but no record can be found of any such casualty. A more detailed account of her cruise will be found in the Home and Atlantic, Naval Staff History, Volume I. The real activity of German U-boats in the Mediterranean did not begin until September 1941.

2 These ships had replaced the *Sussex* and *Shropshire* (Appendix F.(a)), which had left the Mediterranean in October to hunt German raiders in the Cape area.

With a depleted fleet some difficulty was experienced in providing a sufficient number of armed guards for the ships on contraband control duties, but the situation was eased at the end of November when the War Office agreed to the provision of 20 N.C.O.s and 100 other ranks from the Malta Garrison.

17

From November 1939 to March 1940 inside the Mediterranean there reigned a period of uneasy calm, for it was felt that at almost any moment a sudden reversal of Italy's attitude might occur and find us unprepared. Such steps were taken as our reduced forces permitted, and precautionary measures adopted such as keeping the port of Malta closed at night while the blackout was on; also, at Port Said and Alexandria exit only was allowed at night. Twin-screw minesweeping vessels were distributed so as to keep three in the Canal area, one at Alexandria and one at Malta, and officers and men from the 3rd Minesweeping Flotilla at Malta who were additional to war complement were withdrawn and used for armed guards in the contraband patrol ships. Two of the three vessels of the 3rd Minesweeping Flotilla (*Dundalk* and *Dunoon*) were ordered to the United Kingdom on 25th November, and on 22nd November the Vice-Admiral, Malta, reported to the Commander-in-Chief that, with one twin-screw minesweeper at Malta, it would only be possible to carry out a 40 per cent search of the main channels (V.A. Malta 1310/22nd November to C.-in-C. Mediterranean). At the same time the Commander-in-Chief ordered all possible steps to be taken for local craft to be used as auxiliary minesweepers and the necessary personnel trained. By early January ten small craft were available at Malta, two at Alexandria, two at Haifa and three in the Canal area where, also, the Canal Company's tugs were available for sweeping duties. In January, two 6-inch cruisers, H.M.S. *Arethusa* and *Penelope,* left for the United Kingdom, being relieved on contraband control service by the *Caledon* and *Calypso,* and the fleet repair ship *Resource* was transferred from Alexandria to Freetown.

18

A severe earthquake occurred in northern Turkey on 8th/9th January, 1940, and doctors, stores and sick berth attendants were sent from Malta in H.M.S. *Galatea,* and from Alexandria in H.M.S. *Antenor,* to Alexandretta. The doctors were not required, and after unloading the stores the ships returned to their former ports. To a country already badly off for road and rail communications, and generally poor, this earthquake was a severe disaster and not without its effect on military plans. The Commander-in-Chief, Mediterranean, and Commander-in-Chief, Middle East, had been in frequent touch with our Ambassador in Ankara, and various members of their Staffs paid visits to consult with Turkish officials on the possibilities of Turkish co-operation, but for the time being it was clear that Turkey would be too busy putting her own house in order to become involved in external commitments. Periodical meetings with us and with French Staff officers, however, continued.

19

These five months, although as already mentioned forming an uneasy period for the Commander-in-Chief and his Staff, were nevertheless useful as an interval of preparation for a situation where supplies would be jeopardised if the Mediterranean had to be closed for any length of time. In a signal to the Admiralty on 20th January (I853/20/1), the Commander-in-Chief asked that the stores, ammunition and other war material, which had been accumulated in the Mediterranean, should be maintained at a level that would suffice for a considerable fleet. It was pointed out that stores might well be a controlling factor if operations became necessary, and that a settled policy was needed. The Admiralty approved and gave details in Admiralty telegram 2237/4th February (1940). Ammunition and stores for the Fleet,[1] Malta and Alexandria and other bases were not, however, sensibly increased until May 1940, and the defences of Malta were not effectively modernised and strengthened until later in that year. Plans for co-operation with the Army and Air Force were worked out with G.H.Q. in Cairo, conferences were held with the

---

1 See Appendix J.

French at Bizerta and at Beyrouth, and details were arranged for housing the Ministry of War Transport and Sea Transport Departments with Headquarters in Cairo and branch offices in Alexandria, Port Said and Haifa (Appendix D(c)).

20

Early in March 1940, there were signs of a rapidly deteriorating military situation in the Mediterranean. Italian troop movements to Libya increased, the War Office estimating that an additional 27,000,white troops had arrived there during February, making a total of 157,000. A further 19,000 arrived by 18th March. The tone of the Italian Press became pointedly anti-British, particularly *Il Popolo* and the *Giornale d'Italia*. Reports from agents and visitors spoke of bellicose intentions voiced openly by the people; for instance, H.M.S. *Caledon* reported to the Commander-in-Chief, Mediterranean (2355/3rd April) that 'the master of U.S.S. *Hybert* states Italians at Venice are boasting that they are going to take Corfu next week.' Another report worth recording is that of the master of an Italian merchant ship in Alexandria, who on 20th March stated that Germany had recently put strong pressure on Italy to open the Mediterranean to submarine warfare. Italy and Spain were understood to have made a joint refusal after long deliberation. This report was of interest because on the next day a French intelligence report from Bizerta stated that there was great activity among German agents on the East coast of Majorca, suggesting preparations for U-boat warfare in the Mediterranean.

At the same time Italian warships began to show unusual activities, and by the end of March the Commander-in-Chief viewed the position with such disquiet that he began arrangements with the Admiralty to reinforce the Mediterranean Fleet. The result was an Admiralty message (2030/27th March) which informed all Commanders-in-Chief that it might be necessary to concentrate considerable force in the Eastern Mediterranean at short notice, and that as a preliminary action certain depôt and repair ships, and submarines, were being sailed for Alexandria.

VIEW OF HARBOUR

On 12th April, the British Vice-Consul at Dubrovnik reported that the Italians had mined the entrance to the Gulf of Valona and southern approach to Saseno, as well as along Durazzo and San Giovanni di Medua, and on the same day our Naval Attaché at Belgrade reported that the Yugoslav Ministry of Marine suggested that Italy was attempting to cause a move of British men-of-war to the Mediterranean in order to relieve German difficulties in Norway (A.N.A. Belgrade 1300/12th April). This seemed possible as the invasion of Norway and Denmark began on 9th April.

Altogether, so serious did the situation appear at the end of April that, on the 27th, the Admiralty ordered all British merchant ships, except mail steamers which were bound through the Mediterranean, to be diverted round the Cape of Good Hope. This order was cancelled on 8th May but reimposed on 16th

May (Appendix E.7 and 12). On 12th May the British Consul at Bari was instructed to report at once any assembly of transports or store ships at Bari, Brindisi or Barletta (Appendix E.8), and on 15th May a message from the Admiralty outlined the arrangements for cutting cables in the Western Mediterranean.

21

From the end of April reinforcements to the Mediterranean Fleet began to arrive. At Alexandria on 14th May, the Commander-in-Chief rehoisted his flag in H.M.S. *Warspite,* fresh from battle experience at Narvik.[1] Under his command were the battleships *Ramillies, Royal Sovereign* and *Malaya* from convoy duties in the Indian Ocean and Atlantic, the cruisers *Orion* from America and West Indies, *Neptune* from South Atlantic, *Gloucester* from East Indies; sixteen destroyers and three sloops and the netlayer *Protector* from the Home Fleet. In addition, the submarine depôt ship *Medway,* the fleet repair ship *Resource* and the destroyer depôt ship *Woolwich* all assembled in the Eastern Mediterranean, together with store ships, oilers, target service vessels and other auxiliaries.

Admiralty policy in relation to the Mediterranean at this time was referred to in a personal message to the Commander-in-Chief, Home Fleet, from the First Lord of the Admiralty (1939/29/4/40), in reply to a telegram from the Commander-in-Chief, Home Fleet, raising certain questions of policy concerning Norway. An extract from this message reads as follows:–

'The danger of Italy joining the war and the crippling of the German Fleet in recent operation (i.e., Norway) make it possible to concentrate certain forces in the Mediterranean. We are anxious to place as strong a fleet as possible at Alexandria, because the Western Basin can be reinforced at any time. We have not got to Alexandria yet,[2] but we expect it will be all right.' Simultaneously with these arrangements a French squadron was detailed to work with us from Alexandria under the command of Vice-Admiral Godfroy (A/T 1319/30/4 – Appendix E.3, F(b))-

Early in May signs of activity in the Italian Fleet gave added colour to the conviction that non-belligerency was coming to an end. Two super-dreadnoughts had been reported commissioned, the *Littorio* and *Vittorio Veneto*;[3] and the older battleships *Caio Duilio* and *Andrea Doria* were being modernised and refitted at Spezia and Trieste respectively. Motor fishing vessels and tugs were being requisitioned in a similar manner to August 1939, when they had been allocated mainly to North Africa and the Dodecanese.

At this stage very little attempt seems to have been made by the Italians to disguise their intentions; for instance, on 13th May, 1940, a British officer in Malta wishing to book passage home for his wife in an *Ala Littorio* plane was discouraged by officials of the line unless she travelled *before 15th May*. An example of the variety of difficulties concerning the Italians, which the Commander-in-Chief had to cope with, is given by his signal to the Admiralty on the questions of Italian escorted shipping and the passage of Italian bombers passing through Egypt bound for Italian East Africa, which were proposing to use aerodromes near Alexandria (Appendices E.13 and 16). On 19th May, H.Q. R.A.F. Middle East reported to the Commander-in-Chief, East Indies, and Commander-in-Chief, Mediterranean, that immediate general mobilisation of the army and air force in Italian East Africa had been ordered (C.-in-C. East Indies to Admiralty. 093 1Z/ 19/5*)*.

Rumours which could not be ignored came of Italian intentions to block the Suez Canal (Appendices E.14 and 17(2)). Each day brought with it fresh intelligence indicating that shortly the storm would burst. An Admiralty message (0027/21/5/40) to the Commander-in-Chief, Mediterranean, gave a summary of Signor Mussolini's message to the President of the U.S.A., the deduction from which was almost a certainty that Italy was only waiting for the German army to complete their conquest of Norway and overrun northern France before taking action herself (Appendices E.15, 17(1)). Mindful of all this the Admiralty and the Commander-in-Chief decided that our preparations must be intensified, and on 21st

---

[1] He had hoisted his flag on 7th May in the *Malaya* at Alexandria.
[2] See Section 16.
[3] These did not join the Fleet until August, 1940.

May a submarine patrol off Crete was instituted to forestall any attempted landing (A.T.0106/21 to C.-in-C. Mediterranean).

Rome made a cypher message[1] on 21st May addressed to 15 Italian tankers in the Atlantic, Mediterranean and Indian Oceans; but Italian ships were known to be still sailing from the Mediterranean for British ports. From San Francisco came a report that Italian lines had instructed their agents to load their ships with maximum quantities for Italian consumption, that the number of American loading ports was to be restricted, and ships were to proceed homewards at full speed. The British Naval Attaché at Rome reported on 24th May (0114/24/5) that the port of Naples was to be closed to passenger traffic from 5th June and reserved for military transports, that two medium-sized merchant ships were loading mines, and concluded with the statement that there were signs of an Expeditionary Force being prepared with Greece, Egypt or Corsica as probable objectives. Again, on 28th May the Naval Attaché, Rome, reported further indications of Italian intentions and ended by saying that preparations for war short of avowed mobilisation were continuing. Finally, our Ambassador in Italy was informed by Count Ciano on 29th May that Italy's entry into the war was certain.

Contraband and clearing negotiations had been broken off by direct order of Mussolini, who was incensed at the prominence given in the British Press to their expected success. Signor Mussolini was unwilling to enter into any discussions of any sort with the Allies, and the British Ambassador considered the situation graver than at any time hitherto (C.-in-C. Mediterranean War Diary).

Thus closed the month of May 1940 with the predominant question of not whether Italy intended to enter the war but when. At this juncture, both inside and outside the Mediterranean, all eyes were on the beaches of Dunkirk.

---

[1] Admiralty to Commander-in-Chief, Med., 1948/22/5/40. The text of the message was not given; the inference drawn from the fact of it being made to 15 tankers was of a cautionary nature, a 'straw in the wind'.

CHAPTER 3

CHALLENGE TO 'MARE NOSTRUM'

(JUNE 1940)

22

DURING THE early days of June 1940 evidence continued to accumulate that the period of uneasy calm in the Mediterranean was at an end. On the 1st, German aircraft bombed Marseilles and the S.S. *Orford* (20,000 tons) was sunk, an unpleasant foretaste of things to come. Daily reports were received of Italian troopships leaving Brindisi, Syracuse and Naples for Libya, and of Italian merchant ships in South American ports bunkering much larger quantities of coal and oil than normally.

Minelaying off Italian ports, in the Straits of Otranto, off the Albanian coast and the Aegean, was reported from various sources and summarised in a message to the Commander-in-Chief, Mediterranean, from the Admiralty (1154/4/6/40 Appendix E.20), and the Naval Attaché, Rome, reported on the 5th that though there was no general change in the situation yet the steady flow of Italian troops and air personnel to Libya should be noted, that 80 per cent. of reservists of the Italian Force would have been recalled by 10th June, and lastly that the Italian commercial air service *Ala Littorio* had suspended its services to Malta, Athens and Rhodes. Obviously the decks were being cleared for action, and as a consequence our attitude towards Italy underwent a change. The Admiralty directed the Commander-in-Chief to ensure that certain Italian ships were brought in for contraband control and detained, cargoes being reported and no 'holdback' undertakings[1] accepted (1723/5/6/40 from D.E.W.D.). A further signal (1739/6/6/40 from First Sea Lord) added that, in the event of Italy attempting to prevent the exercise of belligerent rights by escorting or convoying their merchant ships, the Commander-in-Chief was to act in accordance with the Naval Prize Manual. We had passed the stage of avoiding incidents which might provoke Italy.

The Greek Government, mindful of the fate of other neutral nations, too weak or too slow to act in time, and confident of our support against Italy, took the precaution of sending four destroyers to Milo ready to set up a patrol between Crete and Capa Malea. In the Western Basin the French prohibited movements of ships in all ports of Algeria and Tunisia and their approaches at night except French and Allied ships, whose arrival or sailing had been previously notified.

Important though these control of trade questions were, however, more urgent and directly naval problems had now to be decided. What action was the Mediterranean Fleet to take if Italy attacked Greece? Would Turkey enter the war on our side? Had we to wait to occupy Crete until Italy attacked Greece? Had we enough forces to serve the initial objects of securing control of communications in the Eastern Mediterranean (including the Aegean), cut off enemy's supplies to the Dodecanese, prevent an attack on Malta by sea, provide covering forces for the Suez Canal, Haifa and Alexandria, cut the Italy–Libya traffic line, and wage an effective anti-submarine war? This last-named object appeared formidable on paper, for

---

1 A 'holdback' undertaking was a guarantee given by a shipper of cargo to the naval authority at the loading port that the cargo was not destined for Germany.

there were 100 Italian submarines in the Mediterranean, all with an endurance of 4,000 miles or over. (See Notes on Italian Submarines, Appendix F(b).) Furthermore there was the rather incalculable difficulty of assessing how much reliance we could place in the French Fleet at this stage and for how long.

An important factor in helping the Commander-in-Chief to decide his course of action was a full appreciation of the Italian Fleet, not only its number and disposition, but the fighting value. Their ships were known to be well built, well armed, fast, and to have exercised at sea to a certain extent, though not to the extent that we had found necessary for efficiency. They had not been tried out against an opposing fleet, except for a few small running fights in the Adriatic against the Austrians in the 1914–18 War. Experience in the Italo-Abyssinian and Spanish Civil wars afforded no guidance to their fighting efficiency since there was no effective naval opposition in the first case, and very little in the second. In the latter, however, they had gained experience of convoy work and submarine patrols, which benefited training in handling their ships at sea under conditions resembling war.

As to the Italian naval policy for a war against France and England some light was given at the time by an article reported to be written by Admiral Cavagnari, the Italian Chief of Naval Staff, early in 1940, which was reprinted in Weekly Intelligence Report No. 14 (June 1940), issued by the N.I.D.[1] He proclaimed a 'short war' policy that would entail their Fleet undertaking an 'offensive to the death'. Ordinarily this would be taken to mean launching an all-out sea and air attack on the British or French forces at the earliest possible moment, and perhaps before war was declared; but when explaining in more detail the use of their naval forces, under the heading of 'Battleships', Admiral Cavagnari stated that their task would be to ensure the predominance of Italian naval power in waters where Italy would need to have full liberty of movement. This could mean retaining their main forces for defence of the Italian coasts, or to cover troop convoys to Libya; it did not look like all-out offensive intentions. This conclusion, formed at the time, is borne out by information available after the war. In reply to a request for a statement explaining Italy's intentions on entering the war, and whether a strategic policy had been arranged with Germany, also what tasks were assigned to each fleet, Admiral Maroni, the Head of the Italian Naval Historical Division, has written:–

'The Directive sent out on 31st March, 1940, by the Head of the Government and Chief of the Armed Forces[2] to meet the eventuality of Italy entering the war, laid down for the navy the general policy "Offensive at all points, in the Mediterranean and outside." Such a directive was interpreted by the Chief of the General Staff[3] as meaning the assumption by the armed forces, especially submarines, of a disposition aimed at cutting the enemy's communications. Nevertheless, the Chief of the Naval Staff[4] explained in a memorandum that adoption of the offensive depended on the existence of a concrete objective, and if this was to be represented by the Anglo-French Fleet such an offensive would soon be exhausted through suffering irreplaceable losses, whilst on the other hand the enemy would be in a position to replace a superiority of force which he already held at the outset. It must be realised that the capacity for action of the Italian naval forces was limited by lack of air strength. For these reasons the policy of the navy could only be defensive.

'With Italy's entry into the war in June 1940 the following arrangements, entered into beforehand with Germany, automatically became operative:–

'Operational spheres. It was agreed not to create a single command, but to leave full liberty of action to each navy in its own area. There was to be suitable exchange of intelligence and mutual study of developments. It was laid down that the German Navy would be responsible for activities in the Atlantic both with surface vessels and submarines; also that the two *Scharnhorsts* would be maintained in the North Sea, so as to keep outside the Mediterranean the greatest possible number of English and French battleships, particularly those of the faster type.

---

1 The Italian Historical Division do not admit that Admiral Cavagnari wrote any such article.
2 Signor Mussolini.
3 Marshal Badoglio.
4 Admiral Cavagnari.

'The Italian Navy would take an active part with submarines in the Atlantic south of the parallel of Lisbon, and possibly operate in the Indian Ocean with surface vessels and submarines.

'In the Mediterranean the Italian Navy would seek to bring to action the greatest number of enemy forces.'[1]

23

A comprehensive statement of policy covering the general strategic situation in the Middle East was issued by the Chiefs of Staff early in July 1940,[2] a shortly after Italy had become actively hostile. The Commander-in-Chief, Mediterranean, had signalled his detailed naval plans to the Admiralty on 6th June (2317/6/6/40, Appendix C.4(b)). He was, of course, well aware that we had not enough ships to meet all objectives at once; he had therefore to decide on a course of action that would serve the most pressing need, bearing in mind that French support was none too sure. However, if we had limitations, so had the Italians; for instance, they could not simultaneously attack Greece, invade Malta, and retain enough forces to protect their long coastline as well as cover traffic to Libya.

The Commander-in-Chief gave priority on the outbreak of war to the occupation of Crete, especially as he required the use of Suda Bay as an advanced fuelling base. He strongly urged that this operation should be undertaken whatever the political situation. His Majesty's Government, however, decided that the occupation of Crete was only to be carried out as already authorised, that is if Italy attacked Greek territory (A.T.1728/30/5, Appendix C.4(a)). The plan of Combined Operations to occupy Crete was, therefore, shelved, but had to be borne in mind whatever else we undertook. It was estimated that British forces would land within 30 hours of the order to move, and the French within 50 hours. The French had four cruisers at Beirut ready to embark troops for Crete, and in addition they proposed to send limited forces to Salonika, Milo, Salamis, Navarino and Argostoli. On the subject of Anglo-French war plans for Greece the Admiralty issued a note of warning (0051/1/6/40 to C.-in-C. Mediterranean) by pointing out the difficulty of reaching finality with the French on account of the critical situation in France (Appendix E.18). Ultimately five months elapsed before the necessary conditions for the occupation of Crete were fulfilled, and by then France was prostrate. When the time came we were afforded every possible assistance by the Greeks in forming a naval base at Suda (S.101).

The next plan to be considered was the action to be taken if Turkey entered the war on our side. This was more complicated than the case of Crete on account of the political issues arising from the proximity of Turkey to Russia, who was at that time a pseudo-ally of Germany. Turkey's assistance, therefore, as pointed out by the Chiefs of Staff,[3] might prove to have political disadvantage so far as the Middle East was concerned. Nevertheless, planning for the possibility of Turkish assistance was necessary, and early in June 1940 a conference was held at Haifa with the French and Turkish authorities (Appendix C.5).

The chief point in the Turkish proposals was the occupation of Rhodes, and though the Commander-in-Chief agreed that it was essential to capture Rhodes as soon as possible, he saw no prospect of success for some time owing to lack of suitable craft, and the fact that the Dodecanese were strongly defended (C.-in-C. Mediterranean, 0436/8/6/40 to Admiralty). The French view was that Turkey would not enter the war on the side of the Allies until we had gained a victory over the Italian fleet. They were, however, attracted by the idea of capturing Rhodes with the co-operation of British aircraft using Larnaca in Cyprus as a base, and sent a battalion to Cyprus to help defend that island. However, as a result of the French collapse on 22nd June the Rhodes plan was dropped for the time being; the first of several plans of attack on that ancient fortress of the Knights of St. John to be jettisoned.

Having decided that neither of the above plans would call for any immediate action by us the Commander-in-Chief concentrated all available forces of the British Fleet for a sweep westward from Alexandria to the Central Mediterranean. At the same time the French Eastern Squadron was to sweep

---

1 See remarks by Vice-Admiral Weichold, Appendix C.3.
2 Appendix C.9(d).
3 Appendix C.9(d).

through the Aegean. This would assert our command of the Eastern Mediterranean from the outset, and also enable us to counter an Italian seaborne attack on Malta, besides testing the enemy's air and submarine strength. The French Fleet was expected to cruise in the Western Mediterranean, thus dividing Italian attention between east and west, making it unlikely that we should meet the whole force of the Italian main Fleet in the Eastern Basin. The possibility of this, however, had always to be taken into account. Much depended on whether the Italian Chief of Naval Staff's expressed intention of an 'offensive to the death' was going to prove genuine or spurious. If they chose to concentrate their six battleships, which included at any rate on paper[1] the two *Littorios* (30 knots, nine 15-inch guns), seven 8-inch cruisers, twelve 6-inch cruisers and forty 'fleet' destroyers, in a determined attempt to give battle to our Eastern Mediterranean Fleet of three battleships (*Ramillies* was in dock), six 6-inch cruisers and 20 'fleet' destroyers with last, but not least, the aircraft carrier *Eagle*, then the outlook was not rosy, especially in view of the large number of submarines that we could expect to meet in a 'set piece' encounter. Their manoeuvres of July 1939 (referred to in the last paragraph, Section 2), pointed to the possibility of such an operation. On that occasion their main Fleet brought the 'enemy' to action off Derna, at a distance well within range of the airfields of Cyrenaica. Moreover, since the French war effort was obviously weakening the Italians could afford to ignore the risk of a large scale attack by the French Fleet. Then in the event of a successful action with us, even if they sustained heavy damage, they would be left in command of the Mediterranean when France fell – Mare Nostrum would have been achieved. All this was fully realised by the Commander-in-Chief, but he knew that even if the two *Littorios* were in commission they would not have had time to 'work up', also he anticipated that the Italian policy would at this stage prove in practice to be one of preserving their main fleet intact.

24

The Middle East Command (G.H.Q. Cairo) assumed administrative control of Egypt, Palestine and the Sudan from 8th June, 1940 (Somaliland was already included). Italian merchant ship sailings were suspended on the 8th, ships at sea were to make for neutral ports, and those in British ports were instructed to sail without delay. On the 9th, Count Ciano informed the British Naval Attaché in Rome that the 'die was cast' and added that the French were expected to leave Rome on the 11th/12th June. Matters had now reached the point where the planning stage was over and operations must begin, and the Commander-in-Chief informed the Admiralty (1209/9/6/40) that he intended to carry out an anti-submarine sweep westward of Alexandria by destroyers on 10th June in case Italian submarines moved out of their declared areas. At 0400/10th June the 2nd Destroyer Flotilla, H.M.S. *Hyperion*, Captain (D) 2, with two flying boats from No. 201 Group, R.A.F., left Alexandria on this sweep which extended to 25° 40' E., some 200 miles away. Submarines located were to be attacked unless they were escorted by a surface vessel. The Admiralty order to commence hostilities was received by the Commander-in-Chief at 2208 in the evening of the 10th (T.O.O. 1916/10/6/40), the British and French Ambassadors in Rome having been informed at 1630/10th by Count Ciano that Italy considered herself at war as from 11th June.

The Mediterranean Fleet came to two hours' notice and an order was broadcast that no merchant ship was to approach within three miles of Malta, Cyprus or Palestine between sunset and sunrise. In the Suez Canal lights were extinguished and navigation suspended during the dark hours.

25

The table on page 22 shows the composition of the Fleet of the Mediterranean Powers in June 1940. Nominal lists and dispositions are given in Appendix F(b). Plan 2 gives a diagrammatic view of the opposing forces.

---

[1] In fact, only the *Cavour* and *Cesare* were active with the Fleet until August 1940, when the two *Littorios* and the *Duilio* and *Doria* rejoined. The *Doria* appears, however, not to have been fully operational until December 1940.

26

Having reported his intentions to the Admiralty (Appendix E.19), the Commander-in-Chief left Alexandria with the Fleet at 0300C/11th June for a sweep towards the Central Mediterranean with the object of attacking enemy forces at sea and countering any Italian action on Malta. The Fleet was composed of two battleships (*Warspite, Malaya*), one aircraft carrier (*Eagle*), five cruisers (Vice-Admiral (D) with *Orion, Neptune, Sydney, Liverpool, Gloucester*), twelve destroyers (2nd and 14th Destroyer Flotillas), and the two old C-class cruisers *Caledon* and *Calypso* which joined at sea later in the day. The Seventh Cruiser Squadron (Vice-Admiral J. C. Tovey) was directed to sweep ahead of the Fleet at 25 knots until dark on the 11th, and then carry out an attack at daylight, 12th June, on enemy patrols off Benghazi and Tobruk, after which they were to rejoin the Fleet.

The R.A.F. co-operated by carrying out a continuous air search ahead of the Seventh Cruiser Squadron on the 11th and on the 12th in an area enclosed between 20° and 22° E., 34° and 37° N. In addition they were to carry out a bombing attack at daylight on 12th June on ships and harbour works at Tobruk. This was to coincide with the naval attack on the patrols outside.

Submarine patrols, French and British, were stationed in the Aegean, and off Taranto, Augusta and Strait of Otranto.

COMPOSITION OF THE FLEETS OF THE MEDITERRANEAN POWERS
June 1940 (*See Appendix F(b) and Plan 2*)

COUNTRY	BATTLE-SHIPS	BATTLE CRUISERS	AIRCRAFT CARRIERS	CRUISERS 8-inch	CRUISERS 6-inch	DESTROYERS	SUBMARINES	ESCORT VESSELS
Great Britain*	5 6	– 1	1 2	– –	9 10	31 38	12	5 5
France†	3 –	2 –	1 –	7 –	7 –	44 –	46 –	22 –
Italy	6²	–	1¹	7	12	44F/67LD 111	7 old 107	10
Spain	–	–	–	1	5	29	5	42
Greece	–	–	–	1	1	23	6	–
Turkey	–	1	–	–	2	4	6	–
Yugoslavia	–	–	1 (small)	–	–	8	4	–
RED SEA
Great Britain	–	–	–	–	4	4	–	5
Italy	–	–	–	–	–	9	8	4

*After the fall of France (22/6/40) Force H was sent to Gibraltar, thus providing 2 Battleships, 1 Battle Cruiser, 1 Aircraft Carrier, 3 6-inch Cruisers, 16 destroyers for Western Mediterranean, with 4 Battleships, 1 Aircraft Carrier, 7 6-inch Cruisers, 22 destroyers for Eastern Mediterranean.

†After the incidents at Oran and Algiers and the demilitarising of ships in the Levant, only one Free French unit (S/M *Narval*) operated in the Mediterranean during 1940.

1 This was the *Miraglia*, which was not an operational carrier.

2 Six was the number believed operational; in fact, five were active in August, and the sixth joined later in the year.

27

In the Eastern Mediterranean French cruisers from Beirut were instructed to sweep towards the Dodecanese and through the Aegean north of Crete, returning to Alexandria p.m. 13th June. In the

Western Basin, French minelaying submarines from Bizerta (*Turquoise*, *Nautilus*, *Saphir*) laid mines off Trapani, Cagliari and Tripoli; also patrols were started north of Messina and off Galita Island.

The Third Squadron (four 8-inch cruisers with destroyers) left Toulon and bombarded the port and shipping of Genoa on the night of the 12th, while the Striking Force (two battle-cruisers, six 6-inch cruisers, with destroyers) cruised along the North African coast from Oran and Algiers.

28

It was soon evident that no spectacular effort of the Italian main fleet was intended. The enemy's naval activities during the first few days consisted of sweeps by two of his cruiser divisions with their destroyers south-east from Messina and Taranto. An outsize network of submarine patrols continued for about a month, when over 50 boats were at sea, but after mid-July they averaged 20. (See Notes on Italian submarines in Appendix F(b), and Plan 2 for disposition on 14th June 1940.)

The presence at noon on 12th June of three *Zara* class cruisers and six destroyers was reported by H.M. S/M *Orpheus* in a position 45 miles S.E. of Syracuse, steering north-west, and early on the same morning D/F reports disclosed several Italian units west of Cephalonia, which may have been the same squadron. Also early on the 12th, D/F reports showed Italian warships north-west of Derna, one being identified as the *Garibaldi*. Owing to pressure of priority W/T traffic, information of this last named movement reached the Commander-in-Chief too late for him to act. This was particularly unfortunate since at the time the enemy was in the middle of a triangle of our forces, H.M.S. *Gloucester* and *Liverpool* being off Tobruk, H.M.S. *Orion*, *Neptune* and *Sydney* off Benghazi, and the battlefleet some 40 miles south of Gavdo Island (Crete), all three forces being about 60 miles equidistant from *Garibaldi*. Owing to chancy visibility she was not sighted by aircraft (Appendix E.21).

At this point it may be as well to explain the arrangements made for taking and utilising D/F bearings in the Mediterranean. D/F stations inside the Mediterranean in June 1940 were located at Malta (Dingli), Alexandria (Sidi Bishr) and Gibraltar (Middle Hill). Stations in the United Kingdom, notably Winchester (Flowerdown) and Scarborough, also listened in on Italian naval wavelengths. In 1941 two more stations were manned at Acre (Nahariya) and Cyprus, and for a short while at Barce, in Cyrenaica. In 1943, when North Africa was cleared of the enemy, and in 1944, stations were set up at Tripoli, Tunis (Protville), Algiers (Draria), Alghero (Sardinia), Oran and Naples. The bearings were transmitted by W/T or landline to Alexandria and plotted at Ras el Tin by the Operations Intelligence Centre.

If a good 'cut' had been obtained, and especially if a call sign could be identified, an 'immediate' signal was made to the Fleet at sea; but at the commencement of the war there was sometimes difficulty over the priority of signals routed by the main W/T station. Enemy sighting reports, either by ship or aircraft, followed the same routine as D/F, but were easier to handle as they were taken in by the special W/T interception sets at Alexandria and handled directly by the O.I.C. At the time of the *Garibaldi* incident these matters were in their infancy, with signal routeing at Alexandria going through considerable birth pangs; but later on methods of receipt and transmission of D/F bearings were speeded up, and probably not more than half an hour elapsed between an enemy signal being made and the Fleet at sea receiving the information. The German submarines which entered the Mediterranean in October 1941 were prolific users of W/T, but the Italian submarines refrained.

29

At 0200/12th June the Battle Fleet was approaching a line of Italian submarines stretching from Cape Littinos (Crete) to Tobruk (Plan 2). H.M.S. *Calypso*, which was eight miles on the port bow of the flagship, was seen to be dropping back, and signalled that she had apparently been struck by a torpedo. H.M.S. *Caledon* and *Dainty* were detached to stand by her, and rescued 24 officers and 394 ratings before she sank at 0330 in 33° 45' N., 24° 32' E. close to the patrol position of the Italian submarine *Bagnolini*, which claimed the *Calypso* as her target. This was one of the very few successes of the Italian submarines in the Mediterranean. The Fleet was lucky on this occasion to have avoided further losses, for they had already passed a line of six submarines off Alexandria before reaching the Crete–Tobruk patrol. The two divisions of the Seventh Cruiser Squadron, which had been detached at nightfall on the 11th, rejoined the Fleet at noon/12th; the First Division (*Orion*) having drawn a blank off Benghazi, whilst the Second Division (*Liverpool*) had engaged six minesweepers off Tobruk and sank one of them. Both the *Liverpool* and *Gloucester* were under fire from shore batteries for 11 minutes without being hit, and had cut mines adrift with their p.v.'s.

The R.A.F. raid at dawn/12th on Tobruk resulted in the cruiser *San Giorgio* being set on fire and beached, also the naval jetty and one ship alongside were set on fire. The *San Giorgio* was acting as depôt ship for destroyers and small craft.

At 1230/12th, the Commander-in-Chief sent the Seventh Cruiser Squadron, less *Neptune*, on ahead at 22 knots to sweep up to a point 120 miles south-east of Cape Santa Maria di Leuca, south-east of Italy, by midnight 12th/13th, whilst the battlefleet continued at 16 knots, course north-west, to a position south-west of Zante. At midnight 12th/13th, courses were reversed, and the Seventh Cruiser Squadron swept down the Ionian Island without incident before rejoining the Flag at 1200/13th, when just westward of Crete.

A/S patrols were provided by H.M.S. *Eagle* throughout the 12th but nothing was sighted. In the afternoon of the 13th, the Seventh Cruiser Squadron was again detached to sweep eastward along the North African coast outside the 150 fathom line, while the remainder of the Fleet continued at 14 knots along the south coast of Crete, increasing speed to 18 knots for the night. At 0530/14th course was altered to the south-east and at 1530/14th the Seventh Cruiser Squadron rejoined, having seen no hostile ships or aircraft.

For the entry of the Fleet into Alexandria full anti-submarine and anti-mine precautions were taken; they included A/S patrols by catapult and carrier aircraft, a patrol by four Sunderland flying boats of 201 Group, and four French aircraft, an A/S sweep by the 10th Destroyer Flotilla from the Swept Channel to the rendezvous 30 miles north-west of Ras el Tin, a sloop to mark the end of the swept channel, and the 2nd Destroyer Flotilla sweeping ahead of the Fleet with T.S.D.S.

These precautions proved successful, though there were two incidents during the approach which caused emergency turns to be made by the Fleet. The *Liverpool* reported a submarine four cables from her and two destroyers carried out a hunt; and the *Nubian*, which was one mile on the *Warspite*'s port beam, made a contact and fired a full pattern of depth charges. No definite result was obtained from these contacts, and the Fleet entered harbour safely.

Carrier aircraft landed at Dekheila, the Fleet Air Arm base, catapult aircraft landing in the harbour.

In his report to the Admiralty (Mediterranean 0587/0710/12 of the 14th June 1940) of this first war cruise, the Commander-in-Chief laid stress on the weakness of our air reconnaissance being a serious obstacle in bringing the enemy to action, and pointed out that this was all the more true in view of the enemy's greater speed and probable reluctance to engage in close action. H.M.S. *Eagle*'s aircraft could supply the Fleet's needs to a certain extent, but were insufficient to provide for both distant and close reconnaissance. The Commander-in-Chief considered that the best remedy would be to find a base in the Greek Islands, preferably Suda Bay, and added that without such a base the unsatisfactory position existed of our not being able effectively to control the Central Mediterranean. After the Fleet had returned to Alexandria the enemy, for a matter of three days, could act with impunity.

In conclusion, the Commander-in-Chief, whilst regretting that the Fleet had failed to make contact with the enemy, felt that the operations were of considerable value in testing the enemy's strength and intentions to fight, in tuning up a fleet of very heterogeneous elements, and in causing the enemy at least some inconvenience.

30

Cross raiding in the air began from the moment Italy entered the war. Malta, as was expected, was the first target of enemy air attack. The defences of Malta at that time were described by the General Officer Commanding, General Sir William Dobbie, as 'woefully meagre and included no aircraft' (R.U.S.I. lecture 21/10/1942. 'The Defence of Malta'). A squadron of T.S.R.'s, a few London Flying boats, and three

Gladiators, known on the island as Faith, Hope and Charity, comprised the available aircraft, and of those, only the Gladiators were technically 'fighter defence'.[1] The first raid was at 0500/11th June, and by 30th June there had been 36, with many more alarms. The military damage was comparatively small, but the proximity of the Sicilian airfields (barely 20 minutes flying distance), coupled with the weakness of the defences, reduced the island's value as an offensive base, and our submarines were moved to Alexandria. The floating dock at Malta was damaged by near misses on 11th and 15th June, and broke in two when being raised on 20th June. France collapsed on 22nd June, which meant more enemy aircraft becoming available, thus reducing the offensive value of the island still further unless and until fighter defence could be provided.

Alexandria experienced its first raid in the early hours of 22nd June when 20 bombs were dropped with no damage to the Fleet, and some minor damage to the Petroleum wharf.

Meanwhile our own air force had begun to harass the enemy. From 12th June, aircraft from the Middle East carried out a series of attacks on enemy airfields, harbours, and shipping, mainly off the North African coast, with Tobruk as the chief target. On 14th June, the Fleet Air Arm Squadron (No. 767),[2] which was based at Hyères, dropped the first bombs on Italian soil in a raid on Genoa, claiming hits on hangars, the power station, and the Ansaldo works, while French aircraft bombed Spezia. Just before the fall of France, the French Naval Air Service carried out attacks on Imperia on the Riviera, on Alghero in Sardinia and on Trapani in Sicily. When France fell, a number of squadrons managed to escape to North African airfields. Our Fleet Air Arm Squadron flew from Hyères to Algiers and Malta, where it acted under the operational control of the A.O.C., Mediterranean and was used for local reconnaissance, A/S patrols and as a torpedo striking force against surface forces within range, also as a reserve for the *Eagle*. Continual air searches by the R.A.F. and F.A.A. were undertaken, especially when the Fleet was at sea, and some patrols produced most effective results. A Sunderland aircraft of 201 Group, R.A.F. No. L.5804, destroyed by bombs on 28th and 29th June the Italian submarines *Argonauta* and *Rubino* in positions west of the Ionian Islands. Also on the 28th and within 20 minutes of an attack on a submarine, Sunderland aircraft No. L.5806 reported (at 1210), three enemy destroyers about 50 miles west of Zante.

At that time the Fleet from Alexandria was at sea for Operation MA.3 (S.32), and Force A, the Seventh Cruiser Squadron, which had sailed from Alexandria 1100/27th June, was in a position some 60 miles south-west of Crete. Course was altered to the northward to intercept, but at 1730 a further report from L.5803 showed that the enemy destroyers were steering south, and in a position about 35 miles west of the *Orion*. At 1735, the Seventh Cruiser Squadron altered course to 220°, speed 25 knots, and formed on a line of bearing 180° in open order, 2nd Division (*Liverpool*) five miles, 180°, from *Orion*.

31

At 1830/28th June, the *Liverpool*, when in a position 60 miles south-west of Cape Matapan, reported three enemy destroyers (*Zeffiro*, *Espero*, *Ostro*), bearing 235° from *Orion*, and three minutes later she opened fire. The 1st Division increased to full speed, course being altered as necessary to close. At 1854 the *Orion* sighted the enemy and opened fire at 1859, range 18,000 yards. All ships were now in action and the enemy returning our fire; their targets were the *Liverpool*, *Gloucester* and *Orion*; the shooting being good for range but bad for line. At 1905, the *Neptune* reported that the enemy had fired torpedoes, and course was altered at 1912 for three minutes to comb the tracks. With the range down to 14,000 yards course was altered to open 'A' arcs and the range increased. Shortly after, the left-hand destroyer was observed to be hit and making smoke. After further alterations the range was brought down again, and the *Espero* was seen to be stopped and sinking. At 2006, when the *Liverpool* reported that she had only 40 rounds per gun remaining, the Vice-Admiral (D) broke off the action. Ammunition expenditure had

---

1 On 18th June the Air Ministry despatched 12 Hurricanes and 12 Blenheims for the Mediterranean, authorising Malta to maintain up to 6 Hurricanes. Owing to bad weather and other mishaps only 6 Hurricanes and 3 Blenheims reached Malta on 21st June. Three days later the Blenheims and one Hurricane arrived in Egypt, so that at the end of June there were five Hurricanes in Malta and seven in Egypt.

2 Later re-numbered No. 830.

been very great, the light was failing badly, also ranging and spotting were rendered extremely difficult by the enemy's clever use of funnel and chloro-sulphonic smoke, and zig-zagging. (Plan 3.)

The *Sydney* was detached to deal with the disabled *Espero*, which eventually sank at 2040 in 35° 18' N., 20° 12' E.; 47 survivors were picked up including many wounded. The other two destroyers, *Zeffiro* and *Ostro*, arrived at Benghazi early 29th June.

This action afforded an early example of the Italian's lack of experience in sea-warfare. The normal tactics for an occasion such as this – that is, three destroyers sighting five enemy cruisers late in the evening – would be to shadow and attack during the night. There was ample sea room, they had a sufficient turn of speed, plenty of fuel, and were in no immediate hurry to reach Benghazi. Yet they continued on a straight course and engaged in a gun duel in daylight against heavy odds (twelve 4.7-inch guns v. forty-eight 6-inch).

On our part, the expenditure of 5,000 rounds of 6-inch ammunition was considered excessive for the results obtained, but the Commander-in-Chief pointed out to the Admiralty that this was the first surface contact in the Mediterranean and that the ships had been concerned to get decisive results. before light failed. (C.-in-C. Mediterranean, 2303/20/7/40.)

32

The action described above occurred in the course of a Fleet operation (MA.3) planned to provide cover for convoys running between the Dardanelles, Greek ports, and Port Said; also between Malta and Alexandria. It was executed under the orders of Vice-Admiral (D), (H.M.S. *Orion*).[1]

The forces employed were:–

(1) ESCORT FORCE FOR THE AEGEAN CONVOY
    Third Cruiser Squadron (2)   *Capetown* (Flag)
                                    Caledon
    Destroyers (4)   *Nubian* (D.14)
                                      Mohawk
                                      Vampire
                                      Garland (Polish)

(2) COVERING FORCES
                                      1st Division
    Force A – Seventh Cruiser Squadron (5)   *Orion* (Flag)
                                      Neptune
                                      Sydney
                                      2nd Division
                                      Liverpool
                                      Gloucester
    Force B – First Battle Squadron (2)   *Royal Sovereign* (Flag)
                                      Ramillies
    Aircraft Carrier (1)   *Eagle*
    Destroyers (7)   *Hyperion* (D.2)
                                      Havock
                                      Hero
                                      Hereward
                                      Hasty
                                      Janus
                                      Juno

---

[1] Mediterranean War Diary, M.022495/40, M.016370/40.

SEC. 34   MEDITERRANEAN, SEPTEMBER 1939–OCTOBER 1940

           Force C – Destroyers (5)   *Dainty*
                                                                                    Decoy
                                                                                    Defender
                                                                                    Voyager
                                                                                    Ilex

(3) AIRCRAFT OF 201 GROUP   *Sunderland flying boats*

The Aegean convoy of seven ships (A.S.1), left Cape Helles 1025/28 June, and four ships joined later. It was twice attacked by enemy aircraft on 29th June, again twice on the 30th with a final attack by four aircraft on 1st July. No hits were received, but of some 85 bombs a few were near misses. The Alexandria portion arrived 1730/2nd July, and the Port Said portion 0800/3rd.

As regards the Malta convoys, one fast (13 K.) and one slow (9½ K.) were organised but did not sail, the operation being postponed early on the 29th owing to the cruiser action described above denuding the cruisers of ammunition, and also owing to numerous submarine reports.

33

As part of the covering operations it was arranged that Force C, which had sailed from Alexandria at 0600/27th June, should carry out a submarine hunt. On the way north from Alexandria to Kaso Straits, at 1830/27th June, the *Dainty* sighted a submarine on the surface, closed to three miles and made the challenge; the submarine dived and the hunt was on. Contacts were made, lost, and renewed, and several depth charge attacks carried out; then, at 1958, *Dainty* and *Defender* observed a submarine on the surface 2,500 yards distant and opened fire. After a few rounds a white light was observed and the crew could be seen jumping overboard. Eventually the submarine – *Console Generale Luizzi* – sank at 2328/27th in 33° 46' N., 27° 27' E.

Force C then re-formed and continued the sweep, passing through Kaso Straits well north of Crete, through the Anti-Kithera Channel, and then shaping course for Malta. No further incident occurred until 0510/29th June when, in a position 130 miles south-west of Matapan, the *Voyager* sighted a submarine on the surface, distant nine miles. Shortly afterwards, when passing an oil-patch at the spot where the first submarine had been sighted, the *Ilex* reported a submarine 300° six miles. *Dainty*, *Ilex*, *Decoy* and *Voyager* all dropped depth charges at 0615/29th and no further contact was obtained; then, at 0642, *Ilex* sighted a third submarine on the surface 330° eight miles. The *Decoy* and *Voyager* remained near the position of the first attack, whilst *Dainty*, *Ilex* and *Defender* proceeded at full speed for the latest position. *Ilex* and *Dainty* attacked, and within three minutes the submarine *Uebi-Scebeli* blew her tanks and surfaced. Fire was opened immediately by all three destroyers and hits obtained on the conning-tower; but firing ceased when the crew came on deck and surrendered. Boarding parties seized a number of confidential books and paper before the submarine was sunk by gunfire in 35° 29' N., 20° 06' E. These documents revealed the position of two other submarines which were hunted for, but without success. Force C returned to Alexandria p.m. 1st July. Later it was learnt that the *Uarsciek* was the submarine first attacked, but she was only damaged; she was destroyed two and a half years later when on patrol south of Malta.

34

Compared with the activities of Force A and Force C, Force B, which had sailed from Alexandria at 1230/28th June, had an uneventful voyage. On the outward journey, when about 50 miles south west of Gavdo at 1347/29th, the *Ramillies* reported two explosions half a mile on her port beam, which may have been torpedoes exploding at the end of their run. During the night (29th/30th) course was shaped well southward of Kithera in order to keep clear of Force A sweeping down past Sapienza Island, and early on the 30th Force B turned to the eastward to pass through 33° 46' N., 23° 10' E. where, according to the captured documents as reported by the *Dainty,* the Italian submarine *Salpa* was on patrol. A submarine was, in fact, sighted in that position by the Air A/S patrol, and bombed, but unsuccessfully. An air search was flown off at dawn on the 30th from the *Eagle* to examine the western approaches to the Aegean as the convoy passed through. Force B sighted the convoy p.m. the next day (1555/1st July) when about 200 miles from Alexandria, and course was altered to the westward to keep clear for the night, returning to Alexandria a.m. 2nd July.

35

After the action with enemy destroyers which ended at 2006/28th, Force A steered towards Malta, and at 0534/29th the 2nd Division (*Liverpool*) was detached to Port Said to replenish with ammunition. The 1st Division (*Orion*) spread and swept towards Sapienza Island, up the Greek west coast to close southward of Cephalonia, and then back towards Kithera during the night of 29th/30th. In view of the reports received of the bombing of the convoy (A.S.1) on the 29th the Vice-Admiral (D) decided to pass close to the convoy to afford protection. The convoy was overhauled at 1315/30th in 35° 11' N., 23° 35' E. During the night 30th/1st July, Force A kept ahead and eastward of the convoy, and at 0625/1 engaged a 'shadower' at long range. Shortly afterwards, as interference by enemy surface forces was no longer likely, course was altered for Alexandria. At 1630/30th a medium bombing attack from 6,000 feet was made by five aircraft (probably B.R.20's) on the *Neptune*; no hits were obtained but *Neptune*'s aircraft was damaged by splinters. Ten minutes later three more aircraft attacked the *Sydney* from 2,000 feet with heavy bombs, but missed ahead. At 1715/30th a single aircraft attacked with two bombs which fell well clear of *Orion*'s port quarter. Resulting from these attacks the Vice-Admiral (D) reported that he considered that a line of bearing formation was unfavourable for such circumstances, and that in future, if attacked when in close formation, he proposed to adopt a triangular or diamond formation with ships one mile apart.

36

Having followed the main Fleet activities, with their accompanying air operations, for the first three weeks of hostilities, it is now desirable to see what was occurring in underwater warfare. At the outbreak of hostilities, on 11th June 1940, there were twelve British submarines in the Mediterranean, six based on Alexandria and six working from Malta, of which two were refitting. During the first fourteen days, three out of the ten available for operations were lost, *Grampus*,[1] *Odin*[1] and *Orpheus*.[1] The *Grampus* had laid mines off Augusta on 13th June and remained on patrol off that port; the *Odin* spent a day or two off Taranto on the 12th/13th and was then to have gone on patrol off Sapienza Island; the *Orpheus* was on patrol north-east of Malta on 12th June and was ordered later to the Libyan coast. All three boats were due to return to Alexandria by 24th/25th June but on 29th June the Commander-in-Chief had regretfully to report that, being more than four days overdue, they must be considered lost. He reported to the Admiralty that the Italians were known to have placed extensive defensive minefields off their ports and in depths of 150 to 200 fathoms, and that consequently these losses were probably due to mines. In future he did not intend to station submarines close off enemy ports, but to place them in strategic positions elsewhere; furthermore, our submarines were not to cross the 200 fathom line except in pursuit of important enemy units. The fourth boat from Malta, *Rorqual*, was more fortunate than her colleagues; she laid mines in a position nine miles east of Brindisi, and then patrolled the Strait of Otranto before returning safely to Alexandria.

As a result of Vice-Admiral Malta's report on 18th June that Malta was becoming unsuitable as a base for submarines on account of frequent air raids (which meant submarine crews having virtually no rest period) the Commander-in-Chief ordered the Malta submarines to shift their base to Alexandria. The submarines working from Alexandria had an uneventful first war patrol except for the *Parthian*, which was watching Tobruk. On 19th June at 1243 she fired two torpedoes at the *San Giorgio* aground in the harbour, but both exploded three-quarters of a mile short of the target (possibly through striking a net).

---

1 From Italian sources we now know the cause of loss:
    Grampus, 16th June, depth charges from Italian torpedo boats *Circe* and *Clio*.
    Odin, 13th June, depth charges from Italian destroyer *Strale*.
    Orpheus, 16th June, depth charges from Italian destroyer *Turbine*.

She was hunted by aircraft and an A/S vessel during that afternoon. While on passage to an area off Derna, at 1502/20th June, in 32° 41′ 30″ N., 23° 49′ E., the *Parthian* fired four torpedoes at an enemy submarine on the surface. All the torpedoes hit, and the enemy submarine (*Diamante*) was seen to sink. Apart from this satisfactory incident the lack of worthwhile targets at this juncture gave small promise of results for our submarines; later on, as the war in Cyrenaica developed, there was no such lack, and it will be seen how our submarines became a thorn in the 'Axis' side.

37

There were 46 French submarines in the Mediterranean command when war broke out. Their disposition is given in Plan 2 and Appendix F. The main submarine bases were at Toulon and Bizerta, the latter possessing facilities for at least 20 submarines and being capable of intermediate dockings and small refits; for large refits submarines usually proceeded to Toulon. With regard to seagoing efficiency our Liaison Officer at Bizerta reported that Commanding Officers seemed to have little idea of attacking. Any range inside 1,000 yards was considered very close, and one submarine had not carried out an attack for over three months. He attributed the poor attacking qualities of Commanding Officers largely to their submarines being fitted with training tubes. Being able to fire in any direction at any time the Commanding Officer was apt not to press home his attack, but to wait for the enemy to come to him. The French method of submarine operations differed widely from ours, their idea being to keep a large number of submarines in readiness in harbour, and on receiving information of enemy movements, to form a barrage of six to ten boats across the expected line of advance of the enemy. They did not favour our method of patrol positions, but preferred 'visiting' two or three enemy ports for a day or two at a time, a procedure which, of course, provided no guarantee that the enemy would choose those particular days to be active. Three of their minelaying submarines, *Turquoise*, *Nautilus*, and *Saphir*, laid mines off Trapani, Cagliari, and Tripoli but no evidence exists of any resultant damage to the enemy. The Admiral Commanding submarines – Contre-Admiral Ven – was described by the B.N.L.O. Bizerta as 'a charming, but easy-going officer', who took little active part in the work, which devolved almost entirely on Commandant Delpuich, who combined the duties of Captain (S), Chief of Staff and Staff Officer Operations. Although he was full of drive and never spared himself the work involved proved too much for him.

38

In view of the large number of Italian submarines available for offensive operations – 100 boats with a radius of action of 4,000 miles or over – the results achieved must have been disappointing to the Italian High Command. For the first ten days of the war in the Mediterranean 57 boats were on patrol; 35 for the period 20th–30th June; 50 from 28th June–12th July; and thereafter approximately an average of 20. (From Italian records.) Before the curtain was raised on the submarine scene the question of their efficiency was the subject of much concern to our operational staff. It was known that they had taken an active part in a curtain-raiser – so to speak – during the Spanish Civil War (1936–1939), that they carried out a certain amount of training at sea, and that their material was reasonably good. The personal element was, however, a doubtful factor. Though known to be weak in team-work, there are many instances of the Italian's skill and daring in individual enterprises, and it is precisely those latter qualities which are required by the Commanding Officers of submarines; what was in doubt was their technical ability.

Fortunately events soon showed that no great harm was to be expected from the Italian underwater menace in the Mediterranean, ominous though it appeared on paper, for before the end of June 1940 ten Italian submarines had been sunk or captured, four in the Red Sea, six in the Mediterranean, six of the ten being accounted for by gunfire or depth charge,[1] two by aircraft bombs, one by torpedo, and one wrecked by stranding. In addition to these total losses, two submarines were known to have been damaged by depth charge attack from our destroyers, the *Cappellini* on 12th June by the *Watchman* off Gibraltar, and the *Uarsciek* on 29th June by the *Dainty*'s force off Matapan. Several other contacts led to depth

---

1 One of these six, the *Provana*, was sunk by the French escort vessel *Curieuse*.

charge attacks by the trawler *Moy* on 11th June, off Alexandria, *Diamond* on 12th and 17th June off Malta, *Voyager* on 13th off Alexandria, an R.A.F. Blenheim bomber on the 19th off Dhaba. Altogether 25 reports of submarine sightings were made between 11th and 30th June. A feature common to many of the reports was the sighting of the submarines on the surface in broad daylight, displaying thereby a lack of proper training.

As a set-off to this heavy casualty list during this period the Italian Senior Officer Commanding Submarines, Rear-Admiral Falangola, could claim as sunk one British light cruiser, H.M.S. *Calypso*, on 12th June, and a Norwegian tanker, *Orkanger*, 8,029 tons, off Alexandria on 12th June, without warning. Three British steamers in the Western Mediterranean were attacked by gunfire from the submarine *Glauco* on 26th June, but escaped unharmed. In one case, that of the S.S. *Baron Erskine*, the fire was returned and at least one hit obtained on the submarine. This action took place off the Algerian coast after arrangements had been made to clear shipping from the French North African ports, all British vessels and those under Allied control in Algerian waters being ordered to leave for Gibraltar as early as possible, in convoy if available, but failing this, independently and taking advantage of darkness and Spanish territorial waters. (A.M.2308/18/6/40.)

39

The first of many coastal bombardments by the Mediterranean Fleet took place on 21st June, Operation MD.3[1] when three cruisers, the *Orion, Neptune, Sydney*, and the French battleship *Lorraine* with four destroyers, under the orders of Vice-Admiral J. C. Tovey, bombarded Bardia, a small port lying some six miles west of the Egyptian Frontier in Libya. The targets consisted of coastal batteries, W/T station, ammunition dumps, power and pumping stations. The bombardment took place between 0548 and 0606/21st June at ranges between 12,000 and 14,000 yards; the coastal batteries did not reply, only A/A guns opening fire at our aircraft, and these were soon silenced by the *Neptune* and *Lorraine*.

The Commander-in-Chief described the action as 'a useful minor operation, fully justifying the expenditure of ammunition.' Air photographs showed that four ammunition huts were destroyed, and considerable damage done to store houses, barracks and administrative buildings. It is possible that more effective results would have been obtained if at the commencement of the operation (actually at the *Sydney*'s second salvo), the *Sydney*'s spotting aircraft had not been mistakenly attacked by R.A.F. fighters, badly damaged, and forced to land at Mersa Matruh. This resulted in *Sydney* firing at only one target throughout. The aircraft identification situation was not improved when the *Lorraine* opened fire on the R.A.F. Gladiators. No enemy aircraft appeared on the scene.

In conjunction with Operation MD.3, R.A.F. Blenheim bombers attacked enemy warships at Tobruk and reported one ship on fire. Also, two other forces were off the Cyrenaican coast: (1) a force of five destroyers under Captain D.2 in the *Hyperion*, which carried out an A/S sweep between Alexandria and Tobruk; and (2) two French cruisers, *Suffren* and *Duguay-Trouin*, and three destroyers of the 14th Flotilla under Captain D.14 in *Nubian*. Both forces returned to Alexandria p.m. 21st June not having sighted any enemy ships. This was the swan song of the French Mediterranean Fleet, for on the next day, 22nd June, it was learnt that the anticipated French collapse had occurred; overnight an asset had become a liability.

40

Doubts about the value of French assistance had been present in the minds of the Admiralty and the Commander-in-Chief, Mediterranean, for some time; even as early as 1st June 1940 these doubts had found expression when the Anglo-French plans for Greece were under review, and the Admiralty had pointed out the difficulty of reaching finality with the French (S.23 and Appendix E.18).

The political side of the question forms a long and tortuous story, and it must be sufficient here to relate briefly a few significant events. On 11th June 1940, M. Reynaud and the French Government retired

---
1 See Naval Staff History, Battle Summary No. 6, B.R.1736(4).

to Tours, and on 14th June they moved on to Bordeaux. Two days later M. Reynaud asked the British Government to release France from her treaty obligations, and on the 17th Marshal Pétain, who had succeeded M. Reynaud, opened negotiations with Germany in a letter to Hitler asking if he was ready to sign with him 'as between soldiers after the fight and in honour, terms that would put an end to hostilities.' During the next four years, the words 'honour' and 'obey' were awkward obstacles to many Frenchmen, for obedience to orders from the Vichy Government meant that they must stop fighting against Germany and Italy, and even in some cases become actively hostile to us. The fact that the voice was the voice of Vichy, but the hand was the hand of Hitler, either could not or would not be recognised, though from their point of view it should be borne in mind that the problem was not a straightforward matter of allegiance. Fear of reprisals on their families acted as a powerful deterrent even to anglophiles, and misrepresentation of our action at Oran, Algiers and Dakar, to which reference will be made later, was stressed by anglophobes as their main reason for remaining loyal to Vichy. Nevertheless, a number of Frenchmen put aside these doubts and fears and continued the fight, some even wearing British uniform to do so. A marked improvement was noticeable in November 1942, when Germany occupied the whole of France, but the unhappy state of divided loyalty, that is whether to serve Marshal Pétain or General de Gaulle, was not really remedied before August 1943 when the French Committee of National Liberation, formed at Algiers in June 1943, was formally recognised by the Allies. This gesture satisfied the finer points of honour of those Frenchmen who had refused to forgo their allegiance to Marshal Pétain. Thereafter, morale improved further and French co-operation on a national scale was resumed, though unfortunately many of their best ships had by that time been destroyed.

41

Despite the feeling of unreliability with which the Commander-in-Chief had to contend, he continued to utilise the French forces up the last possible moment. On 20th June he informed the Admiralty of his intention to take the combined Fleets at Alexandria, less the *Malaya* and *Lorraine,* to sea early a.m. 23rd June in order to carry out a sweep into the Central Mediterranean. He 'proposed to include the French cruisers, who are full of fight, in these operations.' The operation (BQ) was to include a night bombardment of Port Augusta and a raid on the Straits of Messina, as well as providing cover for shipping between Malta and Alexandria. Led by the *Eagle* and 2nd Destroyer Flotilla, at 1700/22nd June the Fleet started to leave harbour, the French squadron, Force D, *Duquesne*, *Suffren*, *Duguay-Trouin* with two British destroyers, being timed to leave at 2230, immediately after the Commander-in-Chief in the *Warspite*, with the *Neptune*, *Sydney* and five destroyers forming Force A. When just clearing the Great Pass, at about 2200, the following signal was received from the Admiralty:–

> MOST IMMEDIATE.
> Your 1211/20 June. Defer proposed
> operation. Acknowledge.
> 2025/22/6/40.

Operation BQ was immediately cancelled and all ships returned to harbour, the Vice Admiral, Malta, being instructed to stop the sailing of the convoy from Malta. The reason for this Admiralty signal was the signing of the armistice between France and Germany on that day, the 22nd of June.[1]

---

[1] Just before the signing of the armistice there had been a proposal before the Chiefs of Staff for withdrawing the fleet from the Mediterranean. This is mentioned in Mr. Churchill's History of the War, Volume II, page 232:
　'Prime Minister to First Sea Lord, 15th July 1940. It is now three weeks since I vetoed the proposal to evacuate the Eastern Mediterranean and bring Admiral Cunningham's fleet to Gibraltar. I hope there will be no return to that project …'
　The proposal was contained in a memorandum by the Director of Plans, Admiralty, and was passed round by the First Sea Lord at a meeting of the Chiefs of Staff Committee on 17th June 1940 (C.O.S.(40), 183rd meeting). The Chiefs of Staff referred it to the Joint Planning Sub-Committee to report on the military implications of the proposed Fleet movement.
　Before the planning sub-committee had rendered their final report the Prime Minister had vetoed the proposal, and on 3rd July 1940 the Chiefs of Staff sent a telegram to all the Commanders-in-Chief concerned and the British High Commissioners in the Dominions explaining that the maintenance of our position in the Middle East was necessary for the successful prosecution of the war. (Section 23 and Appendix C.9(d).)

42

The clause in the Armistice terms relating to the French Fleet stated that 'except that part left free for the safeguard of French interests in the Colonial Empire, ships are to be collected in ports to be specified, demobilized, and disarmed under German or Italian control.' The clause went on to give a solemn undertaking that the German Government had 'no intention of using for their own purposes during the war the French Fleet stationed in ports under German control except those units necessary for coast surveillance and minesweeping.' The final sentence stated that 'except for that part (to be determined) of the fleet destined for protection of Colonial interests, all ships outside French territorial waters must be recalled to France.' In view of what had happened on several occasions when German or Italian promises of this nature were made, it is not surprising that the Admiralty thought it necessary to warn the Fleet that reliance could not be placed on this understanding (Appendix E.40; for signals concerning the period just previous to and after the French collapse see Appendices E.22 to 37).

43

Then began a short period of uncertainty which, if allowed to continue, threatened severely to cramp the operations of the Fleet. On 25th June, the Commander-in-Chief therefore decided to resume activities by running convoys to and from the Aegean and Egypt, also between Malta and Alexandria, with a submarine hunt to fill in time. This was operation MA.3.(S.32). Two incidents served to emphasize the need for resuming activities with a minimum of delay, the first occurring in the Western Mediterranean on 23rd June when three *Cavour* class battleships, two 8-inch cruisers, two 6-inch cruisers, and ten destroyers were reported at 1930 south of Sardinia steering eastward. The second incident was in the Eastern Mediterranean on 25th June when three Italian destroyers bombarded the road near Sollum without, however, causing much damage. The Commander-in-Chief could not allow the French collapse to prevent him putting a stop to such activities and he informed the Admiralty accordingly (Appendix E.38).

The French Squadron at Alexandria under Admiral Godfroy received orders from Bordeaux on 25th June to sail for Beyrouth, but the Commander-in-Chief refused to allow them to sail and reported to the Admiralty that the French Admiral appeared glad to have to bow to 'force majeure'. At other places – Bizerta, Algiers, Oran, Dakar, Beyrouth – matters were not so easily settled, and had not the Admiralty taken prompt action our control of the Western Mediterranean would have virtually ceased to exist on 22nd June, 1940. By that date, however, strong reinforcements from home were approaching Gibraltar.

44

The battle cruiser *Hood* and the aircraft carrier *Ark Royal* with 30 T.S.R.'s and 24 fighters arrived at Gibraltar on 23rd June, from which date Force H began to assemble, eventually consisting of one battle cruiser, two battleships, three cruisers and nineteen destroyers, under the command of Vice-Admiral Sir James F. Somerville K.C.B., D.S.O.[1]

Force H's immediate task was to secure the transfer, surrender, or destruction of the French warships at Oran and Mers-el-Kebir, so as to ensure their not falling into German or Italian hands. After that, subject to any instructions which might be given by the Admiralty, its tasks were to prevent units of the Italian Fleet breaking out of the Mediterranean, and to carry out offensive operations against the Italian Fleet and Italian coasts. In the latter case, careful timing was required to coincide with suitable action at the eastern end of the Mediterranean by the Commander-in-Chief.

Briefly, the proposal of the Director of Plans was that as enemy raiders would now be in a position to make use of the French Atlantic ports, we should be obliged to use capital ships for convoying purposes, and for this it would be necessary to withdraw our Fleet from the Eastern Mediterranean. In a signal to the Commander-in-Chief, Mediterranean (T.O.O. 2330/16/6/40) the First Sea Lord referred to such a possibility, stating that the 'Atlantic trade must be our first consideration.' Admiral Cunningham describes his reaction to this proposal in 'A Sailor's Odyssey' (p.241).

1 M.016021/40.

45

Before describing events at certain French North African ports when force, most unwillingly, had to be used to prevent French ships returning home possibly for the benefit of Germany and Italy, the strategic results of the French collapse in the Mediterranean may be briefly summarised. Formerly, the Anglo-French fleets had exercised almost complete command of the sea with vast stretches of coastline at their disposal (Plan 2). But now, all coasts, except those of Egypt, Palestine, and Cyprus in the east, Malta in the centre, and Gibraltar in the west were closed to the Royal Navy until Greece entered the war, four months later. On the one hand the Allies lost the services of the French Mediterranean Fleet, consisting of three battleships, two battle cruisers, one aircraft carrier, and fourteen cruisers – apart from numerous destroyers, submarines and small craft; while on the other they had arrayed against them the undivided strength of the Italian Fleet of six battleships,[1] nineteen cruisers and a large number of destroyers and submarines. In capital ships, the addition of Force H made up for the loss of the French; but in cruisers and destroyers the Italians attained superiority of numbers (S.25), which fact, combined with the menacing strength of the Italian Air Force of 2,000 aircraft, boded ill for the Mediterranean supply route, especially on occasions when Force H was operating in the Atlantic. In one respect, however, this new development was satisfactory, for it is better to have no friends at all than to be hampered by unreliable allies. *'Praestat habere acerbos inimicos, quam eos amicos qui dulces videantur.'* (It is better to have bitter enemies than those friends who seem to be sweet.)[2]

---

[1] Four of these six were known to be on the point of joining the Fleet, which they did early in August 1940. One, the *Andrea Doria*, was not fully operational until December.

[2] Ascribed to the great Roman statesman, soldier, and writer, Marcus Porcius Cato, 234–149 B.C., surnamed The Censor.

CHAPTER 4

SIGHTING SHOTS

(JULY, AUGUST 1940)

46

THE SECOND month of the war in the Mediterranean opened with the French situation still unsettled, and although the Commander-in-Chief had not allowed the French collapse to keep the British Fleet inactive for a day longer than necessary, yet it was abundantly clear that the prevention of the French Fleet falling into German or Italian hands was a matter of paramount importance to our control of the Middle Sea, and that a solution must be found forthwith. After the Armistice on 22nd June a number of ships remained at ports of the French mainland, but the greater portion, including the most important units, were in the French North African ports of Oran and Algiers. With regard to the remainder, the Eastern Mediterranean Squadron comprising one battleship, three 8-inch and one 6-inch cruisers, three Fleet destroyers[1] and six submarines was at Alexandria or Beirut, whilst at Casablanca and Dakar there were some submarines and destroyers together with the new but uncompleted battleships *Jean Bart* and *Richelieu*, respectively. The two old battleships *Courbet* and *Paris,* four destroyers, six torpedo-boats, seven submarines and various minesweeping and auxiliary craft escaped to ports in the United Kingdom.

Inside the Mediterranean the stretch of coast between Oran and Algiers required special attention with the object of preventing French ships leaving for ports in the south of France; whilst outside it was necessary to watch the West African coast down as far as Dakar, whence French ships might make for Atlantic ports, the West Indies, or through the Strait of Gibraltar to Toulon or Marseilles.

The West African ports of Casablanca and Dakar were the responsibility respectively of F.O.C.N.A. at Gibraltar and Commander-in-Chief, South Africa, at Freetown.

47

The situation at Casablanca, where Admiral Ollive was in command of French naval units, was reported on 24th June by the B.N.L.O., Brest, who had arrived there in the *Jean Bart* on the 23rd. He stated that the *Jean Bart* was commissioning with a crew from Brest who were arriving in large numbers; also that there were present six destroyers and twelve submarines with a few despatch vessels and minesweepers. On the 25th, Captain C. S. Holland, R.N., Chief Staff Officer to the Vice-Admiral (A) in H.M.S. *Ark Royal* at Gibraltar, visited Casablanca and reported that the situation was deteriorating, but that a show of force might restore morale or at least prevent scuttling (2245/25/6). That same day H.M.S. *Watchman*, which had been sent from Gibraltar to Casablanca with orders to shadow the *Jean Bart* if she left harbour was ordered out of Casablanca by Admiral Ollive at 1800/25th. This was complied with and she remained patrolling outside territorial waters. On the next day the Admiralty instructed F.O.C.N.A. that if the *Jean*

---

1 These were termed 'contre-torpilleurs' and were sometimes referred to as light cruisers.

Bart sailed she was to be intercepted by H.M.S. *Resolution* and taken to Gibraltar, and that all means at his disposal were to be used to prevent her getting through the Straits (Adm. 0346/26/6/40). These instructions were, however, later amended by orders to take her to the United Kingdom instead of Gibraltar. Uneasiness about the *Jean Bart* was lessened on 27th June by an Admiralty signal stating that her armament was incomplete and that it was unlikely that any ammunition was on board; also on the same day the B.N.L.O., Brest, who had transferred from the *Jean Bart* to the *Watchman*, said that he believed that no orders for action were contemplated either for that ship or other French ships at Casablanca. Matters remained in a state of uncertainty for the next few days, the *Watchman* being relieved on patrol by the *Velox*, who reported on 3rd July that she was being fired on by shore batteries. Later the same evening the *Velox* returned to Gibraltar to re-fuel, the duty of watching for possible movements being taken over at dawn on the 4th by air reconnaissance. Our aircraft report, p.m. 4th July, showed the *Jean Bart*, one cruiser, nine destroyers, eleven submarines, twelve M/Ls. or M/Ss. and a number of merchant vessels present, but with no obvious activities.

Although the *Jean Bart* was capable of moderate steaming, having proceeded from Brest to Casablanca at 20 knots without a previous basin trial, F.O.C.N.A. had reported that she would require many months to complete even in a home dockyard (1132/9/7/40), that she had no main armament ammunition on board; that only two of her eight I5-inch guns were manned, and that practically no fittings or equipment were in place. The Admiralty therefore decided that operations against her could wait, and that operations at Dakar against the *Richelieu* which, according to the B.N.L.O., Brest, had embarked 15-inch ammunition on 18th June before leaving Brest, and was nearer completion than the *Jean Bart*, should take precedence.

It is interesting to note that the *Jean Bart* remained at Casablanca until August 1945 when she sailed for Cherbourg. Periodically F.O.C.N.A. had to take special precautions on account of rumours that she was going to 'run for it', and there was an interlude of activity in November 1942 when she offered some slight resistance to the American landing operations at Casablanca.

To return to July 1940, relations with Vichy France continued to deteriorate, a process which was hastened by our action on 3rd July against the French ships at Oran, to be described later. French submarines and aircraft were now receiving orders to attack British warships off Casablanca and Dakar. We on our part were endeavouring to avoid unnecessary incidents in this area, our submarines receiving directions from F.O.C.N.A. that no submarine was to be attacked unless obviously hostile within 70 miles radius of Casablanca, an order which was later amended to within 20 miles of the French mainland or colonial territory.

48

At Dakar the attitude of the French Governor General, M. Pierre Baisson, and the naval personnel, was potentially hostile from the start, and the same difficulty was encountered as at all other French Colonial Ports, namely refusal to question the authenticity of signals received from Bordeaux notwithstanding our assurance that evidence showed that the Germans had obtained French naval codes and were issuing instructions purporting to come from Admiral Darlan, the French Minister of Marine and Head of the Navy of the Vichy Government (Appendix E.40(b)). The French ships present were the *Richelieu*, three destroyers, two submarines, seven armed merchant cruisers and some minor vessels. On 7th July it was decided that action must be taken to prevent these ships returning to France and coming under German control. For this purpose Captain R. F. J. Onslow of the aircraft carrier *Hermes* was promoted to Acting Rear-Admiral and directed to take charge of a special force consisting of the *Hermes*, the two 8-inch gun cruisers *Dorsetshire* and *Australia*, and the sloop *Milford*. At the same time he received Admiralty instructions to present to the French authorities at Dakar a demand that in regard to French ships present in the port one of the following four alternative courses of action should be complied with:–

(1) To sail, with reduced crews and without ammunition, under British control to a British port, the reduced crews being repatriated at the earliest possible moment. If this course was adopted we undertook to restore the ships to France at the conclusion of the war or pay compensation if they were damaged.

1. ADMIRAL SIR ANDREW B. CUNNINGHAM, G.C.B., D.S.O.

2. Cairo, showing vicinity of G.H.Q., Middle East

3. H.M.S. *Warspite*

4. H.M.S. *Malaya*

5. H.M.S. *Resource*

6. H.M.S. *Royal Sovereign*

7. Italian Battleship *Vittorio Veneto*

8. French Submarine *Narval*

9. Italian 6-inch Cruiser *Giuseppe Garibaldi*

10. H.M.S. *Calypso*

11. ITALIAN SUBMARINE *Diamante*

12. ITALIAN DESTROYER *Ostro*

13. THE SUBMARINE BASE AT MALTA

14. Gibraltar

15. Vice-Admiral Sir James F. Somerville, K.C.B., D.S.O.

16. BATTLESHIP *Richelieu*

17. FRENCH 6-INCH CRUISERS *Georges Leygues* AND *Emile Bertin*

18. BATTLESHIP *Lorraine*

19. 6-INCH CRUISER *Duguay-Trouin*

20. 8-INCH CRUISER *Duquesne*

21. FORT ON THE HILL OF MERS-EL-KEBIR, WEST OF ORAN

22. THE *Strasbourg* AND THE *Dunkerque*

23. AERIAL TORPEDO HITTING THE *Dunkerque*

24. FRENCH BATTLECRUISER *Dunkerque*

25. FIRST BOMBS FALLING ON THE JETTY AND ROUND THE SQUADRON

26. The *Provence* with her after-deck ablaze

27. French Destroyer *Vauban*

(2) To sail with reduced crews and without ammunition to some French port in the West Indies where the ships could be de-militarised or be entrusted to the United States, the crews being repatriated.

(3) To de-militarise the ships within a period of 12 hours so that they would be incapable of taking further part in the war.

(4) To sink the ships within six hours.

If none of these alternatives were accepted force was to be used to secure that the ships did not fall into German hands. Admiral Onslow, in presenting this demand, stated that he required within four hours a decision as to which alternative would be adopted, this limit being fixed so as not to allow the *Richelieu* time to get under way.

The ultimatum expired at 8.5 p.m. on 7th July, and, in spite of a polite reminder from Admiral Onslow, no answer having been received, he decided to take action (see Plans 5 to 8). The first attack was carried out by a specially prepared motor boat of the *Hermes* commanded by Lieut.-Cmdr. R. H. Bristowe, R.N., who succeeded in getting through the boom defences at 0210/8th and dropping four depth charges under the stern of *Richelieu* so as to damage her propellers and steering gear. The second attack was launched at dawn on 8th July by six torpedo aircraft from the *Hermes*, three being fitted with duplex pistols set to 38 ft. and three with contact pistols set to 24 ft., the depth of water being 42 ft. and the mean draught of *Richelieu* 26 ft 10 in. The Admiralty subsequently informed the Commander-in-Chief, South Atlantic, and the Commanding Officer of the *Hermes* that the setting of the torpedoes to run under the ship should not have exceeded 33ft., six feet greater than the ship's draught, and the contact torpedoes should have been set at 21 ft., six feet less than the ship's draught. The results of the torpedo attack were not satisfactory, as it appears that only one torpedo hit and exploded,[1] whilst the depth charge attack failed to explode on account of the shallow water. When full daylight broke, however, the *Richelieu* was observed to be down by the stern, and during the forenoon she was moved into the inner harbour and berthed at the detached mole, where she rested on the bottom at low water.

The special force was withdrawn on 9th July, and before leaving Admiral Onslow expressed to the French S.N.O., West Africa, Vice-Admiral G. H. Ollive, Headquarters at Casablanca, the hope that the operations, which had to be carried out with great regret, had not caused any casualties to personnel. Subsequently the *Richelieu* played a prominent part in the resistance offered in September 1940 to General de Gaulle's unsuccessful attempt to re-capture Dakar (see Naval Staff History, Battle Summary No.20–C.B. 3081). After that she remained at Dakar until early 1943, when she left for refit in America, returning to Oran in October 1943, shortly afterwards joining the Home Fleet at Scapa Flow, and then proceeding in 1944 to the East Indies for operations against Sabang and Surabaya, thus seeing much active service before finally arriving at Toulon in February 1946, where she was presented with the Croix de Guerre.

49

The French Squadron at Alexandria[2] had carried out several war operations with the British Fleet, and relations between Admiral Godfroy and our Commander-in-Chief had been on a most cordial basis. It was this, coupled with the firmness shown by the Commander-in-Chief when the crisis arose, that enabled the task to be carried out without the use of force of preventing French ships leaving harbour in order to return to France. Nevertheless, the threat of force was undoubtedly a factor. The Commander-in-Chief, from the start, left no doubt in Admiral Godfroy's mind that his ships would not be allowed to return to ports under so-called French control. At Alexandria on 24th June there were present one battleship, the *Lorraine*, three 8-inch cruisers, one 6-inch cruiser and three destroyers. Based on Beirut were six submarines, of which two were on passage to patrol in the Aegean, three returning from patrol and one

---

[1] French reports confirm this. The breach was 25 feet by 20, sternpost fractured, starboard inner shaft distorted and out of action, three compartments flooded. Repairs to ensure seaworthiness took one year to complete at Dakar.

[2] See Appendix F(b).

in harbour. The netlayer *Gladiateur* was on passage from Alexandria to Beirut. The alternatives before Admiral Godfroy were to continue to fight against the Axis under the aegis of General de Gaulle, to remain at Alexandria with the ships in a non-seagoing condition, or to sink his ships. The Commander-in-Chief's immediate anxiety was that if the last alternative was adopted the ships might be sunk at their moorings and partially block the harbour; also, he did not wish to have to land some 4,000 French sailors from sunken ships in Egypt, where the repercussions might have been serious.

Discussions on a more or less amicable basis continued until 3rd July, when the Commander-in-Chief was able to report to the Admiralty that the alternative of remaining at Alexandria in a non-seagoing condition was likely to be accepted, though there was still a possibility of ships being sunk, and that Admiral Godfroy had consented to begin discharging oil from the 8-inch cruisers and to remove torpedo warheads. Early next day, however, matters became critical, for having heard of the action we had taken at Oran Admiral Godfroy declined to continue discharging oil, or to remove any of his men, or indeed to give any undertaking whatever. The 4th July, 1940, in fact, began by being a French version of American Independence Day; and to make matters worse he stated that he would not take the ships to sea voluntarily to be sunk in deep water. The Commander-in-Chief took immediate action. He made a signal[1] during the forenoon to all the French ships, and a personal visit was paid by a senior British naval officer with the object of influencing the officers and the ships' companies against useless resistance to overwhelming force. These efforts proved successful, as at an unofficial post-prandial meeting the captains of the French ships prevailed upon Admiral Godfroy to accept the conditions of demilitarization and to remain at Alexandria. The main points were as follows:–

(1) All oil fuel to be discharged from French ships forthwith.

(2) Ships to be placed immediately in a condition in which they cannot fight.

(3) Discharge of ships' companies to France to be a matter for further discussion.

(4) Admiral Godfroy to place the above in writing and to give the details of paragraph 2.

(C-in-C. Med. 1529/4/7/40 to Adm.)

De-fuelling and disarming of the French ships was completed on 5th July, the latter measure consisting of landing the obturating pads of all large guns, the spares and firing mechanism of small guns and all warheads pistols for custody in the French Consulate-General with the right of inspection. Arrangements were also put in hand for the disembarkation of reservists and their early departure for their own country. By his strong, and at the same time tactful methods in the conduct of negotiations with Admiral Godfroy, the Commander-in-Chief had succeeded in removing the major anxieties concerning these French ships. There still, it is true, remained the anxiety that the ships might be scuttled at their moorings in Alexandria harbour. Fortunately this contingency did not arise, and on 9th July, while the action off Calabria was being fought, the French finally agreed to a reduction of combatant ratings to one-fourth of full complement, and an overall reduction to one-third of full complement. 2,000 men left Alexandria on 10th July in the *Providence* for Beirut and eventual repatriation, followed on the 13th by 1,000 in the *Athos II*.

Supplies and pay for the remaining 140 officers and 1,700 men then became the responsibility of the British Government for the next three years. Though now and again some of the men decided to join the Free French, in the main this large number lived a carefree life in a pleasant climate with only the occasional disturbances of an air raid.

50

Of the several French naval colonial ports concerned with these tragic events, Oran was by far the most important, due to the main strength in surface ships of the French Mediterranean Fleet being based there. Unlike Alexandria, Dakar or Casablanca there were, at the time of the Armistice, no British forces readily available to prevent the French ships sailing as and when they chose. On 22nd June 1940, there were in harbour at Mers-el-Kebir and Oran two battleships (*Provence* and *Bretagne*), two battle cruisers

---

[1] The *Warspite*'s signal log for this period cannot be traced; possibly it was lost in transit from enemy action.

(*Dunkerque*, *Strasbourg*), three 6-inch cruisers (*Gloire*, *Montcalm*, *Georges Leygues*), nine destroyers, four submarines and some auxiliary vessels. The French order to ships at Alexandria to return to French ports was sent out on 24th June (Appendix E.36(a)), and two days later the Admiralty ordered F.O.C.N.A. to institute an air patrol to watch the Oran Toulon route; at the same time the Commander-in-Chief, Mediterranean, sent two submarines (*Pandora*, *Proteus*) to patrol off Oran and Algiers respectively, and on the 30th a destroyer patrol was established westward of Oran.

As at the other ports, hopes were entertained that the French Admiral Gensoul would accept our offer to sail to British harbours and continue the fight with us, or at any rate sail to British harbours with reduced crews, and be demilitarised. Failing these two alternatives the offer was open to sail with reduced crews to West Indian ports, or lastly to carry out Admiral Darlan's final instructions issued before the Armistice, namely that ships should be sunk rather than be allowed to fall into the hands of the enemy (Appendix E.39 and 40).[1] On 25th June, the Admiralty asked F.O.C.N.A. if there was any prospect of the French ships at Oran surrendering to us if a British Force arrived off the port and summoned them to surrender (1025/25/6). An answer to this was provided in a signal to the Admiralty on 28th June from Casablanca, where all the B.N.L.O.s of Mediterranean ports had assembled. This signal contained a suggestion that the arrival of a British Squadron outside the territorial waters of Oran would give the lead required to influence the men to follow their officers, who were unanimous in desiring to continue the war. Furthermore the B.N.L.O.s drew attention to the statements of Admirals Esteva and Rivet at Bizerta, which indicated their determination not to obey orders for giving up the Fleet, if received from the new Government (Appendix E.41). Prior to the receipt of this signal the Admiralty had instructed Vice-Admiral Sir J. F. Somerville to proceed to Gibraltar and assume command of Force H (S.44), whose immediate task was 'to secure the transfer, surrender or destruction of the French warships at Oran and Mers-el-Kebir.'[2]

A plan of operations was drawn up and the Admiralty were informed that the earliest date for its execution would be a.m. 3rd July, code name Catapult.[3] The operations consisted of two separate attacks, the first on 3rd July and the second on the 6th. Force H left Gibraltar at 1730/2nd July and was composed of the battle cruiser *Hood*, battleships *Valiant* and *Resolution*, cruisers *Arethusa* and *Enterprise*, the aircraft carrier *Ark Royal* and eleven destroyers.

Captain C. S. Holland, of H.M.S. *Ark Royal*, who had returned from Casablanca, was given the distasteful task of emissary to Admiral Gensoul, being assisted by two former Liaison Officers, Lieut-Commanders A. Y. Spearman and G. P. S. Davies. At 0630/3rd July the destroyer *Foxhound* went ahead with Captain Holland on board and at 0805 anchored outside the net defence of Mers-el-Kebir, a message having been passed to Admiral Gensoul at 0602 through the Port War Signal Station announcing the object of Captain Holland's visit, and stating that the British Fleet was at sea off Oran waiting to welcome him and his ships. Admiral Gensoul declined to see Captain Holland and at 0847 asked the *Foxhound* to leave immediately. This request was carried out, Captain Holland and his assistants remaining behind in the destroyer's motor boat in order to continue negotiations. About 0900 Captain Holland obtained contact with Admiral Gensoul's Flag-Lieutenant and handed over a sealed envelope with the British proposals, adding that he would remain where he was to await a reply.[4] These proposals, which were passed to Flag Officer, Force H in A.M. 0108/2/7/40, stated that His Majesty's Government had agreed to the French Government approaching the German Government only on conditions that if an armistice was concluded the French Fleet should be sent to British ports. They went on to say that the French Council of Ministers

---

1 Whatever Admiral Darlan's intentions were this did not, in fact, occur. It is known now from the Italian Historical Division that on various dates between the French collapse at the end of June 1940 and the Allies' Armistice with Italy in September 1943, two 6-inch cruisers, ten destroyers, seven submarines, six corvettes, eight minesweepers and one minelayer were transferred to the Italian Navy and manned by the Italians. Only a few were employed on operations.

2 The decision to attack the French fleet at Oran was taken at a War Cabinet meeting on 27th June, 1940. (War Cabinet Minute (40) 184. Minute, 5, Confidential Annex. Appendix C6(c) of this volume.

3 For detailed description see Naval Staff History, Battle Summary No. 1, B.R.1736(1).

4 Eventually Captain Holland saw Admiral Gensoul himself, when he boarded the *Dunkerque* at 1615. See Battle Summary No. 1, sections 10 and 11.

had declared on 18th June that, before capitulating on land, the French Fleet would join up with the British force or sink itself.[1]

'Whilst the present French Government' – continued the proposals – 'may consider that terms of their armistice with Germany and Italy are reconcilable with these undertakings, H.M. Government finds it impossible from their previous experience to believe that Germany and Italy will not at any moment which suits them seize French warships and use them against Britain and Allies. Italian armistice prescribes that French ships should return to metropolitan ports, and under armistice France is required to yield up units for coast defence and minesweeping.

A.M. 0108/2/7/49 continued, 'It is impossible for us, your comrades up to now, to allow your fine ships to fall into the power of the German or Italian enemy. We are determined to fight on until the end, and if we win, as we think we shall, we shall never forget that France was our ally, that our interests are the same as hers, and that our common enemy is Germany. Should we conquer, we solemnly declare that we shall restore the greatness and territory of France. For this purpose we must be sure that the best ships of the French Navy will also not be used against us by the common foe.

'In these circumstances, H.M. Government have instructed me (that is, Admiral Somerville) to demand the French Fleet now at Mers-el-Kebir and Oran shall act in accordance with one of the following alternatives:–

A. Sail with us and continue to fight for victory against the Germans and Italians.

B. Sail with reduced crews under our control to a British port. The reduced crews will be repatriated at the earliest moment. If either of these courses is adopted by you we will restore your ships to France at the conclusion of the war, or pay full compensation if they are damaged meanwhile.

C. Alternatively, if you feel bound to stipulate that your ships should not be used against Germans or Italians, since this would break the armistice, then sail them with us with reduced crews to some French port in the West Indies – Martinique, for instance – where they can be demilitarised to our satisfaction, or perhaps be entrusted to the United States of America, and remain safely until the end of the war, the crews being repatriated.

'If you refuse these fair offers, I must with profound regret require you to sink your ships within six hours. Finally, failing the above I have the orders of His Majesty's Government to use whatever force may be necessary to prevent your ships from falling into German or Italian hands.'

Admiral Gensoul's reaction was similar to that of Admiral Ollive at Casablanca, namely, to assume a non-co-operative attitude.[2] Eventually Admiral Somerville had to resort to force as the only alternative to allowing the ships to escape and at 1754, Force H opened fire on the French ships at 15,000 yards'

---

[1] The French attitude, as described in the first two paragraphs of the British proposals, was obtained from our Ambassador's dispatch of 27th June, 1940, No. C/7541/65/17. In this dispatch Sir Ronald Campbell writes as follows:–

'*18th June.* I was informed that the Council of Ministers had taken the attitude that it was a point of honour for France to receive the armistice terms with her armies and fleet still fighting. A unanimous decision was taken to the effect that any terms whatever which included the surrender of the Fleet would be rejected, and that France would go on fighting as long as she could. Before she capitulated on land the Fleet would go to join up with the British Navy, or, in the last resort, could carry out pre-arranged orders to scuttle itself.'

This action of the French Fleet would, of course, have only become operative if the terms of the armistice included a demand for its surrender – a contingency which did not arise in the full sense of the word. It is not confirmed that the French Government agreed to sending their Fleet to United Kingdom ports before signing the armistice, although it is clear from the Admiralty message (0108/2/7/40) that such was the impression at the time.

[2] In the afternoon Admiral Gensoul received instructions from the French Admiralty to answer force with force. (Appendix E.42). He had sent two messages to the French Admiralty, at 0845 and 1230, stating that the British ultimatum was that they should either join the British Fleet or sink themselves. General Weygand attended the Council of Ministers; meeting at 1500 and states that '… it would appear that Admiral Darlan, whether deliberately or not, or whether he was aware of them or not, I do not know, *did not in fact inform us of all the details of the matter at the time*. It now appears that the terms of the British ultimatum were less crude than we were led to believe, and suggested a third and far more acceptable alternative – namely the departure of the fleet for West Indian waters.' (From 'The Role of General Weygand' by Jacques Weygand.) When under examination by a French Parliamentary Commission of Enquiry in June 1949, Admiral Gensoul expressed regret at not having informed the Council of

range, G.I.C. concentration, with aircraft spotting. The line of fire was from the north-west, so that fire from the French ships was blanked to some extent by Mers-el-Kebir (Plan 9), and risk of damage to civilian life and property reduced. The French shore batteries and the battle-cruisers *Dunkerque* and *Strasbourg* opened fire about a minute after the first British salvo. None of the French projectiles hit, though a number of 13.4-inch shells, presumably from the battleships *Bretagne* and *Provence*, fell close to, and in come cases straddled, the British ships. At 1804, as the French ships were no longer firing, 'Cease fire' was ordered and Force H proceeded westward so that, if necessary, the bombardment could be renewed without causing casualties to men in boats or exposing the British ships unduly to fire from the forts.

When the pall of smoke cleared away the *Dunkerque* was seen to be damaged and aground, the *Bretagne* was sunk, the *Provence* damaged and apparently beached, the aircraft carrier *Commandant Teste* was on fire and the destroyer *Mogador* damaged and beached. During the night 3rd/4th July the *Commandant Teste* escaped and fled to Toulon. At 1820, the *Strasbourg* was reported leaving the harbour and steering east, and at 1830 an air striking force of six Swordfish, armed with 250-lb. S.A.P. bombs and escorted by Skuas, was directed to attack her, whilst the *Hood* with the cruisers and destroyers proceeded to chase at full speed. The bombing attack on the *Strasbourg* was pressed well home and claimed at least one hit. At 1950, six Swordfish aircraft armed with torpedoes were flown off the *Ark Royal* to continue the attack, which they did at 2055, twenty minutes after sunset, and reported two probable hits from explosions seen near her stern amidships. As Force H was getting short of fuel, particularly the V and W class destroyers, the Vice-Admiral at 2020 reluctantly abandoned the chase, and altered course for a position westward of Oran. The *Strasbourg* was then 25 miles ahead, and a few hours later turned north for Toulon together with five destroyers from Oran and an Algiers force of three 6-inch and four 8-inch cruisers, which had been reported at 1730 by the *Pandora* steaming west from Algiers.

A French minelaying escort vessel, the *Rigault de Genouilly*, was sunk by our submarine *Pandora* on the 4th off Algiers, an incident for which the Admiralty expressed deep regret to the French Embassy. Admiralty instructions to all Commanders-in-Chief sent out late on the 3rd (2303/3/7) contained direct orders to H.M. Ships to be prepared for attack but not to fire the first shot. These instructions had not reached *Pandora* when the incident occurred. Her last orders were from Force H (2205/3/7/40) to 'sink French warships'. Not withstanding these general instructions, however, the Admiralty felt it necessary to ensure that the capital ships damaged at Mers-el-Kebir on the 3rd – particularly the *Dunkerque* – could not be refloated and repaired in less than twelve months. Consequently, on the morning of 6th July, Force H carried out an aircraft attack on that ship in three waves. It was thought at the time that five certain and two possible hits were obtained, but later information shows that this was not so. Serious damage was, however, caused by the explosion of a trawler laden with depth charges close alongside, which was hit by a torpedo. Our losses of aircraft in the first attack were five, three Swordfish and two Skuas, of which all the crews were saved except that of one Skua shot down in combat. There were no casualties in the second attack, and it was remarked that French fighters sent up to intercept our aircraft did not press home their attacks. Apart from gunfire from the warships and some indecisive air attacks, the only French reprisal for our action at Oran was a raid by a single aircraft on Gibraltar at 0615/5th which dropped eight bombs in the sea (M.016022/40. A.01523/43. A.0742/3/6/40).

When considering the question of whether the use of force might have been avoided it is clear that much depended on the attitude adopted by Admiral Gensoul, and in this connection it should be noted that on 3rd July he showed Captain Holland a personal copy of orders of 24th June purporting to come from Admiral Darlan.[1] Amongst other things it was stated that it would be the last cypher message from Admiral Darlan, but it should be remembered that messages from Admiral Darlan dated later than 20th

---

Ministers in his 1230 message of the British Government's third alternative. In a previous message, 0103/2/7/40, the Admiralty stated that if Admiral Gensoul made the suggestion that his ships should be demilitarised at Oran under strict British supervision, and within six hours, he (Admiral Somerville) could accept this provided he was satisfied that the ships could not be brought into service again even at a fully equipped dockyard for at least one year. (See Appendix C.6(d.)) Admiral Gensoul, however, made it quite clear to captain Holland that he would only accept orders from his Government or Darlan. (See Naval Staff History, Battle Summary No. 1, Section 11 and report of French Parliamentary Commission of Enquiry into the Oran episode.)

1 Appendix E. – Naval Staff History, Battle Summary No. 1.

June were under suspicion of being German inspired. This suspicion had been reported on 26th June by the Admiralty to F.O.C.N.A., who was asked at the same time to pass the information on to French authorities with whom he was in contact (Adm. 1910/26/6/40 – Appendix E.40(b)). It would appear that either Admiral Gensoul did not take this aspect into account or else refused to believe it, since he reiterated to Captain Holland on 3rd July that he would obey the orders only of his Government and Admiral Darlan. A further message from the French Admiralty received by Admiral Gensoul in the afternoon of 3rd July (Appendix E 42) telling him to meet force with force was again accepted by him at its face value, and although he stated that, if threatened by the enemy, he would go to Martinique or the U.S.A., this did not comply with any of our alternatives laid down for immediate acceptance. To sum up, Admiral Gensoul maintained that the danger of French ships falling into enemy hands was not imminent whereas we maintained that it was. Apart from the importance to us of exercising control of the sea route through the Mediterranean we were deeply concerned in preventing the whole balance of naval power being upset by the addition of the French ships to the existing strength of the Axis naval forces. His Majesty's Government considered that the general situation was far too serious to run such a risk through being dependent on the words of the German and Italian Armistice declarations.[1] That part of the French Fleet which, according to the armistice terms, was to be left free for safeguarding French interests in the Colonial Empire could later have been used by the enemy to 'safeguard' an Axis version of such French interests.[2]

51

The danger of any substantial addition to Axis Forces in the Mediterranean having now been removed, the Commander-in-Chief and the S.O. Force H were free to operate against the Italian Fleet and coasts, and to attack the enemy supply route between Italian and Libyan ports. An additional objective was the enemy shipping in the Adriatic, mainly the bauxite traffic between Yugoslavia and Trieste, and the tanker traffic from the Corinth Canal and Kithera Channel, composed mostly of ships from the Black Sea. The Commander-in-Chief's suggestion of using submarines to attack this valuable bauxite and tanker traffic was approved, as also was his request that existing instructions which restricted submarine attacks on convoys and merchant ships should be amended so as to give freedom to attack all vessels entering or leaving Libyan ports. At this time the Italy-Libya traffic was not very large; but sooner or later it was bound to become so, and in any case, whether large or small, its cessation was a matter of considerable importance to our army in Egypt. Being based at Alexandria, some 600 miles from the nearest enemy route, Taranto to Benghazi, our surface ships were limited to intermittent action; a limitation that was accentuated by the inadequate air defences of Malta, which imposed severe restrictions on operations in the Central Mediterranean, since the task of fuelling light craft and flying boats could, at that time, only be undertaken at night. On 1st July (message 1605/1/7) the Commander-in-Chief, Mediterranean, drew the Admiralty's attention to this point and requested most urgently that immediate consideration be given to sending more fighters to Malta. This, however, could not be done immediately because neither of the two known methods of getting fighters to Malta were then feasible, that is, either from a carrier sent well into the Mediterranean or over an African route via Nigeria and Egypt. Both these methods were adopted later, but meanwhile, in spite of the Island's inadequate air defence, some offensive air operations were possible after the arrival of Fleet Air Arm No. 830 Squadron (Swordfish, ex 767 Squadron), evacuated from Toulon, which operated under the orders of the A.O.C. Mediterranean and frequently attacked oil tanks, refineries and aerodrames in Southern Sicily.

52

At dusk on 5th July, nine Swordfish from Malta launched a dive bombing attack on the hangars and workshops of Catania airfield, starting four big fires. At the same time they reported two 8-inch cruisers, some destroyers, and an oil tanker in Augusta, where on the morning of the 6th, another reconnaissance reported

---

1 Naval Staff History, Battle Summary No. 1 – Sections 11 and 12, and Appendix B of same. For policy with regard to French warships after Oran and Dakar, see Appendix C.8.
2 See Appendix F(b) – Disposition of French Fleet in Mediterranean.

THIRD CRUISER SQUADRON OFF BARDIA

three battleships (really 8-inch cruisers), three cruisers and eleven destroyers. The Fleet Air Arm was also active in the Eastern Mediterranean where, on the evening of 5th July in conjunction with the Royal Air Force, nine Swordfish of 813 Squadron from H.M.S. *Eagle*[1] carried out a dusk torpedo attack on warships and shipping in Tobruk. According to Italian accounts the raid resulted in one destroyer, the *Zeffiro*, being sunk and a second destroyer, the *Euro*, being hit twice forward, all her fore compartments being flooded. A motor vessel, the *Manzoni*, of 4,000 tons was sunk, and the Lloyd Triestino liner, *Liguria*, of 15,000 tons damaged. The *Serenitas*, 5,171 tons, was sunk. Our aircraft met with a hot fire of 'flaming onions',[2] pom-pom and .5-inch machine gunfire with red and green tracers. Seven aircraft fired their torpedoes inside the harbour, and all the nine machines returned to Dekheila safely. The Commander-in-Chief, Mediterranean, reporting this action (1931/6/7) to the Admiralty, recorded that the success of the attack was largely due to excellent R.A.F. co-operation in providing reconnaissance, diversionary attacks and aerodrome facilities.

53

Turning to actions by our surface ships, early on 6th July the Third Cruiser Squadron, Rear-Admiral Renouf in the *Capetown*, with the *Caledon* and four destroyers, bombarded shipping in the port of Bardia, which had already had a severe hammering from the Fleet on 21st June (S.39).

The cruisers opened fire at 0537 at ranges between 9,000 and 10,000 yards from outside the 100-fathom line, but short shots falling on a point of land obscured the target, and two more runs were carried out from inside the 100-fathom line at ranges between 4,000 and 5,000 yards. The destroyers remained outside the 100-fathom line so as to give A/S and A/A protection if required. No opposition was offered and fire ceased at 0631, two military supply ships having been hit. At 0820, three enemy aircraft attacked the squadron from 8,000 feet without causing any damage, and the squadron reached Alexandria safely at 1900/6th July. From the above it will be seen that the process of 'softening' enemy bases had begun, and the Commander-in-Chief, deciding that the opportunity was ripe to pay some attention to the Italian Fleet, if he could find them, took the Fleet to sea for Operation MA.5.

54

This (MA.5) was a large scale operation undertaken primarily to ensure the safe passage of two convoys from Malta to Alexandria, and coupled with this objective was a determination to seize any opportunity

---

1 Operating from advanced airfield at Maaten Bagush.
2 Tracer shell. The term 'flaming onion' is believed to have been first used by us in the First World war to describe German A/A tracer shells.

of bringing the enemy to action. It consisted of an extensive sweep by the Mediterranean Fleet from Alexandria into the Central Mediterranean to within 25 miles of the Italian coast, and was supported by Force H from Gibraltar cruising eastward towards Sardinia with the intention of carrying out an air attack on Cagliari.

The operation happened to coincide with a sortie of the Italian Fleet from Taranto and Sicilian ports towards the Libyan coast;[1] reports of their movements on 8th July, received from H.M. S/M *Phoenix*[2] and Flying Boat 5803, showed a battleship force in the morning steering southward and a cruiser force in the afternoon steering northward. The two forces joined and, at 1610/8th, L.5803 reported the combined force steering 070° in a position 60 miles north of Benghazi. During the same period (0800 to 1600/8th July) the British Fleet, which had left Alexandria in the afternoon of the 7th, was proceeding on a westerly course southward of Crete and being subjected to heavy attacks by aircraft from the Dodecanese Islands of Leros and Rhodes.

From these reconnaissance reports, and owing to the intensity of the Italian bombing, the Commander-in-Chief deduced that the Italian Fleet was covering the movement of a convoy to Libya; and in view of their position in the afternoon he decided temporarily to abandon the operations in hand, and to move the Fleet at best speed towards Taranto so as to get between the enemy and his base.

From his aircraft reports the Italian Commander-in-Chief was aware of our Fleet's movements and he decided to plan a running fight for the afternoon of 9th July in a position where, with his superior speed, proximity to shore-based bombers, and the laying of a submarine barrage, he might inflict some damage on us at a minimum risk to his own forces. Matters did not turn out according to the Italian plan, for in the event both the British objectives were achieved and some damage inflicted on the Italian ships without injury to us. Only lack of speed in our battleships prevented us from closing the range before the enemy literally disappeared in a cloud of smoke. The Italian 8-inch cruisers' shooting was good for the short time it lasted, but the submarine-trap plan failed, because the action took place some 60 miles to the northward of the northernmost submarine, six of which had been placed on a north-south line across the route Alexandria to Augusta.[3]

55

Enemy air attacks were continuous and heavy in daylight hours on 8th July, during and after the action on the 9th and on the 11th and 12th. Many ships had narrow escapes. On 12th July, the *Warspite* with two cruisers and four destroyers in company, was attacked 22 times, some 260 to 300 bombs being dropped. The most unpleasant attack was at 1530/12th July, when 36 bombs fell simultaneously within one cable, 24 along the port side and 12 across the starboard bow. Anti-aircraft fire from the Fleet was described by the Commander-in-Chief as below pre-war standard except for one or two ships, nevertheless it spoiled the bombers' aim and probably accounted for five or six aircraft. Prolonged bombing is very wearing to personnel, and the Commander-in-Chief reported that the system which his predecessor had started of having at least two complete reliefs for the whole A/A armament in battleships and cruisers, was essential for lengthy operations. The action took place out of range of R.A.F. fighter protection from Egypt. The Fleet Air Arm in H.M.S. *Eagle* was normally composed of Swordfish T.S.R. aircraft, but two Gladiators from the F.A.A. reserve had been embarked, and these two aircraft brought down five enemy bombers between the 11th and 13th. During the attacks it was noted that the Fleet was shadowed by aircraft which transmitted 'longs' by W/T at intervals in order to direct attacking aircraft. This knowledge was utilised in subsequent operations by immediate transmission from the Fleet to Alexandria W/T Station of the

---

1 This sortie was in support of a Libyan convoy.
2 H.M.S. *Phoenix* did not return from this patrol; she was sunk by the Italian submarine chaser *Albatros* on 16th July.
3 A detailed description of the whole operation MA.5, including the action with the Italian Fleet, is given in the Naval Staff History Battle Summary No. 8 (B.R. 1736 series).

    Plans 11, 12 and 13 reprinted here were taken from an earlier edition of this Battle Summary, which has recently been re-written.

HIGH-LEVEL ATTACK

wave-length used, and on more than one occasion the 'longs' were jammed successfully enough to prevent the arrival of enemy bombers.

The only serious hit sustained was on 8th July, during the series of attacks on Force A (Seventh Cruiser Squadron) between 1023 and 1837, when during the last attack H.M.S. *Gloucester* was hit on the compass platform; seven officers, including Captain F. R. Garside, C.B.E., and eleven ratings were killed; three officers and six ratings were wounded. The *Gloucester* continued with the operation, steering from aft and using her after gun control.

During the course of these operations general reconnaissance of the area was undertaken by 201 Group's Flying Boats, temporarily working from Malta as follows:–

8th July	On passage Alexandria-Zante-Malta.
9th July 10th July	Continuous patrol of the area between Malta-Cape Spartivento-Cape Colonne-Corfu.
11th July	On passage Malta-Zante-Alexandria.
13th July	To a depth of 60 miles to the westward of Convoy MS.1.

Their reports on 8th July of the enemy's movements were invaluable, for without them the Commander-in-Chief would have continued on a westerly course for operations against the coast of Sicily previous to covering the movements of the two convoys from Malta.

Our own air attacks on the enemy Fleet were launched from H.M.S. *Eagle* at 1145/9th and 1545/9th, both with nine Swordfish torpedo aircraft (Plans 11 and 13). The first attack failed to find the enemy battleships, which had altered course to the southward after the last reconnaissance report (1135) had been received in the *Eagle* giving their course as due North. The rear ship of a cruiser squadron was attacked at 1330; but her high speed and rapid turning saved her from being hit. The second attack was launched while the Fleets were in action at 1545, in three subflights coming in from ahead of a line of ships led by two 8-inch cruisers. Anti-aircraft fire was heavy, but all the aircraft dropped their torpedoes on the leading cruiser's starboard side between her bow and beam bearings. At least one hit was claimed but later information did not confirm this. After the action the *Eagle*'s aircraft maintained reconnaissance duties over the Fleet, and on the night of 10th July launched a torpedo attack on ships in Augusta, sinking a destroyer and a tanker. 'This obsolescent aircraft carrier,' said the Commander-in-Chief in his report on the engagement (M.05369/41), 'with only 17 Swordfish embarked, found and kept in touch with the enemy fleet, flew off two striking forces of nine torpedo bombers within the space of four hours, both of which attacked, and all aircraft returned. Twenty-four hours later a torpedo striking force was launched on shipping in Port Augusta, and throughout the five days' operation the *Eagle* maintained constant A/S patrols in daylight and carried out several searches.'

56

In the action of 9th July the Forces on each side involved were:–

BRITISH	ITALIAN
3 battleships, mounting	2 battleships, mounting
24–15-inch guns	20–12.6-inch guns
32–6-inch guns 4	24–4.7-inch guns

	Max. speed		Max. speed
Warspite, Malaya,	23 knots	*Giulio Cesare, Conte Di Cavour*	26 knots
Royal Sovereign	20 knots		
5 cruisers, mounting		6–8-inch cruisers, mounting	
48–6-inch guns		48–8-inch guns	
		72–3.9-inch guns	
Liverpool, Neptune, Orion, Sydney, Gloucester		*Zara, Pola, Gorizia, Fiume, Bolzano, Trento*	
1 Aircraft carrier, mounting		8–6-inch cruisers, mounting	
9–6-inch guns		68–6-inch guns	
Eagle		52–3.9-inch guns	
17 T.S.R. aircraft		Our Fleet reported engaging	
3 Gladiators		6–8-inch cruisers	
		6–6-inch cruisers	
		Italian report says ten 6-inch cruisers were present; but two appear to have been with the Libyan convoy, leaving eight for the action, of which four possibly joined in the later stages.	
16 destroyers, mounting		32 destroyers, mounting	
69–4.7-inch guns		144–4.7-inch guns	
8–4-inch guns			

In speed the Italian battleships had a 3-knot advantage over the *Warspite* and *Malaya* and six knots over the *Royal Sovereign*. Two of the 8-inch cruisers were three knots faster, and their 6-inch cruisers from three to four knots faster than ours. With regard to maximum gun-range the *Warspite*'s 15-inch was 34,000 yards; *Malaya* and *Royal Sovereign* 24,000; the *Cavour* class, 28,0000.

In aircraft the Italians had potentially vast superiority through proximity of numerous shore bases.

Referring to Plan 12, just before action was joined at 1514, when the enemy 8-inch cruisers of Column C opened fire on the Seventh Cruiser Squadron at 23,600 yards, the *Gloucester* was detached to join the *Eagle*, which had quitted the line to take up a position ten miles east of the *Warspite*. This left Vice-Admiral Tovey, who was flying his flag in the *Orion*, with only four 6-inch cruisers to engage some twelve enemy cruisers, of which six were 8-inch and all of which had the advantage of the sun behind them. The *Neptune* and *Liverpool* opened fire at 1522, range 22,100 yards, followed at 1523 by the *Sydney*, all three engaging enemy cruisers; and at 1526 the *Orion* fired at a destroyer for three minutes before shifting target to the right-hand cruiser at 23,700 yards. As it was urgently necessary to support the heavily out-numbered cruisers, the *Warspite* at 1526 opened fire at 26,400 yards on an 8-inch cruiser. After turning 360° so as to allow *Malaya* to catch up the *Warspite* fired at two 6-inch cruisers in Column D, forcing them to turn away.

Between 1536 and 1548 there was a lull in the action, during which time the Seventh Cruiser Squadron was steering to close the enemy, whilst the destroyers, having been detached from screening, formed up on the disengaged bow (Plan 13).

The second phase of the action began at 1548 when the enemy battleships opened fire on the *Warspite* at extreme range; their shooting was moderately accurate for line but had a wide spread, some of the 'overs' falling amongst our destroyers, which were then between one and two miles east of the *Warspite*. At 1553, the *Warspite* fired at the right-hand battleship (*Giulio Cesare*), range 26,000 yards, obtaining a hit at 1600. This had the immediate effect of making the enemy battleships turn away and break off the action. They soon became obscured by smoke. About this time our cruisers re-opened fire at the enemy cruisers at 23,000 yards, and the *Neptune* successfully straddled and hit her target, the *Bolzano*. Much to their regret the *Warspite*'s consorts could not support her gunfire. The *Malaya* fired seven salvoes at extreme range, but the *Royal Sovereign* could not get within firing distance.

From 1604 onwards gunfire was desultory owing to the great range and the effectiveness of enemy smoke, and by 1641 firing at the heavy units ceased owing to disappearance of the targets. The destroyers were in action from 1554 to 1649, at one time engaging enemy destroyers at 12,000 yards when the latter were apparently making a torpedo attack. After firing their torpedoes at long range the enemy destroyers turned away to the westward making smoke, the second flotilla retiring through the smoke made by the leading flotilla. The *Warspite* and *Malaya* fired a few salvoes of 6-inch at the attacking destroyers, and our destroyers spasmodically engaged targets when they could be seen; but altogether this part of the action was unsatisfactory, except as long-range firing practice at disappearing targets. None of the enemy torpedoes hit, and only a few of their destroyers were hit by our gunfire. Our destroyers chased the enemy, but when finally clear of the smoke screen at 1700 there was nothing in sight. Aircraft reported the various units making off at high speed in the direction of Messina or Augusta. During their retreat enemy ships were repeatedly attacked by their own bombers, but no hits were observed, though from later accounts it seemed that the *Cavour* was hit.[1] The Commander-in-Chief took the battle fleet up to the smoke screen, but did not pass through it as he suspected a submarine trap; instead, he worked round to the northward and windward of the screen beyond which – like the destroyers – he found the enemy had vanished.

The British Fleet continued on a westerly course until within 25 miles of Punto Stilo lighthouse, and at 1740 turned to 220°, still hoping that the enemy would renew the fight. In this hope, however, the Commander-in-Chief was disappointed and as by 1830 it was evident that there was no longer any hope of intercepting the enemy's arrival at Messina the Fleet turned to the south east until 2115, when course was shaped for a position south of Malta.

57

From 0800/10th until 0900/11th the Fleet cruised to the south and east of Malta, the destroyers and the *Royal Sovereign* entering to refuel. A fast convoy of three ships of 13 knots (M.F.1) left Malta for Alexandria 2300/9th, and a slow convoy of four ships of 9 knots (M.S.1) left during the night 9th/10th. By 0900/11th the Fleet's return voyage had started, the Commander-in-Chief in the *Warspite* with four destroyers going on ahead at 19 knots, leaving the R.A.1 in the *Royal Sovereign* with the *Malaya*, *Eagle* and remaining destroyers to maintain a covering position to the westward of convoy MS.1. The Vice-Admiral (D), about 80 miles to the eastward, with the 7th Cruiser Squadron, was covering Convoy M.F.1. Early on 12th July, two of his cruisers (*Liverpool* and *Sydney*) joined the *Warspite*, and the remaining three attended to Convoy M.F.1. Enemy air attacks during the 11th and 12th, as previously mentioned, were continuous and heavy, but no ships were hit and there were only three fatal casualties. Blenheim fighters from 252 Wing, R.A.F., Middle East, provided fighter cover from late p.m. 12th and no more was seen of the Italian bombers.

On the 13th, the R.A. Third Cruiser Squadron, with the *Capetown* and *Caledon* from Alexandria, joined the covering force to MS.1 when 60 miles S.W. of Gavdo Island, also the *Ramillies* with four destroyers

---

[1] The Italian official account states that 27 attacks in all were made by their own bombers between 1643 and 2110, but no ships were hit.

sailed from Alexandria to give additional cover. Early on the 13th the Commander-in-Chief in the *Warspite*, the 7th Cruiser Squadron and four destroyers, with Convoy M.F.1 arrived at Alexandria. The R.A.1 with the other two battleships, *Eagle* and destroyers arrived next forenoon, and Convoy M.S.1 with the *Capetown*, *Caledon* and *Ramillies* A.M. 15th July.

Concluding his remarks on the action of 9th July (M.05369/41), the Commander-in-Chief stated that 'the meagre material results derived from this brief meeting with the Italian Fleet were naturally very disappointing to one and all under my command, but the action was not without value. It must have shown the Italians that their Air Force and submarines cannot stop our Fleet penetrating into the Central Mediterranean, and that only their main Fleet can seriously interfere with our operating there.' After pointing out the need for closing the gun range (when speed permitted) in order to get decisive results, the Commander-in-Chief concluded by affirming that these operations and the action off Calabria 'produced throughout the Fleet a determination to overcome the air menace, and not let it interfere with our freedom of manoeuvre and hence our control of the Mediterranean.' It may be added that though the actual results were disappointing to the Commander-in-Chief himself, nevertheless the British Fleet had continued a running fight with enemy ships to within 25 miles of the Italian mainland, no sustained attempt being made by the enemy to engage in battle, and this notwithstanding the advantage derived from the proximity of Italian shore based aircraft. We had in fact established moral superiority over the Italian navy which had shown little determination to dispute with us the command of the waters of the Mediterranean.

58

In the Western Mediterranean it will be remembered that Force H returned to Gibraltar p.m. 6th July after completion of the operations against the French ships at Oran. Plans were immediately considered for operations against Italy. The Admiralty suggested an aircraft-torpedo attack on warships in Taranto or Augusta (0419/7/7/40), or an attack by surface ships on any warships suitably placed. The Commander-in-Chief, Mediterranean, observed that he intended to launch the Fleet Air Arm at ships in Augusta on 9th July, and added that he did not advise a Fleet Air Arm attack on Taranto until more experience had been gained (1409/7/7/40).

He recommended that whilst Operation MA.5 was in progress Force H should carry out air attacks against ships in Naples, Trapani, Palermo or Messina. Admiral Somerville, however, considered that lack of destroyers with sufficient endurance, added to the little time available for making plans, prevented him from undertaking such operations for the time being. Instead he decided to sail from Gibraltar a.m. on 8th July with the object of carrying out an air attack on Cagliari at dawn 10th July, and thus causing a diversion from Operation MA.5. Force H sailed accordingly at 0700/8th July, the squadron consisting of one battle cruiser, H.M.S. *Hood*, the flagship of the Vice-Admiral, two battleships, the *Valiant* and *Resolution*, three 6-inch cruisers, the *Arethusa*, *Enterprise*, *Delhi*, one aircraft carrier, the *Ark Royal*, flagship of the Vice-Admiral (A), and ten destroyers, being parts of the 8th and 13th Flotillas, with Captain D.8, H.M.S. *Faulknor*, in command. When in a position approximately 50 miles south of Minorca at 1545/9th, enemy air attacks began and lasted until 1840. The first attack was made by two subflights of three aircraft, which were only sighted a few seconds before bombs fell and were consequently only engaged during their withdrawal. The second attack, at 1750, was made by a large number of aircraft, which were heavily engaged while approaching. Some bombs fell in the sea about five miles from the Fleet. At 1836 the third attack developed from the sun sector, the aircraft being sighted and engaged before bomb-release. Altogether some 40 aircraft took part in these attacks, about 100 bombs being dropped, the majority of the attacks being pressed home determinedly and with good accuracy from heights of 10,000 to 13,000 feet. The bombs were dropped in patterns, about 12 being 'near misses', causing some superficial splinter damage but no casualties to personnel. Two enemy aircraft were shot down by our fighters and two by A/A fire, three others were considered to be too badly damaged to reach home and four more were known to have been hit. Immediately after the first air attack a submarine on the surface was reported by reconnaissance aircraft, and the course of the Fleet altered, but the submarine dived before she could be attacked. At the conclusion of the enemy air attacks Admiral Somerville decided that the risk of damage to the *Ark Royal* outweighed the considerations of a minor operation. He therefore cancelled his air attack on Cagliari, and turned westward for Gibraltar, arriving at 0830/11th July.

59

A few hours before the arrival of Force H at Gibraltar, Admiral Falangola scored his second success for the Italian submarines against a British warship. At 0325/11th July the *Forester* reported that she was standing by the *Escort*, which had been torpedoed. Both these destroyers were part of Force H returning to Gibraltar. Having sighted the submarine on the surface on her starboard bow at 0215/11, the *Forester* attacked with gunfire and tried to ram. The submarine, which was the *Marconi*, crash-dived and fired a torpedo from her stern tube, hitting the *Escort*. Unfortunately the *Forester*'s depth charges were set at 'safe', so could not be released at the crucial moment of the first attack, but she continued the hunt and at 0300/11, obtaining a firm contact, released six depth charges, without, however, causing damage to the submarine. The *Escort* eventually sank in a position approximately 35 miles west of Alboran Island with a loss of 20 officers and men. The search for the submarine was kept up by three destroyers throughout the 11th and 12th without success. Two Italian aircraft attacked the destroyers at 1322/11th, but caused no damage.

60

When reporting on these operations (1215/11/7/40 to Admiralty; and C.-in-C. Mediterranean) Admiral Somerville called attention to the limited endurance of even the best V and W class destroyers and the consequent limitation placed on the activities of Force H. Cruising speed of the squadron at sea had to be restricted to 15 knots, whilst from Gibraltar Sardinia was about the limit of distance for these destroyers without refuelling. The E and F class destroyers, on the other hand, could reach Genoa or West Sicily.

As regards Italian air operations Admiral Somerville pointed out that in favourable weather conditions the enemy could locate and attack up to a distance of 250 miles from Sardinia, and that this meant, assuming 16 hours of daylight, that Force H would come under attack for:–

1½ days when attacking Sardinia,

2 days when attacking Genoa or West Sicily,

2½ days when attacking Naples or Taranto.

Admiral Somerville in this same report referred to the *Ark Royal* and asked for guidance as to whether risk to that ship could be accepted in carrying out operations not necessarily of considerable military or political importance. If so, he proposed to use a raiding force of the *Hood*, *Ark Royal*, *Arethusa*, *Enterprise*, with five or six E and F-class destroyers, operating at 25 knots in zones open to air attack. If the *Valiant* was included the force's speed would be reduced to 22 knots, and destroyers would have to be oiled at sea.

There now followed an exchange of telegrams between the Admiralty, the Commander-in-Chief and Admiral Somerville regarding the strength and employment of naval forces in the Eastern and Western Mediterranean.

The maintenance of our position in the Middle East was necessary for the successful prosecution of the war, particularly in relation to ensuring the security of the vitally important Anglo-Iranian oilfields, and also to facilitate our economic blockade of the continent of Europe. In the opinion of the Chiefs of Staff the possibility of a German attack on Egypt was by no means unlikely in the future. Meanwhile they considered that as long as the fleet could be retained in the Eastern Mediterranean our existing forces were sufficient to deal with a purely Italian attack. The policy therefore was to maintain strong naval forces in the Eastern Mediterranean and to strengthen the defences in the Middle East as soon as possible. This latter requirement had to wait, however, as the immediate necessity was to concentrate on repelling the air attack now likely to develop against Great Britain and also to deal with a possible German attempt at actual invasion.

As regards the Western Mediterranean, here also it was considered necessary to retain a force at

Gibraltar as long possible with the object of controlling the Western exit, for possible Atlantic operations, and for carrying out attacks on the Italian fleet and bases. The general conclusion reached was that by the middle of August the forces under the Commander-in-Chief in the Eastern half of the Mediterranean would comprise the battleships *Warspite*, *Valiant*, *Malaya* and *Ramillies*, the aircraft carriers *Illustrious* and *Eagle* and the cruisers *Kent*, *York*, *Gloucester*, *Liverpool*, *Orion*, *Neptune*, *Sydney*, *Calcutta* and *Coventry* together with destroyers and submarines, whilst Force H, working from Gibraltar, would consist of the battle cruiser *Renown*, the battleship *Resolution*, the aircraft carrier *Ark Royal*, the cruisers *Sheffield* and *Enterprise* and destroyers (Appendix C. 7 and 9). In the event of war with Spain the Admiralty directions to Admiral Somerville were to base his plans on going to sea shortly before the outbreak of war if intelligence permitted, or if not immediately afterwards, proceeding to carry out attacks on Ferrol, Vigo or Cadiz. On conclusion of these operations a decision would be taken by the Admiralty as to whether Force H should return to Gibraltar or proceed elsewhere. (Admiralty 1432/28/7 to S.O. Force H.)

While at Gibraltar during the remainder of July Force H carried out exercises in Air Defence, against M.T.B. attack and in concentration exercises with air spotting. Between 23rd and 27th July the Vice-Admiral took the squadron into the Atlantic with the object of launching an air attack on enemy shipping in Bordeaux and Le Verdon, also to intercept shipping not carrying navicerts when bound for Spanish and Portuguese ports. No shipping was located and the Admiralty cancelled the air attacks on French ports.

61

Meanwhile, in the eastern half of the Mediterranean, our operations connected with the attack on enemy shipping and the protection of our own led to an encounter between British and Italian surface forces off Cape Spada on 19th July. To appreciate how this came about it should be noted that Italian shipping passed unescorted through the Aegean to and from the Black Sea and Aegean ports, making use in most cases of the Corinth Canal if bound for Italy or Adriatic ports. This meant a frequent use of the Gulf of Athens. Our shipping consisted mainly of northbound and southbound convoys between the Dardanelles and Egypt, from which individual ships broke off for Aegean ports. British submarines were usually on patrol off the Dardanelles, Doro and Kithera channels, whilst Italian submarines were placed off the southern exits of the Aegean and in the area north of Crete. Opportunities for submarine attacks on Italian shipping were not great because of the use made of territorial waters, and opportunities for attacks by our aircraft were limited owing to the distance from Egypt. Enemy aircraft, on the other hand, being based on Leros and Rhodes, were admirably placed to attack our shipping whether approaching or in the Aegean.

The Commander-in-Chief's general policy with regard to shipping in the Eastern Mediterranean was expressed on 27th June 1940, to the Admiralty as follows:–

- (*a*) Southbound Aegean convoys (AS.) and Northbound Aegean convoys (AN.) to be run periodically to connect with Red Sea convoys.
- (*b*) Local convoys between Haifa, Port Said, and Alexandria for oilers, Armament Store Issuing ships and transports to be run approximately weekly-
- (*c*) Remaining shipping for Cyprian, Syrian, Palestinian and Egyptian ports to sail independently.
- (*d*) When occasion demands a convoy will be run to Malta.

To counter the activities of Italian submarines in areas through which British convoys had to pass, and at the same time attack Italian shipping, the Commander-in-Chief used his light forces for periodic sweeps. One such sweep was undertaken prior to the passage of convoy AS.1 on 27th June and has already been described (S.33). Another was now planned before the sailing of convoy AN.2 and was arranged to start on 18th July. The orders issued by Vice-Admiral (D) arranged for:–

1. A submarine hunt towards the Kaso Strait and round Crete by four destroyers, combined with a sweep by a cruiser and destroyer into the Gulf of Athens for Italian shipping.
2. A further submarine hunt by eight destroyers between Crete and Cyrenaica, starting on 20th July. This force was then to sweep into the Southern Aegean to cover the movement of (3).

3. A convoy to Aegean ports sailing from Port Said on 19th July. The escort of this convoy was to bring back a convoy from Aegean ports to Egypt, arriving about 28th July.

The forces detailed left Alexandria on 18th July. Captain (D) 2nd Destroyer Flotilla, with *Hyperion*, *Ilex*, *Hero* and *Hasty*, was directed to pass through Kaso Strait about 2130/18th and then to proceed along the north coast of Crete through the Anti-Kithera Channel and thence back to Alexandria. In support were H.M.A.S. *Sydney*, Captain J. A. Collins, R.A.N., with H.M.S. *Havock*. This force, after passing through the Kaso Strait, was to proceed to the Gulf of Athens to search for enemy shipping and then through the Anti-Kithera Channel back to Alexandria. Two destroyers *Hereward* and *Imperial* were sent to Port Said to collect ships from there for the Aegean convoy AN.2.

62

Two Italian cruisers, unknown to us at the time, had left Tripoli on 17th July with the object of a raid on our Aegean shipping, and according to a survivor's report expected to be joined by a supporting force, but Italian official sources contain no evidence of this. They were approaching the Anti-Kithera Channel from the west on the morning of the 19th at the same time as our four destroyers were approaching from the eastward. The two forces were in sight at 0722/19th, and the *Hero*'s sighting report reached the *Sydney* at 0733, the latter being at that moment some 40 miles N.N.E. of the Kithera Channel on her way to the Gulf of Athens with the *Havock*. Four minutes later the *Sydney* received an amplifying report from the *Hyperion* giving her own course as 060° and the enemy's as 360°. She immediately turned south and worked up to full speed and shortly afterwards received the Commander-in-Chief's signals to her and Captain (D) 2nd D.F. to join and act together. The *Sydney* sighted the enemy, the 6-inch cruisers *Giovanni Delle Bande Nere* and *Bartolomeo Colleoni*, at 0826/19 and opened fire at 0829 at a range of 20,000 yards on the leading cruiser. The Italians were taken by surprise, the fall of the *Sydney*'s salvoes being the first announcement of her arrival; our destroyers were then out of sight steering N.E. to join the *Sydney*, and probably the Italian lookouts were searching to the eastward. At 0832 the enemy returned the fire, his salvoes falling short at first, then over, with an occasional straddle; simultaneously he altered course parallel to the *Sydney*, and at 0840 turned off to the south-westward, having then been hit but not apparently seriously damaged. At 0846, the *Sydney*'s original target was so obscured by smoke that fire was shifted to the rear cruiser – *Colleoni* – which was engaged by 'A' and 'B' turrets at a range of 18,000 yards. The destroyer division from time to time joined in the fight, but up to 0900 was generally out of range for 4.7-inch guns. For a few minutes after 0901 the *Sydney* shifted target again to the *Bande Nere*, but at 0908 she was obliged to shift back to the *Colleoni*, the range still being about 18,000 yards but closing. It was evident that her fire was having considerable effect. At 0923, the *Colleoni* was seen to be stopped and apparently out of action in a position 250° Cape Spada five miles. She was down by the bows

THE *BARTOLOMEO COLLEONI* UNDER FIRE

and listing heavily, having been brought-to by a shot in the engine or boiler room; all lights went out and electrical machinery, including turret power hoists and steering gear, ceased functioning. The *Bande Nere*, after making a tentative turn towards her stricken colleague, made off to the southward at high speed, chased by the *Sydney* with the *Hero* and *Hasty* at 39 knots. At 1100/19th the *Bande Nere* was in a position 40 miles west of Gavdo island steering 170°, heading for Tobruk. The *Sydney* did not continue the chase after 1030 as she had only four rounds a gun left in 'A' turret, and one round a gun in 'B' turret. The end of the *Colleoni* came at 0929 when she sank in the position given above, having been finished off by torpedoes from the *Ilex* and *Hyperion*. The *Bande Nere* reached Benghazi on the afternoon of the 19th.[1] Hoping that this sign of enemy activity might prove to be a prelude to the movements of larger forces, the Commander-in-Chief took active steps with the rest of the Fleet. The Vice-Admiral (D), with the *Orion* and *Neptune*, left Alexandria at 1915/19th and steered towards Tobruk at 30 knots. If the *Bande Nere* was damaged – and she was known to have been hit[1] – there was a chance of intercepting her, but not otherwise, as at 1100/19th our cruisers had some 260 miles to go to the enemy's 200. The Commander-in-Chief requested the R.A.F. to send bombers to attack the *Bande Nere* on approaching land, and at the same time ordered the *Eagle*'s striking force to be ready to attack Tobruk harbour with torpedoes in the evening. Reconnaissance was undertaken by flying boats of 201 Group, R.A.F. The Commander-in-Chief himself proceeded to sea in the *Warspite* with a destroyer screen at 1100/19th, and the remainder of the Fleet (less the *Royal Sovereign*) sailed at 1230, all sweeping to the westward.

As regards British shipping, directions were given to ships from Port Said for Convoy AN.2 to return to that port whilst the oiler convoy from Alexandria to Port Said proceeded without escort.

During the afternoon of the 19th there was no further sign of enemy activity, nor was any information received regarding the *Bande Nere*, and at 2100 the Commander-in-Chief gave orders for all forces to return to Alexandria, where they arrived the following day. During the night of the 19th/20th Blenheim bombers from Number 55 and 211 Squadrons R.A.F. bombed Tobruk, and No. 824 Squadron F.A.A. from *Eagle* launched a torpedo attack on shipping in the harbour. These attacks did considerable damage and hits were obtained on a destroyer, two merchant ships and an oiler.

63

Five hundred and twenty-five survivors from the *Colleoni*, including the Captain, Umberto Novaro, who died at Alexandria on 23rd July, were rescued by the *Havock*, Commander R. E. Courage, *Ilex* and *Hyperion*. Bombing attacks were carried out by Italian aircraft while survivors were being picked up, and two heavy attacks were made on the *Havock* later. In the second of these attacks a 250-lb bomb burst close by and six feet under water, splinters entering No. 2 boiler room which was flooded. The *Havock*, however, only lost way for five minutes and then proceeded at 24 knots for Alexandria.

Our casualties in the action were negligible, one rating being slightly injured in the *Sydney*, which was hit on the foremost funnel, and two ratings in the *Havock*'s boiler room received minor injuries. The *Warspite* unfortunately lost her aircraft, which had been catapulted at 1700/19th to search the Tobruk area and had to make a forced landing in the sea. Search for the crew by the *Jervis* was unsuccessful, but they were captured the next morning by the Italians, having swum ashore from their scuttled aircraft.

In his covering letter to the Admiralty, written on 21st September 1940 (M.020932/40), the Commander-in-Chief observed that:–

> 'The credit for this successful action belongs mainly to Captain J. A. Collins, C.B., R.A.N., who by his quick appreciation of the situation, offensive spirit and resolute handling of H.M.A.S. *Sydney*, achieved a victory over a superior force which has had important strategical effects. It is significant that, so far as is known, no Italian surface forces have returned into or near the Aegean since this action was fought.'

---

1 The *Bande Nere* was hit twice, first about 0835 by a 6-inch shell passing through the foremost funnel and exploding near the after catapult machinery, killing four ratings and wounding four more. The second hit was at 0950; either a 4.7 or 6-inch shell penetrated the quarter deck and exploded on a divisional bulkhead, killing four ratings and wounding twelve.

He added that the action brought out a few points of particular interest and value as showing how to obtain the best results when the opportunity arrives. The points he emphasised were as follows:–

(i) By preserving W/T silence during his approach to the scene Captain Collins achieved what every commander in war desires, namely, surprise to the enemy.

(ii) Both for accuracy and rate of fire the *Sydney*'s shooting was markedly superior to that of the enemy.

(iii) By turning back immediately at right angles to the enemy's course after sighting the *Sydney*, our destroyers almost certainly headed off the enemy's retirement to the eastward, and so kept them within the *Sydney*'s gun range.

The enemy's tactics appeared faulty; for, when his two cruisers first sighted our destroyers, instead of holding their easterly course and utilising their advantage of superior gunfire, sixteen 6-inch to sixteen 4.7-inch, they immediately turned due North and fired a few rounds at maximum range.

After the action, when survivors were being rescued by our destroyers, the Italian bombing attacks led the Commander-in-Chief to issue a warning to the Fleet that it must be remembered we were waging a relentless war against odds. Practically the whole of the area of our operations was subject to enemy, bombing, and therefore in picking up survivors not only did ships expose themselves to attack under very disadvantageous conditions, but subsequent operations were liable to be delayed. 'Difficult and distasteful as it is to leave survivors to their fate,' said the Commander-in-Chief, 'Commanding Officers must be prepared to harden their hearts, for after all, the operations in hand and the security of their ships and ships' companies must take precedence in war.'

CHAPTER 5

REINFORCEMENTS, AIR AND SUBMARINE ACTIVITIES

(SEPTEMBER 1940)

64

BY THE end of July 1940, the Commander-in-Chief felt that he was in a position to assess the Fleet's task with some degree of certainty, as several encounters with the Italians had enabled him to take their measure. Two of the new *Littorio* battleships were believed to be active,[1] and a further two of the *Cavour* class were nearing completion of their modernisation; these considerations kept alive the chances of a main Fleet action, nevertheless the feeling existed that however impressive their strength appeared on paper – both on and below the surface – yet they would not meet us in open battle Experience had shown their leadership to be faulty and their training inadequate; submarines were sighted time and again on the surface in daylight; except for the 8-inch class cruisers at Calabria, both cruisers and destroyers had shown few signs of skilful handling, and the only two battleships encountered ran for shelter after receiving one hit. So far, Admiral Cavagnari's injunction of an 'offensive to the death' (S.22) had not materialised. The main threat to our command of the sea was from the air. Both the Fleet and the two main bases – Malta and Alexandria, particularly Malta – were endangered, and it was clear that our A/A defences had somehow to be improved.

The lessons of the Fleet action off Calabria on 9th July were that we needed at least two capital ships fast enough to get, and keep, within range of the enemy,[2] also that two 8-inch cruisers were required to control the area ahead of the Fleet. Another aircraft carrier was necessary to provide adequate fighter support to the Fleet when operating in the central Mediterranean since R.A.F. fighter cover could not be relied upon farther west than 23° E, and we had not then advanced into Cyrenaica. Also, we lacked any radar equipment afloat.

The position with regard to ammunition was becoming troublesome; reserves were running low, and replenishments would be even more necessary if reinforcements arrived. In the Western Basin the task of Force H had to be settled; operations against objectives in the Tyrrhenian Sea were limited by enemy air superiority, but our ships could carry out sweeps as far as Sardinia or northern Italian ports and thereby stifle enemy trade; also, on specific occasions, they could act so as to divert attention from the operations of the Mediterranean Fleet in the Eastern Basin, and *vice-versa*.

On the question of the reinforcement of the Mediterranean Fleet [Appendix C.7a. par. M] the Admiralty asked whether ships could pass safely through the Mediterranean, particularly the Sicily-Malta channel, or if they should be sent round the Cape of Good Hope. The Commander-in-Chief, Mediterranean, replied that by carrying out a concerted movement it would be possible to pass reinforcements through the

---

1 The *Vittorio Veneto* and *Littorio* became operational in August 1940, also the *Duilio*. The *Doria* was not fully operational until December.
2 See Section 56.

Mediterranean, but he did not advocate risking the bulk of the ammunition by that route. He advised sending the whole of the reserve of ammunition – less additional 4.5-inch that could be packed into *Valiant* and *Illustrious* – in the fastest ships possible round the Cape (Appendix C.9). The outcome of these interchanges between the Admiralty and the Commander-in-Chief was the planning of Operations Hats and Hurry.

Operation Hats, which was to bring the main reinforcements, was timed for mid-August, and would include a further supply of Hurricane fighters for Malta to be flown from the *Argus*, a first batch of twelve Hurricanes being arranged to reach Malta about 1st August in Operation Hurry (Appendix E.44). The *Argus* left the United Kingdom for Gibraltar with these machines on 24th July, expecting to leave there with Force H on 31st July. The Commander-in-Chief considered that with the additional forces proposed, that is, two battleships, *Valiant* and *Barham*, in place of *Ramillies* and *Royal Sovereign*, the aircraft carrier *Illustrious* with 21 Swordfish and 16 Fulmars, two 8-inch cruisers, *York* and *Exeter*, the A/A cruiser *Carlisle* from the Red Sea, and two convoy sloops from the Red Sea to provide A/A escort for convoys, which hitherto had been provided by cruisers, the Mediterranean could be held indefinitely provided that Malta received proper fighter protection. The *Valiant* would be particularly welcome as she not only possessed radar equipment, but also was armed with a battery of twenty 4.5-inch dual purpose guns which would prove most useful in combating the air menace to the Fleet at sea, as well as giving additional protection to Alexandria harbour, where raids were becoming a nuisance.

65

The Commander-in-Chief took the fleet[1] to sea from Alexandria early a.m. 27th July in order to provide distant cover for the southward passage of convoy AS.2, which left the Dardanelles 0700/27th escorted by C.S.7 in the *Liverpool* with the *Capetown* and four destroyers, which had brought convoy AN.2 up from Egypt. The original intention was for this cruise to coincide with Operation Hurry, but as that had been postponed until 31st July the Commander-in-Chief planned a further cruise in the Eastern Basin from 31st July to 2nd August.

At 1330/27th July reports from Italian shadowing aircraft were intercepted, but the bombers did not arrive until late in the evening, when five attacks developed between 1818 and 1920. A total of 63 bombs were dropped, mostly aimed at and falling close to the *Warspite*, but there were no hits or casualties. The Italian aircraft reports frequently gave our Fleet's position between 30 and 60 miles in error, and knowledge of this fact made the maintenance of W/T silence all the more valuable in preventing enemy shore D/F stations checking our position.

Gladiator fighters from the *Eagle* took off whenever a shadower was reported, and though unable on this cruise to locate and intercept on account of the shadowers' height, their activities undoubtedly kept the enemy at a respectful distance. At 0915/28th, convoy AS.2 and the escort force were sighted clear of the Aegean and proceeding south of Crete for Alexandria, but the Fleet maintained a north-westerly course until reaching a position 50 miles south of Matapan at noon/28th, when course was reversed for the return trip. During the forenoon it was learnt that the Greek ship *Hermione* (440 tons), bound for the Dodecanese with an Italian cargo of 300 tons of aviation spirit and 200 tons of lubricating oil, would clear the Corinth Canal at 1100/28th, and the *Neptune* and *Sydney* were detached to intercept her. When in the Thermia Channel, south-east of the Gulf of Athens, the cruisers were heavily bombed. Shortly afterwards, at 2050/28, the *Hermione* was met and sunk as a military emergency, the master and crew being left in boats close to land.

At 0800/29th the Commander-in-Chief in the *Warspite*, with three destroyers, proceeded ahead to Alexandria, arriving at 2000/29th; but the 1st Battle Squadron remained at sea, eastward of the convoy, until the next day, the 30th. Four air attacks were delivered on the escort force on the 29th, the *Liverpool* being hit by an unexploded bomb which killed one rating; one enemy bomber was shot down by a Gladiator

---

1 H.M.S. *Warspite*, *Malaya*, *Ramillies*, *Eagle*, *Neptune*, *Sydney*, *Jervis* and nine destroyers.

from the *Eagle*. The Rear-Admiral Commanding 7th C.S. reported each attack by W/T; but the rest of the Fleet kept W/T silence and were not attacked.

During the passage of convoys AN.2 and AS.2 attempts were made to divert enemy air attention by demonstrating off Castelorizo. V.A. (D) in the *Orion* with two destroyers appeared off the island on 24th July, and again on the 27th accompanied by two armed boarding vessels, *Chakla* and *Fiona*, representing transports. On neither occasion, however, did enemy aircraft take any action, nor did the shore defences show any sign of resentment.

66

Force H sailed from Gibraltar for Operation Hurry at 0800/31st July with the object of flying off fighter aircraft, 12 Hurricanes and two Skuas, to Malta from H.M.S. *Argus*. The Force consisted of the *Hood*, Flag of Vice-Admiral Somerville, *Valiant* and *Resolution*, *Ark Royal*, Flag of V.A. (A), and *Argus*, *Arethusa* and *Enterprise*, with 10 destroyers. Arrangements were made for two Sunderland Flying Boats from Malta to rendezvous with the *Argus* at dawn on 2nd August to act as navigational escorts for the fighter flights.

In order to hamper enemy air activity while Operation Hurry[1] was in progress an air attack on Cagliari was planned to be carried out by the *Ark Royal*: Operation Crush. A second diversion, Operation Spark, was arranged to take place at 0200/2nd August when the *Enterprise* (Captain J. C. Annesley) would be off Minorca and transmit W/T messages on 366 k.c's. simulating reports of a suspicious vessel in bogus lettered positions, and also burning searchlights.

Enemy aircraft attacked the Fleet in two waves about 1800/1st August, when in a position N.W. of Gulf of Bougie, and both attacks were effectively dealt with by A/A fire from the ships and Skua fighter aircraft of 803 Squadron from the *Ark Royal*. Several enemy aircraft sheered off without dropping their bombs; at least one was brought down by gunfire and another, a Savoia S.79, was shot down by our fighters. Altogether some 80 bombs were dropped, and it was noted that the attacks were not pressed home as determinedly as on 9th July (S.58). Two details in connection with the visibility of ships from the air were mentioned in the *Ark Royal*'s report of these operations. It was found, for example, that the *Argus* was visible from aircraft at five miles greater distance than the *Ark Royal*, owing to her light paint, and that the newly painted sides and bulges of the *Valiant* and *Resolution* gave noticeable reflections of light.

At 2045/1st August Group 1, *Hood*, *Ark Royal*, *Enterprise* and four destroyers, parted company and proceeded to a position 100 miles south-west of Sardinia to carry out Operation Crush; and at 2130/31st the *Enterprise* was detached to carry out Operation Spark, after which she was ordered to intercept the French ship *Gouverneur-General De Gueydon*, believed to have sailed from Algiers at 1600/1st August for Marseilles with M. Daladier, a former French Prime Minister, on board.

Group II, that is the remainder of Force H, under command of the Commanding Officer, *Valiant*, continued on an easterly course until 0445/2nd August when, having reached 37° 40' N., 7° 20' E. (350 miles from Malta), two flights of six Hurricanes and one Skua were flown off the *Argus*. Both flights reached Malta safely, though one Hurricane crashed on landing. Two Flying Boats were picked up by the radar screen, but did not contact the fighters in time for their flight.

Meanwhile the attack on Cagliari was in progress. At 0230/2nd August a striking force of nine T.B.R.'s armed with bombs and three T.B.R's armed with mines took off from the *Ark Royal*. Weather conditions were bad and one aircraft crashed on taking off, the crew being lost. The others were forced to delay their attack until full daylight, when it was pressed well home in face of considerable A/A fire. Direct hits were made on the four hangers of Elmas aerodrome, many buildings and two hangers being set on fire, also several aircraft destroyed or damaged.

Three mines were successfully laid in the gate of the outer harbour net defences. One T.B.R. aircraft forced-landed after being hit by A/A fire and the crew were made prisoners, but the remaining aircraft returned safely at 0720/2nd with only minor damage. Enemy fighter opposition was ineffective, one being

---

[1] M.016108/40. M.01722/40.

driven off by an observer with a service revolver. Group I then proceeded south-eastward to meet Group II returning from the flying-off operation; both forces joined at 0815/2nd and proceeded westward. The *Enterprise* at 1000/2nd reported successful completion of Operation Spark, two enemy aircraft being then over her, and she was ordered to return to Gibraltar. Neither the *Enterprise* nor the *Arethusa*, which was detached at 0930/2nd, sighted the French ship expected to be on her way to Marseilles from Algiers. All forces reached Gibraltar by daylight 4th August, the return voyage being uneventful except for the bringing down of two enemy aircraft by Skuas of 800 Squadron.

The Mediterranean Fleet during the progress of Operation Hurry carried out diversionary operations (MA.9) in two groups, which left Alexandria on 31st July, the object being to give the impression of a general movement into the Central Mediterranean, and so tend to deter surface and air forces in Sicily and South Italy from moving westward.

Force A, comprising C.S. 7 in the *Orion*, with the *Neptune*, *Sydney* and four destroyers, left Alexandria at 0600/31st July with orders to pass through Kaso Strait at dusk the same night, then up to the Doro Channel, sweep through the Gulf of Athens area, and south-west part of the Aegean, return to the Gulf of Athens during the night of 1st/2nd and thence back through Kaso Strait to Alexandria by a.m. 3rd August. Force B, comprising R.A. 1st B.S., Rear-Admiral H. D. Pridham-Wippell, in the *Malaya*, with the *Royal Sovereign*, *Eagle* and eight destroyers, sailed at 1420/31st July to carry out gunnery practices; they were then to proceed westward towards Gavdo Island until after dark on 1st August and return to Alexandria by p.m. 2nd August, but owing to condenser trouble in the *Malaya* the force had to curtail their cruise and returned to harbour on 1st August.

67

Enemy shadowing aircraft reported both Forces A and B at sea several times during the first day, 31st July, when on north-westerly courses. This was satisfactory for our diversionary purpose. The Italian Fleet, however, showed no sign of consequential action. The reason for this was thought at the time to be that both the battleships *Cesare* and *Cavour* were under repair after their injuries on 9th July, when the former was known to have been damaged by shell fire from the *Warspite* and the latter reported hit by bombs from their own aircraft (S.56). Damage to these ships – even if actual – need not have deterred the remainder of the Fleet from taking some action, but whatever the motive they remained in harbour. Some cruisers and destroyers were at sea between 30th July and 2nd August and were reported by the submarine *Oswald* which was on patrol southward of the Strait of Messina. These vessels were acting as escort for a troop convoy to Libya, mainly for Benghazi. Unfortunately the *Oswald*'s report was received in Malta too late for a striking force of Swordfish to take off and intercept them. A further misfortune arose out of the *Oswald*'s enemy reports in that their transmission was D/F'd by the enemy, who ordered a submarine hunt in her vicinity, and on 2nd August she was attacked and sunk by the Italian destroyer *Vivaldi*, the Commanding Officer and 52 of the crew of 55 being taken prisoner.

The question of intercepting enemy troop convoys to Libya was again brought to the fore by this incident, as it served to emphasize the importance of Malta as a base for our light forces. Our ability to attack such convoys at short notice by surface forces working from Alexandria was obviously limited. The enemy was immediately acquainted with our Fleet movements by its daily air reconnaissance and could seize the opportunity to pass fast convoys to Libya. In this case he had been informed of the Fleet's cruise to the west of Crete on 27th/29th July and of their return to Alexandria on the 30th. The Admiralty assured the Commander-in-Chief that they fully appreciated the difficulties and the implication involved. (A.T. 1740/1/8/40.)

68

The need for early arrival of reinforcements for the Fleet, Army and Air Force was emphasized by a message to the Chiefs of Staff from the Middle East on 22nd August (P.16981) which stated that there were indications of an impending attack on Egypt by the Italian army from Libya.

The pressing need of Malta for fighter aircraft having been partially relieved by Operation Hurry, the next step was to proceed with the main plan of reinforcement, known as Operation Hats. The intention to include in the main operation a further supply of Hurricanes for Malta from the *Argus* was abandoned, as it was thought better to send a consignment of 30 Hurricanes fitted with long-range tanks by sea in the *Argus* to Takoradi on the Gold Coast, whence they could be flown across Africa to Egypt and thence, as directed by the Air Officer, Commanding-in-Chief, Middle East, to Malta. The first of these flights left Takoradi on 5th September, and further consignments thereafter were sent from the United Kingdom to Takoradi in merchant ships.

The warship reinforcements from the United Kingdom comprised the battleship *Valiant*, aircraft carrier *Illustrious* with 19 Fulmar fighters and 18 Swordfish T.S.R.'s, the 8-inch cruiser *York*, two A/A cruisers *Calcutta* and *Coventry*. These ships left Home Waters on 21st August 1940, and arrived at Gibraltar at dawn on 29th August. The request of the Commander-in-Chief, Mediterranean, for a second 8-inch cruiser was met by transferring the *Kent* from the East Indies Station early in August. On account of her low freeboard the *Exeter*, as well as the *York*, had been asked for, but she was not available. The 6-inch cruiser *Ajax* was sent to replace the *Neptune*, as the former had the latest type of radar for both warning and gun-ranging.

If any signs developed of an Italian attack on Egypt becoming imminent before the reinforcements reached Gibraltar, the Chiefs of Staff decided on an alternative plan for hastening the arrival in Egypt of the M.T. ships, which had sailed at the same time from the U.K.; Operation Hats, round the Cape, would then be turned into Operation Bonnet, when the transports would pass through the Mediterranean (Adm. message 1043/15/8/40). The two cargoes most urgently required for the Army were in two M.T. ships, the *Waiotira* (17½ knots with cruiser tanks) and *Denbighshire* (16 knots with infantry tanks), and these would accompany the reinforcements through the Mediterranean, leaving the personnel and other equipment in the *Royal Scotsman*, *Sydney Star* and *Duchess of Bedford* to proceed round the Cape. The decision to carry out Operation Bonnet was to be taken any time before the forces reached the latitude of Gibraltar, but not later than midnight 26th/27th August, so that the personnel required for the tanks in the *Waiotira* and *Denbighshire* could be transferred to those ships at Gibraltar. The Commanders-in-Chief, Middle East, were requested to undertake special reconnaissance over Libya and inform the Chiefs of Staff in London of their deductions not later than 0800/26th August.

The final plans for Operation Hats [Appendix E.44 (d) to (f)] provided for the Senior Officer Force H leaving Gibraltar on 30th August, D + one day, with Force B consisting of the *Renown*, *Ark Royal*, *Sheffield* and seven destroyers and Force F consisting of the reinforcements for the Eastern Mediterranean, *Valiant*, *Illustrious* (flying the flag of the Rear-Admiral, Air), *Calcutta* and *Coventry*, both forces passing through the longitude of Galita Island about 1700 on D + three day, 1st September. After passing this longitude, and before dark, the Senior Officer Force H was to alter course with both forces to the north eastward as though heading for Gaeta or Naples, maintaining this line of advance until fully dark, when Force F was to be detached to rendezvous with the Commander-in-Chief, Mediterranean. The latter, with Force I consisting of the *Warspite*, *Malaya*, *Eagle*, *Orion*, flying the flag of V.A.L.F., *Sydney*, *Kent*, flying the flag of R.A. Third Cruiser Squadron, *Gloucester*, *Liverpool*, and twelve destroyers was to be in a position 220° Gozo Light 45 miles at 0800/D + 4. After detaching Force F, Force B was to proceed under the orders of the S.O. Force H to carry out a dawn air attack on Gagliari. Modifications of the above plan were prepared in case Operation Bonnet was ordered. In this event Group X comprising the *Renown*, *Valiant*, *Illustrious*, *Ark Royal* and *York*, with Force H cruisers and some destroyers, would leave Gibraltar a.m., D + one, and Group Y, comprising the two M.T. ships escorted by the *Coventry*, *Calcutta*, and the remainder of Force H destroyers, would sail at dusk D + one day and feint to the westward until dark. On D + two day and the night of D.2/D.3 Group X was to make a feint towards the Balearic Islands with a W/T diversion further north, and then carry out a night bombing of Cagliari aerodrome. Group Y, meanwhile, was to proceed at 30 miles distance from the North African coast until sunrise on D + 3 day, when it was to rendezvous with Group X off the Gulf of Bougie. An escort of fighters for the M.T. ships was to be provided from dawn. Thereafter the plan was the same as for Operation Hats. The separation of Groups X and Y during D + 1 and D + 2 days would enable a preliminary bombing of Cagliari to be carried out, and thereby help to conceal the presence of Group Y until D + 3 day.

The passage through the Sicilian Narrows of these valuable M.T. ships was a matter of considerable anxiety both to the Commander-in-Chief, Middle East, and the Commander-in-Chief, Mediterranean, as well as to the Chiefs of Staff, for the safe arrival of additional mechanical transport in Egypt was a matter of great importance to the Army at this juncture. It was therefore with a feeling of relief that on 25th August the Commander-in-Chief, Mediterranean, reported to the Admiralty that in the opinion of G.H.Q., Middle East, the situation did not justify Operation Bonnet.[1] (C.-in-C. Mediterranean 1959/25/8/40.) The Italian invasion of Egypt did not begin until 13th September, by which date the M.T. ships escorted by the *Ajax* and *York* had arrived at Durban, eventually reaching Suez on 23rd September.

69

The Commander-in-Chief, Mediterranean, had agreed with the Senior Officer, Force H, to send four destroyers designated as Force A to Gibraltar to assist in escorting the reinforcements through the Sicilian Narrows, and these ships left Malta on 22nd August, but at 0317/23rd August, one of them, the *Hostile*, struck a mine and was sunk off Cape Bon. Another, the *Nubian*, had two complete failures of forced lubrication of the main engines and returned to Malta for repairs. The other two, *Mohawk* and *Hero*, also returned to Malta with survivors from the *Hostile*. This was not a good beginning for Operation Hats, but the *Janus* took the place of the *Hostile* and eventually the *Nubian*, *Mohawk*, *Janus* and *Hero* arrived at Gibraltar on 29th August in time to take their part as arranged.

The Commander-in-Chief, in H.M.S. *Warspite*, with the *Malaya* and *Eagle*; the *Orion* flying the flag of the V.A.L.F. with the *Sydney* and ten destroyers; the Rear-Admiral, Third Cruiser Squadron in the *Kent*, with *Gloucester* and *Liverpool* and three destroyers, cleared the swept channel from Alexandria at 0600/30th August, D + one (day), and proceeded westward at 16 knots, being sighted and reported by Italian aircraft at 1530/30th August. The Rear-Admiral, Third Cruiser Squadron's force, made a detour through Kaso Strait and the southern Aegean before meeting the Commander-in-Chief at noon, 31st August, when 50 miles south of Matapan. Aircraft from the *Eagle* were flown off for A/S patrols, and during the 31st a fighter patrol of four Gladiators was maintained over the Fleet. Their presence probably kept the bombers away, but enemy shadowers appeared at intervals, one being shot down by our fighters in the afternoon.

A convoy, M.F.2, comprising the S.S. *Cornwall*, *Volo*, and the R.F.A. *Plumleaf*, all with stores for Malta and escorted by four destroyers, left Alexandria late p.m. on 29th August, and from the morning of 31st August the *Eagle* provided an A/S patrol for this force.

Enemy air attacks on the convoy started at noon 31st August soon after it had passed the south-west corner of Crete, and the Third Cruiser Squadron was detached to provide additional A/A protection, with orders to rejoin the Fleet at 2000. At 1630/31st the *Cornwall* was hit aft by a bomb which destroyed her steering gear, put the W/T out of action, destroyed both her guns, holed her below the waterline and started a fire which spread to her after hold and the magazine blew up. The Master, Captain F. C. Pretty, however, managed to get the fire under control and continued with the convoy, steering by the main engines.

The Commander-in-Chief's hopes of encountering the enemy Fleet were raised at 1815/31st August, when the *Eagle*'s aircraft, duty 'C', reported two battleships, seven cruisers and eight destroyers in a position 140 miles N.W. of our Fleet and steering south-east. The Commander-in-Chief with the main force at that time was 70 miles S.W. of Matapan and steering due south to close the convoy, then some 50 miles to the south-east. At 2130/31st, when 20 miles from the convoy, the Fleet turned to 260°, speed 13 knots, so as to be well disposed if the enemy had intended to attack the convoy. Earlier in the afternoon H.M. S/M. *Parthian* attacked four cruisers and five destroyers in a position 40 miles N.W. of the 1815

---

1 The Prime Minister in his capacity of Minister of Defence had urged the Chiefs of Staff, Admiralty and Commander-in-Chief, Mediterranean, to pass all the ships through the Mediterranean. In the 22nd chapter of Volume II of his 'Second World War', Mr. Churchill states that he thought in 1949 as he did in 1940 that the risk should have been taken.

position, firing six torpedoes at a cruiser of the Zara class. The *Parthian* dived deep and was hunted by a destroyer, so was unable to observe the results of her attack, which in fact had been unsuccessful. There were no incidents during the night, and at 0630/1st September nine aircraft were flown off to search to a distance of 100 miles N.W. and S.E. from the Fleet, whose position was then 220 miles east of Malta and steering 130° to keep clear of the convoy, altering to 210° at 1000 and to 270° at 1120, when the convoy was 18 miles on their port bow. Air patrols were up all day searching up to 100 miles from the Fleet, but no enemy was seen until 1600/1st when Flying Boat on Duty X, working from Malta, reported two battleships ten cruisers and a large number of destroyers 200 miles north of the Fleet and steering for Taranto. Clearly they did not intend to try conclusions with us on this occasion. It is now known from Italian official accounts that the First and Second Squadrons, comprising five battleships, six cruisers and twenty seven destroyers, left their bases of Brindisi and Taranto during the early hours of 31st August and assembled at 1400/31st in 37° 50' N., 18° 30' E., namely about 170 miles south east of Taranto.

At 1800/31st when in 36° 45' N., 19° 25' E. and 140 miles north west of the British Fleet, course was altered to 335°, speed 13 knots, until 0845/1st September in 39° 08' N., 17° 28' E. Course was then altered to 155° until 1400/1st, when all ships were ordered to return to base. Their voyage was prompted by an aircraft reconnaissance report at 1600/30th, made presumably by the aircraft referred to above. At 1600/1st, when the British flying boat on Duty X reported the enemy 200 miles away the distance was probably about 160.

At 0800/2nd September, Force I was in a position 40 miles S.W. of Malta steering 320° to meet Force F, which was sighted right ahead at 0900. Until late p.m./2nd September, the combined forces remained cruising 35 miles south of Malta, during which time the convoy arrived and the destroyers were refuelled in Malta, while the *Valiant*, *Calcutta* and *Coventry* discharged guns, ammunition and stores. An enemy reconnaissance aircraft was shot down at 1120 by Fulmars from the *Illustrious*, shortly after a sighting report of our forces had been made; Fulmars also chased off an attacking force of bombers at 1450, shooting down one and damaging others. Intermittent bombing attacks were made on the Fleet between 1600 and 1900 without causing any damage; two S.79's were brought down by gunfire and one by our fighters. The *Valiant*'s sailing from Malta to rejoin was delayed by air raids until 0130/3rd September, when she took station astern of the line, course 085°, speed 18 knots.

During the return voyage to Alexandria opportunity was taken of attacking enemy air bases in the Dodecanese at Scarpanto and Rhodes.[1] The V.A.L.F. with the *Orion*, *Sydney* and two destroyers, *Ilex* and *Dainty*, on 4th September carried out a dawn bombardment of Pegadia Bay, Scarpanto and heavily plastered the eastern part of Makri Yalo aerodrome. E-boats came out to attack the Squadron, but fared badly, for *Ilex* sank one and damaged the others. At dawn on the 4th, eight Swordfish flew off the *Illustrious* to attack Callato airfield, Rhodes, and twelve Swordfish from the *Eagle* attacked Maritza airfield, Rhodes. Useful results were obtained in both attacks by the destruction of enemy aircraft on the ground, hangars, barrack blocks, ammunition and petrol dumps. One Swordfish was lost from the *Illustrious* through taking off down wind, and four of the *Eagle*'s aircraft failed to return after encountering enemy fighters. The V.A.L.F. rejoined the Fleet during the forenoon of the 4th, and at noon the Commander-in-Chief with the main force was 60 miles S.E. of Scarpanto with the R.A. First Battleship Squadron 40 miles to the southward, course being shaped for Alexandria. The Third Cruiser Squadron, with the *Coventry*, *Calcutta* and two destroyers, were detached on 3rd September to rendezvous with and escort a southbound Aegean convoy, AS.3. Several unsuccessful air attacks were made on the Fleet during 4th September, the Fulmars shooting down one S.79 and damaging three others. In addition to the protection given by the Fulmars at sea and the Fleet Air Arm attacks on Dodecanese air bases, No. 202 Group, R.A.F. from Egypt carried out a number of successful attacks on the Libyan aerodromes, all of which measures produced a noticeably reduced air effort against the Fleet.

Just before noon, 4th September, one of the A/S aircraft on patrol dropped a bomb on a suspected submarine two miles from the *Warspite*, obtaining a faint contact the *Imperial* carried out a depth charge

---

[1] Operation MB.3. A.0978/40, A.0755/41. Operation Hats, M.019144/40, 023713/40, 02964/41.

attack. The only other reminder of the existence of Italian submarines occurred on entering the swept channel to Alexandria a.m./5th September, when *Hereward* obtained an A/S contact and the Fleet made an emergency turn. According to Italian submarine patrol records ten submarines were at sea in the Eastern Mediterranean, and either the *Millelire* or the *Da Procida* may have been involved in this incident. By a.m. 6th September all forces had returned to Alexandria, and convoy AS.3 arrived at Port Said p.m. on the same day.

70

Turning to the Western Mediterranean, Force H left Gibraltar for Operation Hats at 0845/30th August and was divided into two forces, B and F; Force B, *Renown*, *Ark Royal*, *Sheffield* and twelve destroyers; Force F, the reinforcements for the Eastern Mediterranean, H.M. ships *Valiant*, *Illustrious* (Flag of R.A. (A) Mediterranean), *Coventry*, *Calcutta*, together with four destroyers which had arrived from Alexandria the previous day. In the early afternoon of 31st August two reconnaissance aircraft were shot down by Skuas from the *Ark Royal*, the first being chased for 55 miles.

At 2150/31st when in a position 20 miles south of Minorca, two destroyers (*Velox* and *Wishart*) were detached to create a W/T diversion to the north of the Balearics. This was Operation Squawk, which was intended to mislead the enemy into thinking the whole Fleet had steered towards the Gulf of Genoa during the night 31st/1st, and also to cover the *Ark Royal*'s transmission of low power W/T signals used with her aircraft.

Shortly after 2200/31st the Fleet altered course without signal to the south-east, and at 0325/1st September, when 150 miles west of Cagliari, an air striking force of nine Swordfish of 800 and 803 Squadrons from the *Ark Royal* was flown off for Operation Smash, an attack on Elmas aerodrome which took place at 0600/1st, bombs being dropped from 3,000 feet and hits observed on barracks, buildings, and dispersed aircraft. All aircraft returned safely and reported that on their return journey a submarine on the surface was sighted in a position approximately 10 miles ahead of the Fleet. The submarine fired a yellow flare and dived when machine-gunned; two destroyers were detached to locate and attack her with the aid of aircraft A/S. patrol, but beyond sighting a patch of oil the search yielded no result. A total of eleven Italian submarines were at sea in the Western Mediterranean, five of which were on patrol between Sardinia and Bona, and either the *Axum* or the *Alagi* could have been in this position. The striking force also reported seven enemy aircraft in a position 80 miles northward of the Fleet and steering 250°, but no attack developed, the pilots probably not liking the look of our fighter patrols.

At 2200/1st September, when 40 miles north of Keith Rocks, Force B parted company with Force F, which proceeded to rendezvous with the Commander-in-Chief, Mediterranean, south of Malta at 0900/2nd. Force B turned back to the westward in order to carry out a second air attack on Cagliari, Operation Grab, but this proved a failure owing to a combination of fog and mist preventing the flares from showing up the targets. After attacking some searchlights the striking force jettisoned their bombs in the sea, and returned to the *Ark Royal* at 0800/2nd September. Force H returned to Gibraltar at 1100/3rd September.

Two subsidiary movements were planned to take place during Operation Hats. The gunboat *Aphis*, which was to play a prominent part with the Inshore Squadron on the Cyrenaican coast, was to sail from Malta to Alexandria. Owing to prolongation of refit she did not, however, sail until early October. Also, the Polish destroyer *Garland* was to sail from Malta to Gibraltar for the United Kingdom. The *Garland* left Malta on 2nd September with four destroyers of the 13th Flotilla for Gibraltar. The Force was attacked by high level bombers in the afternoon of 4th September when off Algiers, the only damage being sustained by the *Garland* from 'near-misses', which caused leaks in two boilers. She was taken in tow by the *Griffin* for a short time and reached Gibraltar safely on the 5th.

71

Before the fall of France, at the end of June 1940, the Italian naval bombers were mainly concentrated in the north (Appendix F (b) – Part II); but late in July their dispositions were altered southward. In Sardinia, Sicily and Pantellaria their aircraft available for operation against Malta or the Fleet in the Central

Mediterranean totalled some 330 bombers, 55 reconnaissance machines, and 130 fighters. The bombers were mostly S.79's or Cant Z.506, some of the latter being torpedo carriers, and there were 14 dive-bombers, S.85's, at Pantellaria. German dive-bombers had not appeared by August, but reports indicated that they might be on the way, and on 5th September six J.U.87's[1] carried out a dive-bombing attack on Kalafrana aerodrome, Malta. In the Dodecanese there were estimated to be 50 bombers, 10 reconnaissance aircraft and 40 fighters. During August 1940, the enemy carried out numerous air attacks on ships at sea and on Malta, Alexandria, Port Said, Haifa and Tel Aviv. This activity, added to the knowledge of a considerable eastward movement of the Italian Army in Libya, pointed to preparations for an early advance into Egypt. At Haifa, on 6th August, three oil tanks were damaged and 600 tons of crude oil set on fire; at Alexandria, on 15th August, the mooring vessel *Moorstone* was sunk and three mines dropped near Kamaria breakwater by low-flying aircraft; at Port Sudan, on 7th and 8th September, some damage was done to quays and warehouses. In other raids at these places, and in their attacks on the Canal area, negligible damage was done, though one bomb dropped uncomfortably close to 201 Group H.Q.[2] at Alexandria on 22nd August. At Tel Aviv, on 9th September, 100 persons were killed and 150 injured, although there were no military objectives in the vicinity. Malta had a breathing space for the first half of August, and on the 10th the Vice-Admiral, Malta, reported (1223/10/8) the dockyard back to normal conditions, and that light forces could use the Grand Harbour as a temporary base provided care was taken to conceal their movements. On several occasions bombers appeared, but sheered off and kept very high when the Hurricanes went up. The lull did not last long, for on 15th, 20th and 24th August, squadrons of bombers and fighters attacked Hal Far and Kalafrana aerodromes, damaging the main Fleet Air Arm storage depôt and some aircraft on the ground, losing only one of their own aircraft. The dockyard was the target on 7th September when Somerset Wharf was hit, damage was done to buildings in the dockyard, a tug and picket boat sunk and H.M.S/M. *Olympus* damaged in dock. The results obtained by the enemy appear incommensurate with the efforts made, but they were sufficient to cause us some concern and to bring about additional efforts to build up A/A defences; obviously we could not hold the initiative and control the sea routes unless the Fleet could operate from properly protected bases.

72

The rendering safe of Malta as a first step in developing our offensive policy had always been considered by the Commander-in-Chief to be the key to our Mediterranean strategy.[3] (C.-in-C. Med. 2015/22/8/40 – Appendix C. 10.) 'Safety' meant building up supplies as well as increasing defensive powers. Also the maintenance of civilian morale in this bomb-swept island was a vital consideration, and for this purpose the provision of adequate air raid shelters was an early task. The Navy had taken over the development of civil air raid shelter schemes, for which a fundamental requirement was a supply of cement, timber and reinforcing material. The Governor of Malta requested the Consul-General at Alexandria to arrange purchase of these materials and other stores as a matter of immediate urgency.

As regards stores the Vice-Admiral, Malta, reported to the Commander-in-Chief, Mediterranean, that certain army and civil stocks were much below the figure of six months' consumption which he considered a minimum figure. To ensure this minimum he recommended that convoys should be run at least every two months, under which arrangement there would be eight months' reserve immediately after the arrival of a convoy, falling to six months' reserve immediately before the arrival of the next convoy. He also recommended that there should be a common policy for reserve covering the requirements of the Malta Government and the Services, approval for which would mean the possibility of co-ordination and making use of available shipping space to the best advantage.

We now know that the strategic value of Malta was fully appreciated later by Rommel when he took over command of the German forces in Libya.

---

1 From enemy documents, these appear to have been manned by Italian crews.
2 See Appendix F(b), Part II. 201 Group was the Eastern Mediterranean counterpart of Coastal Command. At this time they were billeted in the Italian boat club, Alexandria.
3 See Section 7.

He seems continuously to have urged on the German High Command the importance of capturing the island which he held could have been done in the Summer of 1941. With Malta captured he would be relieved of anxieties as to his vital seaborne supplies and would be free to develop an offensive which aimed at least at the capture of the Suez Canal and envisaged even an advance to the Persian Gulf. It was fortunate that at this juncture the eyes of the German High Command were fixed on Eastern Europe. The North African campaign was looked upon as a side show. In short, the importance of sea power was not understood. It was only when too late, in the Spring of 1942, that plans were made for an operation against the island (Operation Hercules), but this operation, in fact, never matured.

73

While the air menace at Alexandria was less threatening to the civilian population than at Malta, there were occasions when the military and civil authorities experienced some anxiety, for there were large numbers of the Services accommodated in the town. On the whole, the Egyptians deserve a tribute for the way they continued their work in the dockyard and at the loading wharves. The Commander-in-Chief's main concern was with the prevention of restrictions on the Fleet's movements, particularly when mine-laying by low-flying aircraft in the Fleet anchorage and the harbour entrance commenced in August 1940, and when a further threat loomed up in the possibility of attacks on ships by low-flying torpedo-aircraft coming in from seaward over the northern breakwater. During high-bombing attacks by about twelve aircraft on the night of 15th August, two aircraft were observed flying low over the harbour entrance. They passed between the *Gloucester* and *Warspite* and disappeared inland over the oil tanks, dropping three mines or torpedoes between Kamaria breakwater and L.1 to L.4 berths. The positions were buoyed and a skid towed over the area, seven times each way, both red and blue poles, without result. One of the aircraft subsequently forced-landed near Sidi Barrani, 200 miles west of Alexandria, and the crew of five were captured after burning their machine, which was found to be fitted with crutches suitable for carrying two 21-inch torpedoes or mines.

As a result the Commander-in-Chief issued an order to the Fleet that energetic measures must be taken at once to combat this threat to our freedom of movement. The Rear-Admiral, Alexandria, organised special boat watches to report immediately where mines fell, and to take prompt action to clear them. Arrangements were made to fly kites from the outer breakwaters, and all ships ordered to make kites for use at sea or in harbour. An A/T baffle was laid in a position to guard the capital ship anchorage from torpedo-aircraft attack, battle practice targets were secured in tandem and rigged with a mast each end, whilst urgent requests were made to the Admiralty for the provision of small balloons to fly at 1,000 to 2,000 feet from the breakwaters (C.-in-C. Med. 1431/17/8/40).

Ships were instructed to mount their Lewis guns so as to bring the maximum volume of fire on low-flying aircraft approaching over the breakwater. Pans[1] were loaded with a mixture of ball, incendiary A.P., and tracer ammunition.

74

At Haifa the principal threat that concerned the Fleet was damage to the oil tanks and refinery, which was capable of refining 1,000,000 tons of crude oil per annum. In July the Commander-in-Chief informed the Admiralty (1723/17/7 and 1003/25/7) that, if the situation at Haifa continued, it would only be a matter of time before the refinery was put out of action and Haifa would cease to function as a source of supply of fuel to the Fleet. The Vice-Admiral, Second-in-Command, paid a visit in July and pointed out that the work on shipping and at the refinery was already suffering severely owing to the lack of any up-to-date air raid warning system or means of defence. Half the employees and 50 American engineers of I.P.C. had quitted by the end of the month (R.A.(D) Med. 1805/26/7). Fortunately the Italians did not continue their attacks with any persistence, and towards the end of August the output from the refinery had to be reduced, not because of enemy air raids but owing to the tanks being nearly full. The Admiralty had as a

---

1 These were circular trays fitted on top of Lewis guns.

consequence to request that Fleet fuel requirements should be met as far as possible by drawing from Haifa in order to keep the refinery working.

Apart from its importance for fuel, Haifa had been earmarked as the principal mine depôt for the Mediterranean. The policy in regard to the Mediterranean minelaying programme was the subject of discussion between the Admiralty and the Commander-in-Chief (Appendix E.45) towards the end of August 1940. Following this discussion the Admiralty arranged to transfer 400 Mark XVI mine units from the Far East to the Mediterranean by the mine carrier *Berenice*, and to send 1,000 Mark XIV type mine units from the United Kingdom in a mine depôt ship (A.T. 2258/20/8/40). As the Commander-in Chief considered it undesirable to add to the already large stowage of high explosives at Alexandria, and since he did not wish to commence using Haifa before the A/A defences were improved he decided to keep the mine carriers in the Canal area until Haifa was reasonably safe (C.-in-C. Med. 1645/24/8).

75

During the months following the outbreak of war with Italy air activity in Mediterranean waters continued on an increasing scale, calling for correspondingly increased facilities for operational requirements, maintenance and repairs.

In Egypt the Fleet Air Arm shore bases were at Dekheila, Alexandria (H.M.S. *Grebe*). Four squadrons were stationed here. In August 1940 construction work for a land aerodrome to take six disembarked squadrons began at Lake Mariut, Alexandria. In addition to these two sites the A.O.C., Middle East, undertook all negotiations and construction work for a separate F.A.A. reserve storage and repair station at the R.A.F. aerodrome at Fayid in the Canal area.

At Malta our air strength was badly in need of assistance. On 1st August the A.O.C., Mediterranean, whose headquarters were at Malta, represented to the Air Ministry the urgent necessity for the provision of a striking force and general reconnaissance force based on the Island after urgent fighter requirements had been met. At that time sea reconnaissance from Malta was undertaken by Sunderlands from 201 Group, Alexandria, which for reasons of maintenance could only operate from Malta for brief periods. This lack of general reconnaissance force working from the Island prevented the A.O.C., Mediterranean, from meeting urgent calls from Flag Officers operating in the Central Mediterranean (A.O.C. Med. 1841/1/8). He considered that a complete squadron, that is 15 aircraft, of Beauforts or Hudsons, would produce results out of all proportion to the numbers involved. Offensive operations by the F.A.A. Swordfish, 830 Squadron, were limited to targets in Sicily or attacks on enemy ships bound for Libya. What was wanted was the power to strike bigger and better blows. The need for more aircraft of all types was indeed apparent, not only in Malta but with the Fleet and the Army in Egypt. He also stated that two flights of Gladiators, R.A.F. No. 80 Squadron at Amriya in the Alexandria area, which had been used for the defence of Alexandria harbour, had to be sent to the Western Desert to help meet increasing enemy air activity. This was awkward for the Fleet in view of it being an important docking period. The Commander-in-Chief, Mediterranean, had pointed out to the A.O.C., Middle East (G.H.Q. Cairo) that Fleet Air Arm reinforcements could not be expected before the arrival of the *Illustrious* in early September. To meet this gap in fighter air defence over the Fleet during the docking period the A.O.C., Middle East, arranged a standing patrol of two Blenheims over Alexandria harbour.

76

Of air operations during these months the attack on Tobruk by 813 Squadron on 5th July has already been described (S.52). Another Fleet Air Arm attack on that place was launched on 20th July. Six aircraft of 824 Squadron, which had taken off from the *Eagle* at sea on the 19th and had proceeded to Sidi Barrani, carried out a torpedo attack at 0240/20th by moonlight. Driving through heavy, horizontal barrage fire, they succeeded in sinking two destroyers, the *Nembo* and *Ostro*, and in setting an oiler on fire. All six machines returned safely to Sidi Barrani, though three were damaged.

On 6th August, an R.A.F. Flying Boat, 9020, observed some enemy ships between Derna and Tobruk, and before returning at Alexandria attacked them with bombs. The relief on patrol, 9025, was met by Italian fighters and shot down and as a result of this incident the Commander-in-Chief requested the C.O. of 201 Group to impress on flying boat captains the necessity for avoidance of jeopardizing their main duty of reconnaissance and shadowing by attacking surface ships, when the latter might be successfully attacked by forces detailed for the purpose.

In order to be within striking distance of shipping located off the Libyan coast, arrangements were made to maintain three Swordfish of 824 Squadron, with torpedoes, at Maaten Bagush, 200 miles from Tobruk and 120 from Dekheila, where they were placed under the operational control of the C.O. 202 Group, R.A.F. This arrangement soon paid a dividend, for on 22nd August an early morning reconnaissance of Bomba, 250 miles west of Maaten Bagush, had revealed one destroyer, two submarines, a depôt ship and a tanker in the Bay. The C.O. 202 Group despatched the three Swordfish to Sidi Barrani, an advanced landing ground 150 miles from Bomba, where they re-fuelled and took off at 1038/22 August. The flight was commanded by Captain O. Patch, R.M., the other two pilots being Lieut. (A) W. G. Wellman, R.N., and Lieut. (A) N. A. F. Cheeseman, R.N. During the approach a submarine was seen on the surface charging batteries; Captain Patch fired his torpedo at 300 yards and the submarine *Iride* blew up. Lieut. Cheeseman fired at a second submarine which was alongside a destroyer secured to the depôt ship (Plan 15), and Lieut. Wellman fired at the depôt ship herself. Both torpedoes hit and caused severe explosions as well as starting a fire in the destroyer. Photographic reconnaissance confirmed the sinking of all four vessels, and an Italian radio report admitted 'the loss of four warships by an overwhelming force of torpedo bombers and M.T.B's.' It seems possible, however, that the second submarine and the destroyer were salved later, since in the Italian list of losses, only the submarine *Iride* and auxiliary minelayer *Monte Gargano* are shown as sunk in this attack (Plan 15).

All three machines returned safely to Sidi Barrani by 1500/22nd August, having flown a total of 366 miles. After landing, Lieut. Wellman's machine was found unserviceable, having been hit by a bullet in the extension of the main spar. This was surprisingly little damage in view of the fact that all three machines, when four miles from their targets, came down to 30 feet above the sea and had to fly through a barrage of A/A fire from guns, pom-poms, and multiple machine guns.

The Commander-in-Chief summed up this operation[1] as 'brilliantly conceived and most gallantly executed.' He added that 'the dash, initiative and co-operation displayed by the sub-flight concerned were typical of the spirit which animated the Fleet Air Arm squadrons of H.M.S. *Eagle* under the inspiring leadership of her Commanding Officer.'

Another active day for both the Fleet Air Arm and Royal Air Force fighters was 17th August, during the bombardment of Bardia by part of the Mediterranean Fleet (S.80). R.A.F. fighters from 202 Group brought down 10 enemy bombers and broke up their attacks on the Fleet. The ships' own aircraft, F.A.A. 700 Squadron, carried out spotting duties, and were protected from enemy fighters by F.A.A. Gladiators operating under orders of the C.O. 202 Group. The Gladiators brought down one enemy bomber for certain and possibly a second. Neither the R.A.F. nor the F.A.A. suffered any losses.

On 30th August all available F.A.A. aircraft were re-embarked in the *Eagle* for Operation Hats (S.69).

Of air operations carried out from Malta one of interest was on 12th August when 830 Squadron, which had carried out frequent reconnaissance of Sicilian ports, reported that 23 merchant ships were assembled in Augusta.

A striking force of Swordfish with torpedoes and bombs attacked late that night. Air reconnaissance on 14th August showed only nine merchant ships present, with one large vessel close inshore and very low in the water. Two of our machines were lost in the attack and a third forced-landed off Malta on return.

---

[1] A.0947/40, A.0755/41. We now know that the *Iride* and *Gargano* were sent to Bomba for the purpose of carrying out an underwater assault craft attack on Alexandria. The *Iride* had on board three 'chariots'. Captain Patch, therefore, figuratively killed several birds with one stone.

77

As reconnaissance reports of Italian and North African ports continually showed the existence of the highly important Italy-Libyan merchant vessel traffic, the Commander-in-Chief from 14th August stationed submarines specially to intercept it; *Pandora* off Benghazi, *Rorqual* midway between Augusta and Benghazi and four across the Taranto-Benghazi route; *Perseus* in 36° N. 17° E. with *Rainbow*, *Regent* and *Parthian* 070° from *Perseus*, 30 miles apart. The *Rorqual* on 17th August laid mines off Tolmeita Lt., Cyrenaica. On 21st August, off Ras-el-Hillal, she torpedoed, but did not sink, an Italian merchant vessel of 5,000 tons, fully loaded, when in company with another ship and a destroyer; unfortunately she missed the second ship. On 14th August, the Italians reported the loss of their transport the *Leopardi*, 4,000 tons, between Derna and Benghazi, and as no British submarine was in the vicinity her loss was considered to be due to mines previously laid by the *Rorqual* on 21st July.

On 16th August the *Osiris* sank by gunfire the *Morea*, 2,000 tons, 40 miles north of Brindisi, and then had to return to Malta with engine defects, her place on patrol being taken by the *Perseus*. On her next patrol in the Adriatic, on 22nd September, the *Osiris* torpedoed and sank the Italian destroyer *Palestro*, and on that day also the *Truant*[1] sank the S.S. *Providenza*, 8,400 tons, off Naples.

The *Parthian* attacked a squadron of cruisers and destroyers on 31st August during Operation Hats (S.69), before the commencement of which the submarine patrol line had been moved 60 miles 340° from that given above. Up to the end of August 1940 we had lost five submarines, *Grampus*, *Odin*, *Orpheus*, *Phoenix* and *Oswald*, while the Italians had lost ten, of which four were outside the Mediterranean, including one captured by the trawler *Moonstone* off Aden, the *Galilei*. The fact that all five of our submarine casualties had been employed on inshore patrols was an additional reason for adopting the movable patrol line.

Enemy submarines caused us very little trouble during August. Eight to ten were on patrol in the Eastern Mediterranean for the period 20th July to mid-August, and the only evidence offered of their activity was on 31st July when the Greek ship *Loula*, 1,500 tons, on passage from Istanbul to Port Said, was sunk by gunfire from two submarines, probably the *Mameli* and *Speri*, 70 miles S.W. of Crete. Ten survivors reached El Dhaba, 60 miles west of Alexandria, four days later and reported eight of the crew missing. A new minefield was discovered on 12th August 14 miles N.W. of Alexandria. This in all probability had been laid by the same two submarines, which were both fitted for minelaying. Nineteen mines were swept by the 15th August and the area considered clear.

78

From 1200/20th August the Mediterranean Light Forces were reorganised, the Vice-Admiral, Light Forces, and Second-in-Command, Mediterranean (V.A.L.F.), Vice-Admiral J. C. Tovey, retaining direct command of the Seventh Cruiser Squadron (*Orion*, *Sydney*) and the destroyer flotillas; the Rear-Admiral, Third Cruiser Squadron, Rear-Admiral E. de F. Renouf, having under him the *Kent*, *Gloucester* and *Liverpool*. The title of Vice-Admiral (D) lapsed.

The Light Forces carried out two sweeps into the Aegean, between 20th–23rd August and 24th–27th August, with the dual purpose of destroying any enemy forces encountered and affording protection to ships passing from Piraeus or Chanak to Egyptian ports. Thorough searches were made and our merchant ships passed safely through, but the only enemy vessel sighted was a submarine reported by the *Orion* late in the evening of the 22nd, when south of Gavdo Island. No attack developed on the cruisers and the submarine escaped attack, as the destroyers had by that time been detached to escort two merchant ships to Alexandria. The *Kent* was attacked at 0800/27th by a single torpedo aircraft when 60 miles N.E. of Bardia; two torpedoes were dropped from 2,000 yards on the beam from a height of 200 feet, but no tracks were observed (C.-in-C. Med. 2031/27/8/40).

---

1 Four submarines of the 'T' class, *Tetrarch*, *Triad*, *Triton*, *Truant* arrived in the Mediterranean from the United Kingdom mid-September and began a patrol in the Tyrrhenian Sea.

CHAPTER 6

BRITISH COMMAND OF THE SEA ESTABLISHED

(OCTOBER 1940)

79

WE MUST now turn to the military situation in North Africa. The Commander-in-Chief, Middle East, had in August 1940 insufficient forces to undertake an offensive campaign from Egypt into Libya; in fact, on both the western and southern frontiers of Egypt he had to remain on the defensive until December, 1940 (Appendix C. 9 (d)). On the southern frontier the Italians had crossed from Abyssinia into the Sudan early in July 1940, but they occupied only one place of importance, Kassala, 10 miles into the Sudan. Here they halted and, except for a raid up the Blue Nile in October 1940, remained until January 1941, when they were driven out. The Commander-in-Chief, Middle East, had therefore to envisage the possibility of an attack on Egypt from both flanks; for, in the south early in August the enemy had captured British Somaliland, thus releasing a number of troops for operations elsewhere, possibly the Sudan, whilst in the west it was evident that Marshal Graziani intended to invade Egypt. Whether this latter attack would be launched conjointly with an attack from the Sudan, thus forming the proverbial pincer movement so as to conquer the whole of Egypt, or would be merely a limited advance, was a question which for the moment mattered less than how to meet the invasion with restricted resources. With regard to the invasion of Egypt from Libya, the naval task of the Commander-in-Chief, Mediterranean, was to assist the Army by harassing the enemy's communications and bombarding military formations, dumps of ammunition, stores and other military targets within range from seaward.

80

The most important coastal bombardment was on 17th August at Bardia, Operation MB.2. The principal previous bombardment of Bardia had been carried out on 21st June (S.39) by three 6-inch cruisers, four destroyers and the French battleship *Lorraine*, but this time three battleships and an 8-inch cruiser were employed. Italian troops were reported to be assembling at Fort Capuzzo, 11 miles south of Bardia, just on the Egypt–Libya frontier, and numerous dumps of stores and ammunition were in and around Bardia itself. The Commander-in-Chief himself took command and targets were allocated as follows:–

Force	Ship	Guns	Target
Force A	*Warspite* (C.-in-C.)	15-inch 6-inch	Capuzzo concentration area. Any visible targets suitable for direct fire near Marsa el Ramla.[1]
	Kent	8-inch	The gun position area west and north-west of Marsa el Ramla.[1]
Force B	*Malaya* (R.A. 1st B.S.)	15-inch 6-inch	Bardia ammunition dump area. Barracks and W/T station.
	Ramillies	15-inch 6-inch	Camp garage, workshops. Same as *Malaya*.

---

1 A fort on the coast six miles south of Bardia.

A full description and plans of the operation are given in Naval Staff History, Battle Summary No. 6 (B.R. 1736(4)); here it will be sufficient to say that the shoot was carried out according to plan. Very little opposition was met, only a few rounds of small calibre, about 4-inch, falling no closer than 1,000 yards from the ships. The part played by the R.A.F. and F.A.A. has already been described (S.75). Air photographs showed Capuzzo and the southern defences well hit, but the town itself escaped serious damage, being masked by the cliffs. Ground mist hid the targets from the spotting aircraft for the first few salvoes, and later low clouds hindered spotting. Care had been taken to choose zero hour sufficiently soon after first light for navigational 'fixing' and the usual morning mist to be clear, whilst not being late enough to allow enemy fighters time to arrive and interfere with our spotting aircraft.

On this particular morning zero time (0700) proved to be a few minutes too early for the ground mist to have cleared. In his report (M.01146/41) the Commander-in-Chief remarked that 'the Italians have shown themselves skilful in dispersing mechanical transport and stores over wide areas in the Desert; and the targets offered do not justify a repetition of this type of operation with heavy ships so long as warfare in the Western Desert remains static.'

Both Bardia and Bomba were bombarded on the night of 23rd/24th August. At Bardia the gunboat *Ladybird*, just arrived from China, penetrated into the harbour and engaged shore targets at point blank range, Operation MB.1. At Bomba, 36 hours after the F.A.A. attack on shipping (S.75), Captain (D) 10 with the *Stuart*, *Juno*, *Ilex* and *Diamond* bombarded the seaplane base. The *Waterhen*, which had been detached by Capt. (D) 10 to cover the *Ladybird*'s withdrawal, also joined in the bombardment of shore targets. H.M.A.S. *Sydney* acted in support of these forces, and all ships returned to Alexandria by 25th August without any air attacks being launched on them. Presumably the Italian losses of bombers on 17th August acted as a deterrent when our fighters were in the vicinity (M.020979/40).

81

In anticipation of the Italian advance into Egypt the Commander-in-Chief, Middle East, had withdrawn the bulk of his forces from the frontier, leaving only a comparatively light screen to absorb the first weight of the advance before retiring to rejoin the main body. From 11th–14th September the R.A.F. made successful bombing attacks on enemy M.T. concentrations and camps, at Sidi Omar and Sollum, starting large fires and causing considerable damage. On 13th September the long expected Italian invasion of Egypt began when the Italian forces moved through the wire to the Sollum area. Two columns of M.T. and tanks moved along the coastal track on 14th September, penetrating 15 to 20 miles east of Sollum. The British covering force engaged the enemy closely, destroying about 150 vehicles, some of them filled with troops, with a loss to us of 13 vehicles and about 40 casualties; finally rejoining the main forces on 17th September in positions approximately due south of a point 15 miles east of Sidi Barrani, which place the enemy occupied on that date. Here they halted, and began to construct several fortified camps. Their advance did not approach in magnitude the famous Italo-German attack under Marshal Rommel in May–July 1942, when El Alamein was reached and the fate of Alexandria, if not the whole Delta, hung in the balance for some weeks. Small though it was, however, it brought disadvantages to the Fleet and the R.A.F., for the loss of Sidi Barrani deprived us of an advanced landing ground, and thereby lessened the fighter protection which could be given to bombarding ships and convoys along the coast; furthermore it brought enemy bombers within 210 miles of Alexandria and 70 miles of Mersa Matruh. Until we re-took Cyrenaica in December 1940, our westernmost landing ground was at Maaten Bagush, 130 miles from the Egypt-Libyan frontier (Plan 16).

The military reasons for Marshal Graziani's prolonged halt are beyond the scope of a naval chronicle; it is sufficient to note that both on the western and southern fronts the Italians remained inactive for three months. In December 1940 General Wavell advanced into Libya, occupying the whole of Cyrenaica in an eight-weeks campaign. In the south we took Kassala in January 1941, and regained British Somaliland in March 1941.

The Commander-in-Chief, Mediterranean, had prepared plans for withdrawal of stores and ammunition from Alexandria (Message 1101/5/9/40 to Admiralty), but it was soon realised that at this time the invasion threat was insufficient to require any such action.

82

The enemy's move on land was the occasion for energetic action on the part of the R.A.F., F.A.A. and the Fleet in support of the Army. The harbour, sea routes, and the coastal road in the north of Cyrenaica were incessantly bombed and bombarded. Benghazi, the principal port of Cyrenaica, received much attention from our aircraft. On 15th September the Vice Admiral, Light Forces, sailed from Alexandria with the *Illustrious*, *Valiant* and seven destroyers, being joined by the Third Cruiser squadron on the 16th when west of Crete. They proceeded to a point 100 miles north of Benghazi, reaching their destination at 2100, 16th September. Aircraft from the *Illustrious* were flown off, and during moonlight laid six magnetic mines within three cables of the harbour entrance, and dive-bombed two groups of ships inside the harbour. Two destroyers were sunk, the *Aquilone* from a mine, and the *Borea* from bombs, and two other ships were damaged. All our aircraft returned safely. (M.02870/41.)

83

After nightfall on the 17th the V.A.L.F. detached C.S.3 with the *Kent* and two destroyers to bombard Bardia. When some 40 miles from her bombardment position *Kent* was attacked in bright moonlight at 2355/17th by two torpedo aircraft as well as bombers. Two torpedoes were dropped from a height of 150 to 200 feet at a range of 500 yards on the starboard quarter, down moon. One torpedo hit under Y turret, causing extensive damage, starting oil fires, and killing two officers and 30 ratings. She was taken in tow by the *Nubian*, and with three shafts working was able to make 11 knots, reaching Alexandria a.m. 19th September. Special air patrols were arranged to cover her voyage of 250 miles in a damaged condition, and the R.A.F. laid on offensive attacks against enemy aerodromes at Derna, El Tmimi, Tobruk west, and Gazala, causing damage to enemy aircraft and M.T.

After temporary repairs in Alexandria the *Kent* returned in November 1940 to the United Kingdom for permanent repairs. Her departure left only one 8-inch cruiser with the Fleet – H.M.S. *York* – which arrived at Alexandria on 27th September after escorting A.P. one (M.T. transports) round the Cape to Aden, and bringing on A.P.2 from Aden to Suez (S.68). A second eight-inch cruiser, H.M.S. *Berwick*, was sent from the United Kingdom to the Mediterranean early in November but she was transferred in mid-December to the Atlantic trade routes for operations against enemy raiders.

84

R.A.F. Wellingtons carried out heavy bombing attacks on Benghazi on 19th and 20th September, damaging and setting on fire transports and warehouses. On 23rd and 25th September they raided Tobruk harbour and the foreshore. In the latter raid, by 26 Blenheims, hits were obtained on barracks and wharves, and several large fires started. A number of M.T. vehicles were also destroyed. Bardia, Sidi Barrani and Sollum all received a full share of bombing and bombardment. The gunboat *Ladybird* bombarded the escarpment road at Sollum on the night of 17th/18th September, having been unsuccessfully attacked by two torpedo aircraft when 40 miles west of Mersa Matruh. On her return voyage to Alexandria, when 10 miles east of Sollum, she passed unscathed through a small controlled minefield of what appeared to be anti-boat mines, of which about 40 were blown up. The destroyers *Juno* and *Janus*, which were supporting the *Ladybird*, bombarded the town of Sidi Barrani for 25 minutes, and then engaged local targets between Sidi Barrani and Buq Buq, halfway between Barrani and Sollum, before returning to Alexandria. On the early morning of 22nd September four destroyers, *Jervis*, Capt. D.14, *Juno*, *Janus* and *Mohawk*, attacked the aerodrome and motor transport concentrations at Sidi Barrani. The targets were selected by the G.O.C. Western Desert Force, and a military liaison officer embarked. Two runs were made, and later the M.T. concentrations were reported dispersed to the south, and the camp near the airfield broken up. During the night of 23rd September the *Ladybird* bombarded targets in the Sidi Barrani area, and on the way back to Alexandria tried to land a party on Ishaila Island, 33 miles west of Mersa Matruh, with the object of setting up an R.A.F. air lookout post. Unfortunately weather conditions prevented landing. The reason for this post was that enemy aircraft were becoming uncomfortably active – 35 machines raided Matruh on 22nd September – and we did not possess sufficient fighters to maintain continuous patrols.

A concentration of M.T. west of Sidi Barrani was successfully bombarded early a.m. 25th September by the four destroyers *Hyperion*, *Hereward*, *Juno*, *Mohawk*, causing a large fire and a number of explosions. Thereafter for a few weeks the call on the Fleet for large scale coastal bombardments ceased (M.024434/40). At dusk on 28th September two Swordfish of 813 Squadron of the Fleet Air Arm attacked an enemy convoy in the Gulf of Bomba and registered two direct hits on one merchant ship, which did not sink. (A.0755/41.)

These many and varied operations give some idea of the continuous fleet activity in operations designed to harass the enemy ashore and to interfere with his supplies, whilst the Army of the Middle East on the other hand was receiving reinforcements and supplies and building up its strength. Coastal operations against Italian positions ashore were mainly undertaken by the *Ladybird* and *Aphis* in co-operation with the R.A.F. These two gunboats formed the nucleus of Force W, which later on was to expand and become the Inshore Squadron, following the Army along the coast to Benghazi during operations extending from December 1940 to February 1941.

85

Meanwhile, early in September, immediately after completion of Operation Hats (S.68), the bulk of Force H was detached from the Mediterranean to Freetown to operate temporarily under the orders of the Commander-in-Chief, South Atlantic, leaving only the *Renown* and a few destroyers at Gibraltar. Neither Admiral Sir Dudley North, the Flag Officer commanding the North Atlantic, nor Vice-Admiral Sir James Somerville commanding Force H, were at this stage informed of the nature of these operations, which were designed to establish the Free French under General de Gaulle in French West Africa by capturing Dakar from the Vichy French.

The expedition left the United Kingdom at the end of August under the command of Vice-Admiral John D. Cunningham, flying his flag in H.M.S. *Devonshire* with Major-General M. N. S. Irwin as Joint Military Commander. General de Gaulle's French force was carried separately in French transports proceeding in convoy, some hours behind the main assault, ready to disembark at Dakar as soon as British troops had secured military control of the city and local resistance had been overcome. Briefly, British forces were to take Dakar and General de Gaulle's troops were to occupy it.

It was an Atlantic rather than a Mediterranean affair, and details of the operation, known as Operation Menace, will be found in Naval Staff History Battle Summary No. 20, C.B.3081 (13). Connected with the operation, however was the passage of certain Vichy French warships from Toulon through the Strait of Gibraltar. These ships subsequently reached Dakar, and on 16th September, 1940, the War Cabinet decided that their presence there rendered the execution of the Dakar operation impracticable. It was only after strong pressure from the Commanders of the expedition and from General de Gaulle that the War Cabinet eventually agreed that it should not be cancelled.

In the chapter of his 'History of the Second World War' which deals with Dakar, Mr. Winston Churchill speaks of 'the misfortune of the French warships having slipped through the Straits.' As the use of this phrase may be held to imply that there was a naval failure in allowing the ships to proceed through the Strait of Gibraltar, it is necessary to set out the chronicle of events in some detail.[1]

The general instructions for the guidance of Commanders-in-Chief and Flag Officers Commanding Home and Abroad with regard to French warships were contained in an Admiralty message of 12th July, 1940 (see Appendix C.8). This message stated that H.M. Government had decided to take no further action in regard to French ships in French Colonial or North African ports, and went on to say 'We shall of course however reserve the right to take action in regard to French warships proceeding to enemy controlled ports.' Apart from this instruction Admiral North early in September had certain other items of intelligence at his disposal on which to base his appreciation. On 5th September, the British Naval Attaché, Madrid, reported to the Admiralty (repeated to Gibraltar) on the general position in France

---

[1] Winston Churchill's 'The Second World War', Volume II, chapter 24, page 428, on which the text of the signal sent on September 16th also appears.

(1842/5/9/40 received in the Admiralty 0304/6/9/40). The message included a statement from the French Naval Attaché at Madrid that French ships at Toulon remained in a condition to fight; that the attitude of officers and men was much less hostile to us; and that the general French feeling was hope in us and intentions to join in again when possible. Also on the 5th, the Admiralty (D.N.I.) sent out an intelligence report (T.O.O.1928/5/9/40) of moderate reliability to various authorities, including Admiral North and Admiral Somerville. This stated that a source in Lisbon predicted that Germany would occupy the whole of France and particularly Marseilles on the pretext that Pétain was losing control. 'Axis agents,' said the report 'had already been sent to Tunis and Algeria, and possibly Morocco, to incite populations against de Gaulle and present French Government as having collapsed.'

On 9th September, in a message from His Majesty's Consul General at Tangier despatched at 6.50 p.m. and repeated to the Foreign Office, Admiral North was informed that a French squadron in the Mediterranean might try to pass the Strait of Gibraltar within the next 72 hours. Later this was confirmed by a message from the Naval Attaché Madrid (T.O.O.1809/10) which read as follows:

> 'French Admiralty to me begins: "Please advise naval authorities Gibraltar departure from Toulon September 9 three cruisers type *Georges Leygues*, and three French cruisers *Le Fantasquc* class which will pass the Straits a.m. September 11." Ends.
> Destination not known.'

This later message was received by Admiral North at 0008 on 11th and by Admiral Somerville at 0800 on 11th. The message had been repeated by the Naval Attaché, Madrid, to the Admiralty.

Not many hours elapsed between the receipt of the message from the French Admiralty to Admiral North and a signal from the *Hotspur* which, with the *Griffin* and *Encounter*, was hunting a submarine to the eastward of Gibraltar, reporting the sighting at 0445/11 of six ships steering west at high speed and that she was shadowing them. This was reported to the Admiralty by Admiral North in a signal despatched at 0617/11 and received at 0740/11 which read as follows:

> 'H.M.S. *Hotspur* sighted lights of six ships probably warships steering west at high speed 36° 03' N., 004° 14' W. I have directed *Hotspur* to take no action.'

He followed this signal with another one to the Admiralty at 0711:

> 'Intend to keep in touch with this force by air and will report probable destination.'

The force was in fact a French squadron comprising the *Georges Leygues*, *Gloire*, *Montcalm*, *Le Matin*, *Le Fantasque* and *L'Audacieux*.

Admiral Somerville received *Hotspur*'s sighting signal at 0510/11 and noted that it confirmed the intimation given in the Consul-General's, Tangier, message of 9th September. (As stated above, Admiral Somerville did not receive the message from the French Admiralty until 0800/11th.) He ordered the *Renown* to be at one hour's notice for full speed, together with the destroyer *Vidette*.

The French squadron passed through the Strait at 0837 on the 11th, having signalled their names. This information reached the Admiralty at 1043.

No further action was taken during the forenoon of the 11th, and the position at noon was that the French ships were some 70 miles S.S.W. of Gibraltar, steering 213° at 20 knots, under observation by R.A.F. reconnaissance aircraft of 200 Group from Gibraltar, the Admiralty and Air Ministry being kept informed.

Admiral North in his report stated that in early September the predominant impression in his mind was that Government policy was to avoid any incidents which might restore the tension between the French and ourselves (M.023509/40). His appreciation, on receiving information about the possible passage of the French ships which was also based on previous intelligence as to the improvement of our relations with the French navy, was that these French ships were 'taking advantage of an opportunity to leave Toulon for Casablanca in order to escape from the German and Italian control liable to occur at the former port' (M.023509/40). He consulted with Vice-Admiral Somerville, who agreed that 'it was evident the Admiralty wished no action taken in connection with the passage of the ships, notice of which must quite obviously have been received by them.' Admiral Somerville in his report says, 'It seemed to me most improbable that the force would proceed to a Bay port and that Casablanca was the probable destination. So far as I am aware, it was not the policy of H.M. Government to interfere with the movements of French warships to French controlled ports.'

Turning now to the Admiralty side of the story the message from the Consul-General, Tangier, referred to above, although received in the Foreign Office at 7.50 a.m. on the 10th, was not deciphered and ready for distribution until the 14th, the delay being due to the accumulation of work in the cipher department of the Foreign Office and the telegram bearing no special priority mark having to take its turn.

The message from the Naval Attaché, Madrid, containing the information on the same subject from the French Admiralty, was received in the Admiralty at 11.50 p.m. on 10th September. It was deciphered at once and sent to the Duty Captain, who passed it to the Director of Operations (Foreign), reaching him about 0030 on the 11th.

The latter took no immediate action on it and the signal was placed with others for distribution at 0800 on the 11th. Actually the earliest news the First Sea Lord had of the passage of the French warships was F.O.C.N.A's signal 0617 of 11th September which passed the *Hotspur*'s sighting report, and stated that *Hotspur* had been instructed to take no action. This signal, although received in the Admiralty at 0740, did not in fact reach the First Sea Lord until the middle of the morning while he was at a Chiefs of Staff meeting. He at once telephoned the Admiralty to order the *Renown* and destroyers to raise steam. At the War Cabinet meeting at 1230 instructions to be sent to Gibraltar were decided upon, and these were embodied in two Admiralty signals despatched respectively at 1347 and 1429. The former directed Force H to proceed to sea and endeavour to obtain contact with the French force, the latter read as follows:

> If French force is proceeding to southwards inform them there is no objection to their going to Casablanca, but they cannot be permitted to go to Dakar which is under German influence. If force appears to be proceeding to Bay ports inform them this cannot be permitted as these ports are in German hands. Minimum force to be used to enforce compliance.

Admiral Somerville, at 4.30 p.m., proceeded to sea in the *Renown* accompanied by the destroyers *Griffin*, *Velox* and *Vidette*. *Hotspur*, *Wishart*, and *Encounter*, which had been recalled to Gibraltar to fuel, joined Admiral Somerville's force later. Meanwhile, at 4 p.m., aircraft which had been shadowing the French squadron reported that it had entered Casablanca.

Admiral Somerville, in accordance with Admiralty instructions, established a patrol to intercept the French cruisers if they sailed southward from Casablanca. The French ships, however, eventually reached Dakar, an air reconnaissance definitely establishing the presence of the heavy units at that port on 15th September and giving confirmation to a previous Vichy report of the arrival of the ships.

On 8th October 1940, the Prime Minister, speaking in the House of Commons on the War situation, said that 'the whole situation at Dakar was transformed in a most unfavourable manner by the arrival there of three French cruisers and three destroyers which carried with them a number of Vichy partisans, evidently of a most bitter type ...'[1] The policy which His Majesty's Government has been pursuing towards the Vichy French warships was not to interfere with them unless they appeared to be proceeding to enemy controlled ports ... By a series of accidents, and some errors, which have been made the subject of disciplinary action or are now subject to formal inquiry, neither the First Sea Lord nor the Cabinet was informed of the approach of these ships to the Strait of Gibraltar until it was too late to stop them passing through.'

Before this, Admiral North on 2nd October had been directed to report to the Admiralty why no action was taken to order the *Renown* to sea on receipt of the signal from the French Naval Attaché, Madrid, 1809/10 or *Hotspur*'s sighting signal 'in case these ships proceeded northward.' In his reply Admiral North stated that his Intelligence did not lead him to suppose that these ships could be going to a northern port, and he assumed that if the Admiralty thought they were going north he would have been instructed to

---

1 This statement is not confirmed by French records.

act as mentioned in clause (c) of Admiralty message 0241/12/7/40 (App. C.8), under which the British Government reserved the right to take action in regard to French warships proceeding to enemy controlled ports. As it was, in the absence of definite instructions, he considered that the avoidance of incidents was of paramount importance. His Intelligence also led him to believe that the attitude of the French Navy was becoming less hostile.

On receiving Naval Attaché's, Madrid, 1809 of 10th September it appeared to him that some of the naval forces in Toulon intended to break away to French colonial ports. He did not think it desirable on this occasion to order the *Renown* to sea, and as the Naval Attaché's signal had been passed to the Admiralty, there had been time for the Admiralty, if action was required, to give instructions.

Admiral Somerville also reported to the Admiralty, having heard from Admiral North that a report from the latter had been called for. He said that rightly or wrongly both he and Admiral North were of the opinion that in view of what appeared to be the ample warning Their Lordships had received of the intended movement of the French ships it was not desired to interfere with this movement or to provoke any incident.

The Admiralty view was that, since N.A. Madrid had stated that the destination of the French force was not known, it was Admiral North's duty to have placed himself in a position where the force could have been intercepted, either on receipt of instructions from the Admiralty or without such instructions, if the situation developed in such a manner as to need it. This could have been done by ordering the *Renown* to sea at an appropriate moment following receipt at 0008/11th September of Naval Attaché's, Madrid, message.

The Director of Operations Division (Foreign) at the Admiralty was relieved on 20th September, and incurred Their Lordships' displeasure for failing to ensure that the signal from the Naval Attaché, Madrid, was brought to the notice of those responsible for taking any action. Admiral North was relieved of his command on 31st December, 1940. Looking back on these events we now know from German sources that 'on 29th August, 1940, information reached the French that Chad Colony had declared allegiance to General de Gaulle. Realising that the risings might spread to the neighbouring Colonies, the French Armistice Commission, on 30th August requested permission to send three cruisers from Toulon to the West African coast in order to promote respect for the French authority. The German and Italian Armistice Commissions at first turned down the French request.

'On 1st September 1940, however, after the Italian High Command had studied the situation, the French were granted permission to send three cruisers to the West African coast. A guarantee had to be given that the ships would resist any British attack. In the event of a deterioration of the situation in West Africa, the Italian High Command promised to consider the possibility of releasing more of the warships in Toulon.

'On 8th September 1940, the French informed the Italians and Germans that the cruisers *Georges Leygues*, *Montcalm* and *Gloire*, accompanied by three destroyers, would leave Toulon for the West African coast at 1600 on 9th September.

'At 0830 on 11th September 1940, the French warships passed unmolested through the Strait of Gibraltar.' (Source PG/33636-7 Waffenstill-stands commission.)

The story of the rest of our naval activities in the Western Mediterranean during the next few weeks is soon told. From early September until nearly the end of October 1940, units of Force H, including the *Barham* and *Australia*, were operating between Dakar, Casablanca, the Strait of Gibraltar and the Azores, which last place was reported to be under threat of capture by the Germans. (M.020777/40, M.019661/40.)

On 24th and 25th September, by way of reprisal for our assistance to General de Gaulle in West Africa, particularly at Dakar, French aircraft carried out heavy raids on Gibraltar; on the 24th, 40 machines dropping 150 bombs, and on the 25th over 100 machines dropping some 300 bombs. The A/S trawler *Stella Sirius* was sunk and damage to buildings was considerable, but there were very few casualties and only slight damage to dockyard equipment. On 27th September, Radio Lyons stated that the French Admiralty had announced that as the English Squadron had ceased to attack Dakar reprisals on Gibraltar had been suspended. The A/A defence of Gibraltar at that time was dependent on gunfire alone, for fighter aircraft were hard to find during and just after the Battle of Britain. The denial to us of the harbour and dockyard would have been an awkward development, so that the cessation of this threat was welcomed with no small amount of relief.

During this period a few destroyers from Force H kept up A/S duties east of Gibraltar and accounted for two Italian submarines on 18th and 20th October. The *Durbo* was located by a flying-boat of 202 Squadron (R.A.F.) when 65 miles east of Ceuta and sunk by the *Firedrake* and *Wrestler*, which rescued five officers and 43 men and seized her confidential papers before she sank. Information from these papers enabled a hunting force of six destroyers to locate the *Lafole* on 20th October in a position 10 miles S.S.E. of Alboran Island, where the *Gallant*, *Hotspur* and *Griffin* attacked with depth charges and finally sank her by ramming, afterwards rescuing one officer and nine ratings. (M.021645/40.)

At the end of October 1940, F.O.C.N.A. and the S.O. Force H were faced with the possibility of a new task by the decision of H.M. Government that French escorted convoys were no longer to be immune from Contraband Control in the Strait of Gibraltar. An Admiralty message (2327/19/10) ordered that convoyed French ships were to be taken into Gibraltar, the escorts being allowed to proceed. Force was to be employed if necessary. In a further message six days later, however (I835/25/10), the Admiralty stated that the interception of French convoys, Operation Ration, was to be postponed. The purport of the original Admiralty message was not put into effect until early December, 1940. (M.024166/40.)

On 30th October, two Italian under-water craft attempted to attack shipping at Gibraltar, one through the northern entrance to the Admiralty harbour, and the other in the commercial anchorage. Both attacks failed; the first apparently through hitting the breakwater, where parts of the machine and two sets of shallow diving apparatus, damaged by explosion, were recovered by divers. The second machine was salved by the Spaniards from the beach at La Linea, where one Italian officer and one rating were picked up. So far as is known this was the first appearance of such a weapon in this war. (M.024136/40.)

86

During the greater part of September 1940, the Fleet was mainly concerned with the coastal operations already referred to off Cyrenaica, but in the middle of the month a north-bound Aegean convoy (AN.3) was run from Port Said to the Piraeus. The *Calcutta* and two destroyers formed the close escort, while the Third Cruiser Squadron, *Kent*, *Liverpool* and *Gloucester*, with four destroyers, cruised in their vicinity to give A/A support. On 13th September, when south of Kaso Strait, the convoy was bombed four times and was attacked at 1410/13th by torpedo aircraft, but escaped damage and arrived safely on the 15th. Towards the end of the month the Commander-in-Chief decided that while the military situation in the Western Desert remained static any naval assistance required by the Army in Cyrenaica could be rendered by the gunboats *Ladybird* and *Aphis* of Force W, leaving him free to take the Fleet into the centre of the Mediterranean and try to find the Italian Fleet at sea. He had originally intended to sail on 27th September on an operation referred to as Operation MB.5 with the twofold object of passing military and air personnel reinforcements to Malta and of engaging the enemy fleet if it could be found. (C.-in-C. Mediterranean 1637/24/9.) For various reasons, however, departure from Alexandria was postponed, but at 0220/29th September the Fleet was clear of the swept channel and steering 310° at 18 knots. The Commander-in-Chief flew his flag in the *Warspite* and had with him the *Valiant*, *Illustrious*, *Orion* (Flag of V.A.L.F.), *Sydney*, *York* and eleven destroyers, being joined before daylight on the 29th by the *Liverpool* and *Gloucester* having on board 1,200 military drafts with a few airmen and R.A.F. stores for Malta.

Early in the afternoon of the 29th the *Stuart* reported a burst steampipe, so was ordered to return to Alexandria. On her way to harbour at 2215/29th, when some 60 miles north-west of the Great Pass, she contacted an enemy submarine. After a series of depth charge attacks the submarine *Gondar* was forced to the surface, where she was bombed by R.A.F. flying boat L.2166. Eventually the submarine's crew abandoned her and she sank at 0925/30th September, 47 out of the 49 survivors being rescued by the *Stuart*.

The Fleet continued on a westerly course during the 29th, and in the afternoon experienced two bombing attacks by S.79's without sustaining serious damage. Later, at 1641/29th, four torpedo aircraft launched an unsuccessful torpedo attack on the *Illustrious*. Fulmar fighters brought down one of the bombers, having earlier in the day shot down two shadowers (Cant. S.507's), though not before the first of these had reported our Fleet's position. By the afternoon of the 29th therefore, the enemy were aware of our force at sea consisting of two battleships, one aircraft carrier, four 6-inch cruisers, one 8-inch cruiser and ten destroyers. The Italian Fleet available for action at this time comprised five battleships, two Littorios and three Cavours, six 8-inch and ten 6-inch cruisers with some thirty Fleet destroyers, of which the major part were shown by air reconnaissance on the 29th to be in Taranto. The Commander-in-Chief expected to reach the centre part of the Ionian Sea by noon/30th, that is approximately 250 miles from Taranto, so that he had good reason to anticipate an encounter with the enemy on the 30th provided that they left harbour before midnight 29th/30th September.

His expectations were not realised, for although the Italian Fleet left the harbours of Messina and Taranto p.m. on the 29th and steered to the south-east, at noon on the 30th, instead of being presented with enemy sighting reports from our cruiser screen, the Commander-in-Chief received aircraft reconnaissance reports of five battleships, eleven cruisers and up to twenty-five destroyers in a position 110 miles N.N.W. from him, steering 325° at 22 knots. Later in the evening of the 30th aircraft reported part of the enemy fleet returning to Messina and the remainder steering for Taranto.

In view of their preponderance of force, that is, battleships five to two, cruisers eleven to five, destroyers more than two to one, the Italian Fleet's behaviour in avoiding action is difficult to explain. Although the presence of an aircraft carrier with our fleet meant the probability of their battleships running the gauntlet of a torpedo-aircraft attack before the fleets made contact, and though the distance from Sicily or South Italy precluded the presence of shore-based fighter patrols, yet they had a number of shipborne fighter reconnaissance machines, about 40 in all, which ought to have been a sufficient number to provide fighter patrols during the approach. If the reason for not using them was the difficulty of re-embarkation during an action then it would appear to be of small value to carry such machines unless they can be used when most wanted. The most likely explanation seems to be the old story of bad leadership, just as at Lissa, on 18th July 1866, when the Austrian fleet with seven ironclads outfought the Italians with twelve ironclads and double the number of guns. Whatever the reason, the Italian fleet on 30th September 1940 avoided action under conditions favourable to them, with the result that the impression held previously that the enemy did not wish to fight a Main Fleet action thereafter became a conviction.[1]

That this conviction was justified is shown by the following reference to Italian naval official policy in September 1940, which is quoted from Admiral Bernotti's *La guerra sui marittimi*, Volume I, chapter 4, section 12. Admiral Bernotti stated that

'the directive for the policy of our fleet besides the protection, direct and indirect, of the traffic with Libya and Albania, lays down that it must bring the main enemy naval forces to battle whenever favourable conditions permit. In irresponsible and incompetent political circles, signs of growing impatience were being manifested, therefore in the middle of September 1940 the Naval Chief of Staff asked the Chief of the General Staff for a ruling. In his reply, Marshal Badoglio, after some comprehensive considerations on the course of the war in the Mediterranean, framed a directive as follows: "A naval battle can be originated by two causes

(1) a meeting between enemy squadrons of which one is trying to prevent the other carrying out an operation,

(2) a definite search by one of our squadrons for an enemy's squadron to destroy it.

---

1 The Italian Historical (Naval) Division, in reply to an enquiry as to why their shipborne aircraft were not used to form a fighter Screen, said that such aircraft were given the exclusive task of reconnaissance. The fact remains, however, that the aircraft carried in Italian battleships and cruisers, capable of acting as fighters, as described in Jane's 'All the World's Aircraft', were R.O.43's, two-seater fighter reconnaissance single-float catapult seaplanes. They carried two machine guns firing through the airscrew, and one machine gun for all-round fire in the back cockpit. Their maximum speed at 6,500 feet was about 195 m.p.h., and their cruising speed about 130 m.p.h. with a flight period of five hours.

The first case may occur at any time, and in fact did occur at Punta Stilo on 9th July 1940.[1] In such a case our navy will seek to join battle, if there is a chance of succeeding, with extreme determination. In the second case there are no possibilities for us, as we are too weak. If we meet the English navy we shall be ready to join issue. The conception of a naval battle as an end in itself is absurd; it is not worth the trouble of further discussion. Conclusion: carry on as at present".'

Admiral Bernotti then resumes his own description:–

'In order to profit from favourable opportunities of meeting the enemy, each of his sorties called for a corresponding movement of our squadrons, as happened in early September 1940, but without our being able to make contact. Similarly, at the end of September 1940, the attempt we made to join battle in the Central Mediterranean did not succeed, notwithstanding the activity of our principal forces. The strategic position of Taranto was too far away for us to arrange our fleet movements to counter conveniently the moves of the enemy from Alexandria, even when the latter was cruising towards the Central Mediterranean,[2] on the other hand the stationing of a large part of our forces at Augusta was out of the question owing to the extreme proximity of that port to enemy aircraft based on Malta.'

To continue with the British Fleet's story. During the afternoon of 30th September the *Gloucester* and *Liverpool* were detached to Malta, while the rest of the Fleet continued westward until 2300/30th, when course was altered eastward. The *Gloucester* and *Liverpool* rejoined the Flag at 1745/1st October. On the return voyage during the forenoon of 1st October Fulmars from the *Illustrious* shot down an enemy shadower, and on the morning of the 2nd they chased off a formation of enemy bombers. When in a position 120 miles north of Sidi Barrani at 0500/2nd October, an enemy submarine was once more surprised on the surface by the *Havock* and *Hasty*, which attacked with gunfire and depth charges. Two hours later the submarine, which had dived on being attacked, surfaced to allow for the rescue of her crew and then scuttled herself. She proved to be the *Berillo*. Forty-five were saved.

After various exercises the Fleet returned to Alexandria by p.m. 2nd October, except for the *Orion* and *Sydney* which had been detached on the 1st for a sweep through the Aegean. During the night of 2nd/3rd October the two cruisers bombarded Port Maltezana, Stampalia, and returned to Alexandria on the 3rd. (M.022719/40, A-01184/40.)

The opportunity was taken during MB.5 to sail a northbound Aegean convoy (AN.4) from Port Said, escorted by the *Calcutta* and two destroyers. The convoy was shadowed but not bombed, and arrived at the Piraeus on 1st October.

87

Important points which emerged from the events of the 29th/30th September were the need for more adequate long-distance air reconnaissance in the Central Mediterranean, and for ensuring the receipt by the Commander-in-Chief of air reconnaissance reports, particularly those of enemy vessels at sea when our Fleet might be in a position to act on them. The general arrangements for reconnaissance in the Central Mediterranean were as follows:–

(i)	Ionian Sea	Glen Martins and Sunderlands working from Malta in continuous daylight patrols
(ii)	Taranto, Bari, Brindisi, Messina, Augusta, Tripoli	Same aircraft as (i) when occasion required
(iii)	General area between	Swordfish from Malta fitted with extra fuel tanks to give a range of about 900 miles

---

[1] This is referred to by us as the Action of Calabria – Section 51 to 56.

[2] This statement is not in accordance with the events of 29th/30th September, because the Italian Fleet did in fact leave their harbours of Messina and Taranto late on the 29th and could have met the Mediterranean Fleet at noon 30th, as already explained.

The A.O.C., Mediterranean, with his headquarters at Malta, dealt direct with the Commander-in-Chief, Mediterranean, in order to co-ordinate these requirements.

These arrangements were in force at the time of Operation MB.5, but although the enemy fleet was observed at 0620/30th September by a Glen Martin and at 1050/30th September by a Sunderland; and though both these sightings were broadcast yet neither report was received by the Commander-in-Chief (C.-in-C. Mediterranean 1259/2/310, H.Q.R.A.F.M.E. 1127/7/10). The first enemy report actually received by the Commander-in-Chief was at 1126/30th, from aircraft duty 'F' which had been flown off from the *Illustrious* at 1030. At 1210 aircraft 'F' amplified her earlier report, and at 1230 aircraft duty 'D' reported battleships and cruisers, all steering 325° at 22 knots. Shadowing of the enemy was kept up by the F.A.A. until 1600/30th, when an R.A.F. Glen Martin from Malta took over. The Admiralty, in replying to the Commander-in-Chief's, Mediterranean, report on these matters (1259/2/10), assured him that the need for more long distance air reconnaissance was fully appreciated (1943/3/10), and noted his further request for longer-range torpedo-bombing aircraft.

88

In order to continue exercising a constant threat to the enemy Libyan convoys and also with the object of covering Crete against possible enemy attack the Rear-Admiral, First Battle Squadron, in the *Malaya* with the *Ramillies*, *Eagle*, *Ajax*, *Coventry* and eight destroyers, sailed from Alexandria at 0100 3rd October soon after the return of the Commander-in-Chief and ships taking part in Operation MB.5. The squadron proceeded to an area close west of Crete and returned to Alexandria on the morning of 6th October. No enemy aircraft were seen, and apart from a number of submarine contacts the cruise was uneventful. The opportunity was taken of exercising the Fleet Air Arm and *Eagle*, working in conjunction with the newly arrived radar-fitted ship *Ajax* and the A/A cruiser *Coventry*.

89

On account of the Italian Army's advance into Egypt (S.81) the need for exerting a threat to their Libyan convoys had become increasingly urgent. The difficulties of making an effective attack by surface forces from Alexandria on the direct-route traffic from Sicily or Southern Italy to Benghazi or Tripoli have already been mentioned (S.51), and a further point at this period, October 1940, arose from the fact that the enemy did not appear to be using these routes. Air reconnaissance had not provided us with any certainty of evidence of what routes were being used; such evidence as did exist pointed to the majority of traffic passing westward of Sicily and Lampedusa, and thence by Tripoli and the coastal route to Benghazi. Many ships off-loaded at Tripoli, whence road traffic took the supplies on to Cyrenaica.

Later in the war, in the autumn of 1941 and early 1942, when German forces were in Libya and the Luftwaffe were operating in the Ionian Sea, the direct routes from Taranto and Messina to Benghazi and Tripoli were resumed, with the Italian Fleet acting as escort, particularly after our capital ships had left the Mediterranean. But in the autumn of 1940 the threat of attack from our Fleet seems to have been sufficient to keep the Italian Fleet either in or not far away from harbour.

Our submarines maintained a constant threat to enemy supply routes, not only on the direct oversea lines to North Africa, but in the Tyrrhenian Sea and Adriatic. On 4th October, the *Triton* sank the S.S. *Franca Fassio* (1,854 tons) in Vado Roads, Gulf of Genoa, and two days later she torpedoed, but did not sink, a 5,000 ton merchant ship, escorted by two M.A.S. in the Gulf of Genoa. On 9th October the *Regent* torpedoed and severely damaged the S.S. *Antonietta Costa* (5,900 tons) in the Adriatic, off Durazzo. Losses on our part were inevitable and towards the end of October the Commander-in-Chief reported that the *Rainbow*[1] had not returned to Alexandria from patrol in Otranto Strait, and that the Triad had not arrived at Alexandria from patrol off Cape Colonne.

At this period results against the Italy-Benghazi and the North African coastal traffic were disappointingly

---

1 The *Rainbow* was sunk by gunfire by the Italian submarine *Toti* on 15th October, 1940 in 38° 15' N., 1 7° 37' E.

small. On 28th September, however, the *Pandora* sank a 1,000 ton supply ship, the S.S. *Fauingha*, off Ras Aaamer, and early in October the *Rorqual* laid 50 mines in the approaches to Benghazi. The Fleet Air Arm and Royal Air Force continued unceasingly to harry the coastal traffic between Benghazi and Tobruk. Until the arrival of extra surface forces[1] in the Mediterranean, enabling him to keep a raiding force of cruisers and destroyers operating from Malta, the Commander-in-Chief had perforce to continue his previous methods of cruises with the Fleet from Alexandria into the centre of the Ionian Sea, and submarine patrols and air strikes from Malta when targets came within range.

90

Fleet cruises into the centre of the Mediterranean, as previously mentioned, had for their primary object the finding and engaging in battle of the Italian Fleet, but they served also the purpose of escorting convoys to Malta, where supplies were badly needed (S.72). Operation MB.5 had succeeded in drawing the Italian Fleet out of harbour, though only to make a quick run back (S.86), and the First Battle Squadron had had no better fortune. Now, the Commander-in-Chief decided to try again and at the same time to pass a full convoy through to Malta, bringing back some empty ships to Alexandria.

With these objects in view he left Alexandria p.m. 8th October with the whole Mediterranean Fleet, comprising four battleships, the *Warspite*, flying his flag, *Valiant*, *Malaya* flying the flag of the R.A. First Battle Squadron, and *Ramillies*; two aircraft carriers, *Illustrious* flying the flag of R.A. (A), and *Eagle*; the Third Cruiser Squadron, consisting of the 8-inch cruiser *York*, the 6-inch cruisers *Gloucester* flying the flag of the R.A. Third Cruiser Squadron and *Liverpool*;[2] the Seventh Cruiser Squadron, *Ajax*, *Orion* and *Sydney*; together with 16 destroyers of the 2nd, 10th and 14th Flotillas.

At 2000/8th October convoy MF.3 which comprised the four merchant ships, *Memnon*, *Lanarkshire*, *Clan Macaulay*, *Clan Ferguson*, with a close escort of two A/A cruisers, *Calcutta* and *Coventry*, and four destroyers, left Alexandria for Malta.

The enemy Fleet, except for the two *Littorio* battleships and some of the cruisers, were reported by air reconnaissance on 9th October in Taranto, and from Intelligence sources the remaining cruisers were either at Messina, Augusta or Naples. Actually the two *Littorios* were probably at sea outside Taranto, for they were reported to have returned to harbour on the 12th together with the three *Cavours*.

By 1330/10th October, our Fleet was in a position 100 miles south-west of Matapan with the convoy 22 miles astern. During that afternoon the *Ramillies* and six destroyers were detached to fuel at Malta, and the Third Cruiser Squadron was ordered to join the convoy.

No enemy aircraft had been sighted by nightfall on the 10th, the only sign of the enemy being a report from one of our aircraft at 1422/10th of a submarine located and attacked with bombs 20 miles ahead of the Fleet, which was probably the same submarine as that reported by aircraft earlier in the day to the northward. Both the *Vampire* and *Defender* reported submarine contacts during the afternoon.

91

When some 70 miles eastward of Malta at 0800/11th the *Ajax* was detached to join the Third Cruiser Squadron, which was reinforcing the close escort to the convoy. During the forenoon of the 11th destroyers were detached to refuel at Malta. One – the *Imperial* – struck a mine in a position 30 miles south of Delimara Point in a depth of 150 fathoms. Her stern was badly buckled, but she was able to proceed in tow of the *Decoy* into Malta for repairs. The *Coventry* cut a mine with her paravanes in a position four miles south-west of the *Imperial*; several floating mines were also reported. These incidents led the Commander-in-Chief to report to the Admiralty (1156/11/10) that a new enemy minefield existed in this area, and that more minesweepers were necessary for Malta as it was not practicable to keep the channels

---

1 See Appendix C.11 for exchange of signals between Admiralty and Commander-in-Chief Mediterranean on requirements for attack on Libyan communications.

2 The R.A. 7th C.S. (Vice-Admiral J. C. Tovey) was on his way home to become Commander-in-Chief, Home Fleet.

clear with only one minesweeper. The Admiralty consequently ordered the *Huntley* and *Derby* to be transferred from the Red Sea to the Mediterranean.

The convoy arrived at Malta at 1600/11th, and the eastbound convoy – M.F.4 consisting of three ships, the *Aphis, Plumleaf, Volo*, escorted by the *Calcutta, Coventry* and two destroyers – sailed at 2230/11th. During the afternoon of the 11th the Fleet cruised to the south and west of Malta, and at midnight 11th/12th the Commander-in-Chief's position was 50 miles south of Delimara Point in company with the battlefleet, aircraft carrier, and Third Cruiser Squadron – course 090°. The Seventh Cruiser Squadron was spread north eastward of the battlefleet, with H.M.S. *Ajax* in the outermost position.

During the 11th the weather had been overcast with thunder, strong squalls and low visibility; no enemy air activity was detected. The presence of our Fleet seems, however, to have been known to the Italians, possibly from observations on the previous day, for they had sent out a division of destroyers and torpedo boats from Augusta to patrol to the south eastward of Sicily. The first intimation of the presence of enemy forces came just before 0200/12th October, when, in a position 100 miles east of Malta, the *Ajax* sighted and opened fire on a destroyer on her starboard bow, down moon, steering an opposite course. Almost at the same moment a second destroyer was sighted on the port bow and engaged with the port 4-inch guns. These two destroyers were the *Ariel* and *Airone*, commanded by Lieut. Ruta and Lieut.-Commander Banfi respectively, the latter being the senior officer of the 1st T.B. Division.[1] Both vessels sank almost at once, some of the crews being rescued later from rafts. They had fired their torpedoes unsuccessfully, but the *Airone* obtained three hits on the *Ajax* with her 4-inch guns, two on the bridge structure and one amidships above the waterline, causing a fire in the central stores and adjacent compartments.

Before the *Airone* sank the *Ajax* had swung to starboard so as to bring all guns to bear, and while turning she sighted and engaged a third vessel – the destroyer *Artigliere*, leader of the 11th Destroyer Division, commanded by Captain Margottini. A short action followed and the *Artigliere* was set on fire and her guns silenced; her torpedoes missed the *Ajax*, but she obtained a few hits with gunfire; her captain was killed and the command taken over by Lieut. del Greco. Two more destroyers were then sighted steering to the northward, and the rear vessel, probably the *Camicia Nera*, turned to engage *Ajax*, but retired under cover of a smoke screen after a few rounds.

It is of interest to note that the *Ajax* was a newly commissioned ship, and this was her first night shoot; her casualties were two officers and ten ratings killed, one officer seriously wounded and twenty minor injuries. In addition to the structural damage mentioned above she received four more hits from gunfire which put out of action one 4-inch gun, her radar and degaussing gear. Due to gunflash the *Ajax* reported considerable difficulty in appreciating the situation, whereas it was noted that the enemy used flashless propellant and efficient tracers. The ranges on opening fire were, *Ariel*, 4,000 yards; *Airone*, 2,000 yards; *Artigliere*, 3,000 yards.

On receiving a report from the *Ajax* at 0306/12th that two cruisers had been sighted and that she had lost touch at 0333, the Commander-in-Chief, who was then some 70 miles south west of the *Ajax*, anticipating that the enemy might be present in force, ordered the Seventh and Third Cruiser Squadrons to close the Fleet. At 0600/12th aircraft were flown off to search from north-west to north-east. The *Orion* reported at 0645 that one ship was still burning, and at 0710 a flying boat reported two destroyers, one on fire and being towed. The course of the Fleet was altered to 010° and four aircraft were flown off to attack the destroyers, while the Third Cruiser Squadron moved out to investigate smoke on the horizon. On sighting the Third Cruiser Squadron the towing destroyer cast off the tow and proceeded north-west at high speed, being attacked by our air striking force, though not hit.

92

The Third Cruiser Squadron closed the crippled *Artigliere* which hoisted a white flag and was given half an hour to abandon ship. Carley floats were thrown overboard by the Third Cruiser Squadron and the

---

[1] Being of over 600 tons' displacement these craft come under the classification of destroyers, though the Italians called them torpedo boats.

position of the survivors broadcast in Italian on the commercial wave length; but in view of the *Havock*'s experience when rescuing survivors from the *Colleoni* (S.63), and also on account of the proximity of Sicily (90 miles) and of being in submarine waters, the Commander-in-Chief did not consider it justifiable to stop and pick up survivors, though some were picked up by the *Nubian* and *Vampire* at a distance from the Fleet. Eventually, about 0830, the *York* opened fire with gun and torpedo, and the *Artigliere* blew up and sank. The enemy's losses in this skilfully-handled night action were:–

    Sunk: One large destroyer and two small destroyers.

    Damaged: One large destroyer, believed to be the *Camicia Nera*.

At 0930/12th the *Orion*, *Sydney* and *Ajax* rejoined the Commander-in-Chief in a position 085°, 100 miles from Malta.

A report by air reconnaissance of enemy surface forces was received at 1150/12th which gave three 8-inch cruisers and three destroyers 60 miles N.W. of the Fleet and steering N.W. Aircraft of 830 Squadron from Malta were sent to attack but did not locate them. By noon/12th October the Fleet had reassembled, steering 090°, and the Third Cruiser Squadron were detached to join convoy M.F.4, then 50 miles astern of the Fleet (M.06616/41).

93

During the afternoon of the 12th enemy aircraft attacked with bombs at 1232 and 1345. A third attack was frustrated by Fulmars from the *Illustrious*, who forced the enemy to jettison their bombs nine miles from the Fleet and shot down two of them; altogether on the 12th aircraft from the *Eagle* and *Illustrious* accounted for five enemy machines. No further attacks developed until 1435/14th, when five aircraft dropped bombs outside the destroyer screen, and at 1442 three aircraft dropped bombs between the *Warspite* and *Illustrious*.

Another attack developed about 1900/14th from astern of the Fleet, this time with torpedoes as well as bombs. The battlefleet was then in a position 60 miles south of Kupho Nisi at the east end of Crete, with the cruisers spread astern. Heavy barrage fire kept the aircraft from approaching the battlefleet, but the cruisers were not so well protected, and at 1855/14th the *Liverpool* was hit by a torpedo well forward. The *Orion* took her in tow until noon/15th when the tow parted; she had then steamed 100 miles at nine knots; by 1450/15th the tow had again been passed. The damaged portion of *Liverpool*, forward of 'A' turret, dropped off and simplified the towing as it had previously been acting as a drogue. She was eventually brought safely into Alexandria at midday, 16th October. The Commander-in-Chief with the Fleet returned to Alexandria by 0100/16th.

94

During the forenoon of the 13th, when the Fleet was approaching Crete, the R.A. (A) in the *Illustrious*, with the *Gloucester*, *Liverpool* and four destroyers, was detached to carry out a night attack on Leros, rejoining the Fleet a.m./14th south of Crete. Fifteen aircraft carried out the attack on Port Laki at 2300/13th, dropping 92 bombs, and all aircraft returned safely. Hangars at Lepida Cove were set on fire, whilst workshops and probably a fuel tank at San Giorgio were hit.

Early on the 13th the *Ajax*, *Coventry* and two destroyers were sent to meet convoy A.S.4 from Athens to Port Said, and in the morning of the 14th convoys M.F.4 and A.S.4 joined forces off Gavdo Island; both convoys arrived safely on the 15th and 16th, not having been attacked by aircraft. (M.06616/41, M.02062/41, A.0755/41.)

95

Ten aircraft from the *Illustrious* and four from the *Eagle* carried out a minelaying operation off Tobruk on the night of 23rd/24th October. The aircraft had previously been flown to Maaten Bagush to operate under the orders of the O.C. 202 Group, R.A.F. Four dropped bombs in the vicinity of the town, and the remaining ten laid 'cucumbers'[1] to cover the entrance of the harbour. The R.A.F. continued to carry out raids on Tobruk, Bardia and Benghazi. On 16th October the Commander-in-Chief records that the 'shipping at Benghazi has greatly diminished and it is doubtful if any important ships remain except those damaged by air attack.' (Mediterranean War Diary, 16/10/40.)

Also it was noted that naval forces from Benghazi put to sea early in the day and returned by nightfall to act as A/A guardships. The Italians were finding out that Benghazi as a forward supply base was of little use without strong air protection, a difficulty that we, in our turn, encountered later on.

Between Operation M.B.6 and the next event of major importance, which was the entry of Greece into the war on 28th October, there was only one cruise of any importance, namely from 25th to 28th October, Operation M.A.Q.2. The R.A., First Battle Squadron, in the *Malaya*, with the *Eagle*, *Orion*, *Sydney*, *Coventry* and eight destroyers, acted as cover to convoy A.N.5 from Port Said and Alexandria bound for the Dardanelles, with close escort of the *Calcutta* and two destroyers. Destroyers carried out a searching but barren A/S sweep of an area lying across the route from Alexandria to Kaso Strait where enemy submarines were reported to be on patrol, and the *Eagle*'s aircraft attacked Port Maltezana, Stampalia, at dawn 27th October, where hangars were hit and set on fire and about twenty 250 lb. bombs were dropped on barracks and ammunition dump area. There was no enemy air activity and all our aircraft returned safely. The convoy was unmolested by either aircraft or submarines.

96

A change in Flag Officers' appointments was announced on 21st October following the departure of Vice-Admiral J. C. Tovey to become Commander-in-Chief, Home Fleet. Rear-Admiral H. D. Pridham-Wippell, with acting rank of Vice-Admiral, became V.A.L.F. and Second-in-Command, Mediterranean Fleet; Captain H. B. Rawlings, with acting rank of Rear-Admiral, became Rear-Admiral, First Battle Squadron.

Between 7th and 17th October a Turkish delegation, consisting of General Galip Turker, Vice-Admiral Ulgen and two staff officers, visited the Middle East and spent some time in Alexandria with the Fleet. They were given passage back to Mersin in the *Nubian*, and expressed great appreciation at the efforts made to show them the Fleet and its duties under war conditions. On our part no great hopes were entertained of obtaining positive Turkish help; in fact it was felt that if Turkey joined us at this stage we should be expected to supply them with weapons and equipment that we ourselves lacked. Yet it was obviously important to keep alive a friendly attitude, for if the Turks became impressed with German achievements to the point of believing that ultimate victory rested with them then we might have to cope with a hostile country on the borders of Syria and thence of Palestine, meaning an added burden to our Middle East commitments just at a time when it seemed that Greece would be requiring our assistance (Appendix C.12).

97

A number of conferences in Cairo and Alexandria were held at this time which the Commander-in-Chief attended, and at one of them (24th October) the Secretary of State for War, the Right Honourable Anthony Eden, presided. At these conferences plans for dealing with developments in the Balkans were discussed. During September and October 1940, the position in the Balkans had been becoming of more and more concern to the Commander-in-Chief. The Treaty of Neuilly in 1919 awarded to Greece the whole of the Aegean coastline formerly belonging to Bulgaria, and in 1934, by the so-called Balkan pact, Greece received a guarantee in respect to this coastline, the pact laying down that Greece, Rumania, Turkey and Yugoslavia guaranteed mutually the security of their Balkan frontiers. An approach was made to Bulgaria to persuade them to adhere to the pact, but without success, her Prime Minister declaring that he would be ready to agree 'to a pact of non-aggression within the framework of the League of Nations, but would not commit the country to any consolidation of the existing order, in other words, to the renunciation of all claims to treaty revision.'[2]

---

1 Cucumbers – magnetic mines.
2 Annual Register 1934 Bulgaria.

The pact remained in force, but by 1940 had practically become a dead letter consequent on German aggression.

By the end of October in that year the whole of Rumania was under German control. In Yugoslavia there had been an infiltration of thousands of young Germans disguised as tourists, and that country was in a weak position to give us assistance required by the terms of the pact.

In Bulgaria there had been also a steady German infiltration. The position of Greece in these circumstances, with Albania to her west occupied by Italy and with potentially hostile neighbours under German influence to the north, was one of considerable peril, especially as all indications at the beginning of October were pointing to an attack by Italy. We were not in a position to offer Greece substantial military or air assistance, but our naval strength was considerable and could be even more effectively exploited if we could use Crete as a naval and air base.

The Turkish attitude to Balkan questions at this time was referred to in a series of messages from our special envoy in Turkey, Admiral Sir Howard Kelly. He considered that Turkey would assist Greece if attacked by Bulgaria, but not if attacked by Italy. Nor would they fight if German troops attacked Greece through Bulgaria. Turkey had no wish to be drawn into a war with the Axis powers, for her territory in Europe was vulnerable and her position generally quite unprepared for war. By the Anglo-French-Turkish Treaty of 19th October 1939, the Turks were under an obligation to come to the assistance of Great Britain and France:

(*a*) in event of an act of aggression by a European Power leading to war in the Mediterranean area in which the United Kingdom and France were involved, and

(*b*) if the United Kingdom and France were engaged in hostilities by virtue of either of their guarantees to Greece and Rumania of 13th April 1939.

It will be seen, therefore, that the Turkish attitude in October 1940, had undergone considerable change since October 1939 (Appendix C.12, 13).

98

An unpleasant warning of Italian designs on Greece was given on 15th August 1940, when at 0830 the Greek cruiser *Helle*, 2,083 tons, was torpedoed and sunk without warning by an Italian submarine. She was lying at anchor off the island of Tinos during a visit to take part in the Festival of the Assumption. The tail of an exploded torpedo of Italian make was found near the position where the *Helle* was sunk, and the submarine *Tricheco* was known to have been on patrol in that area at that time. Two more torpedoes were fired 15 minutes later at two ships berthed in Tinos harbour, which missed the ships but hit the mole. (N.A. Athens 1900/17/8.) Many casualties were suffered in the *Helle* and a few civilians ashore were injured. The *Tricheco* was herself sunk 18 months later by the *Upholder* off Brindisi, so that it is unlikely if it will ever be definitely known whether this treacherous attack on a neutral warship, performed during a religious festival, was in execution of previous orders like the invasion of Albania on Good Friday, 1939.[1]

99

The *Helle* episode occurred only four days after the Commander-in-Chief had sent a strongly worded telegram to the British Minister at Athens, in which he drew attention to the Greek Government's habit of turning a blind eye to infringements of Greek neutrality by Italian aircraft. Cases had occurred when our ships could not fire on enemy shadowers because they kept over Greek territory, and on one occasion, 8th August, Italian aircraft bombed and machine gunned a number of tugs and lighters which were close inshore at Hierapetra, south of Crete. On 24th July an Italian seaplane forced-landed in Cretan waters and claimed the right to leave after effecting repairs and in spite of protests from the Commander-in-

---

[1] Count Ciano referred to this incident in his diary: '15th August, 1940. A Greek vessel has been sunk by a submarine of unidentified nationality. The incident threatens to become serious. For myself I consider the intemperance of De Vecchi (Governor of the Aegean) at the bottom of it.'

Chief, the Greek Government allowed the seaplane to proceed. The Commander-in-Chief made a further protest, pointing out that existing International Law required the immediate internment of the crews of belligerent aircraft making a forced landing in neutral territory, and that there were plenty of precedents for this in the present war. Shortly afterwards the Greek Government passed a new law prohibiting the recurrence of such an incident. About the same time the Greek Government had sent a note to the British Minister at Athens drawing attention to the presence of British destroyers close to Hydra on 27th July and the bombing of them by Italian aircraft, and requesting us to respect territorial waters in order to avoid such incidents. To this the Commander-in-Chief replied that no British destroyers were near Hydra on the date mentioned, and that he presumed the Greek Government was aware that British warships were fully within the rights of International Law in making a passage through territorial waters. There was no question, he added, of our carrying out patrols in Greek territorial waters, in fact H.M. Ships had orders to remain outside them unless in pursuit of the enemy or on account of navigational considerations.

A temporary change in the Greek attitude towards Italy took place after the *Helle* was sunk. On 17th August, our Naval Attaché at Athens reported that an A/S boom was being laid across the southern entrance to Salamis, and that all Greek men-of-war had been recalled to Salamis except the training ship *Ares*, which was cruising inside Euboea. On 22nd August the situation was reported critical; all leave for the Greek Army was stopped and Senior Officers ordered not to leave Salonika, and a few days later reports from Athens stated that mobilisation had been ordered in West Macedonia and Epirus. Matters, however, developed no further for some weeks and the jolt given by the *Helle* incident was soon forgotten. Towards the end of September the Commander-in-Chief reported to the Admiralty that the Italian policy of intimidating Greece was apparently successful, and suggested the time had come for a firm stand, which would serve the double purpose of reminding the Greeks as to who was controlling the Mediterranean and of enabling them to point out to Italy that they were acting under British pressure (C.-in-C. Mediterranean 0901/23/9).

100

The possibility of the Italians springing a surprise on us by occupying Crete had caused the Commander-in-Chief considerable anxiety for some time, for with Crete in the enemy's hands our difficulties would be heavily increased. It was suggested to the Admiralty that the Greek Government might be urged to mobilise their forces of about one division in Crete and perhaps be offered financial assistance (C.-in-C. Mediterranean 2229/15/8). Also, he informed the British Minister at Athens that although naval forces would, in the event of Greece entering the war, be sent to the assistance of Crete as rapidly as possible unless resistance in that island was immediate and properly organised our naval help could not develop its full weight.

The Commander-in-Chief did not consider that our assistance to Greece should be regarded as being limited to attempts to deny Crete to Italy. The Aegean sea routes were largely in our control, and on the west coast by means of submarine and to a certain extent surface activity we could challenge any attempt to pass forces by sea to Greek ports (C.-in-C. Mediterranean 1129/26/8). To assist Greece further the British Minister at Athens suggested asking the Turks to loan equipment. He considered that we were risking the loss of the mainland of Greece for the sake of a small amount of fighter aircraft and armaments. In particular he pointed to a lack of anti-tank guns on the frontier, but since the Turks themselves were short of equipment (Appendix C.12) no support in that respect was possible from them.

On 15th October the Chiefs of Staff instructed the Commanders-in-Chief, Middle East, to consult the British Minister at Athens about introducing British officers into Crete unobtrusively and in plain clothes, with the purpose of advising locally on defence matters, stimulating Greek resistance and ensuring early and efficient reporting if attack took place (C.O.S. No. 16 1252/15/10). Matters now began to assume a more threatening aspect, for on 22nd October our Ambassador in Washington reported to the Foreign Office that information from Rome indicated that the invasion of Greece was being timed to begin 25th October, and added that the U.S.S.R. had been offered the Dardanelles in return for accession to the Axis (1739/22/10). On the next day the Chiefs of Staff asked the Commanders-in-Chief, Middle East, to prepare for Crete a small force, which could be sent to the island when Greece entered the war (C.O.S. No. 19 1724/23/10). A battalion of the York and Lancaster Regiment with some A/A artillery was at once detailed to stand by for embarkation, and arrangements for the equipment of Suda Bay as a fuelling base with coal, petrol, stores A/S nets, were put in train at Alexandria.

101

The Italian Minister at Athens handed an ultimatum to the Prime Minister of Greece, General Metaxas, at 0300/28th October. Occupation of certain strategic points was demanded, the ultimatum further stating that if Greek consent was not given by 0600 that morning Italian troops would cross the frontier. The ultimatum was refused, and the Italian Minister was told that the Greek Government regarded the demand as a declaration of war. At 0530/28th October artillery fire was exchanged on the Albanian-Greek frontier, and Italian aircraft raided Patras, Preveza, Corinth and Athens, but did not inflict serious damage.

On the 28th the Commander-in-Chief ordered the Fleet to come to two and a half hours' notice for steam, and at 0130/29th October sailed from Alexandria so as to be off the west coast of Crete by dawn 31st October, ready for eventualities and to cover the passage of ships to Suda Bay. The submarine *Pandora* was on patrol in the Strait of Otranto; the Triton in the Gulf of Taranto, and two Greek submarines were stationed off the Ionian Islands, one off Levkas and one off Corfu.

Our air reconnaissance reports up to 1700/28th showed the main Italian Fleet in Taranto and Brindisi, a small convoy of merchant ships eastbound off Taranto, and a few destroyers at sea in the Gulf of Taranto and off Brindisi. No enemy naval activity was observed in the region of Corfu, Cephalonia, or the Gulf of Patras. At dawn on 31st October the Fleet was 20 miles west of Cephalonia, and remained cruising off the west coast of Greece during the day. The Commander-in-Chief in the *Warspite*, with the *Illustrious*, Third Cruiser Squadron and five destroyers, returned to Alexandria p.m. 2nd November.

The A.O.C., Mediterranean, was now requested to institute the maximum scale of air reconnaissance in the Ionian Sea north of 37° N., and to include examination of Taranto, Corfu and Argostoli, together with the western Greek ports.

The first convoy with stores and supplies for Suda Bay left Alexandria at 1400/29th October and consisted of the Royal Fleet Auxiliaries *Olna* and *Brambleleaf*; two Armed Boarding Vessels, *Fiona* and *Chakla*, escorted by two A/A cruisers, *Coventry* and *Calcutta*; the netlayer *Protector*; four destroyers and the minesweeper *Fareham*. The convoy reached Suda Bay early morning 1st November, together with the cruiser *Ajax* bringing an advance detachment of the York and Lancaster regiment. A reconnaissance party of officers of all three Services had previously arrived by flying boat at Suda Bay a.m./29th October, and had got in touch with the Greek authorities. By the afternoon of 1st November one A/S net had been laid by the *Protector*, military personnel disembarked, stores unloaded from the *Fiona* and *Chakla*, and a dump established near Suda Point. The Greek authorities gave every possible assistance, and local labour proved excellent. There was a heavy air raid at 1400/1st November by 25 aircraft on the mainland and harbour entrance, also farther west on Canea, but no appreciable damage was done and at least two aircraft were brought down by the A/A cruisers.

By 3rd November the A/S net defence at the entrance had been laid, and an A/T baffle placed at the western end of the anchorage for protection against aircraft torpedoes dropped in the harbour. Further measures were arranged for, including a table cloth net[1] and four A/T baffles originally intended for the Canal area for which the Admiralty were asked to send replacements (C.-in-C. Mediterranean, 2315/3/11). The Naval Attaché at Athens was asked to provide up to 50 small craft with a speed of not less than seven knots, including tugs, yachts and power caiques manned by Greek crews for A/S, M/S, boom patrol and service requirements for Suda Bay.

From the 6th onwards reinforcements for Crete continued to arrive. A convoy of seven ships (AN.6) had left Egypt on the 4th, and another on the 5th of five ships sailing with convoy MW.3, whose destination

---

1 Small square floating nets intended to foul propellers of small craft.

was Malta. These ships arrived at Suda Bay on the 6th. In addition, the *Ajax* and *Sydney*, which had sailed from Port Said on the 5th, arrived on the 6th with H.Q. 14th Infantry Brigade, one light and one heavy A/A battery and administrative troops. The monitor Terror arrived on the 13th as guardship.

The operation of supplying military forces to Greece and Crete, known as Operation Barbarity, was in general charge of the V.A.L.F., Vice-Admiral Pridham-Wippell, flying his flag in the *Orion*. On 15th November, the Third Cruiser Squadron, consisting of the *Berwick*, *York*, *Gloucester*, *Glasgow*, with the *Sydney* and a convoy of three fast merchant ships, embarked some 3,500 troops including R.A.F. maintenance staff and 1,500 Army ranks for A/A defence and base guard duties. The V.A.L.F., with the *Orion* and *Ajax*, visited Suda, Piraeus and Candia.

A strong covering force was provided by the R.A. First Battle Squadron in the *Barham*[1] with the *Valiant*, *Eagle* and eight destroyers. This Force also provided cover for movements of Greek troop convoys in the Aegean, where six Greek battalions moved from Suda Bay to Salonika and were replaced by a battalion of the Black Watch which embarked on 18th November in the *York* at Port Said. These measures provided against a surprise attack on Crete, and set up an advanced fuelling base at Suda Bay.

The entry of Greece into the war came at a time when our command of the sea in the Mediterranean was established, the Italians showing no signs of attempting to interfere with our free movement of troops and supplies to Crete. This command of the sea was not seriously threatened until the arrival of the German Air Force in the Mediterranean early in 1941. For the time being, therefore, the Commander-in-Chief was able to plan his operations for passage of supplies through the Mediterranean and to Greece without undue anxiety.[2] Military reinforcements, as well as more fighter aircraft, were required in Malta, and the Commander-in-Chief, Mediterranean, asked for the *Barham* and four destroyers to be detached from Force H in order to join his Flag as soon as possible. To cover the above requirements the following operations were planned for early in November (Admiralty 2126/3111).

Operation Coat	Reinforcement of Mediterranean Fleet and passage of military reinforcements to Malta
Operation White	Reinforcement of Hurricanes at Malta
Operation Collar	Passing military transports through to Malta (M.023953/40)

These will be described in the next volume of the Naval Staff History, Mediterranean.

---

1 H.M.S. *Barham* joined the Mediterranean Fleet early November, Operation Coat.
2 A description of the enemy's general attitude towards control of the sea is given in the essays of Admirals Doenitz and Wachold, written after the war and summarised in Appendices C.2 and C.3

APPENDIX A

PRECAUTIONARY MEASURES IN THE MEDITERRANEAN

(AUGUST–SEPTEMBER 1939)

Aug. 19th	Instituted special precautions in cruisers and above to prevent attempts at sabotage.
Aug. 20th	Started mounting 12-pdr. H.A. gun in *Leaf* class oilers, and gun in *Reliant*. Ships to fuse remaining H.E. shell and complete to maximum convenient stowage of ammunition.
Aug. 21st	Two destroyers to guard the Great Pass at Alexandria, by night and day, from attempts at blocking.
Aug. 22nd	Started to mount armament in *Ol* and *Dale* class oilers.
	H.M.S. *Resource* from Alexandria to Port Said with personnel for implementing the Canal Defence Plan.
Aug. 23rd	A/A and coast defences at Alexandria at 12 hours' notice. A destroyer to be secured inside harbour to guard against M.T.B. attack.
	Boat patrol instituted round R.A.F. flying boats at Alexandria by night.
	Reporting Officers directed to report suspicious German, Italian and Japanese vessels – action by officers in Italy restricted.
	Telegram – 'Situation A Germany' received.
Aug. 24th	Vice-Admiral Bedford assumed duty as Senior British Naval Officer, Canal Area.
	Started requisitioning of British ships.
	Limits of station amended – Gibraltar excluded. (A.L. M.00697/39 of Jan. 1939.)
	Cid and *Cisneros* sent to Bitter Lakes in order to reduce number of issue ships in Alexandria.
Aug. 25th	Second and Seventh Divisions of destroyers sent to Red Sea under Commander-in-Chief, East Indies, to escort shipping and cover any troop movements.
	Recognition signals brought into force.
Aug. 26th	War W/T organisation brought into force.
	'Vesca' system brought into force.[1]
Aug. 27th	Mediterranean closed to outside shipping, ships inside to continue voyage.
Aug. 28th	H.M.S. *Protector* arrived Alexandria from United Kingdom.
	H.M.S. *Devonshire* (C.S.1) and 1st Division of destroyers to sea to take over escort of S.S. *Mariette Pasha* from 3rd Destroyer Division coming from Malta.
	Orders given to start sweeping of channels at Malta, Alexandria and Port Said.

---

1 The 'Vesca' system of reporting movements of merchant ship dates back to the First World War and is derived from the first syllables of Vessel and Cargo. Telegrams sent by N.C.S.O.'s with the prefix 'Vesca' called attention to the nature of the message and enabled the appropriate authorities to act immediately. The system was explained in 'Reporting Officers' Instructions' issued before war broke out.

APPENDIX A

Aug. 29th	H.M.S. *Aberdeen* arrived Haifa from Alexandria to put Defence Plan into operation.
	Examination service instituted at Malta.
Aug. 30th	A/S trawlers left Malta for Alexandria on commissioning.
Aug. 31st	Ordered removal of stocks of S.P.s and C.B.s for ships working in Eastern Mediterranean from Malta to Port Said.
	Orders to mobilise and to increase readiness for war received. Censorship imposed (see A.T. 1759/1/8/39).
Sept. 1st	Laying of minefield off Malta started.
	Warning telegram received.
	Telegram 'Suez Canal – Situation C' received.
	Five submarines arrived Malta from United Kingdom.
Sept. 2nd	Orders given by Admiralty to Commanders-in-Chief to send a destroyer flotilla to Gibraltar to prevent the entry of German submarines into the Mediterranean. The 3rd Flotilla (H.M.S. *Inglefield*, D.3), who were en route for patrol between Cape Matapan and Crete with C.S.3 (H.M.S. *Arethusa*), were detailed for this duty and were relieved on patrol by Captain D.2 (H.M.S. *Hardy*) and 3rd Division (H.M.S. *Hero*, *Hereward*, *Hostile* and *Hasty*), who came from Malta. This relief took place about 2100/3rd September. The object of this patrol was to intercept German shipping from the Aegean and to cover British shipping. The Admiralty also ordered the Commander-in-Chief, East Indies (message 1407/2nd September) to send back to the Mediterranean the 7th and 2nd Destroyer Divisions from the Red Sea, and at the same time a division of the 21st Flotilla from China was ordered to the Red Sea.
Sept. 3rd	At 1251 (Zone-2) received orders from Admiralty to start hostilities with Germany.
	SHIPPING. Some 20 British ships were held up at Port Said and Gibraltar, another 20 were on passage in the Mediterranean. Ships between Malta and Egypt were routed to pass close south of Crete.
	FOREIGN. Except for some 10 ships in the Black Sea, all German ships had taken refuge in neutral ports. The majority of the big Italian liners had returned to Italian ports, but local traffic in the Mediterranean continued with little interruption.
	CONTRABAND CONTROL SERVICE. Institution of control services at Haifa, Gibraltar, Suez and Port Said ordered. Italian ships not to be interfered with.
	HOSPITAL SHIP. H.M.H.S. *Atlantis* left Gibraltar for Alexandria.
	EXAMINATION SERVICE. Examination Service was brought into force at Alexandria.
	INDICATOR NETS, ALEXANDRIA. First laying of one and a half miles by H.M.S. *Protector* completed. (Final laying completed on September 10th.)

PERSONNEL

Transport for the additional personnel from the United Kingdom required in war by the three Services was effected by sending two cruisers to Marseilles. H.M.S. *Shropshire* left Alexandria on 19th August and returned on 31st August. H.M.S. *Sussex* left Malta on 21st August and arrived at Alexandria on the 27th.

These ships and H.M.S. *Penelope* also took various sections from Malta to Alexandria including the Operational Intelligence Centre, Staff Officer (Intelligence) Malta, Accounting Staff for destroyers, Fleet repair and Armament Staffs.

H.M.S. *Penelope* also took from Malta a supply of books to equip a Distributing Authority at Alexandria.

APPENDIX B

CONTRABAND PATROL AREAS

(SECTION 10)

CA	Off Dardanelles
CA2	South of Tenedos
CB	Doro, Steno and Mykoni Channels
CC	Elaphonisos, Kithera and Antikithera Channels
CD	Approaches to Gulf of Athens
CE	Cape Matapan
CF	Sapienza Island
CG	Approaches to Gulf of Patras
CH	Straits of Otranto as far north as latitude 40° North
CK	South of Strait of Messina
CL	West of Gavdo Island
CM	Kaso Strait, east of Crete
CN	Gulf of Salonika between Cassandra Point and Kissobo Point
CO	South of Mitylene between Cape Sigri and Cape St. Nikolo, Khios

During February 1940 the following numbers of ships were sent in to Malta by contraband patrols for examination:–

PATROL   NUMBER OF SHIPS SENT IN

	February 1st–9th	*10th–17th*	*18th–24th*	*25th–2nd March*
CA	5	1	2	6
CA2	6	2	–	1
CB	3	–	–	–
CC	3	1	1	–
CD	–	–	–	1
CF	–	–	–	1
CG	–	5	–	1
CH	2	–	1	1

Agreements were concluded early in February between the Ministry of Economic Warfare and the Jadranska Plovidba and the Royal Hungarian Danube lines. These, together with the Greek trade agreement, resulted in a large increase in the number of ships which could be dealt with by the patrols at sea without being diverted to a Contraband Control Base.

APPENDIX C

PLANS AND POLICY

SYNOPSIS

	Section
1. Action against enemy seaborne trade	13
2. Axis policy for the Mediterranean:–	3, 22
(*a*) Objective: Occupation of Eastern Mediterranean.	
(*b*) Campaign in North Africa, causes of failure.	
3. The defensive policy of the Italian Navy	23
4. Commander-in-Chief's, Mediterranean, plans, June 1940	23
5. Haifa Conference – 4th June 1940	23
6. Force H	
(*a*) Need for reinforcements at Gibraltar	44
(*b*) Duties	44
(*c*) Decision to attack French ships at Oran	50
(*d*) A.M. 0103/2/7/450 and French account of Admiral Oden'hal's interview with D.C.N.S. on 1st July, 1940	50
7. British Naval policy in the Mediterranean, July 1940	60, 64
(*a*) Admiralty plan.	
(*b*) Commander-in-Chief, Mediterranean, plan.	
(*c*) S.O. Force H plan.	
8. After Oran and Dakar, policy vis-a-vis French warships	47
9. (*a*) Admiralty proposals for reinforcements and ammunition July 1940	64
(*b*) Commander-in-Chief's, Mediterranean, views on reinforcements and ammunition July 1940	
(*c*) Admiralty decision on composition of Mediterranean Fleet and Force H July 1940	79
(*d*) Chiefs of Staff appreciation of Middle East position July 1940	23, 79
10. Policy for Malta, August 1940	72
(*a*) Commander-in-Chief, Mediterranean.	
(*b*) Admiralty.	
(c) Admiralty.	
11. Requirements for attack on Libyan communications, October 1940	89
(*a*), (*d*) Admiralty.	
(*b*), (*c*) Commander-in-Chief, Mediterranean.	
12. Assistance to Greece and Turkey Chiefs of Staff. Commander-in-Chief, Mediterranean, 23/10/40	86
13. Turkish attitude and Balkan Questions, October 1940	97
(*a*), (*b*), (*c*).	

85

APP. C.2 MEDITERRANEAN, SEPTEMBER 1939–OCTOBER 1940

1
ACTION AGAINST ENEMY SEABORNE TRADE
(Extract – Section IV, para. 80 to 83 of M.00697/39)

(*a*) On the outbreak of war immediate action will be required by naval forces on all stations to round up and seize enemy shipping still on the high seas.

(*b*) Thereafter, with the North Sea and the Gibraltar and Suez Canal entrances under our control, German trade outside the Baltic and Italian trade outside the Mediterranean will be limited to that carried in neutral ships.

When we have established naval ascendancy in the Mediterranean, Italian vessels will be further restricted to coasting and Adriatic trade.

(*c*) Whereas enemy vessels are liable to seizure anywhere outside neutral waters, action against neutral ships trading with the enemy is limited to those which carry contraband, except in so far as it is possible to establish a close blockade of some part of the enemy's coast.

It is anticipated, however, that the contraband list in force will be so comprehensive as to cover practically everything of any value to the enemy in war time.

It will not be permissible to seize enemy exports carried in neutral ships, except when a close blockade is established, unless H.M. Government should decide to take action against enemy exports in retaliation for some breach of international law by the enemy, as was done in 1915.

(*d*) To prevent contraband from reaching the enemy it is necessary to establish patrols to intercept shipping, and bases where shipping may be examined, at the entrances to the North Sea and Mediterranean.

Consideration will also be given to the establishment of control of trade between the Black Sea and Mediterranean as soon as circumstances permit.

2
AXIS POLICY FOR THE MEDITERRANEAN
(Extracts from an essay by Grand-Admiral Doenitz, Commander-in-Chief of German Navy.)
(N.I.D 1/GP/10, 24.9.45.)

(a) *Objective Occupation of Eastern Mediterranean*

Dealing with the cause of the German defeat from the naval point of view Admiral Doenitz gives four decisive periods of the war, two of which (Nos. 2 and 3) were concerned with the Mediterranean.

(1) (*Summarised*) Failure to follow up the rapid success of overrunning France and the Low Countries by the invasion of England, which at that time was virtually unarmed.

(2) Germany's next objective was the occupation of the Eastern Mediterranean by which the British route to the Far East and oil supplies would be cut off. The failure to obtain this objective was due to poor fighting qualities of the Italians, and land supply difficulties of Rommel's Army which, in turn, were due to the fact that the combined German-Italian naval forces in the Mediterranean were insufficient[1] to obtain even temporary command of the sea in that area owing to the relatively small naval forces which we could spare for that theatre.

(3) (*Summarised*) The Invasion of North Africa. Admiral Doenitz laments the failure of German naval forces to interrupt the expedition.

(4) (*Summarised*) The Invasion of the Continent. Germany's failure to oppose this effectively was due to inadequate naval and air forces, poor intelligence, and lack of high speed air reconnaissance craft.

(Extract from Grand-Admiral Doenitz essay – N.I.D. 1/GP/10, 24.9.45.)

(b) *The entry of Italy into the War and the North African Campaign*

After the conquest of France and the entry of Italy into the war in June 1940 the Mediterranean too became a

---

[1] *Comment.* – The term used by Admiral Doenitz to describe the combined Axis naval forces would be more appropriately 'inefficient', for numerically, after the fall of France the Italian Fleet was superior, especially from December 1941 to November 1942.

sphere of interest of our war leaders, and with it North Africa came into the area covered by our own strategic deliberations.

From the appreciation of the Italian fighting forces at that time, which were not indeed equal to the English or German but were still valued too highly, a favourable opportunity seemed to be offered to strike a decisive blow at English interests and to compensate for the failure to invade England, which owing to circumstances could not be undertaken.

In addition it happened that, soon after the French ports were set working, owing to the great danger from the air the Navy wished for Atlantic ports farther to the south near French Morocco and Dakar.

The strategic aim of control of the Mediterranean Sea, which at times even raised hopes of the conquest of the Near East and creation of a sea link with Japan through the Red Sea, was not reached for the most varied reasons, though at times we came near to it.

The already planned attack on Gibraltar was not carried out, because there was no political success in drawing Spain in. The winning and using of French North Africa was only possible with the voluntary support of the French, which was not attained.

When the situation at sea in the Mediterranean took an unexpectedly favourable turn for us after the sinking of the battleship *Barham* by a German U-boat, and the damaging of two other battleships *Queen Elizabeth* and *Valiant* by Italian midget craft in Alexandria, the Italian Fleet, in spite of continual German proposals, failed to make adequate use of it.

The beating down of Malta by the German and Italian Air Forces to a state of helplessness in the winter of 1941–42 did not lead to its conquest, for the Italian Forces were insufficient and German support, considering the commitments in Russia and North Africa, was not available. Moreover, the successful offensive of Field Marshal Rommel in North Africa was prevented from being a strategic victory by lack of adequate land transport to bring up supplies, lack of material, bad leadership of the Italians, and lack of reinforcements.

On the Italian side the Navy suffered from lack of training, inferior technical equipment, and to some extent a lack of offensive spirit – this is not to belittle many incidents of bravery in operations involving the Italian Navy and Merchant Fleet.

On the German side, the final failure of the North African campaign was due to the fact that large forces were tied down in Russia, which prevented any large scale operations by land and sea forces in the Mediterranean.

The German Navy played only a very small role in the Mediterranean campaign, and apart from U-boat support could only use light forces and improvised auxiliaries, and for this reason had to leave the direction of sea warfare in this area largely in the hands of the Italian fleet, over whose operations only limited influence could be exerted.

At the end of January 1941, the Supreme Commander of the Navy was acquainted for the first time with the Fuhrer's opinion that a campaign against Russia was unavoidable, and that plans for this must be formed. Though at the beginning Russia abided loyally by the terms of the Russian-German treaty, she subsequently changed her tactics and exploited the position Germany had been forced into by withholding more and more of her supplies of wheat and oil to Germany, and also flagrantly violated various conditions laid down in the Treaty, with the Baltic States and Rumania.

Besides this, intelligence had been received that Russian armament, which on the face of things could only be used against Germany, had been placed on a war footing and that violent anti-German propaganda was being carried on in the Russian Army; reliable intelligence was later received about the deployment of Russian troops on her western frontier.

3

THE DEFENSIVE POLICY OF THE ITALIAN NAVY

(*Extract from essay, para. 19 to 23, by Vice-Admiral Weichold Chief German Liaison Officer in June 1940, at Italian H.Q., Rome, and German Commander-in-Chief Mediterranean, from November 1941 to March 1943.*)

1. The operational concern of the Italian Navy was limited to a strong defence of the Central Mediterranean and the keeping open of the sea routes to Libya. Neither was Malta, the thorn in the side of Italy's operational

freedom, seized, mined in or blockaded, nor were the many opportunities offered by the enemy taken with the serious object of engaging his forces. The failure to utilize the favourable position in the Dodecanese must also be regarded as a further example of Italy's renunciation of offensive measures. In contrast, the British practically controlled the whole of the Mediterranean east of Crete, including Greek waters, and continually menaced even the Central Mediterranean.

2. Reasons for the far reaching caution of the Italian Admiralty in the conduct of the war:–

(a) The Italian Navy believed it could carry out its task of securing the sea communications with Libya merely on the basis of tactical defence. It did not think it could afford to accept the risk of losses in offensive operations.

(b) Aerial reconnaissance over the sea was insufficient. The weaknesses of the Italian Fleet Air Arm[1] became evident from the beginning of the war.

(c) The Italian Navy's terror of using darkness as a cover for light forces and above all of the night attack of torpedo-carrying craft.

(d) An uncertainty in the direction of operations which in the first place was based on the silent admission of the enemy's superiority in war experience as well as in achievement in the battle of one ship against another.

3. This defensive policy meant the renunciation of a direct attack on the enemy's very important lanes of supply by means of numerous light forces.

In fact his trade was almost unmolested.

4. At the beginning of August 1940, the British reinforced their Air Force in Malta and increased the aerial reconnaissance activity from that base. The head of the German naval liaison staff took the opportunity to express his opinion of the consequences and of the general situation as follows:–

'The British by increasing aerial reconnaissance radiating from Malta in the Central Mediterranean will apparently have a better basis for attacks on Italian sea communications with Libya, as well as for the timely receipt of intelligence concerning operations of the Italian naval forces.

'Should they succeed in this the Italian Navy's freedom of action in the most important theatre of operations will be limited and the vital communications with Libya threatened.[2]

'Under these circumstances the elimination of Malta as a British naval and air base becomes imperative. Going by present experiences this task cannot be left to the Italian Air Force alone. Moreover, the use of naval forces is essential if a combined attempt to seize the island is to be made.'

The German Admiral then instigated a long list of plans for the elimination of Malta as the first condition for control of the Central Mediterranean, with all its advantages for the intensification of the Italian campaign at sea.

5. British naval forces were operating in the Central Mediterranean almost without hindrance from the Italian defences. Already since the night of 9th/10th July 1940, the Italian fleet had given up seizing favourable opportunities for attack especially by night. On 31st August, the Italian naval forces still possessed even by day a great potentiality.

Again no attempt was made to utilize the numerous Italian destroyers in a night attack on the heavy British units. Suggestions on the part of the German Liaison Staff that the operational situation offered an ideal case for night attacks by torpedo-carrying aircraft were of no avail. By remaining in harbour the Italian fleet again allowed the enemy complete freedom of action both in the Central Mediterranean and in the Sicilian channel.

---

1 Properly speaking, there was no Italian Fleet Air Arm, as we understand the term. Aircraft operating over the sea were subject to three authorities:–
   (a) Those carrying out reconnaissance from shore bases, assigned for that duty permanently to the Navy, operated under the orders of area naval commands according to the general direction of the Ministry of Marine.
   (b) Those embarked in ships operated under the orders of the Commander-in-Chief, Afloat.
   (c) All other aircraft formed part of the Air Force and operated, at the request of the Navy, under the orders of the Air Ministry

2 *Comment*. – In view of what actually occurred Admiral Weichold had the gloomy satisfaction of seeing his prophecies fulfilled.

4
COMMANDER-IN-CHIEF'S, MEDITERRANEAN, PLANS, JUNE 1940

(a) *From Admiralty to Commander-in-Chief, Mediterranean, 414*   1840/5/6/40

In view of increasing importance of Mediterranean and the necessity for Admiralty knowing your exact dispositions and intended movements in the immediate future, request you will signal this information more fully than has been previously necessary.

(b) *From Commander-in-Chief, Mediterranean, to Admiralty*   2317/6/6/40

Reference 1840/5th June from Admiralty. My intentions at onset of hostilities are entirely governed by short notice to carry out the operation for occupation of Crete.

The actual occupation will be carried out by two cruisers carrying troops supported by a Division of Destroyers, followed a day later by four French Cruisers now at Beirut ready to embark troops.

2. All rest of the light forces, less Third Cruiser Squadron, together with a substantial part of the Battle Fleet will be required to cover operations and will leave Alexandria for area west of Crete as soon as it is ordered.

3. One of Third Cruiser Squadron is maintained on patrol in Kithera Channel, remainder at Port Said to ensure safety of Canal. The two river gunboats will also shortly be in the Canal Area to assist in the defence.

4. The submarine patrol off Crete will be augmented by patrols off Augusta, Taranto, Straits of Otranto, Tobruk, and Dodecanese. Minelaying at Augusta and off Cape St. Maria di Leuca.

5. It is strongly urged that the occupation of Crete should be proceeded with, whatever the political situation, as it is desired to use Suda Bay as a fuelling base during operations in Central Mediterranean and Aegean.

6. Should the Cretan operation not be ordered it seems operations by the Fleet must be unfortunately governed by Italian action, but when war is imminent it is intended that a strong force including battleships should proceed westward at first, countering Italian action on Malta or in other directions. This movement may be accompanied by sweep of Dodecanese and North African area, or by submarine hunt south of Crete or in Kaso and Kithera channels.

7. Should Malta be subjected to seaborne attack it is intended to move with the whole Fleet to its relief. An attack on Port Augusta may be best method of affording relief to Malta, but it is hoped to test out the enemy's air and submarine strength before operating so close off his coast.

8. If and when adequate reconnaissance has been established, working from Tunisia or Malta, it may be possible to keep a force of cruisers and destroyers in the central area almost permanently to prey on Libyan traffic. They would use Malta or a Greek island for fuelling at night.

9. Should Turkey enter war on our side, operations against Dodecanese will probably be required and it is proposed at outset to interrupt Dodecanese communications with Italy.

10. With reference to paragraph 2 and 6 above, after meeting other calls there are insufficient destroyers remaining to take whole Battle Fleet to sea together.

(c) *From Admiralty to Commander-in-Chief, Mediterranean*   0028/11/6/40

Your 2317/6 para. 5. Regret that for political reasons occupation of Crete can only be carried out as authorised in Admiralty 1728/30/5.[1]

Ref. para. 10. Shortage of destroyers and handicap it imposes on you is fully realised, but situation in Home Waters prevents any further reinforcements.

(*See also Appendix E.18 for Admiralty directive on Italy and Greece.*)

---

[1] *Comment.* – i.e. authority would be given only if Italy attacked Greek territory.

APP. C.6 MEDITERRANEAN, SEPTEMBER 1939–OCTOBER 1940

5
HAIFA CONFERENCE

From Commander-in-Chief, Mediterranean, to Admiralty 0131/7/6/40

Haifa Conference concluded 4th June:–

Dodecanese

    1. (*a*) Turks still wedded to intention capture Rhodes by assault but have no plan ready. No prospect of success for some time.

       (*b*) Franco-British proposal was for capturing smaller islands first.

       (*c*) French pressed strongly for Weygand's proposal to concentrate air forces of three nations for crushing blow, then dispersing and re-concentrating for similar action when opportunity offered.

    2. Turks opposed to any preliminary action against islands until assault on Rhodes, except such naval and air action as needed to obtain command of sea and air. They will provide no air force for 1 (*c*). British also are unable to provide.

    3. Conference considered that decision on para. 1 must be settled now by Commanders-in-Chief.

    4. Agreed essential to capture Rhodes as soon as possible. Planning proceeding.

    5. Project held up until suitable craft for movement of force in dark hours from Marmaris and Fethiyeh to Rhodes are available. Mediterranean being combed. Early despatch of M.L.C's from United Kingdom urged.

    7. Made clear that with Italy hostile Allied Naval force could not be available initially inside Straits or in Black Sea.

    9. Conference considered successful.

    11. French consider Turks will not enter war till after seeing result of first naval action, but British attachés do not agree with this opinion.

6
FORCE H
(*a*) Need for reinforcements at Gibraltar

From F.O.C.N.A. to Admiralty T.O.O. 1522/25/6/40

As result of French collapse there are now no forces in Western Mediterranean between Gibraltar and Italian Fleet base.

    2. Aircraft at Gibraltar, six Londons and three Swordfish are inadequate for reconnaissance necessary to give warning to approach from East of enemy force.

    3. Number of destroyers available at Gibraltar at any time probably not exceeding eight. These are too few to provide for patrol, convoy, escort and screen for three large ships.

    4. No cruiser available to support patrol in event of raid.

    5. If raid by Italian surface force took place first warning might well be arrival of first shot.

    6. There are no alternative bases near.

    7. V.A. (A) and I would like to be informed of future policy for employment of forces now based Gibraltar.

    8. Urgent requirements are (*a*) Sunderlands for distant reconnaissance; (*b*) At least three modern cruisers to support patrol and protect Ark Royal as Hood alone could not deal with divided enemy forces; (*c*) Submarines; (*d*) More destroyers.

(*b*) Duties

From Admiralty to Flag Officers, Home and Abroad (to include Australian Commonwealth Naval Board, New Zealand Naval Board, N.H.Q., Ottawa).

T.O.O. 1724/28/6/40

    1. A detached Squadron known as Force H under the command of Vice-Admiral Sir James Somerville has

been constituted as follows:– H.M. Ships *Ark Royal, Hood, Resolution, Valiant, Arethusa, Faulknor, Foxhound, Fearless, Escapade, Forester, Foresight, Escort.*

2. The following ships will join Force H when they enter the limits of the North Atlantic:–

H.M. Ships *Nelson, Enterprise, Delhi, Fame, Fury,* H.M.C. Ships *St. Laurent, Skeena.*

3. Force H will for the present be based at Gibraltar.

4. Subject to any instructions which may be given by the Admiralty the tasks of Force H will be:–

(*a*) To prevent units of the Italian Fleet from breaking out of the Mediterranean.

(*b*) To carry out offensive operations against the Italian Fleet and Italian coasts. (See below.*)

From Admiralty to S.O. Force H, (R) F.O.C.N.A. 405, V.A.A. 391   T.O.O. 1738/28/6/40

1. Reference para. 4 (*b*)* of my 1724/28. You are to inform Admiralty in advance of your intentions regarding operations against the Italian coast.

2. The 13th Destroyer Flotilla to be placed at your disposal for any operations for which destroyers immediately under your command are not adequate.

3. When Force H is in harbour the destroyers attached to it are to assist in the patrol of the Straits of Gibraltar as required by F.O.C.N.A.

(*c*) *Decision to attack French ships at Oran*

This decision was taken at a War Cabinet meeting on 27th June 1940 (War Cabinet Minutes (40) 184, Minute 5, Confidential Annex), and on 30th June 1940 the Chiefs of Staff produced an Aide-Memoire:– 'Implications of Action contemplated in respect of certain French ships.'

(*Extract of Aide-Memoire, C.O.S. Committee, 30th June, 1940.*)

We have five alternative courses of action in regard to the French Navy:–

(*a*) To ask them to join us actively.

(*b*) To ask them to lie up in our ports, on the condition that they were not used against the Germans, unless the latter infringed the Armistice terms.

(*c*) To induce the French to demilitarize.

(*d*) On the assumption that the above alternatives were unsuccessful to take no forcible action, but hope that events 'will somehow turn in our favour.'

(*e*) In the last resort to take action against the French fleet at Oran.

It is considered that the last alternative should be adopted, and that the operation contemplated against the French Fleet at Oran, Operation Catapult, should be carried out as soon as possible. In reaching this conclusion the main considerations were that:–

(*a*) Unless this action was taken the French Fleet would sooner or later fall into the hands of the Germans and be used against us; for, 'in the light of recent events we can no longer place any faith in French assurances.' If so, the balance of capital ships' strength would be altered in the enemy's favour.

(*b*) We had to concentrate the maximum possible naval strength in Home Waters to meet the threat of invasion; but we must accept, as an unavoidable risk in the meantime, the temporary dispersion of strength entailed by sending a force to Oran.

(*c*) As a result of our action the French might become actively hostile; but if we carried out our intention of including France in the blockade it would only be a matter of time before they became so in any case, and to hasten this hostility did not outweigh the previous arguments.

(*d*) *A.M. 0103/2/7/40 and French account of Admiral Oden'hal's interview with D.C.N.S. on 1st July, 1940*

The text of message 0103/2/7/40 was as follows:–

To F.O. Force H

    repeated C.-in-C., Mediterranean 881   *Date: 2/7/40*

From Admiralty

AIDAC

My 0435/29 and your 1514/29

His Majesty's Government have decided that the course to be adopted is to be as follows:–

(A) French Fleet at Oran and Mers-el-Kebir is to be given four alternatives:

(1) To sail their ships to British Harbours and continue to fight with us.

(2) To sail their ships with reduced crews to a British port from which the crews would be repatriated whenever desired.

In the case of Alternatives (1) or (2) being adopted, the ships would be restored to France at the conclusion of the war or full compensation would be paid if they are damaged meanwhile. If French Admiral accepts alternative 2, but insists that ships should not be used by us during the war you may say we accept this condition for so long as Germany and Italy observe the Armistice terms, but we particularly do not wish to raise the point ourselves.

(3) To sail their ships with reduced crews to some French port in the West Indies such as Martinique.

After arrival at this port they would either be demilitarised to our satisfaction or, if so desired, be entrusted to United States jurisdiction for the duration of the war. The crews would be repatriated.

(4) To sink their ships.

(B) Should the French Admiral refuse to accept all of the above alternatives and should he suggest that he should demilitarise his ships to our satisfaction at their present berths, you are authorised to accept this further alternative provided that you are satisfied that the measures taken for demilitarisation can be carried out under your supervision within six hours and would prevent the ships being brought into service for at least one year, even at a fully equipped dockyard port.

(C) If none of the above alternatives is accepted by the French you are to endeavour to destroy ships in Mers-el-Kebir but particularly *Dunquerque* and *Strasbourg*, using all means at your disposal. Ships at Oran should also be destroyed if this will not entail any considerable loss of civilian life.

(D) Communication to be made to French Admiral follows (message 0108/2/7 attached).

(E) It is most undesirable that you should have to deal with the French Fleet at sea, and consequently about 12 hours' warning, as suggested in your 0812/1, is not acceptable. Hence, you should arrive in the vicinity of Oran with your force, at whatever time you select, and send your emissary ashore, subsequently taking such action as you consider fit with your force in the period before the time limit given expires.

(F) If first alternative is accepted ships should proceed to a United Kingdom port rather than Gibraltar. If second alternative is accepted ships should proceed to a United Kingdom port unless French much prefer Gibraltar.

(G) In view of the strength of the defences at Algiers and the impossibility of avoiding the destruction of the town, it is not considered justifiable to carry out a separate operation against that place.

(H) These are your final instructions, for the case of your finding the French Fleet in harbour which were decided on after receipt of your 1220/1.

(I) Further instructions follow as regards action to be taken if French Fleet is met at sea.

0103/2,
Secretary to 1st Sea Lord.

In connection with para. (B) of message 0103/2/7, the prospect of some of the Vichy French ships demilitarising 'at their present berths', in this case at Oran, was mentioned in all probability as a result of the visit to the Admiralty on 1st July, of the French Naval Attaché, Admiral Oden'hal. There is unfortunately no record amongst British official documents of this visit, but a description of Admiral Oden'hal's interview with Vice-Admiral Philips (D.C.N.S.) is given in French records.

On 30th June, Admiral Darlan telegraphed to the French Naval Mission in London as follows:–

'5202. Situation renders repetition of demand in your 1845 pointless. Stop. Italian Government authorises the stationing of our effective fleet either in Toulon or North Africa. Stop. I have firm hope that the German Government, whose reply is awaited, will also agree. Stop. In these conditions, all the

English pretexts for blockading our forces fall down, and I ask you to insist that our warships and merchant ships are set free.'

This message actually reached Oden'hal on 1st July, in the following form:–

'Italy authorises the location of the fleet with reduced crews at Toulon and in North Africa. I have every hope … (remainder indecypherable).'

Admiral Oden'hal sought and obtained an interview with the D.C.N.S. in the course of which he stated that 'according to a message, the text of which had not been very clear when it reached me, the French government had firm hopes of obtaining permission to station the fleet at Toulon *and* in North Africa.' Thus it seems clear that the part of Darlan's message to Oden'hal relating to the 'location of the fleet with reduced crews at Toulon *and* in North Africa' was delivered verbally by Oden'hal to the D.C.N.S., but not left in writing, and that the Admiralty had this in mind when framing para. (B) of their 0103/2/7.

It will be noted that Darlan's full message referred to 'our effective fleet being stationed etc. …', and that it did not refer to demilitarisation. Moreover, the German and Italian Armistice Commission retained *ultimate* control, nor was there any suggestion at any time of permitting British control of demilitarisation of French ships in a French port. In this respect, of course, the situation at Oran was vastly different from Alexandria.

7

BRITISH NAVAL POLICY IN MEDITERRANEAN, JULY 1940

(a) Admiralty Plan

From Admiralty to Commander-in-Chief, Mediterranean; S.O. Force H T.O.O. 0227/15/7 and 2300/16/7

A. Policy of H.M. Government is to maintain a strong force in the Eastern Mediterranean as long as possible, and also to maintain a force at Gibraltar.

B. The role of these forces would be:–

(i) *Eastern Mediterranean Force*

In accordance with the policy you are adopting.

(ii) *Gibraltar Force*

Control of the western exit of the Mediterranean, and to carry out offensive operations against the coast of Italy as far as possible.

C. Desirable to consider what the composition of the two forces should be in order to carry out the above.

D. In any re-distribution there must be:–

(*a*) A long term policy, as time will be necessary for a re-distribution of ammunition reserves, etc.

(*b*) A short term policy of the re-distributions, which are desirable at the present time.

E. Factors to be taken into account:–

(i) The role of the Eastern Force and Force H, as given above.

(ii) The strength and possible disposition of the Italian Battlefleet.

(iii) Air menace.

(iv) Repair facilities.

F Re E (ii), at the moment the Italian Battlefleet only consists of two ships, but there appears no reason why six ships should not be available in a short time.

G. Re E (iii), appears that Italian high bombing is as good as German, and therefore the situation would not be materially altered if the Germans sent high bombing aircraft to Italy. There has, however, been no mention of dive bombing by the Italians, and if the Germans sent some Ju.88 to Italy, the situation would undoubtedly be altered for the worse.

The range of the Ju.88 is 2,000 miles.

H. Re E (iv), possible that you will be able to judge to what extent damage from bombing can be repaired with your facilities in Eastern Mediterranean.

I. On the assumption that *Barham* might be made available for the Mediterranean, you should report what capital ships should be in the Eastern Force and what in Force H.

J. If repair facilities in the Eastern Mediterranean are inadequate to deal with damage from bombing would it be desirable to maintain a spare battleship of 'R' Class in Canal area.

K. Re carriers. On assumption that both *Ark Royal* and *Illustrious* available for Mediterranean, would you prefer that the *Illustrious* should be in the Eastern Mediterranean and *Ark Royal* in the Western, or vice versa? Armour and number of aircraft carried should be taken into account.

L. Also, in view of the lack of shore fighters, do you consider that carriers in the Mediterranean should have a larger proportion of fighters at the expense of T.S.R's?

M. Should any re-distribution of capital ships or carriers be decided upon, should exchange take place through Mediterranean or round the Cape?

Difficult to assess risk in passing ships through the area between Bone/ Sardinia line and Malta.

(b) Commander-in-Chief's, Mediterranean, Plan

From Commander-in-Chief, Mediterranean, to Admiralty, S.O. Force H   T.O.O. 2259/16/7/40

Reference Admiralty 0227/15 following are my views:–

2. Spain is assumed neutral. France semi-hostile. The vital (? strategical) importance of having the North African coast, at least, is evident.

Italian Policy

3. (*a*) In Western Mediterranean the most direct harm to British interests lies in attacks on Gibraltar or a break out into Atlantic. Both seem unlikely while Spain remains neutral, and there is every reason to suppose that Italian Fleet will not go far from its bases.

(*b*) In Eastern Mediterranean there is a concentration of Italian interests. Italians are used to idea that their main danger lies in Eastern Mediterranean dominated by British Fleet.

(*c*) The vulnerable points on Italian west coast are more easily covered by air protection than those in south, owing to relative position of Sardinia and Sicily. On the other hand (? manufacturing) area vital to industry lies in North West.

(*d*) My conclusion from above is that while Italians will keep a certain portion of force to protect their Western coast, particularly with Force H working from Gibraltar, preponderant force will be based Messina, Taranto and Augusta.

British Tasks

4. (*a*) *East*. Destruction of enemy naval forces; protection of Egypt, Palestine and Syria; interruption of Black Sea and Aegean trade, and of Libyan communications.

(*b*) *West*. Interruption of all trade to Italy and possibly France; attacks on Western coasts; control of exit from Mediterranean.

British dispositions

5. My opinion the more powerful force must be in Eastern Mediterranean. Reasons.

Composition of forces

6. (*a*) *Eastern Mediterranean*. *Warspite, Valiant, Malaya*, possibly *Barham* (see below), *Illustrious, Eagle*, two 8-inch cruisers, one A/A cruiser and two convoy sloops, rest of fleet as at present.

(*b*) Comments on (*a*)

Essential there should be at least two capital ships whose guns can cross enemy line at 26,000 yards and who are fast enough to have some hope of catching up with enemy. It is also necessary to have at least two cruisers who can act similarly in van. On 9th July our cruisers were outnumbered, outgunned and outranged, and thus could not control area ahead of battlefleet. *York* and *Exeter* are particularly required owing to being small targets. I am of opinion we are over insured against air in Red Sea and that *Carlisle* should come to Mediterranean with two convoy sloops to provide A/A escort for convoys now being carried out by large cruisers. The Air Forces in Italian East Africa are a waning effort and this is the one place where our Air Force can really get at them. First convoy (B.D. one) up the Red Sea was not attacked at all.

Illustrious and *Eagle* in combination will provide striking force without which faster Italian Fleet cannot be 'fixed', will double also (? large) measure of fighter support without which experience has shown unjustifiable hazards are incurred when operating in Central Mediterranean.

Intend to employ *Eagle* also in Red Sea against Massawa and shore objectives. Ample reserve of fighter and T.S.R. should be provided so that proportion in carrier can be varied to provide very strong fighter support or a powerful striking force according to operation contemplated. *Valiant* would also provide R.D./F. which no ship of present fleet has got. The 'R' class battleships can be released and sent via Cape to Gibraltar or elsewhere, since in face of present scale air attack they are simply a source of constant anxiety.

If *Barham* were available I should welcome her so as to provide a reserve of force, because unlike Western Mediterranean the passage of any reinforcements will be either a major fleet operation or else mean delay of at least six weeks, and if I was meanwhile reduced to two battleships, capital ship force would be on the weak side.

(*c*) *Western Mediterranean*. *Hood*, *Ark Royal*, four *Arethusa* class, one and a half flotillas, one or two 'R' class battleships.

(*d*) *Comments on* (*c*)

The Western Force for reasons already given should not have to meet very heavy forces and is to my mind primarily a raiding force.

It should attack in Gulf of Genoa with objectives such as Turin and Milan as well as coast ports. The 'R' class battleships could cover Straits of Gibraltar and provide support on which to fall back in emergencies.

7. I consider that with forces proposed the Mediterranean can be dominated and Eastern Mediterranean held indefinitely, provided the following matters also receive attention.

(*a*) *Malta*. Proper fighter protection.

Alexandria. As stated in para. 5.

(*b*) Adequate reserves and spares are essential for repairs.

(*c*) Air co-operation. Replacements for flying-boats are essential.

Passage of Reinforcements

8. By carrying out a concerted movement it should be possible to pass reinforcements through Mediterranean, but it would probably be desirable to do it all in one operation.

(*c*) *Senior Officer, Force H, Plan*

From S.O. Force H to Admiralty, Commander-in-Chief, Mediterranean   T.O.O. 1100/18/7/40
Commander-in-Chief, Mediterranean 2259/16 (C.7 (*b*)).

On assumption Spain is neutral, I concur generally, subject to following remarks.

2. Unless Italian morale can be shaken decisively at reasonable cost to ourselves, raids on Italian coast by Naval Forces alone will not assist national object, which I assume is at present to counter attempts to defeat us before winter and to maintain economic pressure.

3. In existing conditions of visibility and daylight which prevent surprise and evasion, and with present poor asdic conditions advantage lies with the enemy. Necessity for oiling destroyers at sea is also a handicap.

4. Raids would, moreover, provide enemy with opportunity he seeks for reducing us by attrition, which in view of future commitments we can ill afford, especially if Gibraltar becomes unusable.

5. Possibility of attacks on Gibraltar developing while Force H is on four days' expedition to Italian coast with only sufficient fuel to return to Gibraltar must be considered also.

6. My conclusion, raids should only be undertaken in exceptionally favourable weather and if (? aircraft) carrier is available. An R.D./F. ship is also essential.

7. Fully concur with Commander-in-Chief, Mediterranean, that raids on N.W. Italy by bombers from United Kingdom should be resumed.

8. On the other hand, sweep by Force H in Western Basin will stifle trade, cause diversion of Italian effort and relieve pressure on Eastern Mediterranean when specific operations are being undertaken by Eastern Force.

9. Possibility of Spain remaining neutral for prolonged period appears remote, and this should be taken into account in allocation of force between east and west.

10. With Gibraltar unusable there appears to be three methods of maintaining control of Atlantic.

(*a*) Covering Force to westward of Gibraltar.

(*b*) Hunting group in focal area.

(*c*) Escort.

11. Para. 10 (*a*) appears only method sufficiently economical to enable force required by Commander-in-Chief, Mediterranean, to be made available.

12. Using Freetown or United Kingdom as bases, efficient cover would be very low and early capture of base in Canary Islands appears to offer only satisfactory solution.

8

AFTER ORAN AND DAKAR
POLICY WITH REGARD TO FRENCH WARSHIPS

From Admiralty to Commanders-in-Chief and Flag Officers Commanding (Home and Abroad)

T.O.O. 0241/12/7/40

(*a*) *Richelieu* has now been dealt with and *Jean Bart* could not complete for a considerable period even in her building yard.

(*b*) Further maintenance of present state of tension between the French Navy and ourselves is very undesirable and might even lead to war with that country.

(*c*) H.M. Government have consequently reviewed our policy regarding the French Navy and have decided to take no further action in regard to the French ships in French Colonial or North African ports. We shall, of course, however, reserve the right to take action in regard to French warships proceeding to enemy controlled ports. So far as submarines are concerned we shall follow rules which were first generally accepted in the Nyon Convention, and subsequently acted upon during the present war in respect of Italian submarines while that country was neutral. These rules are (1) that submarines found submerged outside certain limited areas to be agreed upon will be treated as hostile; (2) that submarines on the surface outside the same areas will be treated as hostile unless accompanied by a French surface warship.

(*d*) It is desired that this policy as given in para. (*c*) be communicated via Naval channels to the French Admiralty and the Commander-in-Chief, Mediterranean, or in his absence C.S.3 is accordingly requested to inform Admiral Godfroy and to ask that the French will propose submarine exercise areas if they wish to make use of them.

No action is to be taken by other addresses.

(*e*) Pending further instructions ships must be prepared for attack when meeting a French warship but should not, repeat not, fire the first shot.

Admiralty General Message (Home and Abroad) 2326/12/7/40

For the present French warships under control of French Government should be treated as neutral war vessels if approaching a defended port.

9

(*a*) *Admiralty Proposals for reinforcements and ammunition*

To Commander-in-Chief, Mediterranean, Rep. V.A. Force H.55 from Admiralty 19/7/40

Your 2259/16. Part 1 of my 1914/19

A. It is probable that an exchange will be made between *Hood* and *Renown* as the latter has better A/A armament and deck protection. Also, if a battle-cruiser and *Ark Royal* are required to hunt for a raider in the Atlantic *Renown* is more suitable on account of her better endurance.

B. As regard Capital Ship strength in the Eastern Mediterranean. Until the situation clears up as regards invasion it is not considered that *Barham* can be spared from Home Waters. It is proposed therefore that only *Valiant* should join you.

C. *Illustrious* and *Eagle* would both form part of the Eastern Mediterranean Fleet.

D. The only way of providing you with two 8-inch cruisers without weakening the cruiser strength in Home Waters, which would be undesirable at the present time, is to take either *Ramillies* or *Royal Sovereign* for troop convoys in the Indian Ocean, thus releasing 8-inch cruisers.

E. Until such time as you get *Barham* it is presumed you would like to retain the other 'R' class. Part 2 follows.

Part 2 of my 1914/19.

F. The question of how *Valiant* and *Illustrious* can join you is largely linked up with the question of reserve ammunition, which comes under two headings:–

(*a*) 15-inch 6 C.R.H. shell for *Warspite* and *Valiant*.

(*b*) 4.5-inch high angle for *Valiant* and *Illustrious*.

G. As regards 15-inch 6 C.R.H. shell, the present situation in the Eastern Mediterranean is that *Warspite* has on board 800 rounds. In addition there are 360 rounds in reserve at Alexandria.

H. If *Valiant* joins you through the Mediterranean she should arrive with 800 rounds on board less any expended on passage, and there would then be only 360 rounds as a reserve for both *Warspite* and *Valiant*, unless some were brought through in ammunition carriers with *Valiant*.

I. In view of our extremely small reserves of these shells it is not considered that more than 200 should be risked in ammunition carriers, passing through the Mediterranean, and only 100 in one ship.

J. In order to bring the necessary reserve for *Warspite* and *Valiant* up to 1,200 in all at Alexandria 200 are being sent from Halifax and 400 will be sent from the United Kingdom but of these only 150 could arrive in nine weeks. The remainder would not arrive for at least 12 weeks. Part 3 follows.

Part 3 of my 1914/19.

K. As regards 4.5-inch high angle ammunition for *Valiant* and *Illustrious*. At the present time there are 800 rounds at Alexandria.

L. Allowing for:–

(1) Two outfits in reserve for *Valiant* and *Illustrious* which totals 18,000 rounds.

(2) The two ships between them might fire 7,000 rounds on passage through Mediterranean.

(3) *Illustrious* and *Valiant* between them could embark 11,000 rounds in addition to outfit, the amount which would have to go by freight would be 13,200 rounds.

As, however, our total reserves are on the low side it is not considered that more than 3,000 rounds in each of two ammunition carriers should be risked through the Mediterranean, leaving 7,200 rounds to go by the Cape.

M. If *Valiant* and *Illustrious* are to join you through the Mediterranean it will be essential for two ammunition carriers of 16 knots to accompany them, with the possibility that if these ships are sunk or damaged so that they have to scuttle themselves, you might find yourself with very small reserves of ammunition for *Warspite* and *Valiant* as regards 15-inch shells, and for *Valiant* and *Illustrious* as regards 4.5-inch high angle. Part 4 of my 1914/19 follows:–

N. The only alternative to the above and one which would delay *Valiant* and *Illustrious* reaching you is to send the whole of the ammunition out via the Cape, in which case *Valiant* and *Illustrious* could either proceed via the Cape, sailing in the near future, or they could proceed through the Mediterranean in about 2½ months' time so that their arrival coincided with the arrival of their reserve ammunition.

O. If the reinforcement took place in the near future through the Mediterranean the opportunity would be taken to send 2,000 rounds of 6-inch Mark 23 ammunition in each of the ammunition carriers referred to in paragraph (M).

P. If the reinforcement took place through the Mediterranean it would be desirable that in addition to the two ammunition carriers referred to above the following ships should be passed through at the same time.

(*a*) One ship, 15 knots, containing:– 12 Hurricanes for Malta, 12 Hurricanes for Middle East, 12 heavy and 10 light H.A. guns for Malta.

(*b*) One ship, 16 knots with personnel for Hurricanes.

Q. Request your remarks.

(b) Commander-in-Chief's, Mediterranean, views on reinforcements etc.

From Commander-in-Chief, Mediterranean, to Admiralty　　　　　　　　T.O.O. 1301/21/7/40

Reference Admiralty 1914/19 (C.9 (a))

1. I do not consider it would be prudent in present circumstances to risk this precious ammunition through the Mediterranean even in 16 knot ships.

2. 15-inch ammunition situation can be accepted for a time, as even if *Warspite* and *Valiant* expended half an outfit during operation of getting *Illustrious* and *Valiant* through they would not be likely to need any more ammunition for a time. In emergency *Warspite* could adjust her material to use 15-inch 4 C.R.H. ammunition held in reserve for 'R' Class battleships.

3. I propose whole of reserve of ammunition mentioned, less additional 4.5-inch that can be packed into *Valiant* and *Illustrious*, should be sent in fastest ships possible (certainly of not less than 16 knots) round the Cape of Good Hope now or as soon as ships can be loaded. I would arrange special escort through Red Sea. If these ships proceed with utmost despatch they should arrive Alexandria in about five weeks.

4. Meantime suggest sending extra 4.5-inch ammunition to Gibraltar for *Valiant* and sail her and *Illustrious* through the Mediterranean about 14 days after ammunition carrier leaves United Kingdom. They should then be here only two or three days ahead of their meeting.

5. Further 12 Hurricanes for Malta to be flown off by *Argus* as already arranged for first 12. Maintenance personnel and as large a supply of stores as possible to be embarked in H.M.S. *Valiant* who would call at Malta by night.

6. A/A guns for Malta would have to be sent in the fast ammunition ship round Cape of Good Hope though perhaps light guns could go in *Valiant*.

7. With reference to para. 4 is it not possible to obtain some really fast ships of the order of 25 knots for this work, even if not primarily designed to take cargo? This would save at least a week and ships could perhaps also bring some aircraft and stores so badly needed with orders to A.O.C., Mediterranean.

8. As regards 8-inch cruisers on escort work. I have not enough destroyers to take four battleships and *Eagle* to sea simultaneously in any case. Even one 8-inch cruiser would be very welcome at the earliest moment.

9. Docking is a most difficult problem at Alexandria and it is highly desirable that any ship joining eastern fleet should have been recently docked.

(c) Admiralty decision on composition of Mediterranean Fleet and Force H.

From Admiralty to Commander-in-Chief, Mediterranean, S.O. Force H.　　　　　　　　1700/25/7/40

1. My 0142/14/7 to Commander-in-Chief, H.F., and 0227/15/7 to Commander-in-Chief, Mediterranean (Appendix C.7 (a)). Decided that, subject to any change in the general situation, the forces operating under Commander-in-Chief, Mediterranean, and S.O., Force H, will be as follows:–

2. *Mediterranean Fleet*:–

Warspite, *Valiant*, *Malaya*, *Ramillies* being later relieved by *Barham*, *Illustrious*, *Eagle*, *Kent*, *York*, *Gloucester*, *Liverpool*, *Orion*, *Neptune*, *Sydney*, *Calcutta* and *Coventry*.

Destroyers as at present.

Sloops under consideration.

Submarines as at present with reinforcements already ordered from China.

Force H

3. *Renown*, *Resolution*, *Ark Royal*, *Sheffield*, *Enterprise*.

Destroyers as at present.

4. *Royal Sovereign* will join the *Halifax* Convoy Escort Force.

5. It is anticipated that preliminary movements will be completed so that the principal reinforcements for the Mediterranean Fleet will be ready to leave Gibraltar on or about 15th August.

(d) Chiefs of Staff appreciation of Middle East position, 3rd July, 1940.

[C.O.S. (40) 521 – Annex]

On 3rd July, 1940 the Chiefs of Staff sent a telegram to the British High Commissioners in all the Dominions, the Commander-in-Chief in India, and the Commanders-in-Chief, Middle East and the Mediterranean. This message was an answer to messages received between 22nd and 29th June, 1940 from:

(a) The British High Commissioner in Australia
(b) The British Ambassador in Cairo
(c) The British Ambassador in Baghdad
(d) The Commander-in-Chief, India

The Chiefs of Staff stated that the maintenance of our position in the Middle East was necessary for the successful prosecution of the war, and particularly to facilitate our economic blockade of Europe, also for the security of the Anglo-Iranian oilfields.

Our safety depended on the defence of:–

(a) Egypt and the Sudan, centre of the Middle East, which controlled the Suez Canal.
(b) Iraq, for control of oil supplies in Iraq and Iran, and to safeguard the Baghdad-Haifa route.
(c) Palestine, which included Haifa.
(d) Aden, essential to the Red Sea line of communication.
(e) Kenya, our second line of defence in Africa, and a valuable base for operations against Italian East Africa.

Our policy must at present be generally defensive. The possibility of a German attack on Egypt must be taken seriously, but as long as the Fleet could be retained in the Eastern Mediterranean our existing forces were enough to deal with a purely Italian attack. Morale and maintenance in the Italian Air Force were poor; and the German Air Force was likely to be fully occupied in the near future with attacks on Great Britain. If, however, they were able to attack Alexandria it might become untenable as a fleet base. It was hoped that Turkey might oppose a German or Italian attack through the Balkans on the Middle East, but the threat was relatively distant.

It was most important that Syria should not be occupied by the enemy. From the military point of view its occupation by the Turks had much to commend it, but there were political disadvantages. The situation in Syria affected the defence of Iraq, which itself was in a disturbed state, and Iran was growing hostile. It was intended to send a division from India to Iraq.

In the Red Sea area our action against Italian aircraft and submarines had been successful, and though we could not rely on the French being able to hold out at Djibouti the prospects of making the Red Sea route safe was promising.

It was agreed that the defences of the Middle East should be strengthened as soon as possible. But a large scale air offensive against Great Britain, and possibly invasion, were probable; and we were short of equipment necessary to meet even these threats.

The Chiefs of Staff concluded: 'Our policy must therefore be to concentrate our immediate efforts on the defence of the United Kingdom, and to start releasing equipment for the Middle East when we can more clearly judge the situation following the impending trial of strength here. This may not be for two months. Meanwhile we shall endeavour to send anything we can spare.'

10
POLICY FOR MALTA

(a) From Commander-in-Chief, Mediterranean, to Admiralty 2015/2218/40

1. 243. There appears to me to be a need for defining more definitely the policy concerning Malta.

2. In my view that policy should be to bring base defences at the earliest possible moment to such a state that we can operate offensive from island with all three services, secure in the knowledge that defences are efficient to (? repulse) any scale of retaliatory action which enemy may produce.

3. At present various deficiencies, notably lack of civilian air-raid shelters, inadequate anti-aircraft defences, and lack of underground protection for certain vital services are such that if we provoke a really heavy scale retaliation the civilian morale would rapidly fall to a point when the population would become a grave menace

instead of an assistance to the garrison in resisting attack. Moreover until there is greater protection Malta is of little use to us as a base, and its invaluable docking and repair facilities are lost to us.

4. That the Service policy on this subject is not co-ordinated is evident from the fact that whilst N.O.I.C., Malta, holds views expressed above, the War Office are at the moment considering sending a force to be based at Malta for offensive raids into enemy territory, whilst the R.A.F. are about to send bomber squadron to work from Malta against Italian targets.

5. N.O.I.C., Malta, informs me that deficiency referred to in para. 3 can be remedied and all work completed by Spring, 1941, if H.M. Government will decide now to supply materials and if energetic and co-ordinated action is taken to see that requirements are shipped with minimum of delay.

6. The rendering safe of Malta is key to our Mediterranean strategy and provides the first step in developing our offensive policy. As our grip on Italy and the Mediterranean increases so will our need of Malta.

7. Details of requirements will be the subject of separate signal but for the moment I submit that our policy should be as follows:–

(*a*) Offensive action from Malta should be restricted to attacks on sea targets and to reconnaissance.

(*b*) We should aim to be ready to make full use of Malta offensively by April, 1941.

(*c*) That by that date: 1. A force of cruisers and destroyers can be permanently based at island. 2. It will be reasonably safe to carry out dockings, refits, and repairs to H.M. Ships. 3. A submarine flotilla can be based at island. 4. Sufficient protection and aerodromes available to work bomber and reconnaissance squadrons and four squadrons of fighters. 5. Raiding forces of troops can operate based at Malta.

8. It may, of course, be possible that some requirements can be met before April, 1941, but our offensive policy, so far as use of Malta is concerned, should be graded to be such that defences of island are sufficient to deal with any retaliatory action likely to be provoked.

9. Are Chiefs of Staff fully satisfied that Malta with its present defences can stand up to a determined effort to capture fortress backed up by the immense scale air attack that can be brought to bear?

Personally my doubts on this point cause me considerable concern.

(*b*) *From Admiralty to Commander-in-Chief, Mediterranean* 1830/25/8/40

Your 2015/22. Admiralty fully concur as to necessity for bringing base defences of Malta to such a state that we can operate offensively from the Island. Matter is already under discussion in Chiefs of Staff Committee, but delay is, of course, due to provision of necessary forces and equipment.

(*c*) *From Admiralty to Commander-in-Chief, Mediterranean* 1758/30/8/40

My 1830/25. Chiefs of Staff Committee have agreed that anti-aircraft defences of Malta should be built up to strength of 112 Heavy, 60 Light A/A guns by April 1941 and if possible Fighter strength to be brought up to four squadrons. No intention of stationing bomber squadron at Malta at this stage.

Intend to establish a flight of G.R. aircraft there within the next month.

2. Governor and Commander-in-Chief, Malta have been informed of details of manning and provision of A/A guns by the War Office. Air Officer Commanding-in-Chief, Middle East, has been informed of intentions regarding aircraft.

11

REQUIREMENTS FOR ATTACK ON LIBYAN COMMUNICATIONS, AUTUMN 1940

(*a*) *From Admiralty to Commander-in-Chief, Mediterranean,* 185   0040/2/10/40

IMPORTANT – A.I.D.A.C.

A. The intensification of the attack on Egypt possibly with the assistance of Germany must depend to a large extent on sea-borne supplies reaching Libya.

B. It is realised that with the Fleet based at Alexandria and with the present strength of your Fleet and degree of air reconnaissance it is impossible to maintain an adequate force in the Central Mediterranean to cut permanently the Italy-Libya lines of communication.

REQUIREMENTS FOR ATTACK ON LIBYAN COMMUNICATIONS, AUTUMN 1940   APP. C.11

C. The additional submarines now reaching you together with those we hope to send you in the future may cause interruption but cannot stop them altogether.

D. It would appear possible to cut these lines of communication if you had the following:–

(1) Sufficient light forces at Malta to enable the lines of communication between Italy and the Western part of Libya to be controlled.

This requires not only adequate air reconnaissance to prevent these light forces being surprised but also sufficient A/A and fighter aircraft to make Malta tenable as a base for the light forces.

(2) Adequate air reconnaissance to prevent light forces being surprised when operating from Alexandria with the object of cutting Italian communications to the Eastern part of Libya.

E. You will realise that with our many commitments at the present time it is impossible to provide sufficient reinforcements of either surface craft, aircraft or A/A guns to deal with the above.

F. It would be a great help, however, if you could give an indication of the minimum, repeat minimum, reinforcements that would be required under the following categories:–

(1) Cruisers.
(2) Destroyers.
(3) Reconnaissance aircraft at Malta.
(4) Reconnaissance aircraft at Alexandria.
(5) Fighter aircraft at Malta.
(6) A/A guns at Malta.

G. It is realised that the final answer is to base the Battle Fleet at Malta but this would require the full scale of defences of 112 H.A. guns.

The reinforcements referred to in para. F would be those required for an interim period.

0040/2
1st S.L.

(b) From Commander-in-Chief, Mediterranean, to Admiralty, (R) A.O. Commander-in-Chief, Middle East, Commander-in-Chief, Middle East, N.O. I/C, Malta. 179   *184515/10/40*

IMPORTANT

705. Admiralty Telegram 0040/2. There are two opposing aspects of Central Mediterranean problems:– (a) The cutting of Libyan communications, (b) The security of Malta.

2. As regards (a) to do the work effectively three things are needed:– (i) Efficient air reconnaissance; (ii) Suitable light striking forces, surface and submarine; (iii) Suitable air striking force. I feel that if we are to take the risks to security to Malta referred to in paragraph 10 it is essential that the forces at Malta should be of such effectiveness that risk is justified.

3. Effective air reconnaissance. As stated in my 1259/2 our present shore-based reconnaissance failed to locate the enemy on 29th September,[1] though he was at sea with his entire fleet, and it was left to Fleet reconnaissance to do so. Moreover it has to be admitted that our Central Mediterranean reconnaissance has so far been a failure. We have only succeeded in spotting a single convoy on its way across to Libya. We suspect they may be going in driblets via Pantellaria Channel, Tripoli and then coasting to Benghazi but this is still supposition. No convoys have been found going straight across from Eastern Italy.

4. From above it will be seen that what is really needed is all round reconnaissance from Malta. At present attempt is being made to do the Western, Cape Bon-Sicily area by Swordfish but they have not suitable range or speed.

5. A further necessity is periodical examination of Italian bases. This can adequately be done by Glenn Martins.

---

1 It was known later that shore-based reconnaissance machines reported the enemy at 0620/30th and 1050/30th, but neither report reached the Commander-in-Chief. The cause of failure to locate the enemy on 29th September may have been the fact of their not leaving harbour until late in the evening (see Section 86).

6. With reference to paragraphs (*d*) (i) and (ii) of Admiralty Telegram 0040/2. The problem of covering force operating from Alexandria is fortunately the same for those operating from Malta, as Italian forces based outside Italy and Sicily are negligible.

7. I consider to carry out duties in paragraphs four to six we need Glenn Martins now at Malta (for duties in paragraph five) and a force of 10 I.E. and 6 I.R. aircraft of good speed and long range. Not more than half these aircraft should be flying boats owing to their vulnerability; ships are to be at the base. It would appear that Beauforts or craft of equal performance are suitable.

8. Suitable light forces. Our raiding forces must be prepared to deal with an enemy escorting force of four 8-inch cruisers and accompanying destroyers. It must therefore have good speed, gun power and protection, and for this I consider that four *Gloucesters* and four *Tribal* or similar class are desirable. The submarines being provided should be adequate though obviously the more that can be put on patrol at a given time the better.

9. Suitable Air Striking Force. I attach the very greatest importance to this as it provides the only sure way of hitting at enemy heavy ships when our own are out of range on way back to or at Alexandria. Moreover the effect will be to force convoys and Italian Fleet further away from Malta and thus increase time on passage and opportunities for us to get at them. For this duty a T.B. Squadron of Beauforts is suggested.

1845/5 Parts 1 to 9

10. Security of Malta. As no doubt is realised the main difficulty in answering questions on defence (? problems) is that the intensity for attack depends not so much on types and numbers of ships sent to the island as on degree of success they attain against enemy. As stated in my 2015/22/8[1] if we are to avoid a serious threat to Malta itself it appears necessary that in any given period the scale of attack drawn down should not be disproportionate to the state of the defences it has been possible to install. It is only logical therefore to expect the full weight of Italian attack if our light forces work effectively. I cannot therefore well suggest an interim figure to aim at for defences. I feel that (corrupt group) as soon as war appears about to develop successful attack on Libyan communications is becoming essential and hence the need for full scale defences to be built up as quickly as resources will permit, and conditions of accommodation in Malta will allow. All we can do meanwhile is to accept what disparity may exist between scale of attack and means of defence. The risk in fact must be accepted and it will at least be reduced by presence of surface forces. I am in fact prepared now to operate the light force and submarines on scale of (corrupt group) from Malta but surface ships would at present enter harbour at night only.

11. Summary. The answers to paragraph (*f*) of Admiralty Telegram 0040/2 therefore are:–
  (i) Four *Gloucesters* and one 8-inch cruiser. (*Note*. – This force is necessary so long as I can only use Malta by night so as to have a similar force at Alexandria and work relief.)
  (ii) Four *Tribals*.
  (iii) Two, of flying boats and Beauforts.
  (iv) Four I.E. and two I.R. flying boats.
  (v) and (vi) The maximum number of fighters and A/A guns that can possibly be spared, up to the four squadrons of aircraft and (? further) of establishment guns.

Requirements (i) and (ii) are exclusive of present forces in Mediterranean; and rest are inclusive.

12. Another and perhaps more obvious method of stopping the enemy's supplies is not dealt with in Admiralty Message 0040/2. That is making port entries in Libya unusable for shipping by continuous bombing.

This has been to some extent achieved at Tobruk, Derna and Benghazi by the Canal Air Force and Fleet Air Arm, but a much greater scale of air attack is necessary which can only be produced by a large increase in the number of long range bombers in Middle East. Backed by heavy attacks from United Kingdom on embarkation ports in Italy this would be most effective. Tripoli is as yet untouched but I hope to start the process shortly.

Finally I submit that there is much evidence that war is swinging this way. The cardinal factor is time. If we can on this occasion succeed in carrying our disposition ahead of the enemy moves the gain may be immeasurable. It is evident that he will move quickly and the specified (? air attack) when enhanced by German

---

1 Appendix C.10 (a).

aircraft is likely to result in serious (? group omitted) against Malta and might well bring whole of our policy of using island to naught unless we act quickly.

This message is repeated to A.O. Commanding-in-Chief, Middle East, Commander-in-Chief, Middle East, and N.O. in charge, Malta 179. End.

1845/5/10/40

(c) From Commander-in-Chief, Mediterranean, to Admiralty 1155/8/10/40

My 1845/5. Following is a restatement of my requirements for the attack on Libyan communications.

2. Surface forces required extra to those already in Mediterranean all four *Gloucester* class cruisers and one 8-inch cruiser and four *Tribals* or similar class destroyers, allow me to keep a raiding force of four cruisers and four destroyers operating from Malta and to work reliefs for them.

3. Reconnaissance aircraft at Malta should consist of the Glenn Martins already there and a force of about 10 I.E. and 6 I.R. aircraft of good speed and long range. Essential to have longer range torpedo-bombing aircraft than are at present available. Owing to conditions at Malta land aircraft are preferable to flying boats and too great a proportion of the latter is therefore undesirable.

4. As regards protection at Malta it is required to build up to the four fighter squadrons and up to establishment of A/A guns as soon as practicable for reasons given in my 1845/5.

5. At Alexandria four I.E. and two I.R. aircraft boats should suffice.

(d) From Admiralty to Commander-in-Chief, Mediterranean 1144/24/10/40

Your 1845/5. Steps are being taken to bring Hurricanes now at Malta to strength of one squadron. Reconnaissance aircraft at Malta will be increased to total of 12 Glenn Martins. September and October allocation of A/A guns will be advanced in despatch to early November. Thereafter monthly allocations will continue until approved scale is reached.

The two cruisers referred to in para. A of A.T. 0205/18 and the four destroyers accompanying *Barham* are all that can be spared at present. Above represents maximum reinforcements we can spare at present. Hoped it will enable you to do something from Malta if only for short periods.

12

ASSISTANCE TO GREECE AND TURKEY

From Chiefs of Staff, No. 19, Admiralty to Commander-in-Chief, Mediterranean 1724/23/10/40

Following from Chiefs of Staff, No. 19. Considering what we can do to strengthen Greek and Turkish will and ability to resist Axis pressure.

2. *Greece*. We realise importance of preventing Crete falling into enemy hands, hut there can be no question of moving troops into the island until Greece enters the war. In light of reinforcements being sent to you in near future report whether and, if so, when you could prepare a small force for Crete to strengthen local forces or to help them resist Italian attack if already started.

3. *Turkey*. Turkish requirements take the form of complete British air, anti-aircraft and anti-tank units, in addition to material already being supplied under Treaty programme. If assistance were required by Turks now it is obvious that it could only be provided from resources in Middle East, since there would be no time to send anything from United Kingdom. Will you consider and report scale and nature of any support you could provide in this eventuality? If assistance were not required until next spring it might be possible to send help from outside Middle East, but probably even then only at your expense. Your conclusions on possibility of immediate aid should guide Major General Smith during his discussions at Ankara, and he should endeavour to ascertain in detail what Turks would want next spring if threat did not materialise before then.

13

TURKISH ATTITUDE TO BALKAN QUESTIONS, OCTOBER 1940

From N.A., Angora, to Foreign Office (R) Commander-in-Chief, Mediterranean 1700/16/10/40

(a) Turkish Situation

Following from Admiral Kelly begins. Minister for Foreign Affairs came out (? as I) went in for hour's talk with

Marshal Chamak just returned from inspection of Thrace. I understand he was completely satisfied with preparations against any invader. The favourable season also is passed.

2. Turkish Government is unperturbed by Roumanian move, likewise Turkish Embassy in Berlin. They believe it part of encirclement of Russia. German concentration in North Norway threatens Murmansk and Arkangel. Japanese Siberia and Black Sea ports in German hands. Russians are hesitating and will not move unless opportunity favourable for them. Russians are frightened by Polish and French examples and their Finnish experience. Russian plan collapsed on (2 corrupt groups) war of attrition followed by world communism.

3. Turkish Government are prepared for attack both political and military and will stand firm against both. The Turks hold by their treaty with Greece, they will fight if Bulgaria attacks Greece but not if Italy attacks. Greeks refused to include Italy in treaty. Turks will not fight even if German troops attack Greece through Bulgaria. The despatch of Turkish divisions to aid Greece would weaken them and lay them open to attack and easy defeat.

4. Italians (? dislike) prospect of attack from Libya but German support against Turkey would be slow and difficult. Marshal referred to lack of road and rail communications and volunteered that all railways and roads would be destroyed in the event of German successful advance. In the last war Germans with Russians, working from home base in Palestine, could not employ more than two divisions in attack on Egypt.

5. Marshal does not exclude possibility of Russian help to Germany in exchange for freedom of Straits. In 1916 when allied with Turkey, Germany offered to Russia the Straits for a separate peace.

6. Turks have two army corps on Syrian Frontier including cavalry division if Italians give trouble there. Italian efforts to raise Syrian natives unsuccessful. Consider it changes (? picture) for Italians.

7. Air attack on Port Laki heard and seen from Budrum and clouds of smoke from fires.

8. In last war Germans occupied territory greatly superior to present and they laid down their arms. If Turkey and Greece hold out they will do same again.

9. Marshal tells his army if rich and prosperous country like England hold out against air attacks surely poor country like (? Turkey) can run same risks. Turks lost 50,000 in earthquake last year and are willing to lose twenty times that for freedom of their country. (N.A., Angora 1700/16.)

From N.A., Angora, to Foreign Office (R) Commander-in-Chief, Mediterranean   1300/18/10/40

(b) *Assistance for Turkey*

Following from Admiral Kelly ref. tel. 1329 to F.O. from Ambassador Angora, I visited General Asim Gunduz to discuss points raised and informed him I was ready to deal with Naval question at any time.

2. General staff's attitude at present situation.

3. Russian relations with Turkey particularly good but except for material assistance Russia will remain neutral even if Turkey is attacked.

4. If they are in war Turks consider communication with desert very indispensable to ensure corridor to Red Sea and Persian Gulf as well as Egypt.

5. They do not anticipate immediate aggression against Greece, existing Turkish Armies in Thrace on Flank of an advance from North, causing hesitation and possible action against Turkey.

6. General promised great discretion over information given Turkey mission. (N.A., Angora 1300/18.)

From N.A., Angora, to Foreign Office (R) Commander-in-Chief, Mediterranean   1700/18/10/40

(c) *Assistance for Turkey*

Following from Admiral Kelly. My telegram 1300118 and para. 6, Ambassador's telegram 1329 to F.O. I foresee Turks intend this discussion to be confined to questions of help they may expect from us. Following is my interpretation.

2. Naval assistance to an ally does not consist in sending given number of vessels to lie in or even work from ports of that ally. It is given by maintaining command of sea and may be exercised from a distance. We are prepared to accept responsibility for Aegean Sea, except for local defence of Turkish ports, thus leaving whole Turkish naval forces free for Black Sea. Turkish submarines in Black Sea not rigidly bound by restrictions of submarine protocol to work principally against supply ships and transports in attack.

3. Turks will ask for ten destroyers to assist in Black Sea as protection against attacks by hypothetical

submarines from Germany on their sea transport along north coast of Asia Minor, Which must be kept open as long as possible including transport of troops from Caucasus to Thrace. Propose saying naval reinforcements would be available in Mediterranean during winter but how and when they would arrive unforeseeable. If assistance required in Black Sea not yet self-evident as plans for Russian neutrality it would be sent as naval situation permitted.

4. Turks have three lines of defence in Thrace before final European stand at Chatalja and Bulair lines and after will hold Asiatic shore. They can count on full British naval assistance to prevent enemy passage of Marmora and Straits.

5. Naval assistance will be available for any combined operations agreed on either in Syria or Dodecanese. Turkish contribution to be opening of all Turkish contribution to be opening of all Turkish ports to British ships and protection in their defended ports. All possible steps for embodiment of mobile defence to be hurried on. Such obstructions or minefields which cannot be placed before emergency period to be ready at shortest notice. Instructions for entry into defended Turkish ports to be in hands of Naval Attaché well in advance.

6. Turks consider Dodecanese operations will become easier owing to restrictions of blockade.

7. Two things they will press for are naval and air assistance and they do not understand what the first is. (N.A., Angora, 1700/18.)

From Admiralty to N.A., Angora   2230/30/1040

(*d*) *Assistance for Turkey*

Following for Admiral Kelly from First Sea Lord.

Your 1700/18/10.

A. Concur generally in line you propose to take.

B. Your para. 2. Most important that Turks should give their submarines a free hand in the Straits.

C. Your para. 3. Undesirable to enter into definite commitment to send specific numbers. Subject to concurrence of Commander-in-Chief, Mediterranean, you may give general assurance that we shall provide A/S protection if at all possible, but not necessarily with destroyers, and if presence of German submarines proves it necessary.

D. Your para. 4. Concur. All possible naval assistance will be given to prevent enemy passage of Marmora and Straits. The term 'full naval assistance' should not be used as Turks may think this means whole main Fleet.

E. Your para. 5. Presume Turkish ports will be available in all circumstances and not only for combined operations. Use of Turkish port, e.g. Smyrna as advanced base for operation in Sea of Marmora to prevent passage of Straits is essential.

APPENDIX D

(a)

MEDITERRANEAN FLEET COMMAND AND STAFF

AUTUMN 1940

LIMITS OF MEDITERRANEAN COMMAND, 1939/40

Eastern Limit – Suez

Western Limit – Meridian of 5° W. (This passes 20 miles east of Gibraltar. The Rock itself was under the command of the Flag Officer, North Atlantic.)

COMMANDER-IN-CHIEF

Admiral Sir Andrew B. Cunningham, K.C.B., D.S.O.

PERSONAL STAFF

Chief of Staff: Rear Admiral A. U. Willis, C.B., D.S.O.
Captain of the Fleet: Captain R. Shelley
Secretary: Captain *(S)* A. P. Shaw
Flag Captain: Captain D. B. Fisher, O.B.E.
Flag Lieutenant: Lieut. W. A. Starkie
Additional Chief of Staff, R.N., G.H.Q., Cairo: Commodore H. G. Norman

OPERATIONAL AND PLANNING STAFF[1]

S.O. Plans: Captain R. M. Dick, D.S.C.
S.O. Operations: Commander M. L. Power
S.O. Operations and Fleet (N): Commander T. M. Brownrigg
Fleet (T) Officer: Commander W. P. Carne
Fleet (G) Officer: Commander G. Barnard
Fleet W/T Officer: Lieut.-Commander J. Liddell
Fleet Signal Officer: Commander Hon. A Pleydell-Bowerie
Fleet A/S Officer: Commander S. A. Cuthbert
Fleet Aviation Officer: Wing Commander H. L. Macro, D.F.C., A.F.C.
Fleet Engineer Officer: Engineer Captain B. J. H. Wilkinson
Fleet Accountant Officer: Captain (S) E. H. Drayson, O.B.E.

---

1 For full list, see Navy Lists.

MEDITERRANEAN FLEET COMMAND AND STAFF

Fleet Medical Officer: Surgeon Captain C. E. Greeson, M.D., Ch.B.
Fleet Royal Marine Officer: Lieut.-Colonel A. H. G. Reading

INTELLIGENCE STAFF[1]

Chief of Intelligence Staff: Captain H. H. Bousfield
S.O. (I) Mediterranean: Major F. P. C. Lordon, R.M.
S.O. (I) Malta: Major O. M. Haworth-Booth, R.M.
S.O. (I) Alexandria: Captain B. W. de Courcy Ireland, R.M.
S.O. (I) Istanbul: Commander V. Wolfson, R.N.V.R.[2]
Operational and W/T Section: Commander S. N. Blackburn, D.S.C.
   Commander G. A. Titterton
   Lieut.-Commander (S) G. R. Lavers
Submarine Tracking: Mr. R. H. Way
Enemy aircraft plot and enemy air sighting report: Lieut. (S) D. L. Blowers
Merchant Ship Section: Lieut.-Commander A. R. C. Prentis

VICE-ADMIRAL, SECOND IN COMMAND, MEDITERRANEAN FLEET
Vice-Admiral J. C. Tovey, C.B., D.S.O.
(and as Flag Officer Seventh Cruiser Squadron, and V.A. (D), later title –
Vice-Admiral Light Forces (V.A.L.F.))

VICE-ADMIRAL, FIRST CRUISER SQUADRON
Vice-Admiral J. H. D. Cunningham, C.B., M.V.O.

REAR-ADMIRAL, FIRST BATTLE SQUADRON
Rear-Admiral H. D. Pridham-Wippell, C.B., C.V.O.
(*October 1940, became V.A.L.F. and Second in Command, Mediterranean Fleet*)
Rear-Admiral H. B. Rawlings, O.B.E. (*from October 1940*)

REAR-ADMIRAL, THIRD CRUISER SQUADRON
Rear-Admiral E. de F. Renouf, C.V.O.

REAR-ADMIRAL, MEDITERRANEAN AIRCRAFT CARRIERS
Rear-Admiral A. L. St. G. Lyster, C.B., C.V.O., D.S.O.

FLAG OFFICER-IN-CHARGE, MALTA
Vice-Admiral Sir Wilbraham T. R. Ford, K.B.E., C.B.
(*and as Admiral-Superintendent, Malta Dockyard*)

Chief Staff Officer: Captain J. P. Wright, D.S.O.
Flag Captain: E. C. Denison, M.V.O
Secretary: Commander (S) R. H. Johnson

OPERATIONAL STAFF

S.O. Operations: Commander P. H. Calderon
Port W/T Officer: Lieut.-Commander J. M. A. Ennion

---

1 For full list, see Navy Lists.
2 Later, in charge of Security Section under S.O.(I) Mediterranean.

Port A/S Officer: Lieut.-Commander A. H. M. Dunn, D.S.C.
Engineer Captain for Captain of Dockyard's Department: Engineer Captain H. E. Lewis
Supply Officer: Captain (S) F. P. B. Jones
Distributing Authority, Malta (C.B.'s, etc.): Lieut.-Commander (S) A. C. Mathews
Naval Provost Marshal: Major D. A. C. Shephard, R.M. (*Acting Lieut. Colonel from 16/7/40*)

Senior British Naval Officer, Suez Canal Area
(*Short title*: S.B.N.O.S.C.A.)
(*Headquarters*: Ismailia)
Vice-Admiral Sir J. M. Pipon, K.B.E., C.B., C.M.G., M.V.O.

Chief Staff Officer: Captain H. A. Simpson, O.B.E., D.S.C.
Secretary: Commander (S) G. W. Best
Naval Officers-in-Charge:
Port Said: Captain W. B. Hynes, D.S.O.
Port Thewfik: Commander P. R. B. Stevens (Southern entrance to Canal, Suez Bay)
Port Sudan: Commander G. T. Whitehouse, D.S.C., R.N.R.

Rear-Admiral, Alexandria
(*Short title*: R.A. (L))
Rear-Admiral F. Elliott, O.B.E.

Chief Staff Officer: Captain G. H. Creswell, D.S.O., D.S.C.
Flag Captain: Captain R. D. Binney
Captain-Superintendent: Captain W. Y. La R. Beverley
Secretary: Commander (S) H. C. Lockyer
S.O. Operations: Commander C. E. St. Aubyn
A/S Officer: Lieut.-Commander A. S. D. Ryder
A/S Loop Defence (at Agami): Commander E. D. Wallis, V.D., R.N.V.R.
Port W/T Officer: Lieut. A. H. C. Gordon-Lennox
Engineer Captain: L. Gregory, O.B.E.
Commander (S): A. H. Parsons
Surgeon Commander: H. M. Willoughby, M.R.C.S., L.R.C.P., D.P.H., D.T.M. & H.
Base Cypher Officer: Instructor Commander C. W. Winwood-Smith, B.A.
Degaussing Officer: Commander F. J. C. Allen

Naval Officer-in-Charge, Palestine Ports; Base, Haifa
Captain: G. O. Lydekker, O.B.E., D.S.C.
S.O. Operations: Commander G. Warburton, D.S.O.
Secretary: Lieut. (S) J. Hopkins, R.N.V.R.

SHIPS UNDER THE COMMAND OF COMMANDER-IN-CHIEF, MEDITERRANEAN, AUTUMN 1940

FIRST BATTLE SQUADRON

H.M.S.	*Malaya*	Captain A. F. E. Palliser, D.S.C.
	Ramillies	Captain H. T. Baillie-Grohman, O.B.E., D.S.O.
	Royal Sovereign	Captain H. B. Jacomb

MEDITERRANEAN FLEET COMMAND AND STAFF

	Valiant	Captain H. B. Rawlings, O.B.E., A.D.C.
	Warspite	Captain D. B. Fisher, O.B.E.

AIRCRAFT CARRIERS

H.M.S.	*Eagle*	Captain A. R. M. Bridge
		Commander (Flying), Commander C. L. Keighly-Peach
		Air Staff Officer, Lieut.-Commander E. R. S. Jackson
F.A.A.	813 Squadron	Lieut.-Commander N. Kennedy (in command)
	824 Squadron	Lieut.-Commander A. J. Debenham (in command)
H.M.S.	*Illustrious*	Captain D. W. Boyd, D.S.C.
		Commander (Flying), Commander J. I. Robertson
		Air Staff Officer, Commander G. H. Beale
F.A.A.	806 Squadron	Lieut.-Commander C. L. G. Evans, D.S.C. (in command)
	815 Squadron[1]	Commander R. A. Kilroy, D.S.C. (in command)
	819 Squadron	Lieut.-Commander J. W. Hale (in command)

CRUISERS

H.M.S.	*Ajax*	Captain E. D. B. McCarthy
	Berwick	Captain G. L. Warren
	Calcutta	Captain D. M. Lees, D.S.O.
	Caledon	Captain C. P. Clarke
	Calypso	Captain H. A. Rowley
	Capetown	Captain T. H. Back
	Coventry	Captain D. Gilmour
	Delhi	Captain A. S. Russell
	Glasgow	Captain H. Hickling
	Gloucester	Captain F. R. Garside (from July: H. A. Rowley)
	Kent	Captain D. Young-Jamieson
	Liverpool	Captain A. D. Read
	Neptune	Captain R. C. O'Conor
	Newcastle	Captain J. Figgins
	Orion	Captain G. R. B. Back
H.M.A.S.	*Sydney*	Captain J. A. Collins, C.B.
H.M.S.	*York*	Captain R. H. Portal, D.S.C.

DESTROYER DEPÔT SHIP

H.M.S.	*Woolwich*	Captain E. C. Thornton, D.S.C. (from 1st December, 1940)

DESTROYERS, SECOND, TENTH AND FOURTEEN FLOTILLAS

H.M.S.	*Dainty*	Commander M. S. Thomas
	Decoy	Commander E. G. McGregor, D.S.O.
	Defender	Lieut. G. L. Farnfield
	Diamond	Lieut.-Commander P. A. Cartwright
	Gallant	Lieut.-Commander C. P. F. Brown

---

[1] Until 28.7.40, then Lieut. Commander K. Williamson.

APP. D(A) MEDITERRANEAN, SEPTEMBER 1939–OCTOBER 1940

	Greyhound	Commander W. R. Marshall A'Deane, D.S.C.
	Griffin	Lieut.-Commander J. Lee-Barber
	Hasty	Lieut.-Commander L. R. K. Tyrwhitt
	Havock	Commander R. E. Courage, D.S.O., D.S.C.
	Hereward	Lieut.-Commander C. W. Greening
	Hero	Commander H. W. Biggs, D.S.O.
	Hostile	Lieut.-Commander A. F. Burnell-Nugent
	Hyperion[1]	Commander H. St. L. Nicholson, D.S.O. (D2)[1]
	Ilex	Lieut.-Commander P. L. Saumarez, D.S.C.
	Imperial	Lieut.-Commander C. A. de W. Kitcat
	Janus	Commander J. A. W. Tothill
	Jervis	Captain P. J. Mack, D.S.O. (D14)
	Juno	Commander St. J. R. J. Tyrwhitt
	Mohawk	Commander J. W. M. Eaton
	Nubian	Commander R. W. Ravenhill
H.M.A.S	*Stuart*	Captain H. M. L. Waller, R.A.N. (D10)
	Vampire	Lieut.-Commander J. A. Walsh, R.A.N.
	Vendetta	Lieut.-Commander G. L. Cant, R.A.N.
	Voyager	Lieut.-Commander J. C. Morrow, R.A.N.
	Waterhen	Lieut.-Commander J. H. Swain
	Wryneck	Lieut.-Commander R. H. D. Lane
Polish Destroyer	*Garland*	Commander Doroczkowski

SUBMARINE DEPÔT SHIP

H.M.S. *Medway*   Captain S. M. Raw (S1)

SUBMARINES

H.M.S.	*Grampus*	Lieut.-Commander C. A. Rowe
	Odin	Commander K. M. Woods
	Olympus	Lieut.-Commander H. G. Dymott
	Orpheus	Commander C. J. Blake
	Osiris	Lieut.-Commander J. R. G. Harvey
	Oswald	Lieut.-Commander D. A. Fraser
	Otus	Lieut.-Commander E. C. F. Nicolay
	Pandora	Lieut. M. A. Langley
	Parthian	Lieut.-Commander M. G. Rimington
	Phoenix	Lieut.-Commander G. H. Nowell
	Proteus	Lieut.-Commander R. T. Gordon-Duff
	Rainbow	Lieut. E. F. P. Cooper
	Regent	Lieut.-Commander H. C. Browne
	Regulus	Commander J. M. Money

---

1 H.M.S. *Hardy*, Captain B. A. W. Warburton-Lee, Captain (D), 2nd Destroyer Flotilla, in September 1939, left Mediterranean in October 1939.

	Rorqual	Lieut.-Commander R. H. Dewhurst
	Rover	Lieut.-Commander H. A. L. Marsham
	Tetrarch	Lieut.-Commander R. G. Mills, D.S.C.
	Triad	Commander E. R. J. Oddie, D.S.C.
	Trident	Commander G. M. Sladen
	Triton	Lieut.-Commander E. F. Pizey, D.S.O.
	Truant	Lieut.-Commander H. A. V. Haggard

Free French
S/M   *Narval*   Commander Dorous

MONITOR
H.M.S.   *Terror*   Commander H. J. Haynes, D.S.C.

NETLAYER
H.M.S.   *Protector*   Captain R. J. Gardner

REPAIR SHIP
H.M.S.   *Resource*   Captain D. B. O'Connell

FLEET SUPPLY SHIP
R.F.A.   *Reliant*   Master R. C. E. Neyroud

HOSPITAL SHIP
H.M.H.S.   *Maine*   Surgeon Captain M. S. Moore, M.D., B.Ch., D.P.H.

CORVETTES, 10TH GROUP

H.M.S.	*Gloxinia*	Lieut.-Commander A. J. C. Pomeroy, R.N.V.R.
	Hyacinth	Lieut. J. I. Jones, R.N.R.
	Peony	Lieut.-Commander M. B. Sherwood
	Salvia	Lieut.-Commander J. I. Miller, D.S.O., R.N.R.

ARMED BOARDING VESSELS

H.M.S.	*Arpha*	Commander F. M. Smith, R.D., R.N.R.
	Chakla	Commander L. C. Bach, R.D., R.N.R.
	Fiona	Commander A. H. H. Griffith, R.N.R.
	Rosaura	Lieut. L. H. Davies, R.N.R.
	Surf	Lieut.-Commander A. J. McHattie, R.N.R.

ESCORT TRAWLERS, 4TH AND 5TH A/S GROUPS

H.M.S.	*Amber*	Sub. Lieutenant P. Le M. Andrews, R.N.R.
	Bandolero	Lieut.-Commander F. M. W. Harris, R.N.R.
	Beryl	Lieut.-Commander J. C. Bird, D.S.C.
	Coral	Midshipman F. H. Walton, R.N.R.
	Jade	Boatswain J. Hughes
	Loch Melfort	Tempy. Lieutenant F. Graham Browne, R.N.R.
	Lydiard	Tempy. Lieutenant K. Currie, R.N.R.
	Sindonis	Chief Skipper G. Rawding R.N.R.
	Victorian	Chief Skipper M. A. Smith, R.N.R.

APP. D(A)　　　　　　　MEDITERRANEAN, SEPTEMBER 1939–OCTOBER 1940

WHALERS, 28TH A/S GROUP

H.M.S.	*Kingston Coral*	Skipper W. Kirman, R.N.R.
	Kingston Crystal	Lieut.-Commander G. H. P. James, R.N.R.
	Kingston Cyanite	Skipper F. A. Yeomans, R.N.R.
	Wolborough	Lieut.-Commander F. A. W. Ramsay

For list of further small craft – M/S trawlers, drifters, auxiliary M/S 'LL', motor A/S boats distributed Egyptian, North African and Malta ports, see Pink Lists.

GUNBOATS

H.M.S.	*Aphis*	Lieut.-Commander R. S. Stafford (until 7th December, 1940)
		Lieut.-Commander J. O. Campbell, D.S.C. (from 7th December, 1940)
	Ladybird	Lieut.-Commander J. F. Blackburn

MINESWEEPERS; 3RD FLOTILLA

H.M.S.	*Abingdon*	Captain A. R. Farquhar (M.S.3)
	Bagshot	Lieut.-Commander J. F. B. Gage, R.N.V.R
	Derby	Lieut. F. C. V. Brightman
	Fareham	Lieut. W. J. P. Church
	Fermoy	Lieut.-Commander J. G. D. Wetherfield
	Huntley	Lieut.-Commander H. R. A. King, R.N.R.
	Stoke	Commander C. J. P. Hill

28. WALRUS

29. SWORDFISH

30. HURRICANES

31. ITALIAN BATTLESHIP *Conte di Cavour*

32. ITALIAN BATTLESHIP *Giulio Cesare*

33. H.M.S. *Faulknor*

34. H.M.S. *Escort*

35. H.M.A.S. *Sydney*

36. H.M.S. *Eagle*

37. H.M.S. *Ark Royal*

38. H.M.S. *Renown*

39. MALTA – FOOD SUPPLIES

This view of the countryside of Malta was taken from the Victoria lines, with a statue of St. Joseph in the foreground. The soil of Malta is shallow but fertile, sometimes producing three crops a year, and the same is true of the sister island of Gozo. Even so, with a population of over 250,000, and Service garrisons in addition, supplies of food from outside are essential.

40. H.M. SUBMARINE *Rorqual*

41. H.M. Submarine *Osiris*

42. H.M.S. *Kent*

43. H.M.S. *Jervis*

44. H.M.S. *Aphis*

45. H.M.S. *Greyhound* AND *Ladybird*

46. H.M.A.S. *Stuart*

47. H.M.S. *Ajax*

48. ITALIAN DESTROYER *Artigliere*

49. ITALIAN DESTROYER *Camicia Nera*

50. H.M.S. *Liverpool*

51. Greek Light Cruiser H.H.M.S. *Helle*

52. H.M.S. *Protector*

(b)
FORCE 'H'

AUTUMN 1940[1]

FLAG OFFICER COMMANDING
Vice-Admiral Sir James F. Somerville, K.C.B., D.S.O.

PERSONAL STAFF
Chief Staff Officer: Captain E. G. Jeffrey
Secretary: Commander (S) W. J. Farrell
Flag Captain: Captain C. E. B. Simeon
Flag Lieut. Commander: Lieut.-Commander (Sig.) J. R. B. Longden

OPERATIONAL AND PLANNING STAFF
S.O. Plans: Commander A. W. Buzzard, D.S.O.
S.O. Operations: Commander A. G. V. Hubback
Staff A/S Officer: Lieut.-Commander H. C. B. Coleridge, D.S.C.

BATTLESHIPS
H.M.S. *Barham*	Captain G. C. Cooke
Resolution	Captain O. Bevir

BATTLECRUISERS
H.M.S. *Hood*	Captain I. G. Glennie
Renown	Captain C. E. B. Simeon, A.D.C.

AIRCRAFT CARRIERS
H.M.S. *Argus* — Captain H. C. Bovell
  Commander (Flying), Commander E. O. F. Price
F.A.A. 767 Squadron – disembarked, Toulon, June 1940 re-numbered 830 Squadron – operating from Malta, July 1940
H.M.S. *Ark Royal* — Captain C. S. Holland
  Commander (Flying), Commander H. A. Traill

---

[1] Force H began to assemble at Gibraltar on 23rd June, 1940 (Sec. 44). It varied in strength according to circumstances. Some of the ships shown here, notably the *Manchester*, *Newcastle* and *Southampton*, took part in only one operation, namely Collar, at the end of November, 1940 (Naval Staff History Battle Summary No. 9, B.R. 1736 series).

F.A.A.		Air Staff Officer, Commander W. W. R. Bentinck
	800 Squadron	Lieut. R. M. Smeeton (in command)
	801 Squadron	Lieut.-Commander J. R. Sarel, D.S.C. (in command)
	803 Squadron	Lieut.-Commander J. M. Bruen (in command)
	808 Squadron	Lieut. R. C. Tillard (in command)
	810 Squadron	Lieut. M. Johnston (in command)
	818 Squadron	Lieut.-Commander T. P. Coode (in command)
	820 Squadron	Lieut.-Commander J. A. Stewart-Moore (in command)

CRUISERS

H.M.S.	*Arethusa*	Captain Q. D. Graham
	Despatch	Captain C. E. Douglas-Pennant, D.S.C.
	Enterprise	Captain J. C. Annesley, D.S.O.
	Manchester	Captain H. A. Packer
	Newcastle	Captain E. A. Aylmer, D.S.C.
	Sheffield	Captain C. A. A. Larcom
	Southampton	Captain B. C. B. Brooke

DESTROYERS, 8TH AND 13TH FLOTILLAS

H.M.S.	*Active*	Lieut.-Commander E. C. L. Turner
	Douglas	Commander J. G. Crossley
	Duncan	Captain A. D. B. James (D13)
	Encounter	Lieut.-Commander E. V. St. J. Morgan
	Escapade	Commander H. R. Graham, D.S.O.
	Escort	Lieut.-Commander J. Bostock
	Faulknor	Captain A. F. de Salis (D8)
	Fearless	Commander I. R. H. Black
	Firedrake	Lieut.-Commander S. H. Norris, D.S.C.
	Foresight	Lieut.-Commander G. T. Lambert
	Forester	Lieut.-Commander E. B. Tancock, D.S.C.
	Fortune	Commander E. A. Gibbs, D.S.O.
	Foxhound	Commander G. H. Peters, D.S.C.
	Fury	Lieut.-Commander T. C. Robinson
	Hotspur	Commander H. F. H. Layman, D.S.O.
	Isis	Commander C. S. B. Swinley
	Jaguar	Lieut.-Commander J. F. W. Hine
	Kelvin	Commander J. H. Allison, D.S.O.
	Keppel [1]	Lieut.-Commander E. G. Heywood-Lonsdale [1]
	Velox	Commander J. C. Colvill
	Vidette	Lieut. E. N. Walmsley
	Vortigern	Lieut.-Commander R. S. Howlett
	Watchman	Lieut.-Commander E. C. L. Day

---

1 Until 14/8/40, then Lieutenant R. J. Hanson.

Wishart	Commander E. T. Cooper
Wrestler	Lieut.-Commander E. N. V. Currey

ESCORT TRAWLERS, 7TH A/S GROUP[1]

H.M.S. *Arctic Ranger*	Commander J. H. Young
Erin	Commander J. O. Davies, R.N.R.
Haarlem	Tempy. Lieut. L. B. Merrick, R.N.R.
Kingston Chrysolite	Tempy. Lieut. R. L. Green, R.N.V.R.
Leyland	Lieut.-Commander A. Wilkinson, R.N.R.
Lord Hotham	Skipper J. W. Morris, R.N.R.
Stella Sirius	Lieut.-Commander Benson, R.N.V.R.

MINESWEEPING TRAWLERS, 92ND M/S GROUP[1]

H.M.S. *Clyne Castle*	Lieut. T. Fraser, R.N.R.
Empyrean	Tempy. Skipper W. F. Salinius, R.N.R.
Honju	Chief Skipper J. Bowie, R.N.R.
Returno	Skipper G. S. Burr, R.N.R.

CONTRABAND CONTROL SERVICE[1]

12 Armed Boarding vessels (6 yachts, 6 trawlers).

---

1 Under orders of the Flag Officer, North Atlantic, for purposes of Local Defence.

(c)
SEA TRANSPORT SERVICE, MIDDLE EAST 1940

(RESPONSIBLE TO THE DIRECTOR OF SEA TRANSPORT, MINISTRY OF SHIPPING, LONDON)

Principal Sea Transport Officer, *Egypt*: Commodore H. Vaughan-Jones
Divisional Sea Transport Officer, *M.E. Cairo*: Captain G. Langham
    " " " " *Port Said*: Captain P. B. Crohan
    " " " " *Suez*: Captain C. D. Moore
    " " " " *Port Sudan*: Captain W. C. Clark-Hall (from 20th December, 1940)
Sea Transport Officer-in-Charge, *Alexandria*: Commander L. Thompson, D.S.C., R.D., R.N.R.
    " " " " *Haifa*: Commander L. J. Edwards, R.N.R.
    " " " " *Port Sudan*: Commander N. S. Griffiths (from September to 20th December, 1940)
    " " " " *Greece*: Commander J. O. Buckler, R.N.R. (from 1st November onwards)
(offices Athens and Piraeus)
Sea Transport Adviser to British Consul-: Commander N. S. Griffiths (June to September, 1940)
General, Istanbul

Broadly speaking, the work of the Sea Transport Service lay in the movement of Service passengers, cargo and stores in chartered and requisitioned merchant vessels. This entailed arranging and supervising embarkation and loadings, the hire of labour, and the handling of floating plant, such as cranes, tugs and harbour craft, as well as the fuelling and ballasting of ships. Also they were responsible for the fitting out of merchant vessels for special requirements such as the conveyance of cased petrol, ammunition, horses and mules.

The Ministry of War Transport had H.Q. offices at Alexandria and representatives at other ports in order to deal with the large volume of shipping requirements for general trading, and Sir Henry Barker took over this work.

The implications of operating in a neutral country were covered by the setting up of the Anglo-Egyptian Port and Transit Committee under the Chairmanship of Hussein Fahmy Bey, the Director General of Customs. This Committee, on which all British Services were represented, was responsible for the reception and allocation to ports of all in-coming shipping, and exercised its powers through the executive functions of the Director General of Ports and Lights Administration, Rear-Admiral Sir Gerard Wells, Pasha. Special regulations were framed by the Egyptian Government to protect shipowners and others against claims arising out of alleged 'frustrated voyages'.

LIAISON ARRANGEMENTS BETWEEN NAVAL AND MERCANTILE AUTHORITIES

To facilitate arrangements involving merchant shipping with military and naval requirements a liaison officer was appointed to the staff of the Commander-in-Chief, Mediterranean; this was Mr. A. Miller-Stirling, who had served with the Ministry of Economic Warfare in London. A 'Merchant Ship' section of the Commander-in-Chief's Intelligence Staff kept a plot of all merchant ship movements – both British, Allied and Enemy – and issued a daily statement for use by the M.W.T., P.S.T.O., and Commander-in-Chief's operational staff. Lieutenant-Commander A. R. C. Prentis was in charge in 1939/40 and was relieved by Lieutenant-Commander R. Mandley in 1941. From September 1939 to June 1940 the information of movements of enemy merchant ships was utilised by the Contraband Control Committee. This Organisation was also linked to the very comprehensive and detailed Shipping Intelligence Centre set up in the office of P.S.T.O. (E) in which the composition, movements and contents of all merchant ships and convoys passing through the area were carefully docketed and card-indexed. This Centre was in charge of the late Lieutenant-Commander A. C. Bolden, R.N.V.R. (Sp.) from its inception in 1940, until November 1943.

More details of the work of the Sea Transport Service in the Middle East will be found in the departmental history being prepared by the Sea Transport Department.

APPENDIX E

SUMMARY OF SIGNALS

		Section
1.	Importance of Crete to Germany	1
2.	Fall of Poland: British policy unchanged	8
3.	French Squadron for Eastern Mediterranean	21
4.	Merchant ships to be routed via the Cape	21
5.	Instructions to British Merchant Ships	21
6.	Australian convoys	21
7.	Re-opening of Mediterranean	21
8.	Italian Preparations	21
9.	Precautions vis-a-vis Italy	21
10.	Policy re Italian M/V's and Escorts	21
11.	Cable cutting	21
12.	Instructions to Shipping, Mediterranean again closed	21
13.	Use of Egyptian aerodromes by Italian aircraft	21
14.	1-2 Threat to block Suez Canal	21
15.	Italian policy explained to the U.S.A.	21
16.	Aircraft over Egypt	21
17.	1-2 Italian Plans	21
18.	1-2 Italy and Greece	22
19.	British and French Fleets sweep, 11th to 14th June, 1940	26
20.	a-b Summary of minefields reported	22
21.	Commander-in-Chief's report of Fleet sweeps	29
22.	Commander-in-Chief, Mediterranean, reports situation on 19th June, 1940 – The French Collapse	41
23.	Evacuation from Marseilles to North African ports	46
24.	French in Algeria, intention to continue fight	46
25.	Intention of Government to carry on overseas	46
26.	French forces in Middle East	46
27.	French Fleets in North African ports	46
28.	British shipping policy at Gibraltar: closing of Mediterranean route	44
29.	French in Middle East not in touch with North Africa	42
30.	French merchant ships to sail to Beirut	42
31.	Attitude of French in Mediterranean, 22nd June	43
32.	Precautions vis-a-vis French	43

SUMMARY OF SIGNALS

33. a-h Attitude of French in Mediterranean, 23rd June	43
34. British appeal to French overseas authorities, 23rd June	43
35. a-h Situation deteriorates	42 to 46
36. a-b French Squadron at Alexandria ordered home: Commander-in-Chief, Mediterranean, refuses permission to sail	43
37. Withdrawal of British Naval Liaison Officers	42
38. Operations of British Mediterranean Fleet hampered by uncertainty of French situation	46
39. German use of French codes	48
40. a-b Caution necessary in Anglo-French interpretations of Armistice Terms	48
41. a-b Appreciation of French attitude by British Naval Liaison Officers, 28th June, 1940	50
42. Instructions from French Admiralty to French Admiral at Oran to answer force with force	50
43. a-b S.O. Force H intentions for supporting operations to MA.5	58
44. (*a*) Details of proposed movements preliminary to reinforcing the Mediterranean	64 to 70
(*b*) Commander-in-Chief, Mediterranean, to take command of reinforcement operations	64 to 70
(*c*) Commander-in-Chief's, Mediterranean, views on movements of *Royal Sovereign*	64 to 70
(*d*) Commander-in-Chief's, Mediterranean, intentions for reinforcement operations	64 to 70
(*e*) S.O. Force H proposals to modify (*d*)	64 to 70
(*f*) Commander-in-Chief's, Mediterranean, concurrence with S.O. Force H	64 to 70
45. Mining policy for Mediterranean, August 1940	74

APP. E.2   MEDITERRANEAN, SEPTEMBER 1939–OCTOBER 1940

1

IMPORTANCE OF CRETE TO GERMANY

17th June, 1941

From H.M. Ambassador, Angora

Date 19/6/41

Addressed Foreign Office

Assistant Naval Attaché at Istanbul (Constantinople) reports that about a week ago the German Naval Attaché in answer to enquiries from the United States Naval Attaché whether the German sacrifices of men and material to capture Crete had been worth while, stated that the importance of the island to Germany lay principally in opening the Mediterranean route to the Italians for sea borne supplies of oil and grain from the Black Sea, and also emphasized the propaganda value in Spain and Portugal of the German ability to supply Spain with food by this route.

Commander-in-Chief, Mediterranean, informed.

No. T.O.O.

See Section 1 (end) 'whether the German sacrifices of men and material to capture Crete were worth while.'

2

FALL OF POLAND, BRITISH POLICY UNCHANGED

From Admiralty to all Commanders-in-Chief (*Commander-in-Chief, Mediterranean, 581*)

Date 26.9.39; Time 1442

The following summary of a telegram from the Foreign Secretary to H.M. Representatives generally may be useful:–

Criticism that Poland's defeat proves Britain's incapacity to help is a misconception of Britain's basic plan and principles. Both Britain and Poland always assumed that Poland would at once be largely overrun. This was confirmed by a Polish General to our mission and quoted by Prime Minister on 20th September: 'We shall fight. A large part of our country will be overrun and we shall suffer terribly. But if you come in we know that we shall rise again.' Owing to geographical limitations at no time was direct help possible. It was always recognised by Britain that:–

- (i) Poland would probably suffer an early defeat, but could surely be rescued by ultimate victory.
- (ii) that this defeat occurring in three weeks instead of later does not fundamentally alter the character of the war.
- (iii) that Britain is ready for a long war as her declaration of preparation for three years war has shown.
- (iv) that this method is as advantageous to her and her allies, since their power grows, as it is disadvantageous to Germany.
- (v) that accordingly it would have been folly for Britain to try and give Poland direct help, and indirect help by widespread bombing could have only delayed but not avoided the Polish defeat. Such possible spectacular success would have been set off by loss of machines of more effective utility on the West.

Compare the Premier's own words: 'There is no sacrifice from which we will shrink ... But we will not rush into adventures that offer little prospect of success and are calculated to impair our resources and to postpone ultimate victory. Military history teaches that that road leads to disaster. Strategy is the art of concentrating decisive force at the decisive moment.'

1442/26/9/39 D.N.I.

3
FRENCH SQUADRON FOR EASTERN MEDITERRANEAN

From Admiralty to Commander-in-Chief, Mediterranean, 835

Date: 1319/30 April, 40

My 0005/29.

A. Although there is no repetition no apparent change in political situation regarding Italy French have agreed that their Squadron should accompany BRITISH FORCE to Alexandria.

B. It is probable that French escorting destroyers will require to fuel at Malta.

C. Acting Vice-Admiral Godfroy in *Duquesne* with *Tourville* will arrive at Bizerta tomorrow. He will ultimately command French Naval forces in Eastern Mediterranean.

1319/30
Approved by A.C.N.S. (A)

4
MERCHANT SHIPS TO BE ROUTED VIA CAPE
A.C.N.S. 1830/27/4/40

With the exception of mail steamers, all British Merchant Ships bound through, repeat through, the Mediterranean are to be diverted via the Cape of Good Hope.

These instructions do not apply to ships in the Mediterranean and Red Sea.

Routes and arrangements. As the above message is not at present being broadcast to merchant ships arrangements should be made to intercept all ships now at sea and affected by this diversion at Gibraltar and Aden.

5
INSTRUCTIONS TO BRITISH MERCHANT SHIPS
A.C.N.S. 0006/29/4 to Commander-in-Chief, Mediterranean

Instructions to be placed in sealed envelope, only to be opened by instructions from Admiralty. To all British Merchant Ships at sea in Mediterranean, Adriatic or Aegean.

(1) Ships west of 12° E. unless bound for a French or French North African port are to proceed forthwith to Gibraltar.

(2) Ships eastward of 18° E. unless bound for Palestine or Egypt are to proceed forthwith to Port Said.

(3) Ships between 12° and 18° E. if eastbound are to proceed to Port Said and, if westbound, to Gibraltar.

(4) Ships in the Adriatic are to proceed to Port Said.

6
AUSTRALIAN CONVOYS

D.O.D.(F) 2351/30/4

If situation with Italy does not improve, undesirable to pass Australian convoys through Red Sea. Proposed to divert via Cape.

7
RE-OPENING OF MEDITERRANEAN ORDERED ON 8TH MAY
(cancelled later – see E.12)

All British Merchant Ships which left Basra for United Kingdom via the Cape on or after 30th April, are to proceed to Aden for orders. (*D.T.D. 0059/8/5.*)

British Merchant Ships which have been recalled to Aden by G.B.M.S. message are to be instructed to proceed through the Mediterranean. (*D.T.D. 0200/8/5.*)

8
ITALIAN PREPARATIONS

N.A., Rome, 2059/13/5/40

Reports received from various sources that merchant vessels have been requisitioned Leghorn. Six others requisitioned Adriatic are being sent Brindisi. Two ships of Adriatic line being armed at Brindisi. Trawlers being requisitioned Bari. Net defence placed at Leghorn. Mines have been placed off Durazzo (C.2) and other mines being held in readiness for laying off Valona and Port Edda (Santa Quaranta) (B.2) on 15th May to which date significance is attached.

Additional A.A. guns being mounted Brindisi (A.1). Seven troopships Naples 11th May, loading troops, ammunition and foodstuffs.

9
PRECAUTIONS VIS-A-VIS ITALY

D.O.D.(F) 2327/14/5/40

The situation with regard to Italy has apparently deteriorated during the last few days, and although it is not considered that war is likely to break out in the very near future a close watch should be kept on Italian shipping in order that planes for interception may be rapidly put into force.

10
POLICY RE ITALIAN M/V'S AND ESCORTS

D. of Plans 0003/15/5/40 to Commander-in-Chief, Mediterranean, F.O.C.N.A., Commander-in-Chief, E.I. and S.O. Red Sea Force

Unconfirmed report, graded C.3, states that from now onwards Italian merchant vessels will be escorted, *Rex* in particular has been mentioned. While legally it would be correct to stop senior ship of escort to ascertain nature of cargoes and details of passengers, it is at the present moment of very great importance that we should avoid any incident with Italy that might result in war.

Our whole policy is directed to ensuring that if war should come it shall be clear beyond all doubt that it is Italy who has forced it on us. For these reasons no attempt is to be made to interfere with Italian escorts or escorted vessels.

11
CABLE CUTTING

Hd. of M., 1550/15/5/40 to F.O.C.N.A., Commander-in-Chief, Mediterranean

My 1827 of 19/4/40, 1545/26/4/40, and Para. 322 of M.00697/39. Action to be taken in Western Mediterranean should be in order of importance, first Malaga-South America, Malaga-Azores, and Malaga-Lisbon to westward of Strait, and second Malaga-Rome, and Malaga-Barcelona to eastward of Malaga. Cutting of Barcelona-Rome would be undertaken by French. Sub-paras. (*a*), (*b*), (*c*) of para. 322 should be disregarded.

12
INSTRUCTIONS TO SHIPPING, MEDITERRANEAN AGAIN CLOSED

1. *1st Sea Lord 1622/16/5/40*

My 0045/16/5 – Instructions contained in first sentence are cancelled. Ships from west coast of India and Persian Gulf bound through the Mediterranean are to be routed via Cape of Good Hope.

2. *A.C.N.S. 2016/16, 2017/16*

Until further orders no British or Norwegian merchant ships are to be sailed eastbound from Gibraltar, or westbound from Port Said, Alexandria, Haifa or Cyprus.

13
A/A DEFENCES AT ALEXANDRIA AND ITALIAN SHIPPING

Commander-in-Chief, Mediterranean, 1319/17/5/40

Admiralty 0003/15/5 (No. 10 above) re Italian escorts and escorted vessels not to be interfered with, I will withhold order as long as possible but present situation is most unsatisfactory on account of permission given for Italian bombers to pass through Egypt landing at Alexandria. Squadrons are due 19/5 and 26/5 and I consider warning Government to be urgently asked to withdraw this permission or at least prohibit use of aerodromes near Alexandria.

Understand French aircraft are now proceeding via Abadan to Syria so no question of reciprocity arises.

See No. 16 for action taken by the Egyptian Government.

14
THREAT TO BLOCK SUEZ CANAL

B.N.L.O., Marceau, to Admiralty 1850/20/5/40

French Consul, Trieste, received anonymous letter stating Italian intention to block Suez Canal with old warships before declaring war. Same source also reports *Miraglia* arriving Suez 23rd or 24th May with excuse carrying aircraft to East Africa.

First Sea Lord to Commander-in-Chief, Mediterranean, 2342/21/5/40

A report, low graded, received that when Italian seaplane carrier *Miraglia* passes through the Canal on or about 25/5 en route for Massawa she may endeavour to scuttle ship and block Canal. Difficult with present state of tension to delay a warship. Can you suggest any reason for temporarily delaying her passage, or if this is not possible, any means for preventing her blocking Canal should she endeavour to do so?

15
ITALIAN POLICY EXPLAINED TO THE U.S.A.

D.N.I. 0027/21/5/40

Signor Mussolini has replied to President Roosevelt's latest message that latter as realist must understand two fundamental facts.

(1) Italy is and intends to remain allied with Germany.
(2) She cannot remain absent when fate of Europe is at stake.

During last 48 hours it is considered that likelihood of Italy entering war has increased, but cannot be regarded as certainty.

Appears unlikely she will take any action for next five days.

16
AIRCRAFT OVER EGYPT

Admiralty, Head of M. 1830/31/5/40

Egyptian Government have informed Italian Legation that instructions have been issued by the Military Authorities that no foreign military aircraft is allowed to fly over Egypt or to Sudan until further orders, and have made it clear that this applies to all flights including those already sanctioned, and public notice is being issued that aircraft flying over prohibited zones will be fired at with live ammunition, after one warning shot. R.A. Alexandria is being kept informed by H.M. Representative, Cairo, of above arrangements, and also about methods of control of civil aircraft.

17
ITALIAN PLANS

N.A., Rome, 2154/23/5/40

1. Italian entry into war contingent upon German success in France. As soon as this is assured operations against Corsica will commence. Preparations to gain control of Western Mediterranean already made.

Italian submarines left for Balearic Islands, others sent to Cadiz. Intention is to establish submarine bases both places. Attack on Corsica will be combined with attack on Gibraltar with Spanish co-operation followed by attack on Nice from seawards. Inform War Office.

N.A., Rome, 1727/22/5/40

2. Recent measures taken include mounting guns in small 14-knot ships similar to *Brioni* of Adriatic line, requisitioning of trawlers on east coast, and placing of nets and boom defences at principal ports including Benghazi, Zuara and Tripoli. Report (D.4)[1] that 2 or 3 ships are loading cement at Naples for the purpose of blocking Suez Canal, names not obtained. General indication is that warlike preparations are being made by fighting services.

18

ITALY AND GREECE

Admiralty, 0051/1/6/40, to Commander-in-Chief, Mediterranean

Owing to vital defence commitments elsewhere there can be no question of taking Greece under our protection.

2. Action to be taken in event of Italian attack on Greek territory:–

(*a*) Despatch of Allied detachment to Crete to help Greeks.

(*b*) Allied control of East Mediterranean and Aegean Sea communications.

This should limit whole scale of Italian effort against Greece.

3. In addition French propose to despatch limited forces to Salonika, Milos, Salamis, Navarino, Argostoli. These would be a French commitment if carried out.

4. Difficult to reach finality with French in present critical situation in France and our own present limited Air and Land Forces. [See also Appendix C.4.]

S.O.(I) Alexandria 1932/2/6/40 to Admiralty for D.N.I.

Patras reports that in Ankara opinion of effective resistance in event of Italian occupation of Western Greek harbours is doubtful as only inadequate Infantry detachments are available.

19

BRITISH AND FRENCH FLEETS' SWEEPS, JUNE 11TH TO 14TH, 1940

From Commander-in-Chief, Mediterranean, to Admiralty, 2243/10/6/40

Intend to leave harbour at 0300/11th June with H.M. Ships *Warspite, Malaya, Eagle*, Seventh Cruiser Squadron and available destroyers.

Battleships will proceed northwest and then along south coast Crete to reach approximate position 80 miles south of Cape Matapan 1200, 12th June.

Seventh Cruiser Squadron will carry out sweep to westward until dark on 11th June then return to attack any patrol off Benghazi and Tobruk at daylight 12th June, subsequently joining me about 1200, 12th June.

Vice-Admiral Force X has been instructed to proceed from Beirut as soon as possible with what force he thinks fit to sweep towards Dodecanese and Aegean north of Crete returning Alexandria p.m. 13th June.

20

SUMMARY OF MINEFIELDS REPORTED

(*a*) *From Admiralty (D.N.I.) to Commander-in-Chief, Mediterranean (info S.O.(I) Alex.) 1154/4/6/40*

Following is summary of minefields reported. Durazzo C.2, Valona C.2,1 Port Edda B.2, other Albanian ports unconfirmed. Saseno to C. Linguetta B.2.

---

1 The letters and figures indicated degree of reliability of source and information, ranging from A one to E five. C.2 meant a moderately reliable source and reasonably reliable information; D.4 meant, in short, 'not very likely'.

Otranto Channel, Taranto, Spezia, Maddalena, Bari, Barletta, Monopoli, Zara, between Stampalia and Scarpanto, between Leros and Kalymnos, Kos, Gurna and Laki Bays in Leros (all C.O). Partheni Bay D.O. Elba to Sardinia D.3. Naples B.3. Brindisi confirmed.

(b) Mediterranean War Diary – 12th June

The following areas were declared dangerous by the Admiralty:–

(1) All along shores of Italy as far as 500 metres depth limit.

(2) The Straits of Bonifaccio; between Corsica and the Continent.

(3) The area limited by Marittimo, the points 37° 30' N., 11° 30' E 37° 30' N., 11° 20' E. – Pantellaria, Cap San Marco.

(4) The following areas were declared dangerous owing to reported Italian minefields:–

Tobruk and Benghazi.

Pantellaria to Cape Granitola.

Outside Tripoli harbour and along coast.

Rhodes at entrance to harbour.

20 miles N.W. of Ras-el-Tin light.

21

COMMANDER-IN-CHIEF, MEDITERRANEAN, REPORT OF FLEET SWEEP

From Commander-in-Chief, Mediterranean, to Admiralty   1153/13/6/40

355. My 2243/10th June (see E.19). W/T silence precluded earlier reports of operations in hand.

(a) Seventh Cruiser Squadron swept along ZZ line British shipping in Eastern Mediterranean. This appears to have been successfully accomplished.

(b) Subsequently H.M.S. *Gloucester* and *Liverpool* proceeded to Tobruk, encountering some small craft probably minesweepers off port. These were engaged for a short while and thought to have been hit. Shore batteries opened fire apparently with 8-inch guns judging by splinters. Action lasted 11 minutes several straddles on ships but no hits. Both ships cut mines with paravanes. This attack was synchronised with bombing attack by the R.A.F.

(c) No enemy encountered by V.A. (D), Mediterranean, and rest of Seventh Cruiser Squadron at Benghazi.

(d) A.T.1250, 12th June. It is most regrettable that *Garibaldi* is now known to have been the centre of triangle formed by forces in (b), (c) and battle fleet, but due to chancy visibility and restricted air reconnaissance she was not sighted and brought to action.

(e) Meanwhile battleships after a cast to northward steered for a rendezvous with Seventh Cruiser Squadron in position 80 miles south of Cape Matapan at 1200 on 12th June. During the night H.M.S. *Calypso* was sunk, as reported separately.

(f) During the night battleships swept north westward with cruisers spread 40 miles ahead, later reaching position 125° Cape Santa Maria di Lenca 120 miles. Fleet then turned and is now sweeping south eastward. Nothing sighted up to 1100 today, Thursday.

(g) At this moment the need for a base in Greek islands is brought home to me with particular force.

(h) Intend to arrive at Alexandria 1800/14th June; Seventh Cruiser Squadron will sweep along Cyrenaican coast during the night.

THE FRENCH COLLAPSE

22

COMMANDER-IN-CHIEF, MEDITERRANEAN, REPORTS SITUATION ON 19TH JUNE, 1940

Message 1815/19/6/40 to Admiralty

An Order of the Day dated 19th June has been received by Admiral Godfroy from Admiral Darlan stating no Armistice yet signed and that all Naval (? forces) are expected to fight on, to fall back on North Africa if necessary, and to blow up or scuttle themselves in emergency. Order is based on one issued by Pétain. But B.N.L.O. Bizerta is doubtful about intention of Army and Air Force in Tunisia. All French Services at Beirut have met and decided to fight on, basing this on a message from Darlan to fight to the end, and have asked their decision be conveyed to General Wavell and myself.

In general therefore all French Mediterranean Forces appear intended to continue the fight. I have sent suitable message to Senior Officers concerned giving them my sympathy and assuring them of all the support in my power.

The lodging of money at a bank in Alexandria for French Fleet by British Admiralty has created an excellent impression.

23
EVACUATION FROM MARSEILLES TO NORTH AFRICAN PORTS
Admiralty to D.S.T.O., Marseilles 2011/19/6/40

British Government are offering shipping assistance to French authorities for evacuation from Marseilles to N. African ports. On assumption that offer will be accepted, all available British shipping in Southern French ports, except that required for R.A.F. and military unit referred to in my 0041/17 to B.N.L.O., Toulon, is to be placed at their disposal. All British ships in ballast which can reach Marseilles within 48 hours have been ordered to proceed there. Importance is attached to evacuation of 6,000 Czech troops and light equipment who have been directed to contact you and may arrive p.m. 20th.

24
FRENCH IN ALGERIA, INTENTION TO CONTINUE FIGHT
No. 3 Military Mission, Algiers, Personal for C.I.G.S. from Dillon 1315/19/6/40

After careful consideration I am persuaded that if the French Government accepts German Terms, whatever they are, Algeria including troops therein and Navy will continue hostilities. If this happens one thing they have most urgent need of is small arms and machine guns and Lewis guns to arm the many good natives with. No matter how old any number of rifles with a minimum of 500 rounds per arm will be welcome. If they could be sent very soon to Casablanca it would be best.

25
INTENTION OF GOVERNMENT TO CARRY ON OVERSEAS
Admiralty to Commanders-in-Chief 0031/20/6/40

French have decided that on approach of enemy to Bordeaux, President of Republic and some Ministers will proceed overseas to carry on Government. It is possible Weygand will go too.

26
FRENCH FORCES IN MIDDLE EAST; MARSHAL WEYGAND TO GENERAL MITTELHAUSER IN SYRIA
From No. 8 Military Mission to War Office 1920/20/6/40

Gist of telegram received today by Mittelhauser from Weygand. Owing to situation of Army and difficulty of feeding civilian population, we have been obliged to approach German and Italian Governments. This does not mean cessation of hostilities and still less capitulation. Armies although sorely tried and separated are still fighting magnificently. Tell those around you that for moment there is no question of ceasing fire.

2. Commander-in-Chief, Middle East, and Air Officer, Commanding-in-Chief, M.E., flew here this morning to see Mittelhauser. Agreement in principle was reached over following points:–

  (*a*) Mutual assistance between British and French air forces in Syria and Egypt.
  (*b*) Possible assistance and troops in Egypt.
  (*c*) Setting up of joint Middle East planning committee to include French staff officers.
  (*d*) Setting up of Anglo-French War Council for Mediterranean.

Visit was a great success, and in all respects there appears to be common point of view.

3. Although in view of high morale at present existing, likelihood of capitulation here seems remote I suggest broad preparation should be made now in Palestine to receive large influx of French material and personnel in the event of the worst happening here. On all sides wish has been expressed to join British Army if necessary. General Massert commanding expeditionary force here told me he would immediately join Foreign Legion if British formed one.

27

FRENCH FLEET IN NORTH AFRICAN PORTS; INTENTION TO CARRY ON WAR

B.N.L.O., Algiers, to Commander-in-Chief, Mediterranean, and Admiralty   1858/21/6/40

Naval Chief of General Staff, Algiers, states practically all French Fleet now in British or French North African ports. General intention French fighting forces is to carry on war from Africa regardless of terms agreed to by French Government. Naval authorities very anxious to continue co-operation with British. Morale of three services excellent.

28

BRITISH SHIPPING POLICY AT GIBRALTAR; CLOSING OF MEDITERRANEAN ROUTE

Admiralty to Flag Officer Commanding North Atlantic – Gibraltar   0037/21/6/40

Your 1258/19. If emergency sailing from Gibraltar becomes necessary you should be guided by the following:–

(1) British ships and others including neutrals under Allied control should be classified in the two categories;
   (*a*) Ocean-going ships.
   (*b*) Short sea traders.
(2) *Category (a)* to be dealt with as follows:–
   1. Ships bound for the East or for Eastern Mediterranean or Malta to be sailed via the Cape, calling at Capetown for onward routeing, and Freetown or St. Vincent if necessary for bunkers.
   2. Ships in ballast or with coal cargoes for Western Mediterranean ports to be sailed for Sydney, Cape Breton for orders, bunkering at Azores if necessary.
   3. Remainder to be sailed to Milford Haven for orders.
(3) *Category (b)*. Ships to be sailed to Milford Haven for orders.
(4) All ships for United Kingdom to be sailed in convoy with normal convoy escort if available. If not, endeavour will be made to meet convoy as early as possible with escort from United Kingdom. Convoy should be routed far to the westward particularly in vicinity of Finisterre. You should select and report position, date, and time of rendezvous in Western Approaches and convoy route.
(5) Further signal will be made regarding neutral ships not under Allied control.

29

FRENCH IN MIDDLE EAST NOT IN TOUCH WITH NORTH AFRICA

No. 8 Military Mission (Syria) to Commander-in-Chief, Middle East   1900/21/6/40

French here appear to be out of touch with North Africa and do not know attitude of Nogues (Governor-General, North Africa). Indication of the determination of Army in Middle East to continue struggle would be appreciated.[1]

30

FRENCH MERCHANT SHIPS TO SAIL TO BEIRUT

S.B.N.O., Suez Canal Area, to N.O.I.C., Haifa   1046/21/6/40

Your 0210/21. French merchant ships with French escort may sail for Beirut as requested by Admiral, Beirut.

---

1 N.B. – Presumably this means a request to pass on the gist of information given in E.26.

British s.s. *Lesbian* should join convoy. This is considered highly desirable as a matter of policy to meet French wishes. Commander-in-Chief, Mediterranean, concurs.

31
ATTITUDE OF FRENCH IN MEDITERRANEAN, 22ND JUNE

B.N.L.O. Sud (at Toulon) to Admiralty, Commander-in-Chief, Mediterranean 0826/22/6/40

Admiral Darlan's telegram 21/6 nominated Admirals De Laborde, Esteva, Abriol, Gensoul to command French Navy successively in event of Chief becoming unable to function satisfactorily. His orders are Fleet should fight to last, no ship ever to be surrendered, orders from Foreign Government not to be obeyed, but only those of Admiralissimo, naval bases to be defended at all costs under Admiral-Governor. Admiral Levant telegraphed to Admiralty highest morale existing Beyrout, will fight to the end.

32
PRECAUTION VIS-A-VIS FRENCH

Admiralty to F.O.C.N.A. (Gibraltar) 0252/23/6/40

Terms of Armistice signed by French not being yet fully known attitude of French Navy is not certain. *Dorsetshire is* to sail for Dakar with moderate despatch, and one destroyer[1] forthwith for Casablanca.

33
ATTITUDE OF FRENCH IN MEDITERRANEAN, 23RD JUNE

(a) Commander-in-Chief, Mediterranean, to Admiralty 1851/23/6/40

Have had talk with Godfroy who has not yet any official intimation of terms of Armistice. He says Darlan still in control of Fleet but has issued no instructions since Armistice terms agreed. Darlan urging that he should fight on and he is obviously considering his position should his ships fight under British Crown in event of there being no French Government willing to order continuance of struggle at sea. He considers good proportion of his men would volunteer to continue to fight their ships. He shows no inclination to leave Alexandria, in fact states he cannot leave. I think, however, he will be finally influenced by orders he receives and for that reason I do not intend to take French Squadron to sea for operations. Godfroy also stated that if it had not been for Spanish Government threatening to join Axis the French would have continued the war from North Africa.

(b) No. 8 Military Mission (Syria) to Commander-in-Chief, Middle East 1940/23/6/40

France will continue to fight here. Danger will arise if French Army in Syria remains inactive. Seems essential that Frenchmen of suitable age and prestige should set up Government in Algiers and take over energetic direction of affairs otherwise danger of hesitation and timidity spreading. De Gaulle considered too young.

(c) No. 8 Military Mission (Syria) to Commander-in-Chief, Middle East 1920/23/6140

Certain ships ordered 22/6 to French ports. Suspected that message emanates from German sources and that Germans have French cypher. Admiral Carpener has no intention of carrying out such orders. Spirit of French Navy here is high.

(d) B.N.L.O. to Commander-in-Chief, South Atlantic Force (French) to Admiralty 1920/23/6/40

Convinced French ships to avoid scuttling would surrender willingly small display of British Naval Forces. Matter is urgent.

(e) S.N.O. Dakar to Admiralty 2030/23/6/40

Decided that British intervention most undesirable at this juncture. *Richelieu* has only A/A ammunition on board and main armament is incomplete. Great importance attached to pronouncement from some form of recognised Government in North Africa.

(f) H.M.S. Watchman at Casablanca to Admiralty 2359/23/6/40

Jean Bart now at Casablanca. Situation:– Senior Officers apathetic. Many junior officers and men willing to continue. Possibly French ship would sail with small armed guard under British escort.

---

1 H.M.S. *Watchman.*

(*g*) *F.O.C.N.A. (Gibraltar) to Admiralty*

I understand necessary instructions exist for scuttling and wrecking of vital material. Fleet has recently been to sea and morale is good, but officers very dejected. Gensoul unfavourably impressed by speech of Mr. Churchill's, most distressed at possibility of any cleavage between Britain and France. He thought French North Africa would not continue the fight owing to insufficiency of material and ammunition.
(E-24, 27).

(*h*) *B.N.L.O., Bizerta, to Commander-in-Chief, Mediterranean, Admiralty*   2230/23/6/40

Esteva sent officer to France for orders this morning. Am left with following impression after talk again Admiral Esteva today.

    (*a*) While wearing his country's uniform consider it his duty to obey all orders of his Chief and see others do likewise with exception never to surrender the fleet or any other units.

    (*b*) If supreme command devolves on him he would similarly accept all Government orders except surrender.

Generally an air of resignation is set in. Officers who often themselves have lost all, would like to continue with British, but do not appear prepared to demand sacrifice from their men of loss of families, upon whom reprisals are indicated.

34
BRITISH APPEAL TO FRENCH OVERSEAS AUTHORITIES, 23RD JUNE

Admiralty to Commanders-in-Chief   0406/23/6/40

Foreign Office telegram to British Consuls in French Colonial territory, appealing to Civil and Military Authorities of all French Overseas territories to continue to fight even against the orders of the Government in France, and guaranteeing funds to all such territories, sent in full to Commanders-in-Chief.

35
SITUATION DETERIORATES

(*a*) *B.N.L.O. Sud (Toulon) to Admiralty*   0744/23/6/40

Situation:– Peruton, staff and local authorities will not permit anything conducive in slightest degree to strengthen will of Colonies to resist.

(*b*) *H.M.S. Velox (at Port Vendres)*[1] *to Admiralty*   2037/23/6/40

H.M.S. *Velox* and *Keppel* arrived at Port Vendres early 22nd to supervise embarkation of Czech and Polish troops from there and Sete for Gibraltar.

    1. At least 300 French officers and men main air personnel wish to proceed to England to continue fight. Not allowed by local French orders. Our policy unknown to me. Request instructions. Transport available.

Admiralty to H.M.S. Velox, repeated F.O.C.N.A., Gibraltar   0117/24/6/40

    2. Your 2037. Personnel referred to should be embarked. Our policy is that all French armed forces who wish to continue the struggle should be encouraged and assisted to do so.

(c) War Diary – 23rd June

Censor, Freetown, has held up two telegrams from Government, Bordeaux, for confirmation from London in view of B.B.C. announcement that British Government no longer recognises Government at Bordeaux.

(*d*) *F.O.C.N.A. (Gibraltar) to Admiralty*   1144/23/6/40

Serious situation arising with large numbers of civilians and evacuated troops arriving from French Mediterranean ports. Food reserves are being seriously depleted, imperative that ships expected with Czech and Polish troops be diverted elsewhere forthwith even if only for food, fuel and water.

(*e*) *No. 8 Military Mission (Syria) to War Office*   1315/23/6/40

Am assured of Mittelhauser's determination to fight on. Only sign of defeat which has reached me concerns

---

[1] Port Vendres, on French coast at frontier with Spain in Mediterranean.

Senior air staff officers. This does not reflect general feeling. All that is wanted is a firm lead from a responsible French Government in London or Algiers. Mittelhauser has just sent following telegram to Commander-in-Chief, Mediterranean. My sincere thanks for cover afforded by your fleet and my cordial wish announcement early Anglo-French naval victory that may be won under your orders.

(f) *No. 3 Military Mission (Algiers) to War Office* 0055/24/6/40

All military opinion disgusted with Armistice and looking for sign of British help which is thought to be always too late. Political opinion here is extremely defeatist. Doubtful whether Nogues will continue war; and Army, though wanting to fight, is thought to be deterred by lack of material. Much depends on immediate support well broadcasted.

(g) *B.N.L.O. Brest in H.M.S. Watchman (at Casablanca) to Admiralty* 1120/24/6/40

Situation deteriorating beyond point suggested. Senior Officer preparing to demilitarize Fleet to support Pétain Government. Some C.O's might disobey order to scuttle, but demilitarization in French or French Colonial harbours seems probable, though many junior officers might re-act against demilitarization if given the chance. If North African Government accept peace terms, force will be required to release French Fleet.

(h) *F.O.C.N.A. (in H.M.S. Douglas) to F.O.C.N.A., Gibraltar* 0136/24/6/40

B.N.L.O. Casablanca 1930/23 (See E.33(D)). Two destroyers if available with Captain D.13 are to proceed Casablanca forthwith to deal with situation.

36

FRENCH SQUADRON AT ALEXANDRIA ORDERED HOME; COMMANDER-IN-CHIEF, MEDITERRANEAN, REFUSES PERMISSION TO SAIL

(a) *Commander-in-Chief, Mediterranean, to Admiralty* 1059/24/6/40

My 1851/23 (see E.33). Message received by Admiral Godfroy from French Admiralty early a.m./24th begins 05123:– If Armistice is signed between France on one side and Germany and Italy on the other, you are to cease all operations or hostilities and return to French ports, to which I shall order you probably Bizerta. You are to embark F.L.O.'s and disembark B.L.O.'s Acknowledge. 1700/23. *Ends.*

    2. It is of course my intention that French ships shall not leave Alexandria.

(b) *Commander-in-Chief, Mediterranean, to Admiralty* 0131/25/6/40

Godfroy has received orders and officially requested that his squadron may be allowed to sail for Beyrout today, Tuesday.

    2. I have refused his request.

    3. Our relations exceptionally friendly, I rather feel he and many of his officers are very glad to have to bow to force majeure. I anticipate no difficulty.

    4. I hope the intention with regard to these ships may be made known to me as soon as possible as Godfroy may have trouble with ships' companies.

37

WITHDRAWAL OF BRITISH NAVAL LIAISON OFFICERS

F.O.I.C., Malta, to Admiralty, Commander-in-Chief, Mediterranean 2101/24/6/40

B.N.L.O., Bizerta, reports French Admiralty orders all B.N.L.O.'s to be withdrawn forthwith. Leaving shortly for Gibraltar, Syko called in. 1650/24.

The Armistice between France on the one hand and Germany and Italy on the other came into force at 0035/25th June 1940.

38

OPERATIONS OF BRITISH MEDITERRANEAN FLEET HAMPERED BY UNCERTAINTY OF FRENCH SITUATION

Commander-in-Chief, Mediterranean, to Admiralty 1939/25/6/40

Operations of Fleet at present severely cramped by uncertainty regarding French Squadron. Am therefore taking opportunity of running a southbound convoy from Dardanelles and Greek ports to Port Said.

Escort Third Cruiser Squadron and 14th Destroyer Flotilla sail 26th June to rendezvous with convoy off Dardanelles. Air and submarine reconnaissance will be provided to west of Crete and a force kept at short notice in Alexandria.

39

GERMAN USE OF FRENCH CODES

F.O.I.C., Malta, to Commander-in-Chief, Mediterranean   1355/26/6/40

Germany has got French codes and are passing out messages in French codes purporting to come from Admiral Darlan. Have seen Darlan's last apparently genuine order dated 20/6 which finishes by saying 'Whatever orders be received, never abandon to enemy a ship of war intact.'

40

CAUTION NECESSARY IN ANGLO-FRENCH INTERPRETATION OF ARMISTICE TERMS

(*a*) *Admiralty to Vice Admiral (A) in H.M.S. Ark Royal*   1537/26/6/40

Supplementing instructions already sent communication to be made to *Richelieu*, it should be explained that we do not doubt Admiral Darlan's good faith and believe he would do his utmost to fulfil his pledge that no unit of the French Fleet shall fall into enemy hands. It must however be observed that under the armistice now signed with Germany and Italy, French naval vessels have to be demobilised and disarmed under German and Italian control, i.e., handed over as fighting units to Germany and Italy.

From that moment Admiral Darlan will no longer have the power, though he would no doubt have the inclination, to carry out his promise, and we should have nothing to rely on but German and Italian declarations, which are obviously valueless. Therefore, in taking steps to prevent French naval vessels from falling into German and Italian hands, H.M. Government are not only endeavouring to safeguard their vital interests, but are also giving Admiral Darlan the opportunity to fulfil his pledge. H.M. Government are quite prepared to discuss the future of French naval units and are only concerned to make absolutely secure that in execution of the Armistice Terms no unit of French Fleet should fall into German or Italian hands.

(*b*) *Admiralty to A.I.G. 9,*[1] *F.O.C.N.A.*   1910126/6/40

To further our policy of obtaining effective co-operation of units of French Navy point out to French Authorities with whom you are in contact that we have evidence to show Germans have obtained French Naval codes and are issuing instructions to the French Navy and Marine purporting to come from Admiral Darlan. It can be assumed that this procedure has been used since 20/6. Under these circumstances policy of waiting to receive orders from Admiral Darlan can only result in playing still further into German hands. Emphasize that Darlan's last message dated 20th June finished by saying:– 'Whatever be the orders received never abandon to the enemy a ship of war intact.'

41

APPRECIATION OF FRENCH ATTITUDE BY BRITISH NAVAL LIAISON OFFICERS

(*a*) *From B.N.L.O. (Sud) to Admiralty, Commander-in-Chief, Mediterranean, and F.O.C.N.A.*   1003/28/6/40

Following undertakings obtained verbally before leaving Bizerta. From Admiral Esteva that if orders for giving up Fleet or units were received from Government and not his chief he would not obey. From Prétet-Maritime that he would never give up Dockyards. Charges already in place to blow nerve centres.

(*b*) *From B.N.L.O. (Sud) at Casablanca to Admiralty, Commander-in-Chief, Mediterranean, and F.O.C.N.A.*
    1108/28/6/40

Following is joint opinion of all B.N.L.O.'s Mediterranean ports meeting at Casablanca.

1. French Army and Air Force at present much more determined than Navy to carry on war in North Africa and to resist attack, although no attempted resistance can be maintained without supply of munitions.

---

[1] Commanders-in-Chief, Home Fleet, Mediterranean, East Indies, A. and W. Indies, Africa, Commodore Commanding New Zealand, Naval Board, Melbourne, Naval Service H.Q. Ottawa, Naval Board, Wellington, Navy Office, Bombay.

2. French Navy. Morale of crews at Dakar deteriorating, some ships have failed to be paid, others fear the same. British Government offer of pay and pensions probably not known by men. Promised terms published in papers today must have caused strong feelings. Pay and *immediate lead* would undoubtedly influence them to follow their officers who are unanimous in desiring to continue war.

3. The best form this lead could take would be arrival of British Squadron outside territorial waters of Oran. Morale would then immediately improve and Admiral Commanding might launch last appeal to French Admiral to his C.O's. If French battleships put to sea all forces would probably follow suit.

4. Reference B.N.L.O's Sud 1003/28 (E.41(a)) British Admiral could stress undertakings given by Admirals Esteva and Rivet which if carried out would render treaty null, therefore French Admiral's action in taking Fleet to sea would be in keeping with these undertakings.

42

INSTRUCTIONS FROM FRENCH ADMIRALTY TO FRENCH ADMIRAL AT ORAN TO ANSWER FORCE WITH FORCE

From Admiralty to S.O. Force H 1613/3/7/40

Following received from French Admiralty to Admiral, Oran, timed 1330/3 G.M.T.
Begins:–
You will inform the British Representative that the Commander-in-Chief has given orders to all French Naval Forces in the Mediterranean to join you immediately in fighting order. You are empowered to give orders to these forces. You are to answer force with force. Call in the submarines and aircraft if necessary. The Armistice Commission has been informed. Signed Leluc.
Ends.

43

S.O. FORCE H, INTENTIONS FOR SUPPORTING OPERATIONS TO M.A.5

(*a*) *From S.O. Force H to Admiralty and Commander-in-Chief, Mediterranean* 1430/7/7/40

After appreciation with V.A.(A) consider taking Force H into S.E. corner of Tyrrhenian Sea for air attack on Taranto or Augusta not worth results likely to be achieved for following reasons:–

(*a*) Surprise would be most unlikely.

(*b*) Striking Force would be only 12 T.S.R. and 9 Skuas.

(*c*) Attacks would be better carried out from East or from Malta without taking capital ships into dangerous area with little prospect of using them.

(*d*) Consider therefore that unless favourable target is presented proposal be limited to Cagliari area where surprise may be achieved and 'V' and 'W' class destroyers can be used. Only five destroyers could accompany force.

2. Such attacks would be 'pinprick' only, but can be synchronized with Commander-in-Chief, Mediterranean, operation.

3. Disadvantage of 'pinprick' policy putting Italians on their guard.

4. Alternative is to fly 12 T.S.R. off *Ark Royal* from position south of Sardinia to arrive Malta dawn. Aircraft to attack from Malta and be retrieved at subsequent date.

Ark Royal would then be left with nine T.S.R. and 18 Skuas.

5. Important requirement for operations against Italian ships in southern harbours is air reconnaissance from Malta giving exact position of ships up to last moment before attack.

6. Substitution of longer endurance destroyers for 'V' and 'W' class would be of great assistance for future operations of this type.

7. Propose sailing p.m. 8th July.

(*b*) *S.O. Force H to Commander-in-Chief, Mediterranean, and Admiralty* 1720/7/7140

Reference Commander-in-Chief's, Mediterranean, 1409/7. 'Lack of destroyers' with sufficient endurance and time to formulate proper plans prevent me from undertaking operations you suggest at present. I will sail a.m./8th July and carry out air attack on Cagliari at dawn 10th July as this should cause a diversion.

(*c*) *S.O. Force H to Commander-in-Chief, Mediterranean and Admiralty* 1750/7/7/40

My 1720/7. Intend to employ whole of Force H for this operation.

DETAILS OF REINFORCEMENT MOVEMENTS

44

(*a*) PROPOSED MOVEMENTS FOR PRELIMINARY OPERATIONS

From Admiralty to Commander-in-Chief, Mediterranean, S.O. Force H T.O.O. 1950/25/7/40

1. My 1700/25/7 (Appendix C.9(*c*)). The following is the general intention for the movements preliminary to the operation of reinforcing the Mediterranean.

2. On conclusion of Operation Hurry, the following ships to return to the United Kingdom.

   (*a*) *Hood* to replace *Renown* as flagship of B.C.S. Flags V.A.B.C.S. and S.O. Force H to be exchanged on arrival at Scapa.

   (*b*) *Valiant* to dock and embark reserve ammunition, H.A. guns and other stores for Malta and the Middle East.

   (*c*) *Arethusa* to be taken in hand for repairs, subsequently to join H.F.

   (*d*) *Argus* to embark Hurricanes for repetition of Operation Hurry, which will form part of reinforcement operation.

   (*e*) All destroyers at Gibraltar except 13th Flotilla.

3. On completion of 2 (*b*) and (*d*) the following ships will sail together for Gibraltar:–

   Renown, Valiant, Illustrious, Argus, York, Sheffield, Calcutta and destroyers as in 2 (*e*).

(*b*) COMMANDER-IN-CHIEF, MEDITERRANEAN, TO TAKE COMMAND OF ALL FORCES ENGAGED

From Admiralty to Commander-in-Chief, Mediterranean, S.O. Force H T.O.O. 1953/25/7/40

1. My 1700/25 (Appendix C.9(*c*)) and 1950/25 (Appendix E.44(*a*)). You are requested to take under your command all forces engaged in the operation of reinforcing the Mediterranean Fleet, after the completion of the preliminary movements from United Kingdom to Gibraltar.

2. Report whether you consider it advisable that *Royal Sovereign* should be passed through to Gibraltar at the same time in view of the added complication to an already difficult operation.

(*c*) MOVEMENTS OF H.M.S. *Royal Sovereign*

From Commander-in-Chief, Mediterranean, to Admiralty, S.O. Force H T.O.O. 1437/26/7/40

Admiralty 1953/25 (Appendix E.44(*b*)). Do not consider it advisable to pass *Royal Sovereign* through to Gibraltar in view of her low speed and added complications. *Royal Sovereign is* badly in need of docking and it is proposed that she should sail now round the Cape, docking en route at Durban. Escort to Aden will be arranged from Mediterranean Fleet.

(*d*) COMMANDER-IN-CHIEF'S, MEDITERRANEAN, INTENTIONS FOR OPERATION HATS

From Commander-in-Chief, Mediterranean, to Admiralty, S.O. Force H T.O.O. 1757/28/7/40

Admiralty 1953/25 (Appendix E.44(*b*)). Following is outline of my intentions for operation which will be known as Hats.

A. Composition of forces:–

   Force A – *Argus* and escort.

   Force B – *Renown* and *Ark Royal*.

   Force F – Reinforcements for Eastern Mediterranean.

   Force I – Mediterranean Fleet.

B. Day 1. Forces A and B sail in company for reaching approximately 08° E. at dawn Day 3. Force F sails p.m. to be near Galita Island at dusk Day 3. Force I sails p.m. from Alexandria to be nearing Malta at dusk Day 3.

Day 2. All forces on passage to initial positions.

Day 3. Force A flies off Hurricanes to Malta and retires to Gibraltar Force B parts company with A during forenoon and proceeds to make detour towards Balearic Islands, to reach position for air attack on Genoa as ordered by F.O. Force H. Force F passes Galita Island at dusk and proceeds at high speed to be well to the South East of Pantellaria at dawn.

Day 4. Force I arrives near Malta as shown and starts fuelling destroyers in Malta. Force B launch air attack on Genoa and retire at high speed, reassembling on completion.

Force I and F rendezvous S.W. of Malta.

Valiant to Malta to discharge stores and rejoin.

Calcutta, *Coventry* and Force F destroyers to Malta to fuel and rejoin. Fuelling of Force I destroyers at Malta continues.

On completion of fuelling Force I and F proceed to Alexandria.

Day 5. Force A arrives Gibraltar. Remaining Force on passage to base.

Day 6. a.m. Force B arrives Gibraltar. p.m. Mediterranean Fleet arrives Alexandria.

C. A small convoy including Oiler *Plumleaf* will be sailing from Alexandria to Malta under cover of Force I to arrive night of Day 3/Day 4. (? an Oiler) and possibly a store ship from Malta will be sailing from Malta on Day 4 from Alexandria.

(*e*) S.O. FORCE H PROPOSALS TO MODIFY COMMANDER-IN-CHIEF'S, MEDITERRANEAN PLAN

From S.O. Force H to Commander-in-Chief, Mediterranean, Admiralty T.O.O. 211 1/30/7/40

Your 1757/28 (E.44(*d*)). Following are my remarks.

1. (*a*) Withdrawal of Force B from Force A during forenoon of Day 3 will leave *Argus* protected by *Resolution* and one cruiser only from air attack, for remainder of day.

(*b*) Retirement of Force A during Day 3 will probably disclose Force F and enemy aircraft, rendering subsequent diversion by Force B largely ineffective.

(*c*) Division to Genoa starts from position south of Sardinia exposing *Ark Royal* to prolonged bombing and cannot be accomplished without oiling destroyers at sea, which is undesirable unless essential for achievement of main objects.

(*d*) Three weak forces will be widely spread p.m. on Day 3 advantageously to Italian Fleet. Should they venture to westward Force F would be without support.

(*e*) To summarise – Force B provides neither adequate support nor adequate diversion for Forces A and F.

2. Following modification to group is proposed after consulting with V.A. (A).

(*a*) Force A to be abolished and *Ark Royal* to carry 6 to 9 Hurricanes on flying deck. This will allow torpedo spotter reconnaissance to be operated.

(*b*) Forces B and F to leave Gibraltar together p.m. Day 1, Force F proceeding as in plan. Force B to use maximum speed for approach p.m. Day 2 and night Day 2/3 thus probably avoiding bombing altogether. *Ark Royal* to fly off Hurricanes dawn Day 3 at longitude 7° 20' E.

(*c*) Force B then either (1) to make diversion to north-west at high speed drawing enemy air from Force F and bombing Alghero aerodrome dawn Day 4 or (2) to reinforce Force F against air and for surface attack during Day 3, parting company after dark and bombing Cagliari aerodrome dawn Day 4.

(*d*) I favour (*c*) (2) above, as this provides formidable concentration of ships, fighters and A/A guns. It might be possible to adopt (*c*) (1) (1 group) and revert to (*c*) (2) if and when Force F is found by enemy air.

3. If required further Hurricanes can be transferred by *Ark Royal* later.

(*f*) COMMANDER-IN-CHIEF'S, MEDITERRANEAN, CONCURRENCE WITH S.O. FORCE H

From Commander-in-Chief, Mediterranean, to S.O., Force H, Admiralty 1007/1/8/40

In general agreement with your 2111/30/7(E.44(*c*)) except para. 1 (*d*) 0 which I think there is little change. I also favour your proposal 2 (*c*) (2). This formidable concentration might well have excellent after effects. 2 (*c*) (2) has further the advantage that it makes for economy in destroyers. Operational orders will now be made out based on my 1757/28/7(E.44(*d*)) as amended by your 2111/30/7, para. 2.

45
MINING POLICY FOR MEDITERRANEAN, AUGUST 1940

From Commander-in-Chief, Mediterranean, to Admiralty   1641/24/8/40

As long as the war is confined to the present belligerents the principal areas for the development of mining offensive are:–

    (*a*) The Adriatic.

    (*b*) Off the Libyan coast.

Should the war extend to Greece and Yugoslavia, the importance of mining in the Adriatic will be enhanced and there will be large areas off the Greek coast where mines could profitably be laid. Until fast surface minelayers are available there is unfortunately nothing to be done to increase the minelaying effort, as the only minelayer, *Rorqual*, does the work at every opportunity, using Malta as her mining base.

APPENDIX F

DISPOSITION OF FLEETS OF THE MEDITERRANEAN POWERS
(a)
SEPTEMBER 1939

GREAT BRITAIN

ALEXANDRIA
  Battleships (3)   *Warspite* (Fleet Flagship)
                                     Barham (Flag of V.A., 1st B.S.)
                                     Malaya
  Aircraft Carrier (1)   *Glorious* (T.S.R. 36, Fighters 6)
  Attendant Destroyer   *Bulldog*
  8-inch Cruisers (3)   *Devonshire* (V.A.C., 1st C.S.)
                                     Sussex
                                     Shropshire
  6-inch Cruisers (3)   *Arethusa* (R.A., 3rd C.S.)
                                     Penelope
                                     Galatea (V.A.(D) Medn. destroyers)
  A.A. Cruisers (1)   *Coventry*
  Destroyers (26)   *Grenville* (D1)
                                     Grafton, Gallant, Greyhound, Glowworm (1st Div.)
                                     Garland, Gipsy, Grenade, Griffin (2nd Div.)
                                     Hardy (D2)
                                     Hero, Hereward, Hostile, Hasty (3rd Div.)
                                     Afridi (D4)
                                     Gurkha, Mohawk, Sikh (7th Div.)
                                     Cossack, Maori, Zulu, Nubian (8th Div.)
                                     21st Flotilla –
                                     Delight, Defender, Decoy, Duchess (42nd Div.)
  Sloops (4)   *Aberdeen, Fleetwood, Grimsby, Deptford*
  Submarines (2)   *Salmon, Snapper*
  Netlayer (1)   *Protector*
  Minesweepers (4)   *Pangbourne, Sutton, Ross, Lydd*
  A/S Trawlers (4)   *Beryl, Moonstone, Coral, Jade*

DISPOSITION OF FLEETS OF THE MEDITERRANEAN POWERS APP. F(A)

Depôt Ships (3)	*Resource* (Fleet Repairs)
	Woolwich (Destroyer)
	Maidstone (Submarines)
Oilers (7)	*'War'* class (7,500 tons) – 2
'Dale' class (11,000 tons) – 3	
'Leaf' class (5,000 tons) – 2	
Storeships (6)	*Bacchus, Cisneros, Foreland, Philomel, Reliant, Rutland*
Hospital Ships (2)	*Atlantis, Maine*

GIBRALTAR
Destroyers (18)	*Keppel* (D13)
	Douglas, Wrestler, Active, Wishart (25th Div.)
	Watchman, Vidette, Velox, Vortigern (26th Div.)
	Inglefield (D3)
	Imogen, Ilex, Isis, Imperial (5th Div.)
	Intrepid, Icarus, Ivanhoe, Impulsive (6th Div.)

MALTA
Submarines (7)	*Sealion, Shark, Porpoise, Cachalot, Oswald, Osiris, Otway*
M.T.B.s (12)	Nos. 1 to 6 and 14 to 19
Minelayer	*Medusa*
Minesweepers (3)	*Dundalk, Albury, Dunoon*
Depôt Ships (2)	*Cyclops* (Submarines)
	Vulcan (M.T.B.s)

PORT SAID
Minesweepers (4)	*Fermoy, Saltash, Crescentmoon, Landfall*
Oilers (1)	*'Dale'* class (11,000 tons)
Petrol Carrier (1)	*Petrella*

HAIFIA
Minesweepers (2)	M.M.S. 1 and 2
Storeships (1)	*Atreus*

RED SEA
Destroyers (3)	*Duncan* (D.21)
	Dainty, Daring (41st Div.)

FRANCE

HIGH SEA FORCE[1]

TOULON
Battleships (3)	*Provence, Lorraine, Bretagne* (2nd Div. of the Line)
8-inch Cruisers (6)	*Algerie, Dupleix, Foch* (1st Div.)
	Duquesne, Tourville, Colbert (2nd Div.)
Destroyers (18)	*Tartu, Vauquelin, Chevalier Paul* (5th Div. C.T.)
	Vautour, Albatros, Gerfaut (7th Div. C.T.)
Destroyers (cont.)	*Maille Breze, Kersaint, Cassard* (9th Div. C.T.)

---

1 Force de Haute Mer. On 30th September, 1939, this force was re-named Mediterranean Fleet.

APP. F(A)   MEDITERRANEAN, SEPTEMBER 1939–OCTOBER 1940

La Palme, Le Mars, Tempete (1st Div. T.)
Le Fortune, La Railleuse, Simoun (3rd Div. T.)
Tramontane, Tornade, Typhon (7th Div. T.)
(C.T. – *Contre-Torpilleur*)
(T. – *Torpilleur*)

INSTRUCTIONAL SQUADRON

Battleships (2)	*Paris, Courbet*
Minelaying (1)	*Pluton*
Submarine Chasers (4)	Chasseur 79, 85, 103, 108

SPECIAL FORCE UNDER ORDERS OF COMMANDER-IN-CHIEF, SOUTH

Escort vessels (4)	*Lassigny, Amiens, Les Eparges, Dedaigneuse*
Submarines (8)	*Redoubtable, Vengeur* (7th Div.)
	Galatee, Naiade, Sirene, Argonaute (19th Div.)
	Diamant, La Perle (2nd Div.)

SPECIAL FORCE, COMMANDER-IN-CHIEF, SOUTH

ALGIERS

Destroyers (5)	*Tigre, Lynx* (4th Div. C.T.)
	Baliste, La Bayonnaise, La Poursuivante (13th Div. T.)
Submarines (18)	*Le Heros, Le Glorieux, Le Tonnant, Le Conquerant* (1st Div.)
	Protee, Acteon, Fresnel, Acheron (3rd Div.)
	Pegase, Monge (5th Div.)
	Doris, Thetis, Calypso, Circe (13th Div.)
	Iris, Venus, Pallas, Ceres (15th Div.)
Submarine Chasers (6)	Chasseur 1, 3, 4, 105, 110, 116

ORAN

Destroyers (3)	*Bordelais, L'Alcyon, Trombe* (8th Div. T.)
Air Carrier (1)	*Commandant Teste* (1 Bomber Sqdn. (10), 1 Reconnaissance Sqdn. (12))
Submarines (12)	*Minerve, Junon, Orion, Ondine* (12th Div.)
	*Diane, Ariane, Eurydice, Dana*e (14th Div.)
	Lapsyche, Oreade, Meduse, Amphitrite (18th Div.)

BIZERTA

1. STRIKING FORCE

6-inch Cruisers (4)	*Marseillaise, La Galissonniere, Jean de Vienne, Emile Bertin* (3rd Div.)
Destroyers (6)	*Vauban, Lion, Epervier* (1st Div.)
	Guepard, Verdun, Valmy (3rd Div.) (C.T.)

2. LOCAL COMMAND

Destroyers (4)	*La Pomone, Bombarde, L'Iphigenie* (12th Div. T.)
	Aigle (attached to S/Ms.)
Escort Vessels (3)	*Ypres, Tapageuse, Engageante*
Minelayer (1)	*Castor*

138

DISPOSITION OF FLEETS OF THE MEDITERRANEAN POWERS   APP. F(A)

Submarine Chasers (4)	C. 102, 113, 114, T-369
Submarines (11)	*Phoque, Espadon, Dauphin* (10th Div.)
	La Vestale, La Sultane, L'Atalante, L'Arethuse (17th Div.)
	Turquoise, Rubis, Saphir, Nautilus (20th Div.)

LEVANT
BEIRUT

Destroyers (1)	*Milan* (C.T.)
Escort Vessel (1)	*D'Iberville* (Sloop)
Submarines (6)	*Caiman, Morse, Souffleur* (9th Div.)
	Marsouin, Narval, Requin (11th Div.)

(*Source* – Minister des Armies, Etat Major General, 2eme Bureau, No. 13 E.M.G./2 (N.I.D.9988/45). O.U.6161. Various W.I.R.s.

ITALY

FIRST SQUADRON

TARANTO

Battleships (2)	*Cavour, Cesare*
8-inch Cruisers (4)	*Fiume, Gorizia, Zara, Pola*
6-inch Cruisers (2)	*Abruzzi, Garibaldi*
Destroyers (12)	*Saetta, Dardo, Freccia, Strale, Baleno, Fulmine, Folgore, Lampo, Alfieri, Gioberti, Oriani, Carducci*
Torpedo Boat (1)	*Stocco*

AUGUSTA

Destroyers (4)	*Maestrale, Grecale, Scirocco, Libeccio*
Seaplane Carrier (1)	*Miraglia* (15 planes), 12 Fighter-Bomber (M.18), 3 Bomber-Reconnaissance (Cant 25) (fitted with catapults for flying off)

SECOND SQUADRON

PALERMO

8-inch Cruisers (3)	*Trieste, Trento, Bolzano*
Destroyers (4)	*Aviere, Artigliere, Geniere, Camicia Nera*

NAPLES

6-inch Cruisers (4)	*Savoia, D'Aosta, Attendolo, Montecuccoli*
Destroyers (4)	*Bersagliere, Alpino, Fuciliere, Granatiere*

MESSINA

6-inch Cruisers (3)	*Da Barbiano, Diaz, Di Giussano*
Destroyers (5)	*Lanciere, Ascari, Grabiniere, Corazziere, Da Noli*

SPEZIA

Destroyer (1)	*Da Mosto*

SCHOOL OF COMMAND

SICILY

6-inch Cruisers (2)	*Bande Nere, Cadorna*
Destroyers (2)	*Vivaldi, Da Recco*

APP. F(A)   MEDITERRANEAN, SEPTEMBER 1939–OCTOBER 1940

    Torpedo Boats (16)   *Lupo, Lira, Lince, Libra, Cigno, Centauro, Castore, Climene, Circe, Clio, Calliope, Calipso, Partenope, Pleiadi, Polluce, Pallade*
    M.T.B.s (12)   509, 432, 437, 424 (7th M.A.S. Div.)
         512, 513, 514, 515 (9th M.A.S. Div.)
         516, 517, 518, 519 (10th M.A.S. Div.)

LIBYA (TOBRUK)
    Cruiser (1) old   *San Giorgio*
    Destroyers (6)   *Zeffiro, Borea, Espero, Ostro, Euro, Nembo*
    Escort Vessels (3)   *Valoroso, Palmaiolo, Alula* (Gunboats)

TRIPOLI
    Destroyer (1)   *Usodimare*
    Torpedo Boats (4)   *Airone, Alcione, Ariel, Aretusa*

DODECANESE
    Destroyers (5)   *Zeno, Tarigo, Pigafetta, Malocello, Pessagno*
    Torpedo Boats (3)   *Vega, Sagittario, Perseo*
    Minelayer (1)   *Legnano*
    M.T.B.s (7)   520, 521, 522, 431, 433, 434 (11th M.A.S. Div.)

UPPER TYRRHENIAN COMMAND (SPEZIA-LEGHORN-GENOA)
    Battleship (1)   *Duilio*
    Destroyers (4)   *Crispi, Ricasoli, Sella, Nicotera*
    Torpedo Boats (13)   *Monzambano, Curtatone, Castelfidardo, Calatafimi, Papa, Chinotto, Cascino, Montanari, Altair, Aldebran, Antares, Andromeda, Audace*
    Submarine Chaser (1)   *Albatross*
    M.T.B.s (13)   *Turr* (S.O.) 438, 439, 440, 441 (1st M.A.S. Div.)
         505, 506, 507, 508 (5th M.A.S. Div.)
         510, 511, 524, 525 (8th M.A.S. Div.)
    Escort Vessels (2)   *Rimini, Matteuci* (Gunboats)

LOWER TYRRHENIAN COMMAND (NAPLES, SICILY, SARDINIA)
    Destroyer (1)   *Cantore*
    Torpedo Boats (12)   *Orsa, Pegaso, Procione, Orione, Cassiopea, Canopo, Spica, Astore, Dezza, Cairoli, Schiaffino, Abba*
    Minelayers (6)   *Buffoluto, Panigaglia, Vallelunga, Durazzo, Pelogosa, Buccari*
    M.T.B.s (4)   501, 502, 503, 504 (4th M.A.S. Div.)

UPPER ADRIATIC COMMAND (VENICE-POLA)
    Battleship (1)   *Doria*
    Cruiser (1)   *Taranto* (old)
    Destroyers (2)   *Mirabell, Pancaldo*
    Torpedo Boats (9)   *Cosenz, Medici, Bassini, Fabrizi, Solferino, S. Martino, Confienza, Palestro, Sirio*
    Minelayers (3)   *Albona, Laurana, Rovigno*
    M.T.B.s (3)   423, 426, 430 (6th M.A.S. Div.)
    Escort Vessel (1)   *Giovannini* (Gunboat)

DISPOSITION OF FLEETS OF THE MEDITERRANEAN POWERS   APP. F(A)

Ionian and Lower Adriatic Command (Taranto-Brindisi)
Cruiser (1)	*Bari* (old)
Destroyers (3)	*Aquilone, Riboty, Turbine*
Torpedo Boats (7)	*Carini, La Masa, Prestinari, Pilo, Mosto, Missori, Sirtori*
Minelayers (2)	*Viesti, Azio*
Escort Vessels (4)	*Otranto, Gallipoli, G. Lante, Cirene*

SUBMARINE DISPOSITIONS

Spezia (21)	*Balilla, Toti, Sciesa, Calvi, Finzi, Tazzoli, Jalea, Jantina, Macalle, Ametista, Berillo, Micca, Foca, Zaffiro, H.1, H.2, H.4, H.6, H.8, Cappellini, Faa di Bruno*
Naples (11)	*Millelire, Mocenigo, Veniero, Glauco, Nani, Provana, Barbarigo, Emo, Morosini, Adua, Torricelli*
Sardinia (8)	*Fieramosca, Marcello, Dandolo, Alagi, Aradam, Axum, Diaspro, Corallo*
Messina (8)	*Turchese, Medusa, Mameli, Capponi, Speri, Da Procida, Onice, Iride*
Trapani (9)	*Des Geneys, Colonna, Pisani, Bausan, Atropo, Zoea, Corridoni, Bragadino, X.2*
Augusta (8)	*Tricheco, Squalo, Narvalo, Delfino, Bandiera, Menotti, Manara, Santarosa*
Taranto (12)	*Gemma, Perla, Archimede, Galilei, Ferraris, Settimo, Settembrini, Salpa, Smeraldo, Diamante, Malachite, Topazio*
Brindisi (5)	*Sirena, Galatea, Naiade, Fisalia, Argonauta*
Fiume (1)	*Rubino, X.2*
Pola (2)	*Ambra, X.3*
Libya (8)	*Ondina, Nereide, Anfitrite, Serpente, Dessie, Dagabur, Uarsciek, Uebiscebeli, Turchese*
Dodecanese (8)	*Gondar, Scire, Neghelli, Ascianghi, Durbo, Tembien, Beilul, Lafole*

Red Sea
Massawa
Destroyers (7)	*Pantera, Tigre, Leone* (5th Div.)
	Battisti, Nullo, Sauro, Manin (3rd Div.)
Torpedo Boats (2)	*Orsini, Acerbi*
Escort Vessels (4)	*Eritrea, Ostia* (Sloops)
	Biglieri, Porto Corsini (Gunboats)
M.T.B.s (5)	Nos. 204, 206, 210, 213, 216 (21st M.A.S. Div.)
Submarines (4)	*Brin, Argo, Velella, Otaria*

Source – N.I.D.3/DW. of 28/12/45 O.U.6161

SPAIN

Ferrol (2 days' steaming from Mediterranean)
8-inch Cruisers (1)	*Canarias*
6-inch Cruisers (5)	*A. Cervera, Navarra, M. de Cervantes, Galicia, Mendez Nunez* (last 3 at 2 months' notice)

APP. F(A)   MEDITERRANEAN, SEPTEMBER 1939–OCTOBER 1940

    Destroyers (8) — *Ulloa, Ciscar, Jorge Juan, A. Valdes, Escano, Ceuta Melilla, Alsedo* (last 3 at 2 months' notice)
    Torpedo Boats (2) — Nos. 7, 9
    Minelayer (1) — *Neptuno*
    [1]Escort Vessels (9) — *Mar Cantabrico, Mar Negro, Tito, Apagador, Argus, Tritonia, Dirizia, Fantastico, Galana*

CADIZ
    Destroyers (5) — *J. L. Diez, Lepanto, Lazaga, Teruel, Heusca* (last 2 at 2 months' notice)
    Torpedo Boats (2) — Nos. 16, 19
    [1]Escort Vessels (10) — *Lauria, Dalvo Sortel, Calvo Sortelo, Mallorca, Reyjaime I, Alcaza, Marquess de Chavarri, Galdanes, Domine, Plus Ultra*
    M.T.B.s (20) — L.A.S. 11 to 18, 21 to 26, LT. 11, 12, 14 to 17

MALAGA
    Destroyer (1) — *Gravina*
    M.T.B.s (4) — *I.2, Sicilia, Candido, Perez*

CARTAGENA
    Destroyers (4) — *A. Antequera, S. Barcaiztegui, Churruca, A. Galiano* (last 3 at 2 months' notice)
    Torpedo Boats (5) — Nos. 14, 17, 20, 21, 22
    Submarines (3) — B.1, B.2, B.4
    Minelayer (1) — *Jupiter*
    [1]Escort Vessels (4) — *G. Dato, Magallenes, Cano, Cabo Menor*
    M.T.B.s (6)

VALENCLA
    [1]Escort Vessels (4) — *Laya, Urllobo, Terensa, Planella*
    Minelayer (1) — *Marte*

TANGIER
    Minelayer (1) — *Vulcano*

ALGECIRAS
    M.T.B. (1) — *Napoles*

BALEARIC ISLANDS
PALMA
    [1]Escort Vessels (13) — *Cuidad de Alcudia, Cuidad de Ivizia, A. Lazarro, Cuidadela, V. Puchol, Santa Urbana, Miguel, Pedro I, Juan Mary, Canovas del Castillo, Jose Canalejas, A. Cervera, Ebro, Pacifico*

PORT SOLLER
    Destroyers (2) — *Velasco, A. Miranda*
    Submarines (2) — *Mola, Sanjurjo*

VINAROZ
    [1]Escort Vessels (2) — *Camamile, J. J. Sister*

---

1 Escort Vessels includes gunboats, armed merchant cruisers, armed transports, armed trawlers.

DISPOSITION OF FLEETS OF THE MEDITERRANEAN POWERS   APP. F(A)

M.T.B.s (3)   *Oviedo, Falange,* (?)

Source – N.A., Madrid RS/292/45 – N.I.D.9988/45 O.U.6161

GREECE

Main Base – SALAMIS
Minor Bases – POROS, SALONIKA, VOLO, SUDA BAY
  8-inch Cruiser (1)   *Giorgios Averoff*
  6-inch Cruiser (1)   *Helle*
  Destroyers (10)   *Vassileus Georgios, Vassilissa Olga, Paul Coundouriotis, Hydra, Spetsai, Psara, Leon, Panther, Ierax, Aetos*
  Torpedo Boats (13)   *Niki, Aspis, Thyella, Sphendoni, Pergamos, Proussa, Kios, Kyzikos, Kydonia, Arethousa, Alkyoni, Doris, Aigli*
  Submarines (6)   *Katsonis, Proteus, Triton, Glaucos, Papanicolis, Nereus*
  M.T.B.s (2)   *T.1, T.2*

Source – O.U.6161

TURKEY

IZMID
  Battle-Cruiser (1)   *Yavuz*
  6-inch Cruisers (2)   *Mecidiye, Hamidiye*
  Destroyers (4)   *Adatepe, Kocatepe, Tinaztepe, Zafer*
  Gunboats (2)   *Berk, Peyk*
  Submarines (6)   *Birinci Inonu, Ikinci Inonu, Sakarya, Dumlupinar, Gur, Saldiray*
  Minelayers (2)   *Yardim, Resid*
SMYRNA (IZMIR)
  Minelayer (1)   *Uyanik*

Source – O.U.6161

YUGOSLAVIA

TIVAT AND CATTARO
  Seaplane Carrier (1)   *Zmaj* (6 aircraft)
  Destroyer (1)   *Dubrovnik*
  Torpedo Boats (6)   T.1, 3, 5, 7, 8
  Minelayers (6)   *Sokol, Orao, Galeb, Labud, Jastreb, Kobac*
  Submarines (4)   *Hrabri, Nebojsa, Smeli, Osvetnic*
  M.T.B.s (8)   *Orjen, Velebit, Dinara, Triglav, Suvobor, Rudnik, Kajmakcalan, Durmitor*

Source – O.U.6161

BLACK SEA
BULGARIA

VARNA
  Torpedo Boats (6)   *Derzki, Hrabri, Smeli, Strogi, Shumni, Letoutschy*

RUMANIA

CONSTANZA AND SULINA
- Destroyers (2) — *Regele Ferdinand, Regina Maris*
- Torpedo Boats (3) — *Sborul, Naluca, Zmeul*
- Gunboats (4) — *Locot-Cdr. Stihi, Cpt. Dumitrescu, Locot. Lepri Remus, Sublt. Ghiculescu*
- Submarine (1) — *Delfinul*

GALATZ
- Destroyers (2) — *Marasti, Marasesti*

DANUBE FLOTILLA
- Monitors (7) — *Ioan C. Bratianu, Alexander Lahovari, Lascar Catargiu, Mihail Kogalniceanu, Basarabia Bucovina, Ardeal*
- Vedettes (7) — Nos. 1 to 7
- River Gunboats (3) — *Bistritsa, Oltul, Siretul*

U.S.S.R.

Main Bases – SEVASTOPOL, ODESSA
Minor Bases – NIKHOLAEV, SUKHUM, NOVOROSSISK

- Battleship (1) — *Pariskaya Kommuna*
- 7-inch Cruisers (2) — *Krasni Kavkaz, Komintern*
- 5-inch Cruisers (2) — *Profintern, Chervonnaya Ukrainia*
- Destroyers (16) — *Alma Alta, Bezposhtchadni, Bezupredni, Bodri, Budenni, Bystri, Felix Dzherzhinski, Frunze, Kharkov, Kiev, Moskva, Nezamozhnik, Ordzhonikidze, Petrovski, Shaumyan, Volochaevka*
- Torpedo Boats (9) — *Likhoy, Sassoviets, Shkval, Shtorm, Serp, Sibirisk, Sokki, Sovnarkum, Stamor*
- M.T.B.s (50) — Approximate number
- Submarines (25) — Out of 43 S/Ms reported in Black Sea, 25 was the maximum number considered effective

Source – C.B1815

(b)

JUNE 1940
I. SHIPS, INCLUDING SEABORNE AIRCRAFT

GREAT BRITAIN

	Ship	Aircraft [1]
ALEXANDRIA		
Battleships (4)	*Warspite* (Fleet Flagship), *Malaya,*	2 T.S.R. (each)
	Ramillies, Royal Sovereign	Nil

---

[1] Type of aircraft. – T.S.R. – Torpedo, Spotting, Reconnaissance.
L.R. – Light Reconnaissance.
A.B.R. – Amphibious Boat Reconnaissance.

DISPOSITION OF FLEETS OF THE MEDITERRANEAN POWERS APP. F(B)

	Ship	Aircraft
Aircraft Carrier (1)	*Eagle*, 813, 824 Squadrons, F.A.A.	18 T.S.R. (Swordfish) 4 fighters (Gladiators)
6-inch Cruisers (6)	*Orton*, *Neptune* (Vice-Admiral D)	2 L.R. (each)
	Sydney	1 A.B.R.
	Gloucester, *Liverpool*	2 A.B.R. (each)
	Capetown (Rear-Admiral 3rd C.S.)	Nil
Destroyers (21)	*Hyperion* (D.2), *Havock*, *Hero*, *Hereward* (3rd Div.)	
	Hostile, *Hasty*, *Ilex*, *Imperial* (4th Div.)	
	Stuart (D.10)	
	Waterhen, *Vampire*, *Voyager* (19th Div.)	
	Dainty, *Diamond*, *Decoy*, *Defender* (20th Div.)	
	Nubian (D.14)	
	Mohawk, *Janus*, *Juno* (27th Div.)	
	Garland (Polish)	
Submarines (6)	*Osiris*, *Oswald*, *Pandora*, *Parthian*, *Phoenix*, *Proteus*	
Netlayer (1)	*Protector*	
Minesweepers (5)	*Abingdon*, *Bagshot*, *Fareham*, 2 Trawlers	
Anti/Submarine Trawlers (8)	5th and 28th A/S Groups	
Armed Boarding Vessels (2)	*Chakla*, *Fiona*	
Depôt Ships (3)	*Resource* (Fleet Repairs)	
	Medway (Submarines)	
	Dumana (R.A.F.)	
Oilers (12)	'British' class (7,000 tons) – 2	
	'Chartered' (total 30,000 tons) – 6	
	'Leaf' class (5,000 tons) – 2	
	Fleet Attendant (2,000 tons) – 1	
	R.A.F. (*Pass of Balmaha*) – 1	
Store Ships (2)	*Calderon*, *Reliant*	
Hospital Ship (1)	*Maine*	
Cable Ship (1)	*Retriever*	

GIBRALTAR (under F.O.C.N.A.)

Battleship (1)	*Resolution*	1 T.S.R.
Aircraft Carrier (with Force H)	*Ark Royal*, F.A.A. Squadrons 800, 808, 8Io, 818, 820	30 T.S.R. 24 Fighters
6-inch Cruiser (1)	*Arethusa*	Nil
Destroyers (9)	*Watchman*, *Vidette*, *Velox*, *Vortigern*, *Keppel* (25th Div.)	
	Douglas, *Wishart*, *Active*, *Wrestler* (26th Div.)	
Minesweepers (4)	Trawlers	
Anti/Submarine Vessels (5)	Seventh A/S Group	
Cable Ship (1)	*Mirror*	

APP. F(B)   MEDITERRANEAN, SEPTEMBER 1939–OCTOBER 1940

	Ship	*Aircraft*
MALTA		
Destroyer (1)	*Vendetta*	
Submarines (6)	*Odin, Olympus, Orpheus, Otus, Grampus, Rorqual*	
Monitor (1)	*Terror*	
Minesweepers (9)	*Fermoy*, 8 Auxiliary M/S.	
Anti/Submarine Vessels (5)	Fourth A/S Group, 2 motor A/S boats	
PORT SAID		
6-inch Cruisers (2)	*Caledon, Calypso*	
Armed Boarding Vessels (3)	*Rosaura, Arpha, Surf*	
River Gunboats (2)	*Aphis, Ladybird*	
Minesweepers (4)	*Stoke*, 2 Trawlers, 1 Auxiliary M/S.	
HAIFA		
Minesweepers (2)	Auxiliary M/S Nos. 1 and 2	
RED SEA (*under Commander-in-Chief, East Indies*)		
6-inch Cruisers (3)	*Leander, Hobart*	1 A.B.R. (each)
	Ceres	Nil
	Carlisle	Nil
ADEN		
Destroyers (4)	*Kandahar, Kimberley, Khartoum, Kingston* (28th Div.)	
Sloops (5)	*Auckland, Flamingo, Grimsby, Cornwallis, Shoreham*	
Anti/Submarine Vessels (2)	*Amber, Moonstone*	

FRANCE

THIRD SQUADRON

TOULON		
8-inch Cruisers (4)	*Algerie, Colbert, Dupleix, Foch* (1st Div.)	2 F.P.R. (each)
Fleet Destroyers (19)	*Tartu, Le Chevalier Paul* (5th Div. C.T.)	
	Vautour, Albatros (7th Div. C.T.)	
	Kersaint, Cassard, Vauquelin (9th Div. C.T.)	
	La Palme, Le Mars, Tempete (1st Div. T.)	
Employed on escort duties, and under orders of Admiral of Striking Force from Oran	*Simoun* (3rd Div. T.)	
	Brestois, Boulonnais (5th Div. T.)	
	Tramontane, Tornade, Typhon (7th Dov. T.)	
	Bordelais, L'Alcyon, Trombe (8th Div. C.J.)	
Submarines (14)	*La Vestale, La Sultane, Atalante, Arethuse* (17th Div. S/M)	
	Galatee, Naiade, Sirene, Argonaute (19th Div. S/M)	
	Le Diamant, La Perle (21st Div. S/M)	
	Iris, Venus, Pallas, Ceres (15th Div. S/M)	
Escort Vessels (15)	*Sampierro Corso, Marigot, Cyrnos, Sidi Okba, Ville D'Ajac, Cio, Pascal Paoli* (1st Squadron)	

DISPOSITION OF FLEETS OF THE MEDITERRANEAN POWERS   APP. F(B)

	Ship	*Aircraft*
Escort Vessels (cont.)	Chamois, Commandant Bony, Gazelle, Annamite, La Surprise, La Curieuse (5th Squadron)	
	Dedaigneuse, La Gracieuse (Unattached)	
Submarine Chasers (7)	Nos. 1, 3, 4, 79, 85, 103, 108	

STRIKING FORCE

ALGIERS
- 6-inch Cruisers (3): *Jean de Vienne, La Galissonniere, Marseillaise* (3rd Div.) — 4 F.P.R. (each)
- Fleet Destroyers (6): *Aigle, Vauban, Lion* (1st Div. C.T.)
  Guepard, Verdun, Valmy (3rd Div. C.T.)
- Escort and Local Defence Destroyers (3): *Baliste, La Bayonnaise, Poursuivante* (13th Div. T.)
- Submarine Chasers (3): Nos. 105, 110, 116

ORAN
- Battleships (2): *Bretagne, Provence* — 4 F.P.R. (each)
- Battle Cruisers (2): *Dunkerque, Strasbourg* — 4 F.P.R. (each)
- Aircraft Carrier (1): *Commandant Teste* — 10 F.P.B. / 12 F.P.R.
- 6-inch Cruisers (3): *Georges Leygues, Gloire, Montcalm* — 4 F.P.R. (each)
- Fleet Destroyers (10): *Mogador, Volta* (6th Div. C.T.)
  L'Indomptable, Le Malin (8th Div. C.T.)
  Le Fantasque, Le Terrible, D'Audacieux (10th Div. C.T.)
  Tigre, Basque, Panther (4th Div. C.T.)
- Submarines (6): *Diane, Ariane, Eurydice, Danae* (14th Div.)
  La Psyche, L'Oreade (18th Div.)
- Escort Vessels (4): P. 136, P.137, P.138, P.139

BIZERTA
- Escort and Local Defence Destroyers (3): *La Pomone, Bombarde, Iphigenie* (12th Div. T.)
- Submarines (18): *Le Tonnant, Le Conquerant* (1st Div.)
  Fresnel (3rd Div.)
  Le Centaure, Argo, Pascal, Henri Poincare (4th Div.)
  L'Espoir, Pegase, Monge (5th Div.)
  Redoutable, Vengeur (7th Div.)
  Caiman, Morse, Souffeur (9th Div.)
  Turquoise, Saphir, Nautilus (20th Div.)
- Minelayer (1): *Castor*
- Escort vessels (2): *Tapageuse, Engageante* (2nd Squadron)
- Submarine Chasers (4): C.102, 113, 114, T.369

SOUSSE
- Submarines (2): *Marsouin, Narval* (11th Div.)

APP. F(B) MEDITERRANEAN, SEPTEMBER 1939–OCTOBER 1940

	Ship	*Aircraft*
LEVANT		
ALEXANDRIA		
Battleship (1)	*Lorraine*	
8-inch Cruisers (3)	*Duquesne, Tourville, Suffren*	
6-inch Cruiser (1)	*Duguay-Trouin*	
Fleet Destroyers (3)	*Le Fortune* (3rd Div. T.)	
	Lynx, Forbin (9th Div. T.)	
Netlayer (1)	*Gladiateur*	
BEIRUT		
Submarines (6)	*Protee, Acteon, Acheron* (3rd Div.)	
	Phoque, Espadon, Dauphin (10th Div.)	
Escort Vessels (1)	*Lassigny*	

ITALY

TARANTO		
		(F.R. – Fighter Reconn.)
Battleships (3)	*Cavour, Cesare*	Nil
	Vittorio Veneto	3 F.R.
8-inch Cruisers (3)	*Zara, Fiume, Gorizia* (1st Div.)	2 F.R. (each)
6-inch Cruisers (5)	*Abruzzi, Garibaldi* (8th Div.)	4 F.R. (each)
	Diaz, Di Giussano, Savoia (4th Div.)	3 F.R.
Fleet Destroyers (20)	*Freccia, Dardo, Saetta, Strale* (7th Div.)	
	Folgore, Fulmine, Baleno, Lampo (8th Div.)	
	Vivaldi, Da Noli, Pancaldo, Malocello (14th Div.)	
	Da Masto, Da Verazzano, Pigafetta, Zeno (15th Div.)	
	Da Recco, Usodimare, Pessagno, Tarigo (16th Div.)	
Escort and Local	*Stocco, Carini, La Masa, Prestinari* (3rd T.B. Div.)	
Defence Destroyers (8)	*Pilo, Mosto, Missori, Sirtori* (6th T.B. Div.)	
Submarines (22)	*Gemma, Diamante, Malachite, Topazio, Marconi,*	
	Smeraldo, Salpa, Settimo, Settembrini, Sirena,	
	Galatea, Naiade, Fisalia, Argonauta, Atropo, Zoea,	
	Corridoni, Bragadino, Brin, Argo, Velella, Otaria	
Escort Vessels (4)	*Otranto, Gallipoli, G. Lante, Cirene* (Gunboats)	
Minelayers (2)	*Vieste, Azio*	
M.T.B.s (8)		
NAPLES		
Battleship (1)	*Littorio*	3 F.R.
6-inch Cruisers (4)	*D'Aosta, Attendolo* (7th Div.)	3 F.P.R. (each)
	Montecuccoli, Colleoni (2nd Div.)	3 F.P.R. (each)
Fleet Destroyers (4)	*Granatiere, Fuciliere, Bersagliere, Alpino* (13th Div.)	
Escort and Local	*La Farina, Cantore* (Unattached)	
Defence Destroyers (14)	*Cairoli, Schiaffino, Abba, Dezza* (5th T.B. Div.)	
	Vega, Sagittario, Perseo, Sirio (10th T.B. Div.)	
	Lupo, Lira, Lince, Libra (8th T.B. Div.)	

DISPOSITION OF FLEETS OF THE MEDITERRANEAN POWERS　　　　APP. F(B)

	Ship	*Aircraft*
Submarines (11)	*Millelire, Mocenigo, Veniero, Glauco, Nani, Provana, Barbarigo, Emo, Morosini, Adua, Da Vinci*	
Minelayers (3)	*Buffoluto, Panigaglia, Vallelunga*	

SICILY

MESSINA AND AUGUSTA
8-inch Cruisers (4)	*Pola, Bolzano, Trieste, Trento* (3rd Div.)	2 F.R. (each)
6-inch Cruisers (3)	*Da Barbiano, Bande Nere, Cadorna* (6th Div.)	2 F.P.R. (each)
Fleet Destroyers (16)	*Alfieri, Oriani, Carducci, Gioberti* (9th Div.)	
	Artigliere, Camicia Nera, Aviere, Geniere (11th Div.)	
	Lanciere, Carabinieri, Corazziere, Ascari (12th Div.)	
	Maestrale, Libeccio, Grecale, Scirocco (10th Div.)	
Seaplane Carrier (1)	*Miraglia* (15 Planes), 12 fighter bomber, M.18, 3 bomber reconnaissance, Cant 25. Fitted with catapults for flying off	
M.T.B.s (8)		

SYRACUSE-PALERMO-TRAPANI
Submarines (17)	*Medusa, Mameli, Capponi, Speri, Da Procida, Desgeneys, Colonna, Pisani, Bausan, Tricheco, Squalo, Narvalo, Delfino, Bandiera, Menotti, Manara, Santarosa*
Escort and Local Defence Destroyers (12)	*Cigno, Centauro, Castore, Climene,* (11th T.B. Div.) *Circe, Clio, Calliope, Calipso* (13th Div.) *Partenope, Pallade, Polluce, Pleiadi* (14th Div.)
Minelayers (2)	*Durazzo, Pelagosa*
M.T.B.s (12)	

SARDINIA (CAGLIARI)
Escort and Local Defence Destroyers (8)	*Orsa, Pegaso, Procione, Orione* (4th T.B. Div.) *Cassiopeia, Canopo, Spica, Astore* (9th T.B. Div.)
Submarines (18)	*Fieramosca, Marcello, Dandolo, Alagi, Aradam, Axum, Torelli, Diaspro, Corallo, Finzi, Tazzoli, Calvi, Bianchi, Iride, Onice, Bagnolini, Tarantini, Giuliani*
M.T.B.s (6)	
Minelayer (1)	*Buccari*

DODECANESE (LEROS)
Fleet Destroyers (4)	*Crispi, Ricasoli, Sella, Nicotera* (4th Div.)
Escort and Local Defence Destroyers (2)	*Solferino, San Martino* (15th T.B. Div.)
Submarines (8)	*Gondar, Scire, Neghelli, Ascianghi, Durbo, Tembien, Beilul, Lafole*
M.T.B.s (20)	
Minelayer (1)	*Legnano*

LIBYA (TOBRUK)
Fleet Destroyers (8)	*Zeffiro, Borea, Espero, Ostro* (1st Div.)

APP. F(B)   MEDITERRANEAN, SEPTEMBER 1939–OCTOBER 1940

	Ship	*Aircraft*
Fleet Destroyers (cont.)	*Euro, Nembo, Aquilone, Turbine* (2nd Div.)	
Submarines (9)	*Ondina, Nereide, Anfitrite, Serpente, Dessie, Dagabur, Uarsciek, Utbiscebeli, Turchese*	
Escort Vessels (3)	*Valaroso, Palmaiolo, Alula* (Gunboats)	
Depôt Ship (1)	*San Giorgio* (Cruiser)	

TRIPOLI

Escort and Local Defence Destroyers (4)	*Airone, Alcione, Ariel, Aretusa* (1st T.B. Div.)

ADRIATIC (TRIESTE-FLUME-POLA)

Battleship (1)	*Andrea Doria*	Nil
Escort and Local Defence Destroyers (6)	*Confienza, Palestro* (15th T.B. Div.) *Cosenz, Medici, Bassini, Fabrizi* (7th T.B. Div.)	
Escort Vessel (1)	*Giovannini* (Gunboat)	
Submarines (4)	*Ambra, Rubino*, X.2, X.3	
M.T.B.s (8)		

BRINDISI-BARI

	Ship	
Fleet Destroyers (2)	*Mirabello, Riboty*	
M.T.B.s (8)		

SPEZIA

Battleship (1)	*Caio Duilio*	Nil
Escort and Local Defence Destroyers (13)	*Altair, Antares, Aldebaran, Andromeda* (12th T.B. Div.) *Monzambano, Curtatone, Castelfidardo, Calatafimi* (16th T.B. Div.) *Papa, Cascino, Chinotto, Montanari* (2nd T.B. Div.) *Audace* (Unattached)	
Submarines (18)	*Balilla, Toti, Sciesa, Jalea, Jantina, Console Generale Liuzzi, Ametista, Berillo, Zaffiro, Micca, Foca, Cappellini, Faa di Bruno,* H.1, 2, 4, 6, 8	
M.T.B.s (20)		
Escort Vessels (2)	*Rimini, Matteuci* (Gunboats)	
Submarine Chaser (1)	*Albatros*	

RED SEA

Fleet Destroyers (7)	*Pantera, Leone, Tigre* (5th Div.) *Battisti, Nullo, Sauro, Manin* (3rd Div.)
Escort and Local Defence Destroyers (2)	*Orsini, Acerbi*
Escort Vessels (4)	*Eritrea, Ostia* (Sloops) *Biglieri, Porto Corsini* (Gunboats)
M.T.B.s (5)	
Submarines (8)	*Archimede, Ferraris, Galilei, Torricelli, Galvani, Guglielmotto, Macalle, Perla*

Spain
Greece
Turkey
Yugoslavia
} No change from September, 1939, (Appendix F (a))

Bulgaria
Rumania
U.S.S.R.
} *Black Sea*
No change from September, 1939, (Appendix F (a))

NOTES ON ITALIAN SUBMARINES

1. *Endurance*

With the exception of the five H class and two X class boats (400-tons) there were in June 1940 100 submarines reported ready to operate from Italian bases in the Mediterranean, all of which possessed an endurance of 4,000 miles or more at surface cruising speed.

Type	No	Endurance at Cruising Speed
Grande Crociera (over 1,500 tons, normal displacement)	20	10 to 12,000 miles
Media Crociera (1,000 to 1,500 tons, normal displacement)	34	7 to 9,000 miles
Piccola Crociera (700 to 1,000 normal displacement)	46	4,000 miles
	100	

2. *Patrols*

At any given moment it was assessed that 20 boats would be under repair, leaving 80 available for operations. Not less than 20 might be expected at sea on offensive patrols, and this would entail a further 40 in harbour in order to maintain the 20 at sea. (During the 1914/18 war the proportion of German U-boats at sea to total numbers worked out at approximately 1/3rd, and in their case greater distance from their bases had to be considered.)

The remaining 20 boats were likely to be kept ready for defensive patrols, minelaying cruises, reserves, and special striking force to be despatched to selected places in the event of Allied Squadrons approaching Italian waters.

Of the 20 expected on offensive patrol it was considered 10 would be found in each half of the Mediterranean. With regard to the Eastern Mediterranean it was estimated that 6 would be stationed on a line from the west end of Crete to Derna in North Africa; 2 off Malta, and 2 off Alexandria; whilst in the Western Basin they would be found off Gibraltar, Algiers, Toulon and on a line southward from Sardinia to Bona in North Africa.

3. *Mines*

Twelve of the large and eleven of the medium-sized boats were fitted for minelaying.

Four (*Atropo, Foca, Micca, Zoea*) carried 36/40 mines, two (*Bragadino, Corridoni*) carried 32, and the remainder 10/18.

When mines were carried they took the place of spare torpedoes.

4. *Torpedoes*

The large and medium sized boats carried six to eight 21-inch torpedoes, and the smaller boats six 21-inch torpedoes.

APP. F(B) MEDITERRANEAN, SEPTEMBER 1939–OCTOBER 1940

II. SHORE-BASED AIRCRAFT JUNE 1940

GREAT BRITAIN

	Type	No. (R.A.F.)
GIBRALTAR	Bomber Reconnaissance	1 Squadron London flying boats
MALTA	Torpedo Spotting-Reconnaissance	1 Squadron (Unit Detachment) No. 3 A.A.C. and 1 Squadron (F.A.A.) Swordfish from July.
EGYPT	Fighters	3 Squadrons, Gladiators
	Bombers	6 Squadrons, Blenheims
	Special minesweepers	1 Unit D.W.I., Wellingtons
	Bomber Reconnaissance (201 Group)	2 Squadrons, Sunderland flying-boats
HAIFA	Fighters	1 Flight (French aircraft)

N.B. – R.A.F. Squadrons vary in numbers of aircraft:–
    Bombers and Fighter Squadrons   18 to 21 aircraft
    Flying boat Squadrons   9 to 12 aircraft

Source – Air Ministry, Historical Section

FRANCE

	Type	No.
S. FRANCE	Long Reconnaissance	5 Breguet Bizerta flying boats
BERRE	Bomber	32 L.E.O. (257) BIS. float planes
	Torpedo Bomber	10 Latecoere (29) float planes
HYERES	S.S. Fighter	15 Dewoitine (373) land planes
	Reconnaissance	8 C.A.M.S. (37) flying boats
	Reconnaissance	5 Autogyros
	Fighters	21 (9 S.S. Dewoitine (501) land planes, 12 multi-seater Potez (630/1) land planes)
MARIQUANE		
N. AFRICA		
BIZERTA (KAROUBA)	Long Reconnaissance	6 Loire (70) flying boats
	Reconnaissance Bomber	8 C.A.M.S. (55) flying boats
		18 L.E.O. (257) BIS. float planes
BIZERTA (SIDI AHMED)	Bomber	12 Bloch (200)

Source – O.U.6161

DISPOSITION OF FLEETS OF THE MEDITERRANEAN POWERS APP. F(B)

ITALY

	Type	No.
Upper Tyrrhenian		
Spezia	Reconnaissance	45 Cant Z.501
Leghorn		
Nisida	Fighter (S.S.)	18 R.O. 44
Vigna di Valle		
Orbetello	Bomber[1]	54 (36 Savoia S.55X, 18 Cant Z.506B)
Lower Tyrrhenian (*including Sicily Channel and Sardinia*)		
Augusta		
Syracuse		
Marsala	Reconnaissance	81 Cant Z.501
Elmas		
Terranova		
Pantellaria	Bomber	9 S.81
Taranto	Reconnaissance	9 Cant Z.501
Adriatic		
Brindisi	Reconnaissance	18 Cant Z.51
	Bomber[1]	18 Cant Z.506B
Pola	Reconnaissance	9 Cant Z.501
Dodecanese		
Leros	Fighter (S.S.)	18 R.O. 44
	Bomber	9 Cant Z.506B
	Reconnaissance	9 Cant Z.501 land planes
Rhodes	Fighter (S.S.)	18 C.R. 30
	Bomber	30 (18 S.79, 12 S.81)

Reconnaissance Squadrons were directly under Naval Command, but Bomber and Fighter Squadrons formed part of the independent Metropolitan Air Force.

Seaborne aircraft (including those in the *Miraglia*) totalled about 60, making the number of aircraft available for naval warfare approximately 400.

Source – O.U.6161; "All the World's Aircraft".

---

[1] Cant. Z.506B were alternative torpedo-bombers.

APPENDIX G

SUMMARY OF ACTIVITIES OF THE GREEK FLEET

I. BEFORE COLLAPSE OF GREECE
OCTOBER 1940 TO APRIL 1941

October 1940

Immediately after the Italian attack on Greece their naval vessels were employed escorting convoys of their troopships for mobilisation of the Greek army and to destinations for defence of their country.

November

The Greek naval authorities co-operated with the British in providing tugs, salvage craft, coastal and other small craft for defences of ports, minesweeping etc., especially during the installation of defences at Suda Bay, which place was an invaluable advance base for the British Fleet operating against the Italians.

Our convoys through the Aegean to Piraeus became more frequent and important, aircraft and stores being sent to support Greece. A British naval mission was sent to Greece, and advice given on A/S work and defences. A Greek delegation was received at Alexandria to study our methods and close contact was maintained.

December

The Commander-in-Chief requested that the Greek destroyers could be employed, (a) to protect trade north of the Doro Channel, (b) to escort convoys between Suda Bay and Piraeus, (c) to escort lightly escorted convoys through the Kaso Strait. This was done, and the Commander-in-Chief remarked that their standard of efficiency was satisfactory, the naval authorities being exceedingly anxious to co-operate.

January 1941

Greek destroyers escorted a convoy from Port Said to the Piraeus and many small convoys between Suda Bay, Piraeus and other Aegean ports. Greek submarines operated with considerable success against the Italian lines of communications and in the Adriatic.

March

The transport of two Divisions with stores etc. (Lustre) began, the Greek authorities assisted with personnel ships and destroyers for escort work.

28th March – Battle of Matapan – Greek destroyers were sent out to assist but took no actual part in the action, though they rescued a large number of Italian survivors next day.

April

On the 6th, Germany attacked Yugo-Slavia and Greece.

Evacuation of British forces from Greece commenced on 24th April.

II. AFTER COLLAPSE OF GREECE
MAY 1941 TO APRIL 1944

The Greek Government withdrew to Crete by the 23rd April, 1941 and offered the services of surviving Greek warships to act under the orders of the British Commander-in-Chief, Mediterranean. This offer was accepted by the Commander-in-Chief, Mediterranean, as follows:– 'Please inform Greek Admiralty that I am delighted to accept their offer, and shall welcome valued assistance of His Hellenic Majesty's ships.' (C.-in-C., Mediterranean, to N.A., Athens 2158/24/4/41).

On 23rd April, 1941 the Greek destroyers *Queen Olga*, *Ierax*, and *Panther* were at Suda Bay, while the cruiser *Giorgios Averoff*, repair ship *Hephestos*, destroyers *Paul Kondouriotis*, *Aetos*, *Spetsai*, submarine *Glaucos*, and torpedo boats *Aspis* and *Niki* arrived at Alexandria. Other arrivals at Alexandria shortly before or after that date were the torpedo boat *Sphendoni*, four minesweepers, and the submarines *Katsonis*, *Nereus*, *Papanicolis* and *Triton*. In 1942 and 1943 the Greek Navy took over 8 *Hunt Class* destroyers, renamed *Adrias*, *Crete*, *Kanaris*, *Miaoules*, *Navarinon*, *Pindos*, *Salamis*, *Themistocles*. After a short period of rest and refit the Greek Squadron under the directions of Admiral Sakellariou continued the fight as part of the British forces under Admiral Sir Andrew Cunningham, taking full share of escort duties, patrols, bombardments, anti-submarine work, minesweeping etc. Greek crews were recruited for manning supply schooners, and small craft supplying Tobruk. Their work was of high value and continued as such until April 1944, when political unrest interfered with their naval activities for some months.

Details of individual ship records are attached. Greek warship losses while working under the command of the Commander-in-Chief, Mediterranean, were as follows:–

	Sunk	Damaged
Destroyers	1	1
	(*Queen Olga*)	(*Adrias*)
Submarines	4	
	(*Glaucos*, *Katsonis*, *Proteus*, *Triton*)	
Minesweepers	2	

III. GREEK WARSHIPS' SERVICES DURING THE WAR

In Alphabetical Order According to Classes
Cruisers 2; Corvettes 4; Destroyers 19;
Submarines 7; Torpedo Boats 3

CRUISERS

1. *Giorgios Averoff*

Arrived at Alexandria 23.4.41 – Flying flag of Greek Admiral 25.4.41. Based on Bombay on *convoy and escort duties* in November 1941. – In July 1942 returned to Mediterranean – Berthed in Leonlos Harbour at Piraeus at end of 1944. Regent of Greece visited Salonika in *Giorgios Averoff* on 2nd March, 1945.

2. *Helle*

Sunk in Tinos Harbour by Italian submarine 15.8.40.

CORVETTES

3. *Apostolis* (ex *Hyacinth*)

Transferred to Greek Navy 1st November, 1943 – *escorting Mediterranean Convoys*. – On 28th March, 1944 joined 47th Mediterranean Escort Group.

4. *Kriezis* (ex *Coreopsis*)

Transferred to Greek Navy 14th November, 1943 – On *convoy escort* from Liverpool January 1944. – With Convoy ECM6 (Operation Neptune) 13th June, 1944. Joined Mediterranean Fleet 27.10.44.

5. *Saktouris* (ex *Peony*)

Transferred to Greek Navy 26.6.42. – *On escort duties in Levant* and Libyan coast till June 1943. *In Operation Husky* (landing in Sicily) July 1943. – *escorting convoys* in Mediterranean till end of 1943.

6. *Tompazis* (ex *Tamarisk*)

Joined Greek Navy 22.11.43. *In Operation Neptune* June 1944. *In Operation Pluto* 12th August, 1944. Joined Mediterranean Fleet October 1944.

DESTROYERS

7. *Admiral Hastings*

Escort to TAM 26 with *Bleasdale* 22.12.44. – convoy in North Sea.

8. *Adrias* (ex *Border*)

On escort duties with convoys to West Africa from United Kingdom in January 1943. On 13th February, 1943 *attacked U/B in* 3° 52' N., 6° 33' W. (off Freetown). Received a congratulatory message from Admiralty regarding this attack on 16th March, 1943.[1] – On *escort duties* in Eastern Mediterranean in August 1943. *Mined* and severely damaged off Leros on 22nd October, 1943.

9. *Aegean* (ex *Avondale*)

Due in Eastern Mediterranean end of April 1944, but her sailing from the United Kingdom was cancelled owing to political unrest.

10. *Aetos*

Arrived Alexandria 23.4.41. Refitting in East Indies from November 1941 to March 1942. Unsuccessfully attacked an enemy S/M S.W. of Colombo on 23rd March, 1942. Working in Eastern Mediterranean till July 1943. – *Attacked a U/B* on 15th June, 1943 in Lat. 32° 20' N., 34° 34' E.

11. *Crete* (ex *Hursley*)

Transferred to Greek Navy on 2nd December, 1943. In *Operation Shingle* (landing at Anzio) in January 1944. *In Operation Dragoon* (landing on French S. Coast). August 1944.

12. *Hydra*

At Alexandria 17th April, 1941, *sunk* in air raid on Piraeus 22nd April, 1941.

13. *Ierax*

Arrived Alexandria 25th April, 1941 – In East Indies March 1942 to August 1942. – Returned to Eastern Mediterranean, Cyprus etc. With *Southern Isle attacked a S/M* in 31° 43' N., 34° 01' E on 24th April, 1943. – Proceeded to Kavalla, December 1944 (Greek disputes).

14. *Kanaris* (ex *Hatherleigh*)

Destroyer *escort to convoy* W.S.23 (round the Cape to Durban) at end of September 1942. In 1943 *on convoy escort duties* in Eastern Mediterranean. – In *Operation Husky* July 1943. – Escorting MKF convoys till March 1944.

15. *King George I*

Damaged by bombing *and sunk by own forces in enemy* air attack on Piraeus 24th April, 1941. Salved by Germans in June 1941.

16. *Kondouriotis* (formerly *Paul Condouriotis*)

Left Mediterranean for Aden and East Indies on 18th April, 1942. Arrived back in Mediterranean in September 1942 – on *escort duties with MW. convoys* till July 1943. – *Attacked a U/B* in 32° 40' N., 23° 08' E. on 17th February, 1943.

17. *Miaoules* (ex *Modbury*)

On *escort duties with convoys* to West Africa and Mediterranean from January 1943. Allocated to 5th Destroyer Flotilla (Mediterranean) 27th February, 1943. – In *Operation Husky* (landing in Sicily) July 1943. On 7th October, 1943, joined *Penelope* and *Sirius* in *attack on enemy convoy* off Stampalia. Destroyed 2 E-boats and 1 small M/V at Port Akli on 17th October, 1943 – on 21st October, 1943 with *Aurora* bombarded Rhodes – landed personnel on Leros night of 26th October, 1943 – Bombarded Kos Roads on 5th December, 1943. *Attacked U/B* on 5th January, 1944 in 32° 08' N., 25° 36' E.

---

1 Later information showed the U/Boat was not sunk.

18. *Navarinon* (ex *Echo*)

In Eastern Mediterranean from end of August 1944 on *escort duties*. Landed troops on Skopelos on 23rd October, 1944 and destroyed German Headquarters at Livahdia Bay on 31st October, 1944.

19. *Panther*

Arrived at Alexandria 23rd April, 1941. – To East Indies and refit at Calcutta in June 1941. On *convoy escort duties* Bombay-Aden during 1942 and early 1943. In Eastern Mediterranean till October 1943.

20. *Pindos* (ex *Bolebroke*)

On *escort duties with convoys* to West Africa and the Cape in August 1942. Joined Mediterranean Station at end of October 1942. – In *Operation Stoneage* (M/V's to Malta) at end of November 1942. – In *Operation Husky* (landing in Sicily) July 1943, Assisted in *sinking U/B 458* in 36° 25' N., 12° 39' E. on 22nd August, 1943. Received congratulations from Commander-in-Chief, Levant – Bombarded enemy positions Leros 14th November, 1943.

21. *Psara*

Hit and badly damaged in air attack on Piraeus 20th April, 1941 and *sunk* 24th April, 1941.

22. *Queen Olga*

Arrived Alexandria 23rd April, 1941 – to East Indies in October 1941 for refit Calcutta – Returned to Mediterranean end of January 1942 and joined 5th Destroyer Flotilla. On 15th December, 1942 with *Petard* captured *Italian S/M Uarsciek* in 35° 0' N., 14° 45' E., which sank later in 35° 18' N., 14° 25' E. Escorting convoy *Operation Pamphlet* (in February 1943). – *In convoy escort work* from Malta and patrol duties till June 1943. On 2nd June, 1943 sank a 1,500 ton M.V. off Cape Spartivento. In *Operation Husky* (landing Sicily) July 1943. In *Operation Avalanche* (attack on Naples) August 1943. *Sunk* in air attack on Leros Harbour 26th September, 1943.

23. *Salamis* (ex *Boreas*)

Transferred to Greek Navy on 10th February, 1944. *On escort duties* in Mediterranean during 1944.

24. *Spetsai*

Arrived Alexandria 23rd April 1941. Proceeded to East Indies for refit Calcutta July, 1941. In Eastern Mediterranean from July 1942. *Attacked U/B* on 12th February, 1943 in Lat. 32° 48' N., 34° 48' E. and *also on* 23rd April, 1943 in Lat. 31° 19' N., 29° 46' E.

25. *Themistocle*s (ex *Bramham*)

Arrived Levant end of September 1943 on anti-shipping patrol in Crete/Rhodes area. On 7th October 1943 *attacked U/B* in 34° 47' N., 32° 08' E. At end of November 1943 in *Operation Strangle* (A/S Operations Mediterranean). In *Operation Shingle* January 1944 (landing at Anzio) and *Operation Dragoon*. August 1944 (landing on South French coast).

SUBMARINES

26. *Glaucos*

Arrived Alexandria 19th April 1941. In *Operation Demon* from Greece) 25th April 1941 – on patrol in Central Mediterranean till end of year. Torpedoed a M/V of 3,000 tons off Heraklion on 10th November, 1941, *sunk* in air raid on Malta 1st April 1942.

27. *Katsonis*

Arrived Alexandria 24th April, 1941. Sank at Port Said in July 1941 after refit. – Raised and refitted and on patrol in Eastern Mediterranean from November 1941. – Sank a Spanish M/V close in-shore West of Thermia on 5th April, 1943. On 9th April, 1943 sank a 1,000 ton M/V during patrol in Aegean – on 2nd June, 1943 scored a probable hit on a 7,000 ton transport in Karlovassi (Samos) Harbour. Was *sunk* off Skiathos (Gulf of Athens) on 14th September 1943 (by ramming).

28. *Matrozos* (ex Italian *Perla*)

On *patrol duties* in Eastern Mediterranean from April 1944 – till October 1944.

29. *Nereus*

Arrived Alexandria 24th April, 1944. *On patrol in Eastern Mediterranean* on 27th July, 1942. Sank three Caiques and scored a probable hit on a 7,000 ton merchant vessel in Dodecanese waters. Sank a 1,500 ton merchant vessel on 28th September, 1942 while on patrol in Aegean.

30. *Papanicolis*

Arrived Alexandria 27th April, 1941. – Operating in *Eastern Mediterranean and Aegean waters* – On 11th August, 1942 successfully intercepted Caique which left Samos for Piraeus with important allied prisoners on board – On 30th November, 1942 sank a 6,000 ton merchant vessel Lat. 36° 15' N., 27° 44' E. – Between December 1942 and May 1943 captured 2 and sank 4 Caiques in Aegean waters.

31. *Pipinos* (ex *Veldt*, ex. *P.71*)

In operation *Stonewall* (anti-blockade Biscay area) patrol. In January 1944. – Patrol in Aegean March 1944. – On 9th August 1944 *sank* Italian destroyer *Calatafimi* outside Karlovassi (Samos).

32. *Proteus*

Sunk by Italian Destroyer on 29th December, 1940.

33. *Triton*

Arrived Alexandria 24th April 1941. – *Operating in Eastern Mediterranean and Aegean*. In June 1942 sank three Caiques in Aegean waters. – July 1942 on patrol off Tobruk. In November 1942 on patrol in Aegean, and on 28th November was reported as overdue and considered lost – claimed by the enemy. (Doro Channel.)

TORPEDO BOATS

34. *Aspis*

Arrived at Alexandria 23rd April, 1941. In *Operation Demon*, evacuation from Greece.

35. *Niki*

Arrived Alexandria 23rd April, 1941.

36. *Sphendoni*

Attacked by Italian submarine on 11th March, 1941. In Eastern Mediterranean at Alexandria April 1941 and working from there.

MINESWEEPERS

37. 28, of which two Y.M.S. were *sunk* by mine off C. Turko, Piraeus, 15th October, 1944.

DEPÔT AND REPAIR SHIPS

38. *Corinthia* – Greek Captain (S) at Alexandria.

39. *Ioni*a – Ashore, Refi Island, Skiathos. December 1944 (may be total loss).

40. *Hephaesto*s – Submarine and destroyer depôt ship at Alexandria.

APPENDIX H

MONTHLY REPORT FOR SEPTEMBER 1940 OF THE SEA TRANSPORT OFFICER, PORT SUDAN[1]

Port Sudan.
4th October 1940.

From The Sea Transport Officer, Port Sudan *to* The Principal Sea Transport Officer i/c Egypt, Port Said.
SUBJECT:– MONTHLY REPORT. PORT SUDAN. 31.8.40/30.9.40
I forward herewith in quadruplicate, monthly report of proceedings for the period ending 30th September, 1940.

Establishment of Office and Staff appointments

Lieut.-Commander J. R. Davies, R.N.R., and Paymaster Lieut. I. Jones, R.N.V.R., arrived from Port Said on 31st August, 1940 to take up duties as Acting S.T.O. i/c and Secretary.

Commander N.S. Griffiths, R.N., arrived Port Sudan from Istanbul on 10th September, 1940 and took over duties as S.T.O. i/c.

Lieut. A. B. Vaughan, R.N.R., arrived from United Kingdom via Suez on 18th September, 1940. In view of this Officer's age and the fact that he had volunteered for service in Egypt, I requested P.S.T.O.E. to replace him as soon as possible. No request or complaint had been received from Lieut. Vaughan, but it was obvious that owing to climatic conditions and the amount of outside work to be done, it was essential that the Staff here should, so far as possible, be composed of younger Officers. A relief has been appointed and Lieut. Vaughan will be posted to Suez on relief.

2. It was anticipated that on my arrival I should find Lieut. O'Halloran and Lieut. Jones from Mombasa and Berbera already at Port Sudan, and Lieut.-Commander Davies was to return to Port Said. Both these Officers, however, were still en route, and not expected before the end of September. It was therefore essential to retain Lieut.-Commander Davies pending their arrival.

On arrival I signalled P.S.T.O.E. that I considered the following minimum Staff essential:–
S.T.O. in charge. S.T.O. 11. 2 S.T.O's 111 or IV. Secretary. Writer or confidential clerk.
These are unobtainable in the Sudan and at the date of this report, the Staff consists of:–
S.T.O. in charge. S.T.O. 11. 1 S.T.O. 111 and Secretary.

It is hoped that these requirements will be met as early as possible. As I have pointed out in my P/S 15 of 16th September to P.S.T.O.E., in addition to the actual work involved, air attacks on Port Sudan are likely to increase and casualties are a possibility that must be reckoned with. In one air attack on the 7th September, H.E. bombs were dropped narrowly missing the office and exploding within 20 yards of Lieut.-Commander Davies and Pay Lieut. Jones.

General Remarks. Prior to the arrival of Lieut.-Commander Davies, the Naval Officer i/c (Commander Whitehouse R.N.R.) had kindly obtained offices, very conveniently situated near the Main East Quays, with necessary minimum furniture and light, telephones and power. These offices which consist of a three-roomed wood and tin-roofed bungalow are rented from Messrs. Gellatly, Hankey & Co. (Agents) at £E 5 per month,

---

1 See Section 5, last sentence.

with £E 1 per month use of furniture. Light, power and telephones extra. A direct line has also now been installed between Naval Officer i/c and S.T.O.

A very full report on Port Facilities was obtained by Lieut.-Commander Davies from the Port Manager and forwarded to P.S.T.O.E. A further complete copy is attached to this report for the information of the Director of Sea Transport.

The Port generally is under the supervision of the Port Manager who is the representative of the Sudan Government. The lay-out is ideal for easy working, and all local authorities do their utmost to assist in every way. Close liaison has been established between S.T.O. and N.O. i/c and Military and R.A.F. Headquarters and Movement Control. If subjected to intense aerial bombardment however, it is possible that considerable damage may be done, as railway sidings, quays, storage sheds and cranes are all situated in compact and exposed positions.

The mooring bollards marked in the attached Harbour Plan enable large vessels to moor stern on at this point, and it has been suggested to the Harbour Authorities that a ramp should be built up from the shore to the bollards, when by means of 90 ft. pontoons, troops could be rapidly marched over the side direct ashore, or conversely marched straight on board for rapid embarkations. This has been favourably considered and will, I hope, be put into immediate effect.

Port Stevedoring Facilities. There are two main Agencies (British) at Port Sudan, Messrs. Gellatly, Hankey & Co. (Sudan) Ltd., and Messrs. Cotts, Darke & Co. Ltd. Both have efficient organisations with European supervisors, but the position obtaining on my arrival at Port Sudan was that Messrs. Gellatly, Hankey & Co. were in the most favourable position owing to the fact that the majority of their Agencies had not been interfered with by present circumstances, whereas Messrs. Cotts, Darke & Co. had lost a very considerable number of their Agencies since the outbreak of war. As it was quite obvious that the resources of both Agencies would be required to the fullest extent, and that if as under normal conditions, Messrs. Gellatly Hankey obtained the working of 80 per cent of the Transports using this port, I arranged a meeting with the Directors of both firms, and informed them that under the Clause in T.99 Charter Party, covering the question of Agencies (Article 9), the Agencies and stevedoring would be divided between the two firms, allowing a slight proportion in favour of Messrs. Gellatly, Hankey & Co. as the official Government Agents. This is working well so far, and has enabled Messrs. Cotts, Darke & Co. to retain their full organisation, and the division of the work has ensured the maximum speed and efficiency in off-loading large numbers of ships in the least possible time, a most essential factor under present circumstances. Examination of the details of vessels dealt with in the Niblick Echelon scheme to date will show that a very rapid turn-round has been effected in every instance. The added possibility of enemy aerial attacks makes it essential that vessels should be discharged with all speed, and where it is essential that vessels should be completed in a specified period to avoid missing convoys, work has been carried on after dark hours, but this is only done when absolutely necessary.

With regard to the working of the 1st Flight of ships, I should like to take this opportunity of pointing out that although Lieut.-Commander Davies had only arrived a week previously, that he and Pay Lieut. Jones did most excellent work in carrying out the necessary preliminary arrangements and that the discharge and turn-round of these ships was carried out without a hitch, and work was completed by 1500 hrs. on the 10th September on the last ship. This was in spite of the fact that an air raid occurred the day previous to the arrival of the Flight, when bombs were dropped near the office and the quays, and also on the day of their arrival in harbour. These air raids naturally disorganise the native labour considerably and cause delays owing to the shutting down of current throughout the Port. Lieut.-Commander Davies and Pay Lieut. Jones had already started an efficient organisation, and there was little for me to do but amplify the arrangements already made.

Bunkering. Owing to the shortage of coal supplied, it has only been possible to bunker ships where essential, and where existing bunkers were insufficient to carry the ship in question to Indian ports. Water is plentiful and reasonable in price, and is easily and quickly supplied ex quay or barge. It was possible to supplement local supplies with 300 tons ballast coal ex *Bankura* and this I carried out owing to the local shortage.

Passages. The following passages were arranged:–

	1st	2nd	T/D
H/T *Varsova* to Suez 10.9.40	6	29	29
S.S. *Northmoor* to Suez 16.9.40	–	3	–

Local Contracts. A car is being hired through the Sudan Government at a rate of Pts. 80. per day – this is below general obtaining price. A launch has been obtained as from 1st October from Messrs. Gellatly, Hankey & Co. Ltd., at a cost of £E 10 – per month, covering all maintenance. Petrol and oils to be supplied by this office from Government sources.

Transports and Freightships dealt with (see separate sheet). Between 8th September and 26th September 18 personnel and M.T. ships were dealt with.

Freightships (*Stores*). The following additional vessels were dealt with:–

Mathura	7.8.40	Army and Navy personnel and stores
El Amin	15.9.40	Army personnel and stores
El Hak	15.9.40	Army and R.A.F stores
Gorgistan	17.9.40	Army and R.A.F. stores
Northmoor	16.9.40	Discharged 1,500 tons coal

Commercial cargo shipped. The following commercial cargo was shipped in Transports:–

Ship	Date sailed	Destination	Cargo bales cotton	Gross Freight (without deductions)	Where Payable
Felix Roussel	7.9.40	Bombay	4792	£E. ms. 3,731.630	D.S.T.
Islami	22.9.40	Bombay	838 "	690.180	D.S.T.
	22.9.40	for U.S.A.	195 tons gum arabic	2,282.180	D.S.T.
Jalamohan	22.9.40	Aden	Cattle	508.000	S.T.O. Aden

Government stores shipped

Ship	Date	Description	Destination
H/T. *Talma*	25.9.40	Army Medical stores	Bombay
H/T. *Islami*	21.9.40	Army Medical stores	Bombay
H/T. *Harpalycus*	23.9.40	Naval stores and ammunition ex H/T *Nurmahal*	Suez

General

The question of Officer's allowances is one which requires urgent settlement. Living expenses are approximately 100 per cent above those obtaining in Egypt, and N.O. i/c has requested inclusion in scale laid down for Colombo.

APP. H   MEDITERRANEAN, SEPTEMBER 1939–OCTOBER 1940

TABLE OF TRANSPORTS AND M.T. SHIPS. PORT SUDAN. SEPTEMBER 1940

Echelon and Flight	Ship	Time and date Arrival	Time and date Completed	Time of sailing	Remarks
1st Echelon – Flight 1		September	September	September	
	Karagola	1100/8th	1430/9th	1600/10th	Air raid 1100 8.9.40.
	Erinpura	1400/8th	1200/10th	1610/10th	Two warnings p.m. 9th September.
	Varsoua	1500/8th	1115/10th	1640/10th	
	Jaladuta	1215/8th	1300/10th	1615/10th	
	Jalakrishna	1215/8th	1500/10th	1630/10th	
Flight II	*Varela*	0630/13th	1600/15th	1630/15th	
	Amra	0645/13th	0830/15th	1630/15th	
	Nevasa	0700/13th	0200/14th	1630/15th	
	Subadar	0715/13th	0900/16th	0100/17th	
	Jalavihar	0730/13th	1900/15th	0100/17th	
Flight III	*Islam*	0900/18th	1030/21st	1700/22nd	Shipped cargo (commercial).
	El Medin	0850/18th	0700/19th	1700/22nd	
	Nurmahal	0930/18th	1400/21st	1700/22nd	
	Jalamohan	0915/18th	1750/20th	1700/22nd	Shipped cattle for Aden. Air raid 1220 22.9.40.
2nd Echelon –				October	
	Bankura	0845/23rd	1730/25th	1700/2nd	
	Talma	0700/23rd	1530/26th	1700/2nd	In harbour awaiting escort 26.9.40 to 2.10.40.
	Akbar	0900/23rd	1700/26th	1700/2nd	Air raid 0920 23.9.40.
	Santhia	0830/23rd	0715/26th	1700/2nd	

2. The following signals have been received and sent by N.O. i/c and are quoted without comment:–

To N.O. i/c Port Sudan (R) C.-in-C. E.I. from S.N.O.R.S.

'You have ably effected a very quick turn round of first and second flights'

T.O.O. 1616Z/16/9/40.

from N.O. i/c Port Sudan to S.N.O.R.S. (R) C.-in-C. in E.I. and S.T.O. Port Sudan (by letter)

'"Niblick Flights" With reference to your message 1616/16/9 ... the quick handling of the Niblick flights is due to the efficiency of the civil authorities in charge of the port organisation, who have been informed of your appreciation and to the co-operation with the Sea Transport Officer of the two stevedoring companies'

17.9.40

To N.O. i/c Port Sudan (R) S.N.O.R.S. from C.-in-C. E.I.

'You are doing very well in these *busy* times with your small staff'

T.O.O. 0552z/28/9/40
(Sd.) Chas. S. Griffiths
Commander R.N.
S.T.O. Port Sudan

APPENDIX J

ROYAL NAVAL ARMAMENT SUPPLY – EASTERN MEDITERRANEAN

1939–1940

[From information supplied by the Director of Armament Supply]

AMMUNITION

Determined that the grave situation, due to shortage of reserve ammunition, which would have occurred had the Fleet been involved in hostilities during the Abyssinian campaign should not be repeated, an adequate number of Armament Supply Issuing Ships (A.S.I.S.) had been taken up by the Admiralty and drafted to the Eastern Mediterranean by August 1939. In addition, several Armament Supply Carriers (A.S.C.) to replenish the A.S.I.S. had also been requisitioned. Thus, when war broke out in September 1939 the position with regard to ammunition reserves caused no concern. The only question was that of dispersal. Although a scheme had been prepared after Munich and a site chosen for a naval armament depôt in the Dekheila area, it was now decided – due to the threat of invasion – that all reserves should be afloat. It was clearly undesirable, however, that these should be concentrated in Alexandria harbour.

Ready use reserves only were, therefore, retained at Alexandria where two A.S.I.S. were berthed, the remainder being stowed in three A.S.I.S. which were removed to the Great Bitter Lake. A further dispersal was arranged in Alexandria harbour by means of a number of cotton lighters which were hired and loaded with ammunition for light forces. These lighters were then moored at safe distances apart in a prohibited and patrolled area of the harbour. Besides affording additional security by this dispersal, the arrangement of lighters provided a ready and more expeditious means of ammunitioning destroyers as they entered harbour. While berthing, lighters would be brought alongside and stores embarked without delay. Eventually 84 lighters and 16 tugs were used for this purpose. Non-explosives stores and offices were established on Mahmoudieh Quay, the whole of which was finally taken over by the Navy at an annual rental of £5,000 for various stores and workshops.

When it became clear that there was no immediate threat from Italy, the armament stores accumulated were gradually dispersed, a quantity off-loaded at Malta and A.S.C.'s paid off. The Bitter Lake organisation was closed down in November and, early in 1940, the special lighters at Alexandria were also paid off. Throughout the spring of 1940, reserves of naval armament stores continued to fall without any attempt being made to replace them, and it was not until May that they began to arrive once more in the Eastern Mediterranean.

By the time Italy declared war, the situation was once more similar to that which had existed in September 1939. But with this difference. A year before, the fleet had included four 8-in. cruisers and only three 6-in. cruisers, and it was understood that this proportion of cruisers would be retained. The fleet that had now assembled at the end of May included eight 6-in. cruisers and none of the larger ones. This meant that there was insufficient 6-in. reserve ammunition, but the situation was retrieved by taking advantage of the *Liverpool*'s trip to Aden with the 1st Battalion Black Watch for British Somaliland to bring back to the Mediterranean much of the reserve 6-inch ammunition held on the East Indies Station.

Apart from this one deficiency, there was no real anxiety at any time, such as prevailed at home, that the demands of the Fleet would exceed the supplies available. But the disadvantage – and danger – of keeping all the reserve ammunition afloat was brought home when the A.S.C. *Arron* was hit by a bomb in Alexandria harbour on 25th July and set on fire. On the other hand Italians were massing on the frontier of Egypt, the country was under the threat of invasion, plans were advanced for a temporary withdrawal from Alexandria and the stabilisation of a line running south from that port. So it was not considered opportune to disperse naval ammunition stores in the site selected to the west of Alexandria where they might be overrun by the enemy. Arrangements were, nevertheless, made for a small quantity of stores (80 tons of depth charges) to be stored in Fort Tewfikieh, situated in the R.A.F. Depôt at Aboukir in September 1940.

The Naval Armaments organisation had, so far, been able to meet all requirements, and as an indication of what these requirements were, it is recorded that between the entry of Italy into the war and 1st September 7,417 rounds of 6-inch and 12,576 rounds of Q.F. 4-inch had been issued to the Fleet among other items.

When the Army of the Nile swept forward in their December 1940 offensive, arrangements were immediately made for naval armament stores to be transferred to special 25-ton dumps near Dekheila at Gebel el Ilwa, 3 miles to the west of Alexandria. This area had been quarried and re-quarried for over 3,000 years, it was broken up into a stretch of rubble spread in mounds and ridges and was eminently suitable for the purpose. By March 1941, 120 of these dumps had been established, a number which was to be increased to 300 by October of that year. Meanwhile, further reserve stores had gone ashore into similar dumps on the south shore of Lake Timsah in the Canal area where 135 magazines were being set up as well as the main workshops. By October 1941, another 100 dumps had been built near Port Said, 150 were under construction at Attaka in the Gulf of Suez, 25,000 tons of storage space had been taken up at Abu Sultan on the N.E. shore of the Great Bitter Lake, and after the Italian collapse in Abyssinia, former enemy depôts in Eritrea were utilised for an additional storage of 4,500 tons of naval armament supplies.

As the fighting fronts moved or new ones came into being, additional stores for naval armaments were set up in Crete, at Tobruk and Mersa Matruh, Syria and Palestine. Sometimes, though not often, these stores were overrun by the enemy, but the organisation for their evacuation in case of necessity was generally effective. A thousand tons of destroyer and A.A. ammunition was fed into Crete where most of it was lost: bombarding ammunition for gunboats was made available at Mersa Matruh, and, at Tobruk, dumps were built up in the caves and tunnels on the north side of the Bay.

From a small organisation comprising a handful of men, the naval armament staff grew within the space of one year to a body of 4,500 of 29 different nationalities.

TORPEDOES

In January 1940 there were 120 spare torpedoes in the Eastern Mediterranean. As war approached, this number was augmented and storage space was taken up on Mahmoudieh Quay in Alexandria where torpedo workshops were also established. A dispersal store for 100 torpedoes was requisitioned at Port Said and others were scattered in the different A.S.I.S. As demand increased, culminating in 1941 in the issue of 643 torpedoes to H.M. Ships alone, additional space for the storage of 200 was taken up on Mahmoudieh Quay which, although frequently bombed, suffered no really serious damage. Torpedoes for Malta were supplied by submarine from Alexandria.

MINES

During the Italo-Abyssinian war it was decided that Haifa should be the Fleet mine base, both for offensive and defensive mining, in the event of hostilities, and for this purpose a number of mines were landed and stowed in transit sheds on the quays. In 1936 they were re-embarked and taken back to the United Kingdom, but it was realised that, if war broke out, all the transit sheds at Haifa would be required by the Army and that there would in future be no space available for mines. If Haifa was to be the mine depôt then a depôt must be built, and plans were laid accordingly to provide a floor space for 2,500 mines. But the months passed and nothing appeared to have been done towards the establishment of this base and, even in January 1940, the Treasury still hesitated to give approval.

It was then discovered that, while all these arguments had been taking place, the Army had, unknown to the Navy, built the mine depôt at Haifa in accordance with the original plans. They did not know why they were doing it – even if they understood the purpose for which the building was intended – but it was a situation which the Navy accepted with gratitude. By Xmas 1940, staff and gear began to arrive and, five months later, the depôt was in full operation.

In point of fact, comparatively little minelaying was carried out in the Eastern Mediterranean, the fast minelayers when they arrived being used for other purposes. Only two big minelaying operations actually took place, one deep field off Perim to catch submarines passing through the Bab-el-Mandeb Straits and the other between Greece and Crete in early May 1941. The mine depôt at Malta, however, functioned from the beginning of the war and was used for submarine minelaying operations off the coasts and ports of Italy. Other fluvial mines intended for the Danube were discovered at Alexandria and used off Tobruk.

GUN MOUNTING AND FIRE CONTROL

The gun mounting organisation which worked in close liaison with that of the naval armament stores was largely an improvisation which owed its success to ingenuity, resource and no little cunning. It never failed to meet the requirements demanded of it and when, for instance, new gun barrels were not available, they were taken from damaged ships whose own replacements were effected at the ports to which they eventually proceeded for repairs or, if these repairs were done locally, from ships damaged in the meanwhile or from new supplies subsequently received. But it is true to say that if so many ships had not been damaged, it would not have been possible to maintain the fighting efficiency of those ships which were intact. The work was extensive and after every Malta operation, for example, new gun barrels would be required for those ships which had taken part.

The Gun Mounting Depôt was also set up on Mahmoudieh Quay where, in spite of air raid damage, it managed to extend its activities to the repair even of compasses and chronometers. Here captured Italian materiel was converted to naval purposes, and if Breda guns were required for H.M. Ships local labourers would be infiltrated into the queue disembarking them for the Army, deposit their booty in the naval shed and then return for more. When the Army found a discrepancy between the number embarked and the number received, it was dismissed as just one of those mysteries which do occur in war time.

But if the Navy sometimes scored over the Army in the matter of Bredas, assistance was readily given in the supply and erection of several guns for the Alexandria shore defences and, in the early days of the war, when naval guns originally destined for Turkey were held up at Alexandria, this organisation was able to get them installed at Tobruk, Benghazi or other points where they could be of more immediate value.

Tribute was constantly paid both to the willingness and skill of the local labour employed. The Arab appeared to be a natural mathematician and the speed and efficiency with which heavy weights were manhandled into position was always most praiseworthy.

APPENDIX K

NAVAL MEDICAL ARRANGEMENTS – EASTERN MEDITERRANEAN

[from information supplied by the Medical Director General]

HOSPITALS

Shortly after the Munich crisis, the question of naval medical facilities in the Eastern Mediterranean was raised by the Admiralty. Was there sufficient hospital accommodation to deal with the generally accepted war estimate of 10 per cent sick and wounded per year of total personnel? On 11th November 1939, the Commander-in-Chief, Mediterranean, was asked to remark on the position. He replied that hospital arrangements were far from satisfactory during the recent crisis, only the Anglo-Swiss Hospital at Alexandria with 50 beds being available. Consultations with the Army had, however, resulted in a proposal that the Army should arrange hospital accommodation for naval personnel in Egypt additional to their own requirements as follows:–

Alexandria	600 beds.
Canal Zone	100 beds (50 at each terminal port)

Army to provide medical stores.
R.N. to provide part staff (10 M.O.s, 40 nurses, 100 S.B. ratings)

This arrangement was subsequently confirmed between the Admiralty and War Office, and Victoria College at Alexandria was taken up and converted into what was known as the 64th General Hospital. By October 1939 it was open. In the first instance the staff was built up from nursing personnel transferred from the military hospital at Ras-el-Tin and from a small naval unit sent out from the United Kingdom just before war was declared. Established under Army control, it was thus the first occasion where the two Services had worked together in one building. Resources were pooled and no attempt was made to create a dividing line between the two Service elements. In this manner it functioned until the end of the war in North Africa and served as the eventual model for similar combinations in India and the Far East. It also led to a considerable measure of standardisation of equipment.

At Port Said, the Seamen's Hospital was taken over by the Navy, the civilian doctor in charge being granted the rank of Surgeon-Commander, R.N.V.R.

HOSPITAL SHIPS AND CARRIERS

Early in 1939 it was proposed that a hospital carrier should be sent out to the Mediterranean and, later, a hospital ship to augment the *Maine*. The *Atlantis* was, therefore, taken up to be prepared as a carrier and arrived on the Station in September 1939. But, shortly afterwards, she was sent home and did not return. The *Maine*, meanwhile, in spite of her age – she was built in 1902 for the P. & O. Company – continued to function alone as the base hospital ship at Alexandria where she virtually became a Casualty Clearing Station and a base for specialist consultations. On an average she treated over 100 patients a day and dealt with approximately 260 specialist consultations a week. From time to time she became infested with cockroaches, ants, rats, bed bugs and carpet beetles, which necessitated the temporary evacuation of all personnel and the subjection of the vessel to fumigation and dis-infestation, and on one occasion she suffered air raid damage from a near miss which killed four of her complement, including the Senior Medical Officer, and wounded twelve others.

In spite of the fact that complete replenishments for Fleet requirements in medical stores at Alexandria were destroyed on three separate occasions, the medical service functioned satisfactorily throughout the war.

MALTA

By the end of 1940 the Naval Hospital at Bighi was so damaged that the nursing staff was transferred to the Military Hospital at Imtarfa. Only a skeleton staff then remained at Bighi which was used as a centre for outpatients and minor casualties.

BIBLIOGRAPHY

DOCUMENTS

Naval War Memorandum (European), M.00697/1939.
C.I.D. Papers, Vols. I and II (plans and policy).
Admiralty War Diary.
Commander-in-Chief, Mediterranean, War Diary.
Vice-Admiral, Malta, War Diary.
Senior British Naval Officer, Suez Canal Area, War Diary.
Reports of Proceedings from Flag and Commanding Officers, now held at the Admiralty as M. Documents, are quoted at relevant places in the text.
Reports of Proceedings from Sea Transport Officers, Port Said, Suez, Alexandria, Haifa and Port Sudan. (Example given in Appendix H.)
Weekly Intelligence Reports, issued by N.I.D.

FRENCH

Papers and Reports from French Naval Historical Service, General Staff, Ministry of National Defence.

ITALIAN

Admiral Cavagnari, Italian First Sea Lord – article entitled 'Short War Theory', reprinted in W.I.R. No. 14, 1940.
Submarine Patrol Charts.
Captured documents, P.I. series, issued by N.I.D.
Admiral Bernotti, 'La guerra sui mari'.
Ministry of Marine, Rome, official narratives.

GERMAN

Essays on the War at Sea by:–
  Admiral Doenitz and Vice-Admiral Weichold.
Documents from:–
  N.I.D., 1/G.P. Series.
  War Diaries and reports from Foreign Documents' Section/TSD/HS.

OFFICIAL BOOKS

The War at Sea, 1939–45 – B.R., 1738
A preliminary narrative of the operations of the Mediterranean Fleet and Force H, June to December, 1940
Battle Summaries, 1, 2, 3, 6, 8 – B.R., 1736, 1 and 4

} TSD/HS

Geographical Handbook series, issued by N.I.D.:–
   Italy, Vol. IV – B.R. 517C.
   Greece, Vol. II – B.R. 5l6A.

BOOKS

A History of Europe – A. J. Grant.

Modern Europe, 1789–1914 – Sydney Herbert.

Anzacs into Battle – Tahu Hole.

So Immortal a Flower* – Cecil Roberts.

Mr. Winston Churchill's Memoirs, Volumes I and 2.

AUTHORITIES CONSULTED

Cabinet Historical (Military) and R.A.F. Historical Departments, especially where large scale inter-Service planning and operations were involved – vide Chapter IV (Sections 79 to 82).

Director of Sea Transport Service (Appendix D(c)).

Head Librarian, Foreign Office, Sections 1, 2, 3, 100.

PUBLICATIONS PREPARED BY THE MINISTRY OF INFORMATION

'East of Malta, West of Suez' – The Admiralty account of the Naval War in the Eastern Mediterranean. September 1939 to March 1941.

'Merchantmen at War' – Ministry of War Transport account of the Merchant Navy, 1939–1944.

'Fleet Air Arm' – Admiralty account of Naval Air Operations, 1939–1943.

---

* A story of the fighting in Crete.

INDEX

Aberdeen, 8, 83
Abyssinia, xv, 1, 63 *see also* Italo-Abyssinian War/campaign
Acre, 20
Actium, Battle of (31 BC), 1
Aden, 10, 65
Admiralty, xii, xiii, 3, 4, 6, 8, 9, 10, 11, 12, 13, 15, 17, 18, 19, 21, 23, 25, 27, 28, 29, 31, 32, 33, 34, 35, 37, 38, 39, 44, 45, 46, 48, 50, 51, 53, 55, 59, 60, 66, 67, 68, 69, 70, 73, 74, 75, 79, 80, 89, 90, 93–4, 95, 96–7, 98, 99, 100–1, 103, 105, 120, 121, 123, 124, 125, 126, 127, 128, 129, 130, 131, 132, 133, 134, 135
Adriatic, 8, 16, 38, 62, 73
Aegean, xii, 1, 3, 8, 15, 18, 19, 23–4, 25, 29, 33, 46, 47, 51, 53, 55, 56, 62, 70, 72, 77, 79
Air Ministry, 5, 60, 67
Air Officer Commanding (A.O.C.) Mediterranean, 38, 60, 73, 80
Air Officer Commanding (A.O.C.) Middle East, x, 54
Airone, 75
Ajaccio, 10
Ajax, 54, 55, 73, 74, 75, 76, 80, 81
Ala Littoria airline, 13, 15
Alagi, 57
Albania, 3, 15, 71, 78
Alboran Island, 45
Alexandretta, 11, 12
Alexandria, xii, xiii, xix, 2, 4, 5, 6, 8, 9, 10, 11, 13, 15, 17, 18, 19, 20, 21, 22, 23, 24, 25, 27, 28, 29, 31, 33, 34, 35, 38, 39, 40, 41, 43, 44, 46, 47, 48, 50, 51, 53, 55, 56, 57, 58, 59, 60, 62, 64, 65, 70, 72, 73, 74, 76, 77, 80, 123, 130
Algeria, xiii, 15, 27, 67, 126
Alghero, 20, 22
Algiers, xii, 9, 20, 22, 28, 29, 31, 35, 37, 52, 53, 57
Allied Supreme Council, xiii
Amriya, 60
Andrea Doria, 13
Anglo-French-Turkish Treaty (1939), 78
Anglo-Iranian oilfields, 45
Ankara, 11
Annesley, Captain J.C., 52
Ansaldo works, 22
Antenor, 10, 11
Anti-Comintern Pact, xiv

Anti-Kithera Channel, 24, 47
Antonietta Costa, 73
Aphis, 57, 66, 70, 75
Aquilone, 65
Arethusa, 10, 11, 35, 44, 45, 52, 53
Argonauta, 22
Argostoli, 17, 80
Argus, 10, 51, 52, 54
Ariel, 75
Ark Royal, 29, 31, 37, 44, 45, 46, 52, 54, 57
Army, xii, xiv, 4, 5, 11, 54, 55, 63, 65, 66, 70
Artigliere, 75–6
Athens, 15, 76, 79, 80; British Minister at, 78, 79
Athos II, 34
Atlantic, 16, 17, 65
Atlantis, 10
Augusta, xv, 19, 28, 38–9, 40, 41, 42, 43, 44, 61, 62, 72, 74, 75
Australia, 32, 69
Austro-Prussian War (1866), 1
Axis, xvii, 3, 86–7
Axum, 57
Azores, 69

Badoglio, Marshal Pietro, xvi, xvii, 71–2
Bagnolini, 20
Baisson, M. Pierre, 32
Balearic Islands, xv, 54, 57
Balkans, xii, 2, 3, 77–8, 103–5; Balkan pact (1934), 77–8
Bande Nere (*Giovanni delle Bande Nere*), 47, 48
Banfi, Lieut.-Commander, 75
Barce, 20
Bardia, 27, 39, 61, 62, 63–4, 65, 77
Barham, 10, 51, 69, 81
Bari, 13, 72
Barletta, 13
Baron Erskine, 27
Bartolomeo Colleoni, 47–8, 76
Beauforts, 60
Beirut, 4, 5, 9, 10, 17, 19, 31, 33, 34, 127–8
Benghazi, xx, 19, 20, 21, 23, 38, 40, 48, 53, 62, 65, 66, 73, 74, 77
Berenice, 60
Berillo, 72
Berlin, xiv

171

Bernotti, Admiral, 71, 72
Berwick, 65, 81
Beyrouth, 12, 29
Bizerta, xii, xiii, xvi, 12, 20, 26, 29, 35
Black Sea, 7, 38, 46
Black Watch, 81
Blenheims, 27, 43, 48, 60, 65
Blue Nile, 63
Bolzano, 42, 43
Bomba, 61, 64
Bona, 57
Bordeaux, 28, 29, 32, 46
Borea, 65
Bosforo, 8
Brambleleaf, 80
Brest, 31, 32
Bretagne, 34, 37
Brindisi, 13, 15, 25, 56, 62, 72, 78, 80
Bristowe, Lieut.-Cmdr, R.H., 33
British Minister at Athens, 78, 79
British Naval Liaison Officers (B.N.L.O.s), 35, 131–2; in Brest, 31, 32
British Somaliland, xvii, 18, 63, 64
British Vice-Consul at Dubrovnik, 12
Bulgaria, 77, 78, 143
Buq Buq, 65

C.O. 202 Group, R.A.F., 61
Cabinet, xiii, xix, 5
Cabinet Defence Requirements Committee, 3
Cadiz, 46
Cagliari, xv, 20, 26, 40, 44, 45, 52, 54, 57
Caio Duilio, 13
Cairo, xii, 4, 5, 12, 77 *see also* G.H.Q. Middle East/G.H.Q Cairo
Calabria, action off (9 July, 1940), xviii, 1, 34, 43–4, 50
Calcutta, 46, 54, 56, 57, 70, 72, 74, 75, 77, 80
Caledon, 11, 12, 19, 20, 23, 39, 43, 44
Callato airfield, Rhodes, 56
Calypso, 11, 19, 20, 27
Camicia Nera, 75, 76
Canal Company, 11
Canal Zone/area, xiii, 5, 6–7, 11, 58, 60
Candia, 2, 81
Canea, 80
Cape Bon, 8, 9, 55
Cape Colonne, 41, 73
Cape Helles, 24
Cape Littinos, 20
Cape Malea, 15
Cape of Good Hope, xix, 12, 50, 51, 54, 65, 121
Cape Santa Maria di Leuca, 21
Cape Spada, 46, 47
Cape Spartivento, 41
Cape Trapani, Battle off (241 BC), 1
Capetown, 10, 23, 39, 43, 44, 51

Cappellini, 26
Captain (D) 2nd Destroyer Flotilla, 47
Captain D.2, 8, 27
Captain D.8, 44
Captain (D) 10, 64
Captain D.14, 27, 65
Capuzzo, 63, 64
Carlisle, 51, 94
Casablanca, xii, xviii, 31, 32, 33, 35, 67, 68, 69
Caspian Sea, 5
Castelorizo, 52
Castille, Malta, 10
Catania airfield, 38
Caucasus, 5
Cavagnari, Admiral Domenico, xiv, xvii, 16, 50
Cavour (*Conte Di Cavour*), 42, 43, 53
Cavour-class battleships, 29, 42, 50, 71, 74
Cephalonia, 20, 25, 80
Cesare (*Giulio Cesare*), 42, 43, 53
Ceuta, 70
Chad Colony, 69
Chakla, 10, 52, 80
Chanak, 62
Cheeseman, Lieut. (A) N.A.F., 61
Cherbourg, 32
Chiefs of Staff, xix, 3, 6, 17, 45, 53, 54, 55, 79, 98–9, 103
Churchill, Winston, xviii, 2, 6, 66
Ciano, Count, 14, 18
Clan Ferguson, 74
Clan Macaulay, 74
Colbert, 10
Colleoni (*Bartolomeo Colleoni*), 47–8, 76
Collins, Captain J.A., 47, 49
Comintern, xiv
Commandant Teste, 37
Commander-in-Chief, East Indies, 13
Commander-in-Chief, Home Fleet, 13, 77
Commander-in-Chief, Mediterranean, xii, xvi, 3, 4, 5, 8–9, 10, 11, 12, 13, 15, 16, 17, 18, 19, 20, 21, 23, 25, 27, 28, 29, 31, 33, 34, 35, 38, 39, 40, 41, 43, 44, 45, 46, 48–9, 50–1, 53, 54, 55, 56, 57, 58, 59, 60, 61, 62, 63, 64, 70, 71, 72, 73, 74, 75, 76, 77, 78, 79, 80, 81, 89, 90, 93, 94–5, 96, 98, 99–100, 101–3, 104, 120, 121, 122, 123, 124, 125–6, 127, 128, 129, 130, 131, 132, 133–4, 135; ships under command of, 108–12
Commanders-in-Chief, Middle East, 11, 18, 54, 55, 63, 64, 79, 101, 127, 128
Commander-in-Chief, South Africa, 31
Commander-in-Chief, South Atlantic, 33, 66
Communist International, xiv
Console Generale Luizzi, 24
Consul General, Tangier, 67, 68
Conte Di Cavour, 42, 43, 53
Convoy: AN.2, 47, 48, 51, 52; AN.3, 70; AN.4, 72; AN.5, 77; AN.6, 80; AS.1, 24, 25, 46; AS.2, 51, 52; AS.3, 56, 57; AS.4, 76; BLUE 1, 8; GREEN 1, 8;

INDEX

M.F.1, 43, 44; M.F.2, 55; M.F.3, 74; M.F.4, 75, 76; MS.1, 43, 44; MW.3, 80–1
Corfu, 41, 80
Corinth, 80
Corinth Canal, 38, 46, 51
Cornwall, 55
Corsica, 14
Courage, Commander R.E., 48
Courbet, 31
Coventry, 46, 54, 56, 57, 73, 74, 75, 76, 77, 80
Crete, 1–2, 9, 14, 15, 17, 19, 20, 21, 22, 40, 46, 47, 51, 53, 55, 62, 65, 73, 76, 78, 79, 80, 81, 120; Battle of (1941), 2; Cretan insurrection (1897–98), 1
Crimean War (1854–55), 1
Cunningham, Admiral Sir Andrew B., 3
Cunningham, Vice-Admiral John D., 66
Cyprus, 4, 7, 17, 20, 30, 46
Cyrenaica, xv, xix, 18, 20, 26, 27, 46, 50, 57, 62, 64, 70, 73
Czechoslovakian crisis, xv, xvii

D'Iberville, 10
Da Procida, 57
Dainty, 20, 24, 26, 56
Dakar, xviii, 28, 29, 31, 32, 33, 66, 68, 69
Dardanelles, 22, 46, 51, 77, 79
Darlan, Admiral, xii, xiii, xviii, 32, 35, 37, 38, 92–3
Davies, G.P.S., 35
Decoy, 24, 74
Defence Plans (Policy) Committee, 3
Defender, 24, 74
Dekheila, 21, 39, 60
Delhi, 44, 91
Delimara point, 74, 75
Delpuich, Commandant, 26
Denbighshire, 54
Denmark, 12
Derby, 75
Derna, xix, xx, 18, 20, 26, 61, 62, 65
Devonshire, 10, 66
Dhaba, 27
Diamante, 26
Diamond, 27, 64
Dingli, 20
Director of Operations (Foreign), 68, 69
Djibouti, xvii
Dobbie, General Sir William, 21
Dodecanese, the, 2, 10, 13 15, 17, 19, 40, 51, 56, 58, 90
Doro Channel, 46, 53
Dorsetshire, 32
Draria, 20
Duchess of Bedford, 54
Duguay-Trouin, 27, 28
Duncan, 10
Dundalk, 11
Dunkerque, 35, 37

Dunkirk, xix, 14
Dunoon, 11
Duquesne, 28
Durazzo, 12, 73
Durban, 55
Durbo, 70

Eagle, 18, 19, 21, 22, 23, 25, 28, 39, 40, 41, 42, 46, 48, 51, 52, 53, 54, 55, 56, 60, 61, 73, 74, 76, 77, 81
East Africa, xvi, 5, 7, 13
East Indies, 33
Eden, Anthony, 77
Egypt, xiii, xv, xix–xx, 3, 4, 5, 7, 13, 14, 18, 29, 30, 34, 38, 45, 46, 47, 51, 53, 54, 55, 58, 60, 62, 63, 64, 73, 80, 123; Egyptian campaigns (1882–85), 1
El Alamein, 64
El Dhaba, 62
El Tmimi, 65
Elmas aerodrome, 52, 57
Encounter, 67, 68
Enterprise, 35, 44, 45, 46, 52, 53
Epirus, 79
Escort, 45
Espero, 22, 23
Esteva, Admiral, 35
Euboea, 79
Euro, 39
European Appreciation 1939–40, 3
Exeter, 51, 54

F.O.C.N.A., 31, 32, 35, 38, 68, 70, 90, 127, 128, 129–30, 131
Falangola, Rear-Admiral, 27, 45
Fareham, 80
Fashoda incident (1898), 1
Fauingha, 74
Faulknor, 44
Fayid, 60
Ferrol, 46
Fez, 1
Fighter Command, xix
Fiona, 10, 52, 80
Firedrake, 70
First Battle Squadron, 23, 51, 56, 74, 81
First Cruiser Squadron, 10
First Lord of the Admiralty, 6, 13
First Punic War, 1
First Sea Lord, 3, 68, 122, 123
First World War (1914–18), 1, 2, 3
Fisher, Admiral Sir W.W., 3
Fiume, 42
Fleet Air Arm (FAA), 22, 39, 40, 44, 56, 58, 60, 61, 64, 65, 73, 74; 700 Squadron, 61; 767 Squadron, 22; 800 Squadron, 53; 803 Squadron, 52; 813 Squadron, 39, 60, 66; 824 Squadron, 48, 60, 61; 830 Squadron, 38, 60, 61, 76

173

Flowerdown, 20
Force A, 22, 23, 25, 41, 53, 55, 63
Force B, 23, 24–5, 53, 54, 57, 63
Force C, 24
Force D, 28
Force F, 54, 56, 57
Force H, xix, 29, 30, 35, 36–7, 40, 44, 45, 46, 50, 51, 52–3, 57, 66, 68, 69, 70, 81, 90–3, 98, 113–15
Force I, 54, 56
Force W, 66, 70
Foreign Office, 67, 68, 79, 103, 104
Forester, 45
14th Destroyer Flotilla, 19, 27, 74
14th Infantry Brigade, 81
Foxhound, 35
Franca Fassio, 73
France *see* French/France
Franco, General, 1
Free French, 34, 66
Freetown, 10, 11, 31, 66
French/France, xii, xiii, xviii, xix, 1, 2, 3, 4, 5, 6, 7, 8, 9, 10, 11, 12, 13, 15, 16, 17, 18, 19, 20, 22, 26, 27–8, 29, 30, 31–8, 66–9, 70, 78, 91, 92–3, 96–9, 121, 124, 125–32, 137–9, 146–8, 152
French Committee of National Liberation, 28
Freyberg, General, 2
Friedrichshafen conference (1939), xvii
Frost, General, 2
Fulmars, 51, 54, 56, 71, 72, 76

G.H.Q. Middle East/G.H.Q. Cairo, xix, 4, 11, 18, 55
G.O.C. Western Desert Force, 65
Galatea, 10, 11
Galilei, 62
Galita Island, 9, 20, 54
Gallant, 70
Garibaldi, 20
Garland, 23, 57
Garside, Captain F.R., 41
Gaulle, General de, 28, 33, 34, 66, 67, 69
Gavdo Island, 20, 24, 43, 48, 53, 62, 76
Gazala, 65
Genoa, xv, 20, 22, 45
Gensoul, Admiral, 35, 36, 37, 38
Georges Leygues, 35, 67, 69
Germans/Gemany, xiv, xvi, xvii, 1, 2, 3, 4, 5, 6, 8, 12, 13, 15,16, 28, 29, 32, 36, 58, 59, 67, 69, 73, 78, 81, 86, 87, 120, 131
Gibraltar, xiii, xix, 4, 5, 6, 8, 9, 10, 20, 26, 27, 29, 30, 31, 32, 35, 37, 40, 44, 45, 46, 51, 52, 53, 54, 55, 57, 66, 67, 68, 69, 70, 90, 127
Giovanni Delle Bande Nere, 47, 48
Giulio Cesare, 42, 43, 53
Gladiateur, 34
Gladiators, 22, 27, 40, 51, 55, 60
Glasgow, 81

Glauco, 27
Glen Martins, 72, 73
Gloire, 35, 67, 69
Glorious, 10
Gloucester, 13, 19, 20, 21, 22, 23, 41, 42, 46, 54, 55, 59, 62, 70, 72, 74, 76, 81
Godfroy, Admiral, 13, 29, 33, 34
Gold Coast, 54
Gondar, 70
Gorizia, 42
Government Code and Cypher School, xix
Grampus, 25, 62
Graziani, Marshal, 63, 64
Great Pass, 6, 28
Grebe, 60
Greco, Lieut. del, 75
Greece, 1, 2, 3, 10, 14, 15, 17, 23, 25, 27, 30, 77, 78, 79, 80, 81, 103, 124, 143, 154–8; Greek War of Independence (1821–30), 1
Grenville, 9
Griffin, 57, 67, 68, 70
Gulf of Adalia, 10
Gulf of Athens, 46, 47, 53
Gulf of Bomba, 66
Gulf of Bougie, 52, 54
Gulf of Gaeta, xv
Gulf of Genoa, 73
Gulf of Patras, 80
Gulf of Taranto, 80
Gulf of Valona, 12

H.Q. 14th Infantry Brigade, 81
H.Q. R.A.F. Middle East, 13
Haifa, 4, 5, 6, 7, 11, 12, 15, 17, 46, 58, 59–60; conference, 90
Hal Far aerodrome, 58
Hardy, 8
Hasty, 23, 47, 48, 72
Havock, 23, 47, 48, 72, 76
Helle, 78, 79
Hereward, 23, 47, 57, 66
Hermes, 32, 33
Hermione, 51
Hero, 23, 47, 48, 55
Hierapetra, 78
Hitler, Adolph, xvii, xviii, 2, 28
Holland, Captain C.S., 31, 35, 37, 38
Hong Kong, xiii
Hood, 3, 29, 35, 37, 44, 45, 52
Horn of Africa, xvi
Hostile, 55
Hotspur, 67, 68, 70
Hudsons, 60
Huntley, 75
Hurricanes, xix, 51, 52, 54, 58, 81
Hybert, 12

INDEX

Hydra, 79
Hyères, 22
Hyperion, 18, 23, 27, 47, 48, 66

Ilex, 24, 47, 48, 56, 64
Illustrious, xix, xx, 46, 51, 54, 56, 57, 60, 65, 70, 71, 72, 74, 76, 80
Imperia, 22
Imperial, 47, 56–7, 74
Indian Ocean, 10
Inglefield, 83
Inshore Squadron, 57, 66
Ionian Islands, 22, 80
Ionian Sea, 71, 72, 73, 74, 80
Iran, 5
Iraq, 2, 5
Iride, 61
Irwin, Major-General M.N.S., 66
Ishaila Island, 65
Ismailia, 5
Istanbul, 62
Italians/Italy, xii, xiii, xiv–xvii, xvii–xxviii, xix–xx, 1, 2, 3, 4, 5, 6, 7, 9, 10, 11, 12, 13, 14, 15, 16, 17, 18, 20, 21, 22, 23, 26, 28, 29, 30, 36, 38, 40, 42–3, 44, 46, 47–8, 49, 50, 51, 53, 55, 56, 57–8, 59, 61, 62, 63, 64, 69, 70, 71–2, 73, 74, 75, 78, 79, 80, 86–7, 87–8, 122, 123–4, 139–41, 148–50, 151, 153
Italo-Abyssinian War/campaign (1935–36), 3, 4, 16 *see also* Abyssinia

Janus, 23, 55, 65
Japan, xiv, 3, 6, 7
Jean Bart, 31–2
Jervis, 48, 65
Joint Intelligence Centre, xii
Joint Planning Staff, xii
Ju87s, xiv, 58
Juna, 10
Juno, 23, 64, 65, 66

Kalafrana aerodrome, Malta, 58
Kamaria breakwater, Alexandria, 58, 59
Kaso Strait, 24, 46, 47, 53, 55, 70, 77
Kassala, 63, 64
Kelly, Admiral Sir Howard, 78
Kent, 46, 54, 55, 62, 63, 65, 70
Keyes, Admiral Sir Roger, 3
Kithera, 24, 25; Channel, 38, 46, 47
Kupho Nisi, 76

L'Audacieux, 67
La Linea, 70
La Spezia (Spezia), xv, 13, 22
Ladybird, 64, 65, 66, 70
Lafole, 70
Lake Mariut, Alexandria, 60

Lampedusa, 73
Lanarkshire, 74
Larnaca, 17
Lascaris Barracks, Malta, 10
Lausanne, Treaty of (1924), 2
Le Fantasque, 67
Le Havre, 10
Le Matin, 67
Le Verdon, 46
Leopardi, 62
Lepida Cove, 76
Leros, 40, 46, 76
Levant coast, 4
Levkas, 80
Libya, 1, 2, 5, 7, 12, 15, 16, 17, 25, 27, 38, 40, 53, 54, 56, 58, 60, 61, 63, 64, 71, 73, 100–3
Liguria, 39
Lisbon, 67
Lissa, 71
Littorio class battleships, xv, 13, 18, 50, 71, 74
Liverpool, 19, 20, 21, 22, 23, 25, 42, 43, 46, 51, 54, 55, 62, 70, 72, 74, 76
London flying boats, 21
Lorraine, 27, 28, 33, 63
Loula, 62

Maaten Bagush, 61, 64, 76
Maidstone, 10
Majorca, 12
Makri-Yalo aerodrome, 56
Malaya, 10, 13, 19, 28, 42, 43, 46, 53, 54, 55, 63, 73, 74, 77
Malta, xii, xiii, xv, xvi, xix, 4, 5, 7, 9, 10, 11, 15, 17, 18, 19, 20, 21–2, 23, 24, 25, 27, 28, 29, 30, 38, 39, 41, 43, 46, 50, 51, 52, 53, 54, 55, 56, 57, 58–9, 60, 61, 62, 70, 72, 73, 74, 75, 76, 81, 99–100
Mameli, 62
Mandakes, Colonel, 2
Manzoni, 39
Marconi, 45
Margottini, Captain, 75
Mariette Pasha, 82
Maritza airfield, Rhodes, 56
Maroni, Admiral, 16
Marsa el Ramla, 63
Marseilles, 9, 10, 15, 31, 52, 53, 67, 126
Matapan, 24, 26, 51, 55, 74
Mediterranean Light Forces, 62
Medway, 13
Memnon, 74
Mers-el-Kebir, xiii, xviii, 29, 34, 35, 36, 37
Mersa Matruh, 27, 64, 65
Mersin, 77
Messina, 20, 43, 44, 71, 72, 73, 74
Metaxas, General, 80
Middle East, xv, xix, 3, 5, 17, 22, 45, 53, 66, 77, 98–9, 126–7 *see also* names of countries

Middle East Air Force (MEAF), xix, xx
Middle East Command *see* G.H.Q. Middle East/G.H.Q. Cairo
Middle East Intelligence staffs, xix
Middle Hill, Gibraltar, 20
Milazzo, xv
Milford, 32
Millelire, 57
Milo, 15, 17
Ministry of War Transport Department, 12
Minorca, 44, 52, 57
Mogador, 37
Mohawk, 23, 55, 65, 66
Montcalm, 35, 67, 69
Monte Gargano, 61
Moonstone, 62
Moorstone, 58
Morea, 62
Morocco, 67
Morosini, General Francesco, 2
Moscow, 2
Moy, 27
Mussolini, Benito, xiv, xvi–xvii, xviii, 13, 14

N.O.I.C., Haifa, 5
Nahariya, 20
Naples, xv, 5, 14, 15, 20, 44, 45, 74
Nautilus, 20, 26
Naval Attaché: Angora, 103–5; Athens, 79, 80; Belgrade, 12; Madrid, 66–7, 68, 69; Rome, 9, 14, 15, 18, 122, 123–4
Naval Chief of Staff, Cairo, 5
Naval Intelligence Centre, 4
Naval War Memorandum, 6, 7
Navarino, 17
Nelson, Lord, 1
Nembo, 60
Neptune, 13, 19, 20, 21, 22, 23, 25, 27, 28, 42, 43, 46, 48, 51, 53, 54
Neuilly, Treaty of (1919), 77
Nile Valley, 5
Norfolk, 10
North, Admiral Sir Dudley, 66, 67–8, 68–9
North Africa, xv, xvi, xix, 2, 3, 4, 8, 13, 20, 21, 22, 27, 30, 31, 59, 62, 63, 73, 86–7, 126, 127 *see also* names of countries
North Sea, 16
Norway, 12, 13
Novaro, Captain Umberto, 48
Nubian, 21, 23, 27, 55, 65, 76, 77

Odin, 25, 62
Ollive, Admiral, 5, 31, 33, 36
Olna, 80
Olympus, 58
Onslow, Admiral R.F.J., 32, 33

Operation: BQ, 28; Barbarity, 81; Bonnet, 54, 55; Catapult, 35; Coat, 81; Collar, 81; Crush, 52; Grab, 57; Hats, 51, 54, 55, 57, 61, 62, 66, 133–4; Hercules, 59; Hurry, 51, 52, 53, 54; MA.3, 22, 23–4, 29; MA.5, 39–40, 44; MA.9, 53; M.A.Q.2, 77; MB.1, 64; MB.2, 63–4; MB.5, 70, 72, 73, 74; MB.6, 77; MD.3, 27; Menace, 66; Ration, 70; Smash, 57; Spark, 52, 53; Squawk, 57; White, 81
Operational Intelligence Centre, 10, 20
Oran, 9, 20, 28, 29, 31, 32, 33, 34, 35, 36, 37, 44, 91, 132
Orford, 15
Orion, 13, 19, 20, 21, 22, 23, 25, 27, 42, 46, 48, 52, 53, 54, 55, 56, 62, 70, 72, 74, 75, 76, 77, 81
Orkanger, 27
Orpheus, 20, 25, 62
Osiris, 10, 62
Ostro, 22, 23, 60
Oswald, 10, 53, 62
Otway, 10

Palermo, 44
Palestine, 5, 7, 18, 30, 46, 77
Palestro, 62
Pandora, 35, 37, 62, 74, 80
Pantellaria, 57, 58
Panther, 1
Paris, 31
Parthian, 25, 26, 55–6, 62
Patch, Captain O., 61
Patras, 80
Pegadia Bay, 56
Penelope, 10, 11
Perseus, 62
Persian Gulf, 5, 59
Pétain, Marshal, 28, 67
Phoenix, 40, 62
Piraeus, 62, 70, 72, 81
Playfair, General I.S.O., xi, xiii
Plumleaf, 55, 75
Pola, 42
Poland, xvii, 5, 6, 120
Port Laki, 76
Port Maltezana, 72, 77
Port Said, 4, 6, 7, 8, 9, 10, 11, 12, 23, 24, 25, 46, 47, 48, 57, 58, 62, 70, 72, 76, 77, 81
Port Sudan, 58
Portsmouth, 10
Pound, Admiral Sir Dudley, 3
Pretty, Captain F.C., 55
Preveza, 80
Pridham-Wippell, Rear-Admiral, H.D., 53, 77
Protector, 13, 80
Proteus, 35
Protville, 20
Provence, 34, 37

INDEX

Providence, 34
Providenzia, 62
Punto Stilo, Battle of (1940), xviii, 72 *see also* Calabria, action off
Punto Stilo lighthouse, 43

R.N.G.H.Q., Cairo, 5
Raeder, Admiral Erich, xvii
Rainbow, 62, 73
Ramillies, 10, 13, 18, 23, 24, 43–4, 46, 51, 63, 73, 74
Ranpura, 10
Ras Aamer, 74
Ras-el-Hillal, 62
Ras el Tin, 4, 20, 21
Rawlings, Captain H.B., 77
Rear-Admiral (A), 76
Rear-Admiral, Alexandria, 59
Rear-Admiral, First Battle Squadron, 73, 77
Rear-Admiral, Gibraltar, 8
Rear-Admiral, Third Cruiser Squadron, 55, 62
Red Sea, 4, 5, 7, 26, 46, 51, 75
Regent, 62, 73
Renouf, Rear-Admiral, 39, 62
Renown, 46, 54, 57, 66, 67, 68, 69
Resolution, 32, 35, 44, 46, 52
Resource, 4, 11, 13
Reynaud, M., 27–8
Rhodes, 15, 17, 40, 46, 56
Richelieu, 31, 32, 33
Rigault de Genouilly, 37
Rivet, Admiral, 35
Rocks, Keith, 57
Rome, xiv, xvi, 9, 14, 18, 79; Naval Attaché in, 9, 14, 15, 18, 122, 123–4
Rommel, Marshal, 58–9, 64
Rorqual, 25, 62, 74
Rosaura, 10
Roskill, Captain Stephen, xi
Royal Air Force (R.A.F.), xii, xiv, xix, 4, 11, 19, 21, 22, 27, 39, 48, 50, 61, 64, 65, 66, 70, 74, 77; 55 Squadron, 48; 80 Squadron, 60; 200 Group, 67; 201 Group, 21, 22, 24, 41, 48, 58, 60, 61; 202 Group, 56, 61, 76; 202 Squadron, 60; 211 Squadron, 48; 252 Wing, 43
Royal Scotsman, 54
Royal Sovereign, 13, 23, 42, 43, 48, 51, 53, 133
Rubino, 22
Rumania, 77, 78, 144
Russia *see* U.S.S.R.
Ruta, Lieut., 75

Salamis, 17, 79
Salonika, 8, 17, 79, 81
Salpa, 24
San Francisco, 14
San Giorgio, 21, 25

San Giorgio, Leros, 76
San Giovanni di Medua, 12
Saphir, 20, 26
Sapienza Island, 24, 25
Sardinia, xv, 20, 22, 40, 45, 50, 52, 57
Saseno, 12
Savoia-Marchetti aircraft, xvi
Scarborough, 20
Scarpanto, 56
Sea Transport Service, 4, 12, 116–17
2nd Destroyer Flotilla, 18, 19, 21, 28, 47, 74
Secretary of War, xiii
Senior British Naval Officer, Suez Canal Area (S.B.N.O.S.C.A.), 5, 8
Senior Naval Officer, Levant Area (S.N.O.L.A.), 5
Senior Officer (1) Alexandria, 9
Senior Officer Force H, 38, 54, 55, 70, 93, 95–6, 98, 132–3, 134
Serenitas, 39
Seventh Cruiser Squadron, 19, 21, 22, 23, 41, 42, 43, 44, 62, 74, 75
Sheffield, 46, 54, 57
Sicilian Channel/Sicilian Narrows, xv, 55
Sicily, xv, 5, 9, 22, 38, 40, 41, 45, 50, 53, 57, 60, 61, 73, 75
Sidi Barrani, 59, 60, 61, 64, 65, 66, 72
Sidi Bishr, 20
Sidi Omar, 64
Sikh, 10
Skuas, 37, 52, 53, 57
Sollum, 29, 64, 65
Somerset Wharf, Malta, 58
Somerville, Vice-Admiral Sir James F., 29, 35, 36, 44–5, 46, 52, 66, 67–8, 69
South America, 15
Spain, xiv, xv, xviii, 1, 2, 3, 12, 46, 141–3; Spanish Civil War, xv, 1, 3, 16, 26
Spartivento, Battle of (1940), 1
Spearman, Lieut. Commander, 35
Speri, 62
Spezia (La Spezia), xv, 13, 22
Staff Office (Intelligence) Mediterranean, 10
Stampalia, 72, 77
Stella Sirius, 69
Straits: Gibraltar, 31, 66, 67, 68, 69, 70; Kaso, 24, 46, 47, 53, 55, 70, 77; Messina, 8, 28, 53; Otranto, 15, 19, 25, 73, 80
Strasbourg, xviii, 35, 37
Stuart, 10, 64, 70
Suda Bay, 17, 21, 80, 81
Sudan, 5, 18, 63
Suez, 6, 55, 65
Suez Canal, xiii, xix, 5, 7, 10, 13, 15, 59, 123; Canal area/Zone, xiii, 5, 6–7, 11, 58, 60; Canal Company, 11; Suez Canal Convention, 6
Suffolk, 10

Suffren, 27, 28
Sunderlands, xvi, 21, 22, 24, 52, 60, 72, 73
Swordfish, xx, 37, 38, 39, 40, 41, 51, 53, 54, 57, 60, 61, 66, 72
Sydney, 19, 20, 23, 25, 27, 28, 42, 43, 46, 47, 48, 49, 51, 53, 54, 55, 56, 62, 64, 70, 72, 74, 76, 77, 81
Sydney Star, 54
Syracuse, 15, 20
Syria, xii, 2, 5, 46, 77

Takoradi, 54
Taranto, xv, xx, 19, 20, 38, 40, 44, 45, 56, 62, 71, 72, 73, 74, 80
Tel Aviv, 58
10th Destroyer Flotilla, 21, 74
Terror, 81
Thermia Channel, 51
Third Cruiser Squadron, 23, 39, 43, 55, 56, 65, 70, 74, 75, 76, 80
Third Minesweeping Flotilla, 11
Tinos, 78
Titterton, Commander G.A., xi
Tobruk, xix, xx, 19, 20, 21, 22, 25, 27, 39, 48, 60, 61, 65, 74, 76, 77
Tolmeita Lt. Cyrenaica, 62
Toulon, xiii, xviii, 9, 20, 26, 31, 33, 37, 38, 66, 67, 69
Tours, 28
Tourville, 10
Tovey, Vice-Admiral J.C., 8, 19, 27, 42, 62, 77
Transjordan, 5
Trapani, 20, 22, 26, 44
Trento, 42
Triad, 73
Tricheco, 78
Trieste, 8, 13, 38
Tripoli, xix, 20, 26, 47, 72, 73
Triton, 73, 80
Truant, 62
Tunis, 20, 67
Tunisia, xii, xiii, 5, 15
Turker, General Galip, 77
Turkey, 1, 2, 3, 11, 15, 17, 77, 78, 79, 103–5, 143
Turquoise, 20, 26
Tyrrhenian Sea, 50, 73

U.S.S.R./Russia, 2, 3, 5, 6, 17, 79, 144
Uarsciek, 24, 26
Uebi-Scebeli, 24
Ulgen, Vice-Admiral, 77
United States, xviii, 13, 33, 36, 123
Upholder, 78

V.A.L.F. (Vice-Admiral, Light Forces), 56, 62, 65, 77, 81
Vado Roads, 73

Valiant, 35, 44, 45, 46, 51, 52, 54, 56, 57, 65, 70, 74, 81
Vampire, 10, 23, 74, 76
Velox, 32, 57, 68
Ven, Contre-Admiral, 26
Vendetta, 10
Venetians, 2
Venice, xv, 1, 12
Vice-Admiral (A), 44, 131
Vice-Admiral, Bizerta, 8
Vice-Admiral (D), 22, 23, 25, 43, 46, 48, 52, 62
Vice-Admiral, Light Forces (V.A.L.F.), 55, 56, 59, 62, 65, 77, 81
Vice-Admiral, Malta, 11, 25, 28, 58
Vice-Admiral, Second-in-Command, *see* Vice-Admiral, Light Forces
Vichy Government/Vichy France, 28, 32, 66, 68
Vidette, 67, 68
Vigo, 46
Vittorio Veneto, 13
Vivaldi, 53
Volo, 55, 75
Voltaire, 10
Voyager, 10, 24, 27
Vulcan, 10

Waiotira, 54
War Cabinet, xviii–xix, 66, 68, 91
War Office, xiii, 11, 12
Warspite, 5, 10, 13, 19, 21, 28, 40, 42, 43, 44, 46, 48, 51, 53, 54, 55, 56, 59, 63, 70, 74, 76, 80
Washington, 79
Watchman, 26, 31, 32
Waterhen, 10, 64
Wavell, General, 64
Wellington bombers, xix, 65
Wellman, Lieut. (A) W.G., 61
West Africa, 31, 66, 69
West Indies, 33, 35, 36
West Macedonia, 79
Western Desert, xii, xiii, 60, 64, 70
Willis, Rear-Admiral A.U., 3
Winchester, 20
Wishart, 57, 68
Woolwich, 10, 13
Wrestler, 70

York, 46, 51, 54, 55, 65, 74, 76, 81
York and Lancaster Regiment, 80
Yugoslavia, 2, 12, 38, 77, 78, 143

Zante, 21, 22, 41
Zara, 42
Zara-class cruisers, 20, 56
Zeffiro, 22, 23, 39
Zhukov, Marshal, 2

MEDITERRANEAN AND BLACK SEA, POLITICAL MAP.

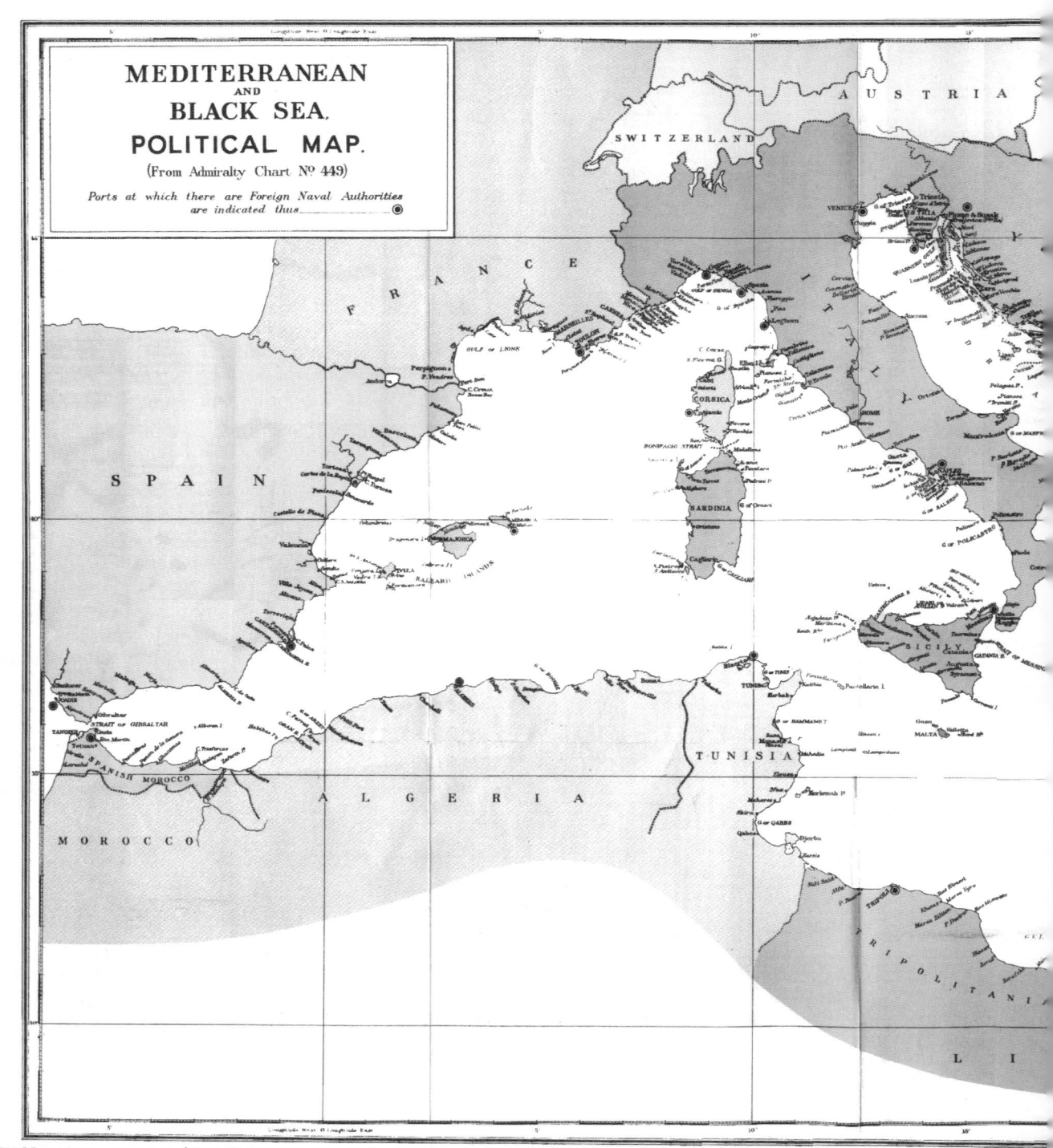

(From Admiralty Chart No. 449)

Ports at which there are Foreign Naval Authorities are indicated thus⊙

Naval Staff (I.D.) 1930. Revised July 1937

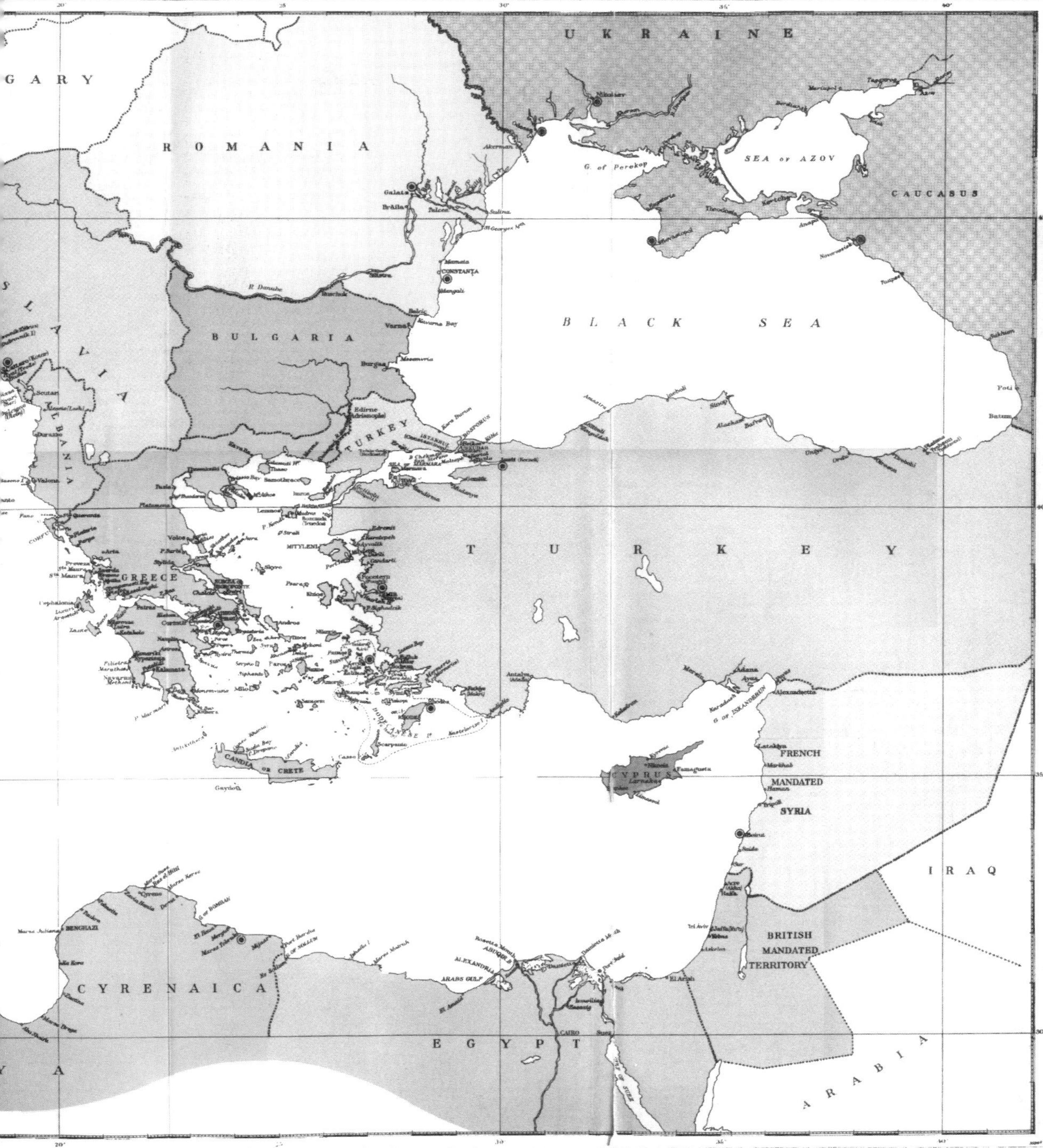

the Superintendence of Rear Admiral H.P. Douglas, C.B., C.M.G., *Hydrographer*

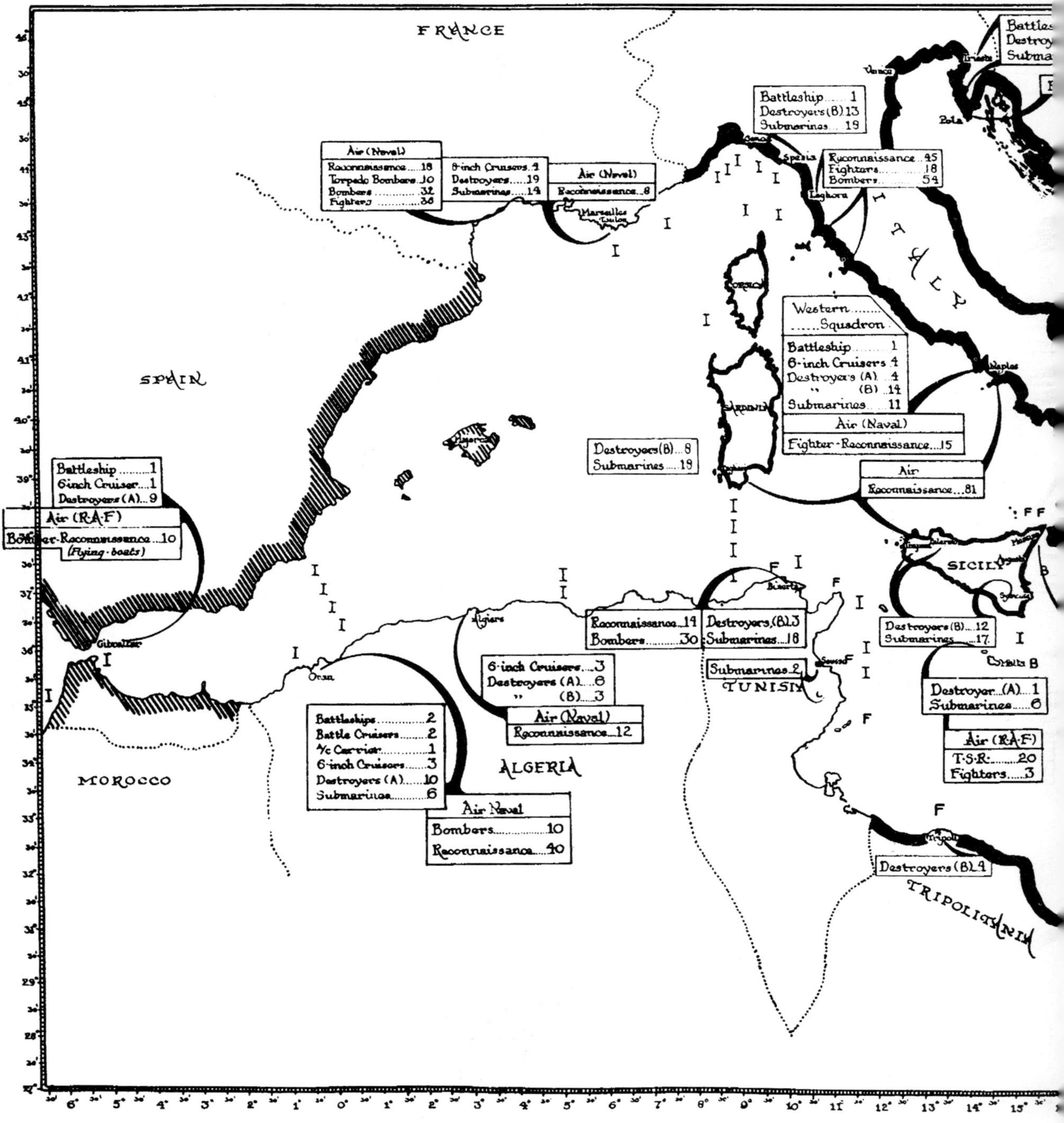

FRANCE
SPAIN
MOROCCO
ALGERIA
TUNISIA
ITALY
SICILY
TRIPOLITANIA
Battleship 1
Destroyers(B) 13
Submarines 19
Genoa
Spezia
Leghorn
Reconnaissance 45
Fighters 18
Bombers 54
Venice
Trieste
Pola
Air (Naval)
Reconnaissance 18
Torpedo Bombers 10
Bombers 32
Fighters 36
6-inch Cruisers 4
Destroyers 19
Submarines 14
Air (Naval)
Reconnaissance 8
Marseilles
Toulon
Corsica
Western Squadron
Battleship 1
6-inch Cruisers 4
Destroyers (A) 4
" (B) 14
Submarines 11
Air (Naval)
Fighter-Reconnaissance 15
Naples
Sardinia
Majorca
Destroyers(B) 8
Submarines 19
Air
Reconnaissance 81
Battleship 1
6inch Cruiser 1
Destroyers (A) 9
Air (R.A.F)
Bomber-Reconnaissance 10
(Flying-boats)
Gibraltar
Palermo
Trapani
Messina
Augusta
Syracuse
Bizerta
Reconnaissance 14
Bombers 30
Destroyers (B) 3
Submarines 18
Destroyers (B) 12
Submarines 17
Algiers
Oran
6-inch Cruisers 3
Destroyers (A) 6
" (B) 3
Air (Naval)
Reconnaissance 12
Submarines 2
Sousse
Malta
Destroyer (A) 1
Submarines 6
Air (R.A.F)
T.S.R. 20
Fighters 3
Battleships 2
Battle Cruisers 2
A/c Carrier 1
6-inch Cruisers 3
Destroyers (A) 10
Submarines 6
Air Naval
Bombers 10
Reconnaissance 40
Tripoli
Destroyers (B) 4

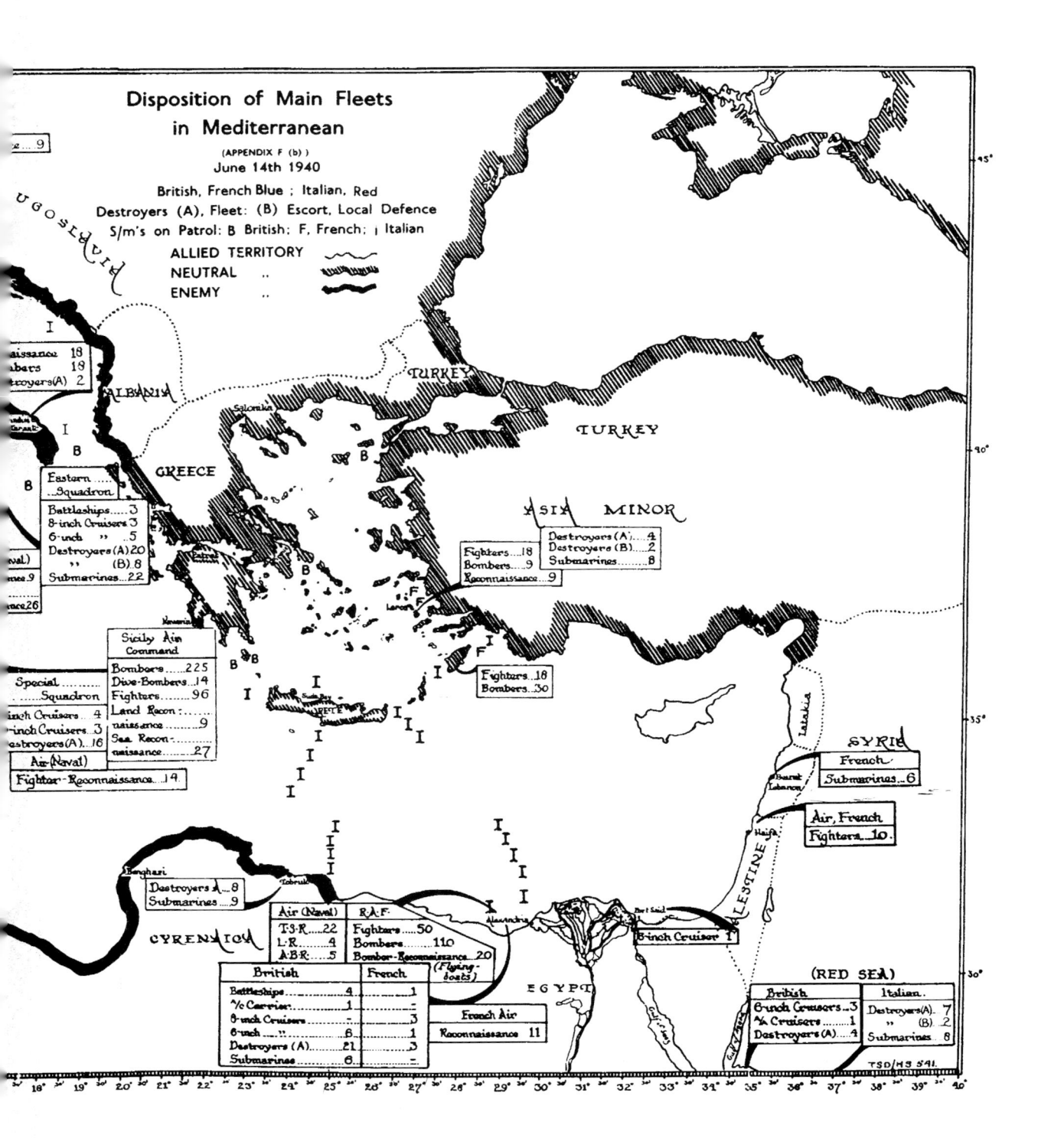

Disposition of Main Fleets in Mediterranean

(APPENDIX F (b))
June 14th 1940

British, French Blue ; Italian, Red
Destroyers (A), Fleet: (B) Escort, Local Defence
S/m's on Patrol: B British; F, French; I Italian

- ALLIED TERRITORY
- NEUTRAL
- ENEMY

(Albania area)
- Reconnaissance 18
- Bombers 19
- Destroyers (A) 2

Eastern Squadron
- Battleships 3
- 8-inch Cruisers 3
- 6-inch 5
- Destroyers (A) 20
- " (B) 8
- Submarines 22

(Asia Minor area)
- Fighters 18
- Bombers 9
- Reconnaissance 9
- Destroyers (A) 4
- Destroyers (B) 2
- Submarines 8

Sicily Air Command
- Bombers 225
- Dive-Bombers 14
- Fighters 96
- Land Recon
- naissance 9
- Sea Recon-
- naissance 27

Special Squadron
- 8-inch Cruisers 4
- 6-inch Cruisers 3
- Destroyers (A) 16
- Air (Naval)
- Fighter-Reconnaissance 14

(Crete area)
- Fighters 18
- Bombers 30

Syria — French
- Submarines 6

Air, French
- Fighters 10

(Cyrenaica)
- Destroyers (A) 8
- Submarines 9

Air (Naval)
- T.S.R. 22
- L.R. 4
- A.B.R. 5

R.A.F.
- Fighters 50
- Bombers 110
- Bomber-Reconnaissance 20 (Flying-boats)

	British	French
Battleships	4	1
½ Carrier	1	—
8-inch Cruisers	—	3
6-inch "	6	1
Destroyers (A)	21	3
Submarines	6	—

French Air
- Reconnaissance 11

(Port Said)
- 8-inch Cruiser 1

(RED SEA)

British	Italian
6-inch Cruisers 3	Destroyers (A) 7
A.A. Cruisers 1	" (B) 2
Destroyers (A) 4	Submarines 8

TSD/HS 541

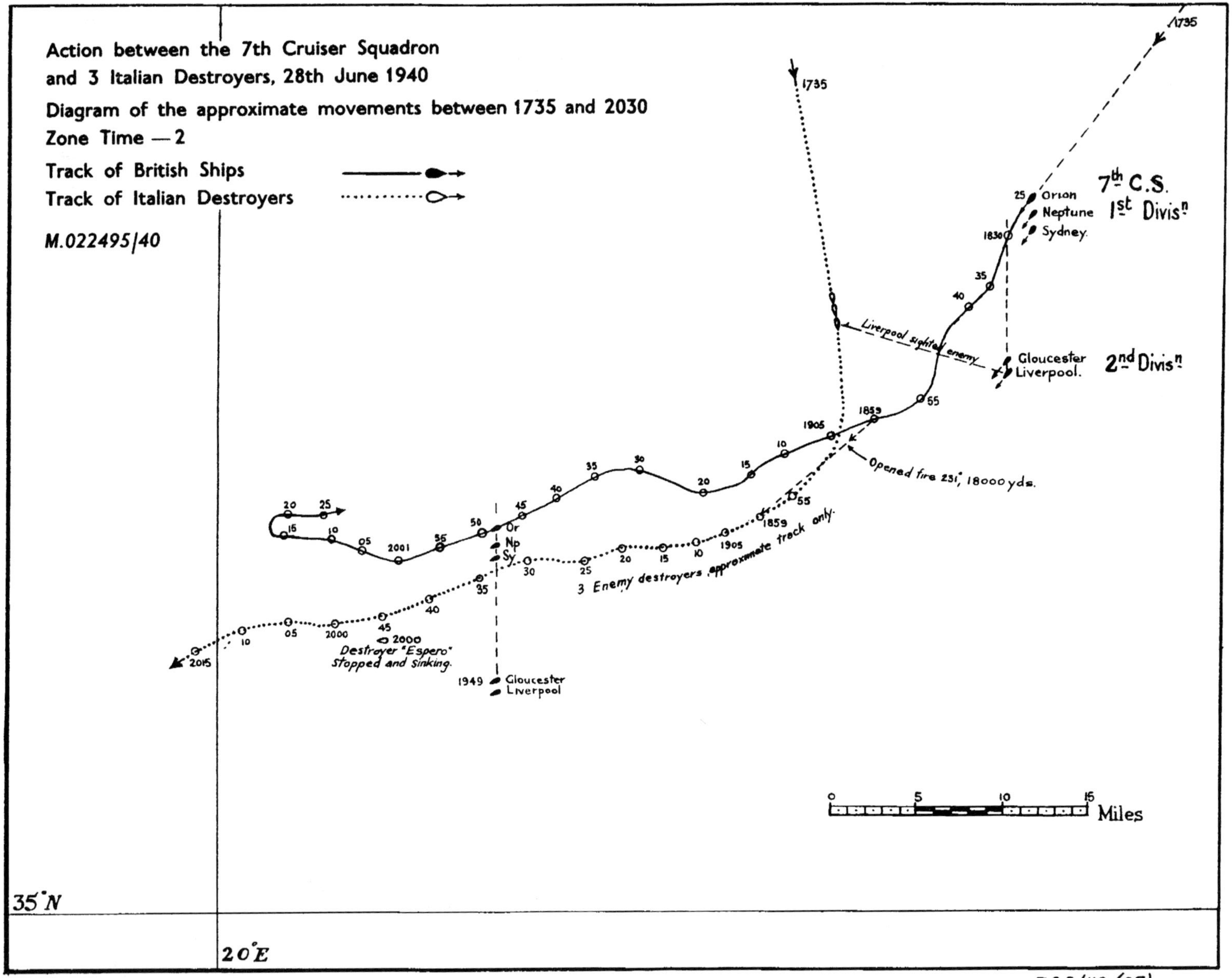

Action between the 7th Cruiser Squadron
and 3 Italian Destroyers, 28th June 1940
Diagram of the approximate movements between 1735 and 2030
Zone Time — 2
Track of British Ships
Track of Italian Destroyers
M.022495/40
7th C.S.
1st Divisn
Orion
Neptune
Sydney
2nd Divisn
Gloucester
Liverpool.
Liverpool sighted enemy
Opened fire 251°, 18000 yds.
3 Enemy destroyers approximate track only.
Destroyer "Espero" Stopped and sinking.
1949 Gloucester Liverpool
Or
Np
Sy
1735
1830
1859
1905
2000
2001
2015
Miles
35°N
20°E

TSD/HS.(97).

PLAN 4

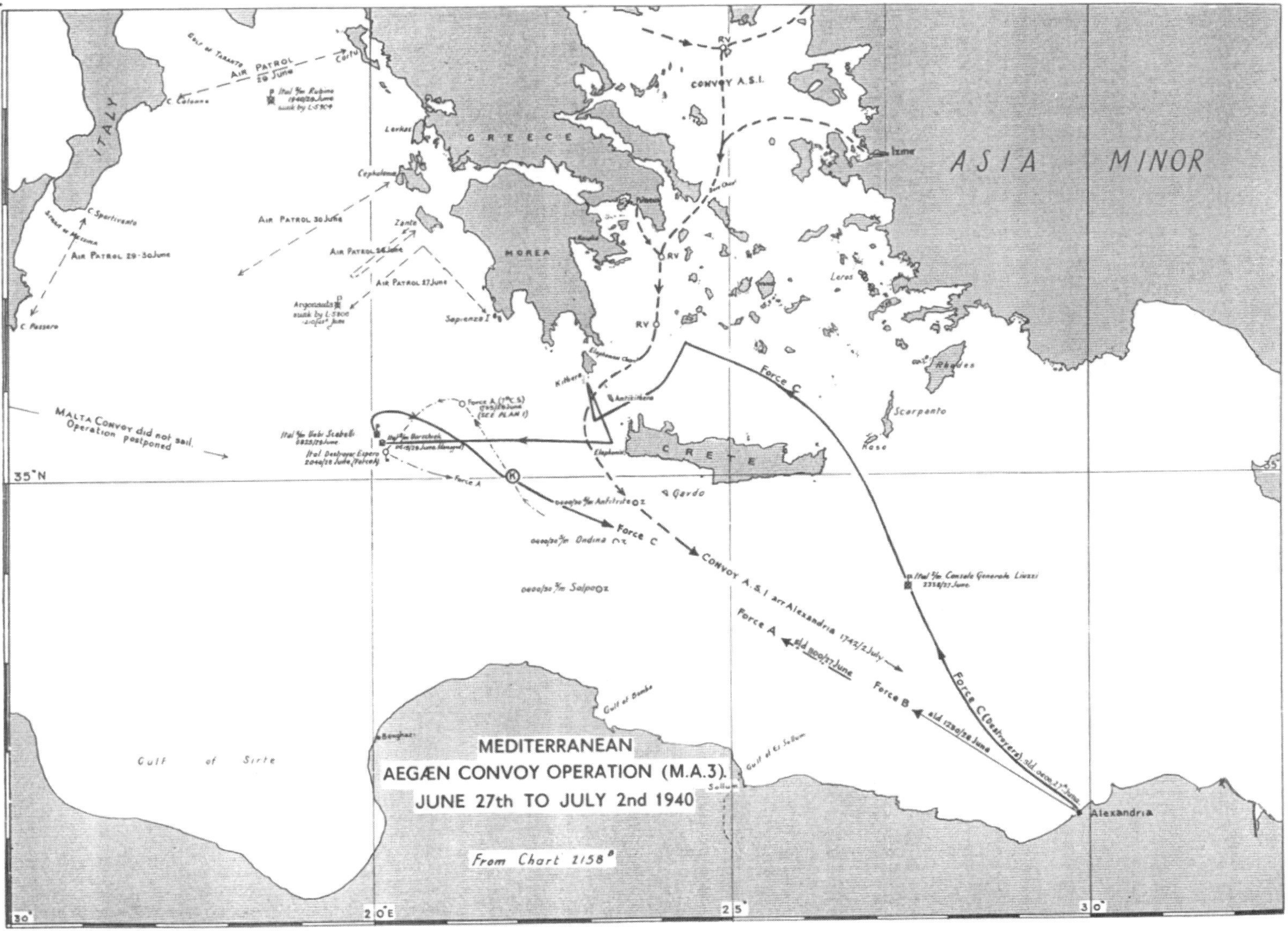

MEDITERRANEAN
AEGEAN CONVOY OPERATION (M.A.3)
JUNE 27th TO JULY 2nd 1940

PLAN 5

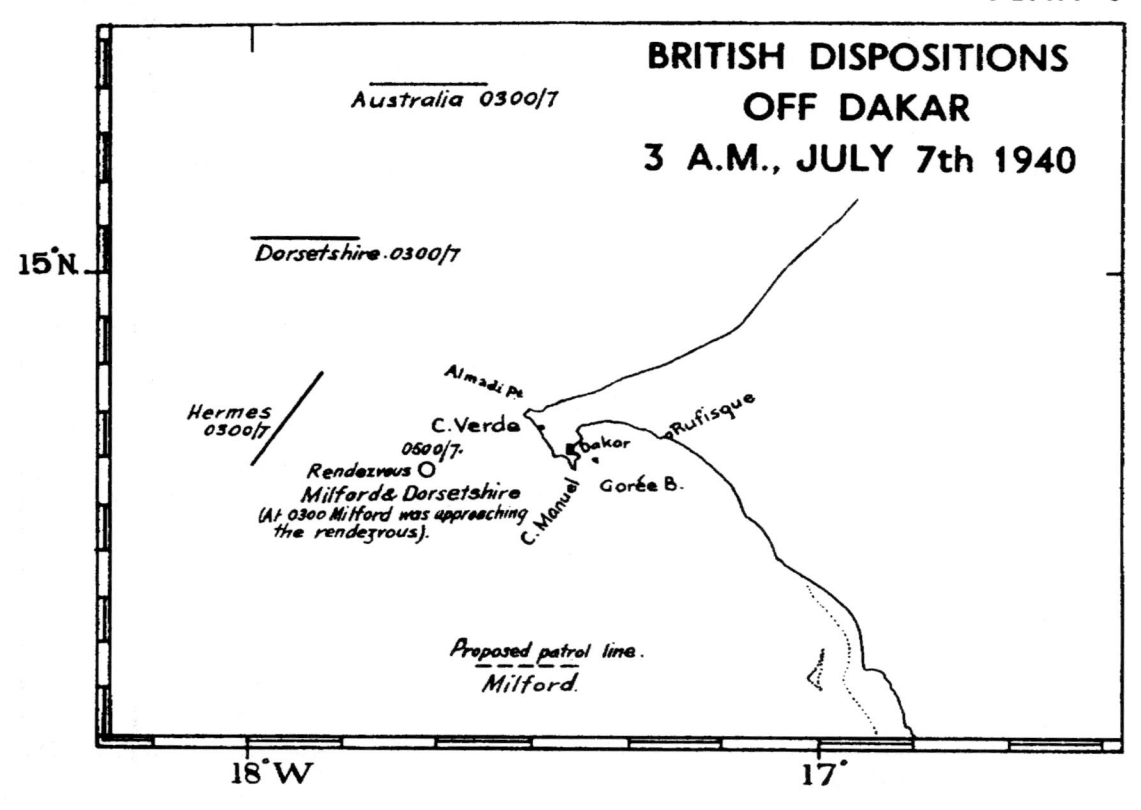

BRITISH DISPOSITIONS OFF DAKAR 3 A.M., JULY 7th 1940

Australia 0300/7

15°N

Dorsetshire 0300/7

Hermes 0300/7

Almadi Pt.
C. Verde 0500/7.
Rendezvous ○
Milford & Dorsetshire
(At 0300 Milford was approaching the rendezvous).
C. Manuel
Dakar
Gorée B.
Rufisque

Proposed patrol line.
Milford.

18°W   17°

PLAN 6

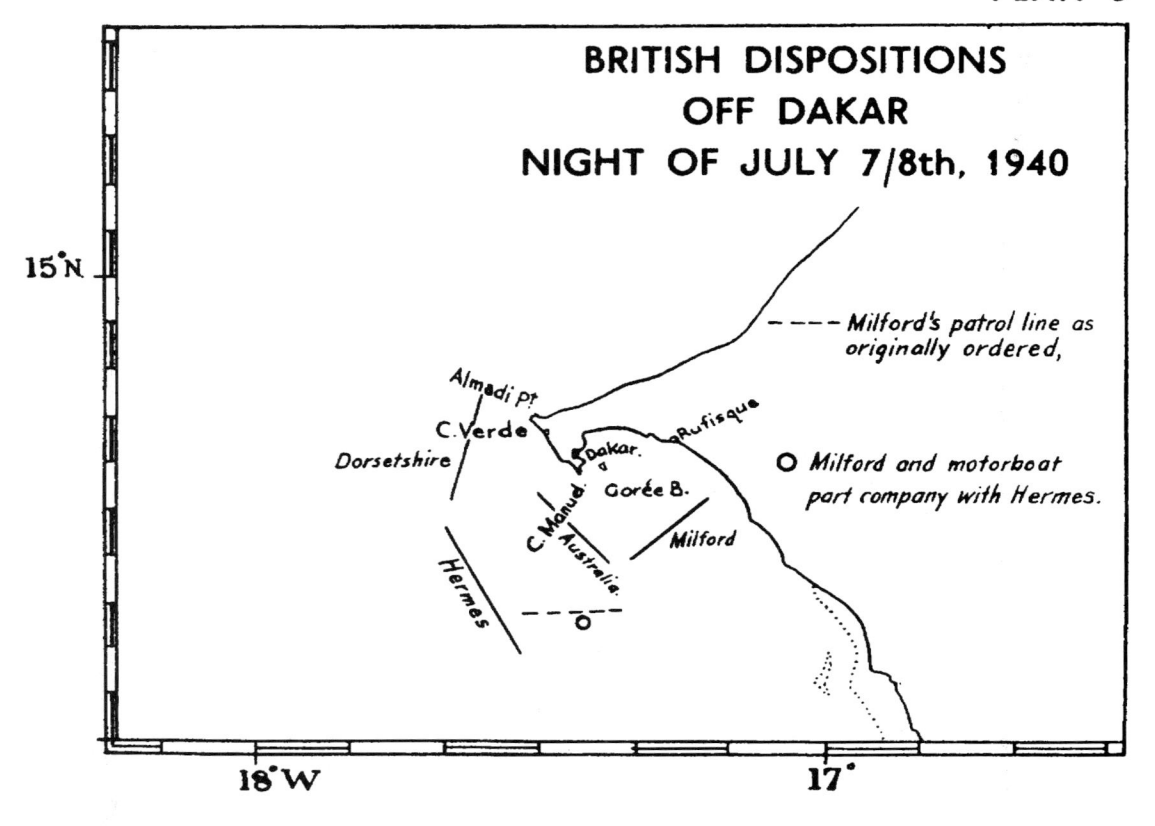

BRITISH DISPOSITIONS OFF DAKAR
NIGHT OF JULY 7/8th, 1940

- - - - Milford's patrol line as originally ordered.

O Milford and motorboat part company with Hermes.

PLAN 7

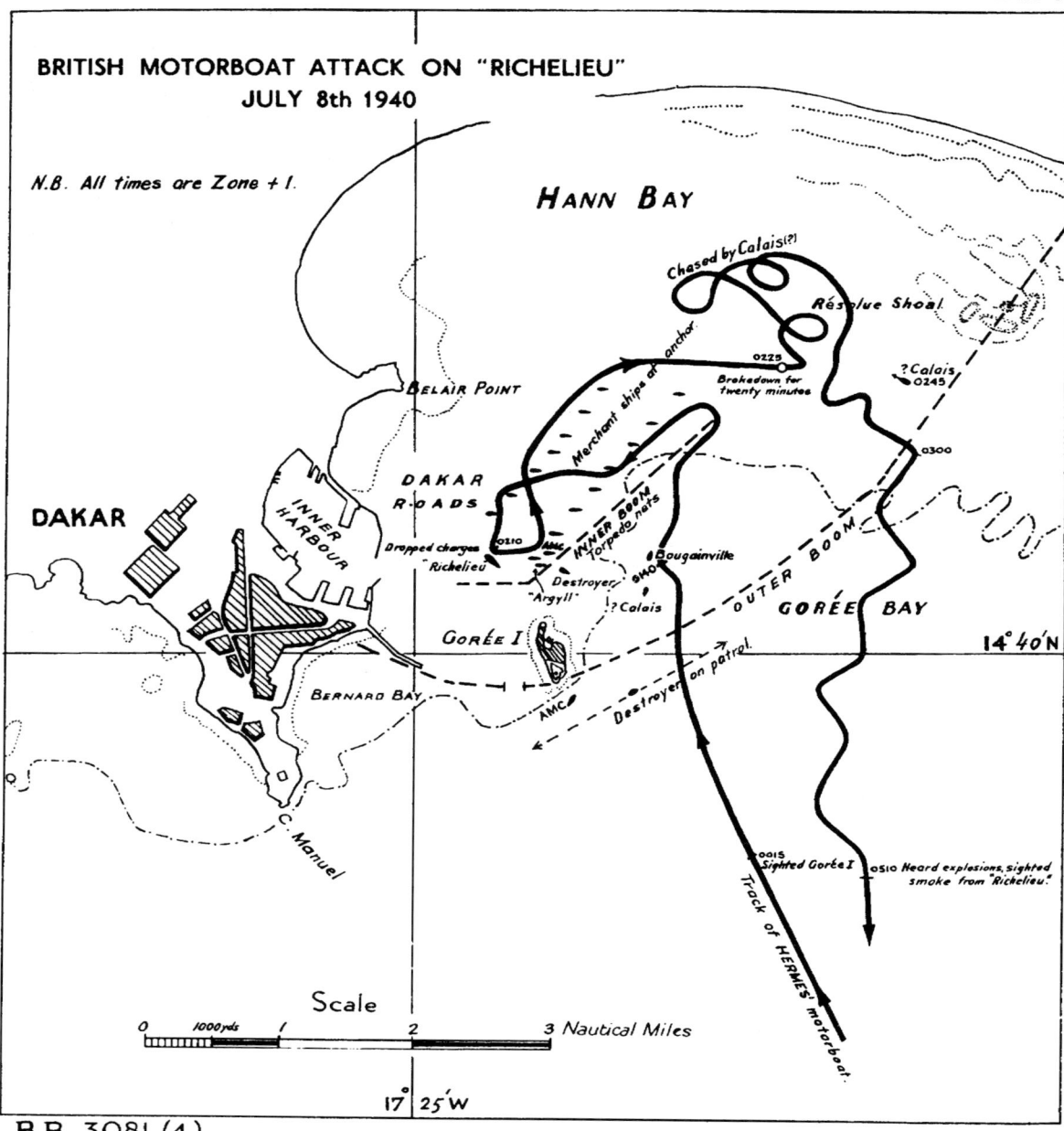

**BRITISH MOTORBOAT ATTACK ON "RICHELIEU"
JULY 8th 1940**

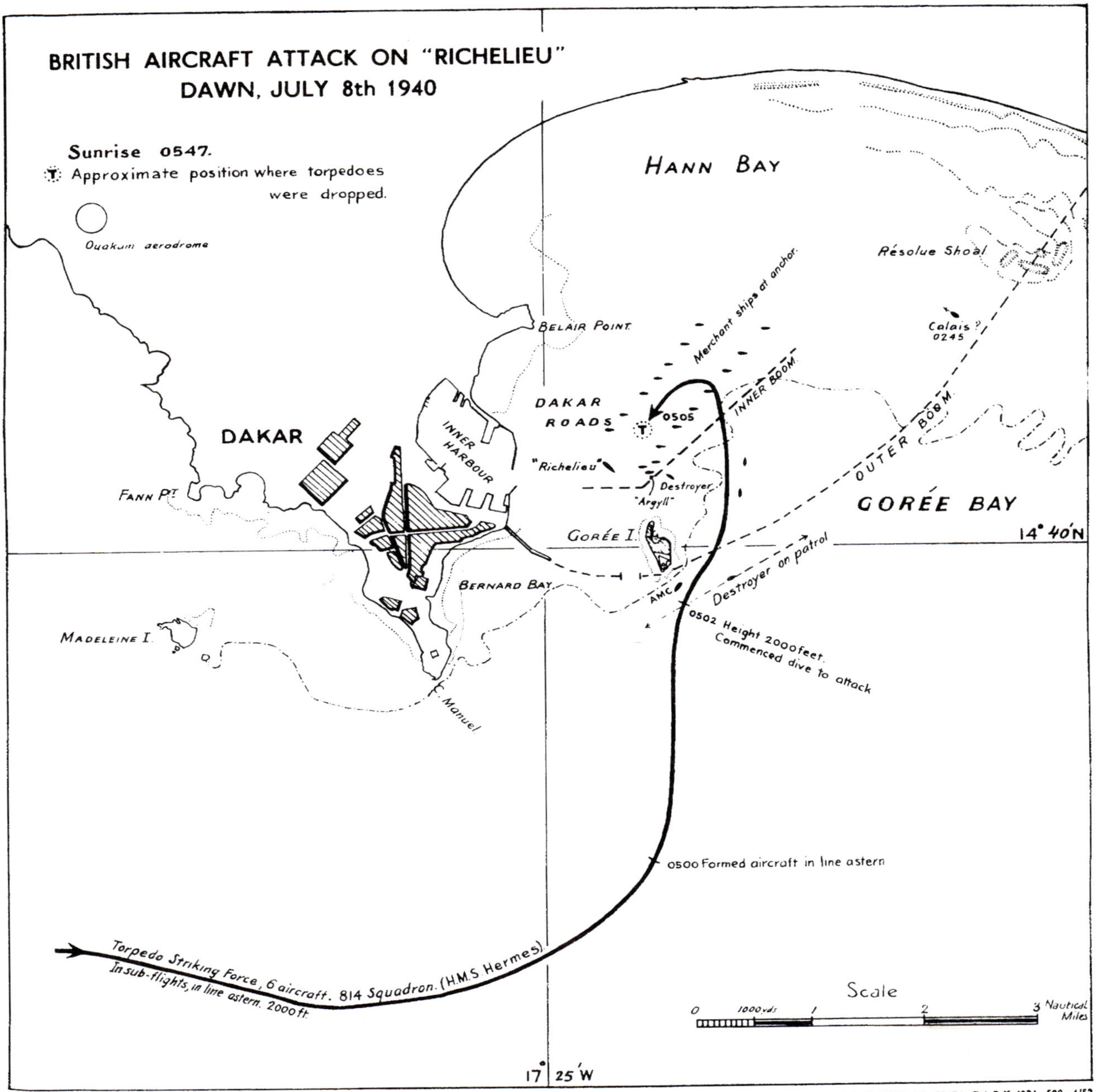

C.B.H. 21453 - Wt. 29474 - Dd. P.K. 4021 - 500 - 4/52

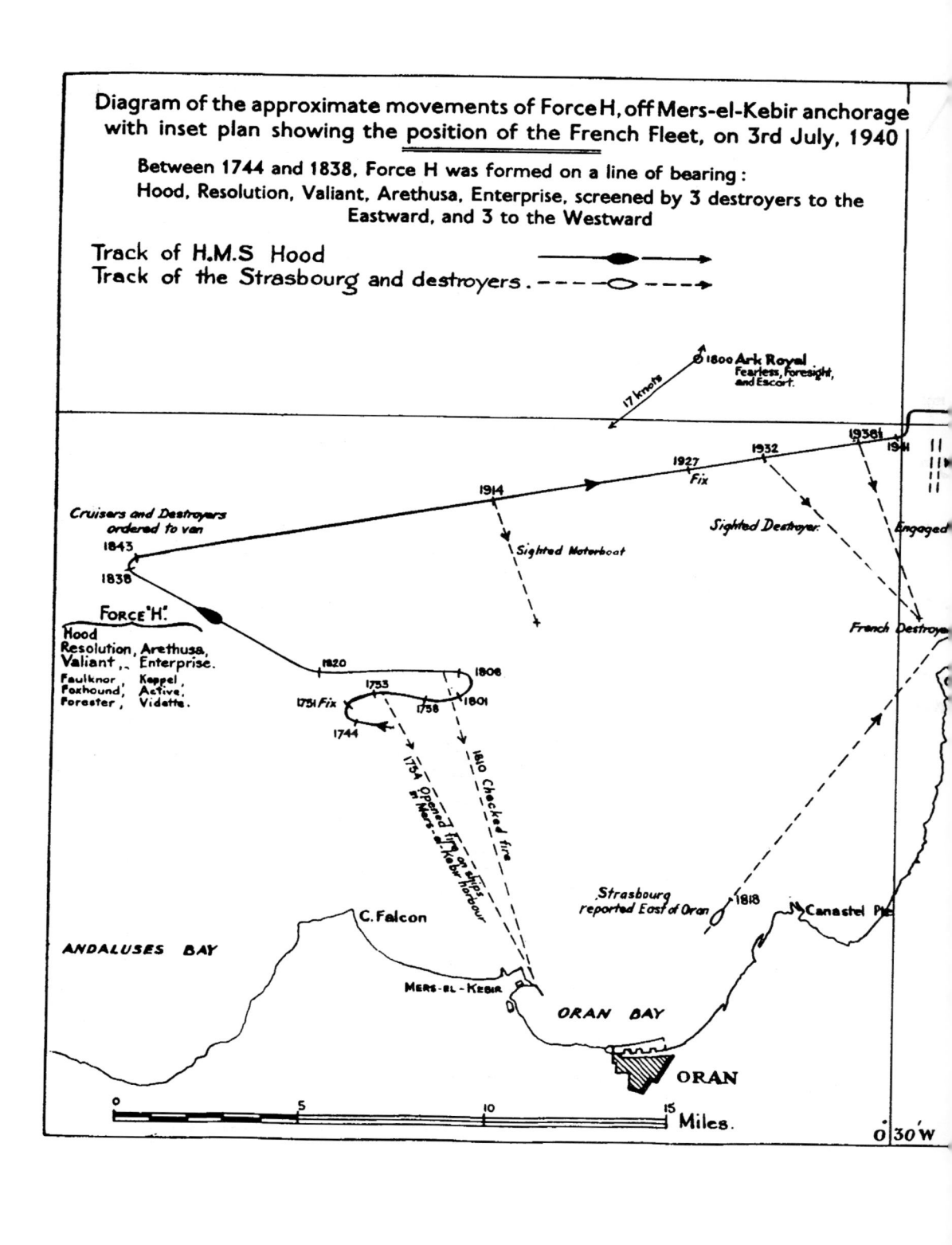

Diagram of the approximate movements of Force H, off Mers-el-Kebir anchorage with inset plan showing the position of the French Fleet, on 3rd July, 1940

Between 1744 and 1838, Force H was formed on a line of bearing:
Hood, Resolution, Valiant, Arethusa, Enterprise, screened by 3 destroyers to the Eastward, and 3 to the Westward

Track of H.M.S Hood
Track of the Strasbourg and destroyers.

1800 Ark Royal
Fearless, Foresight, and Escort.
17 knots

1936
1914   1927   1932   1941
       Fix
                Sighted Destroyer.
Sighted Motorboat
                              Engaged
Cruisers and Destroyers
ordered to van
1843
1838
                              French Destroyer
FORCE "H"
Hood
Resolution, Arethusa,
Valiant, Enterprise.
Faulknor, Keppel,
Foxhound, Active,
Forester, Vidette.
              1820   1806
              1753
       1751 Fix   1801
              1758
       1744
                1754 Opened fire on ships in Mers-el-Kebir Harbour
                1810 Checked fire

                              Strasbourg
                              reported East of Oran 1818
         C. Falcon   Canastel Pt
ANDALUSES BAY
              MERS-EL-KEBIR
                         ORAN BAY
                              ORAN

0   5   10   15 Miles

0° 30′ W

PLAN 9

Plan of Mers-el-Kebir anchorage

PLAN 10

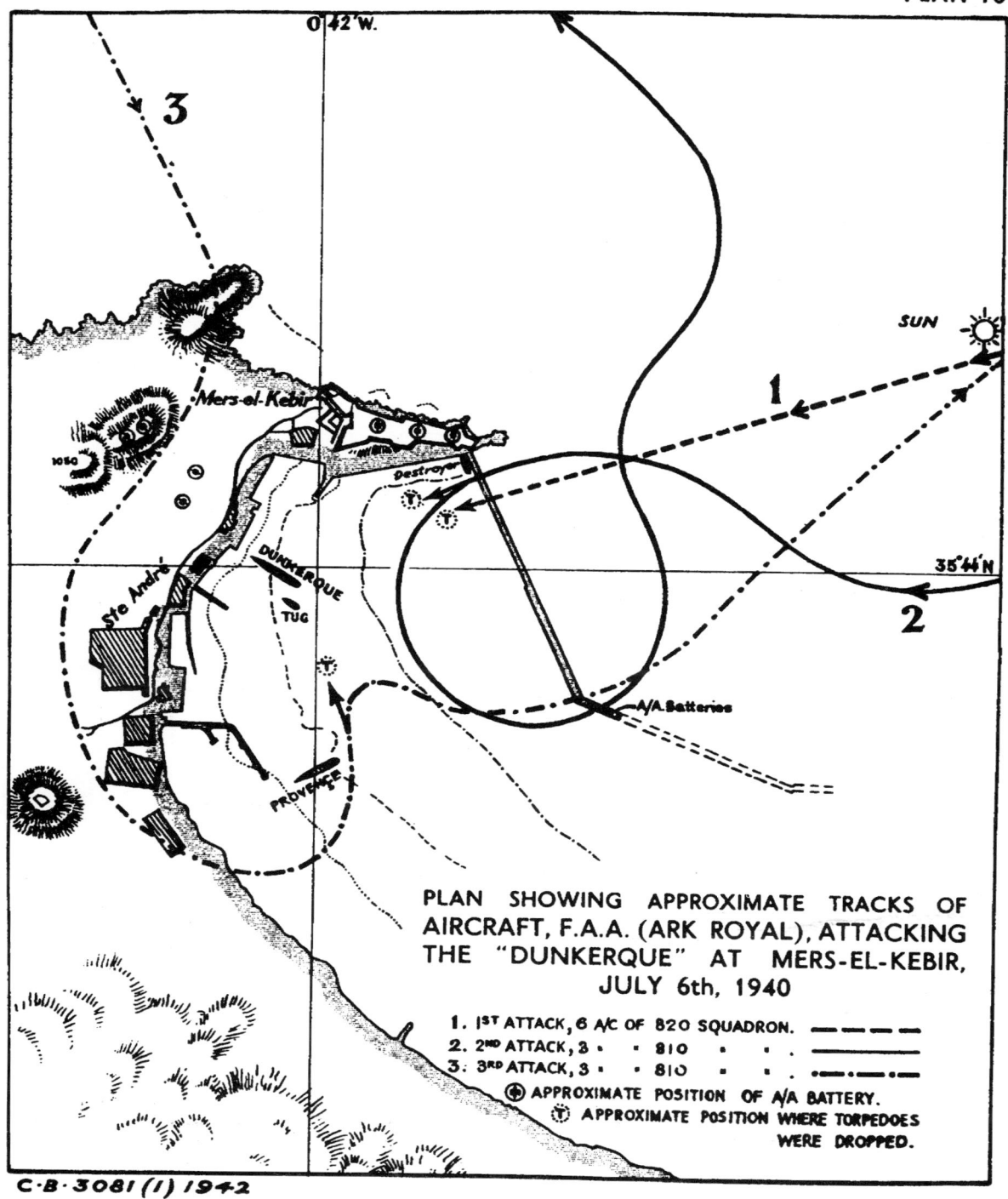

PLAN SHOWING APPROXIMATE TRACKS OF AIRCRAFT, F.A.A. (ARK ROYAL), ATTACKING THE "DUNKERQUE" AT MERS-EL-KEBIR, JULY 6th, 1940

1. 1ST ATTACK, 6 A/C OF 820 SQUADRON. — — —
2. 2ND ATTACK, 3 " " 810 " ————
3. 3RD ATTACK, 3 " " 810 " —·—·—
⊕ APPROXIMATE POSITION OF A/A BATTERY.
Ⓣ APPROXIMATE POSITION WHERE TORPEDOES WERE DROPPED.

C.B.3081(1) 1942

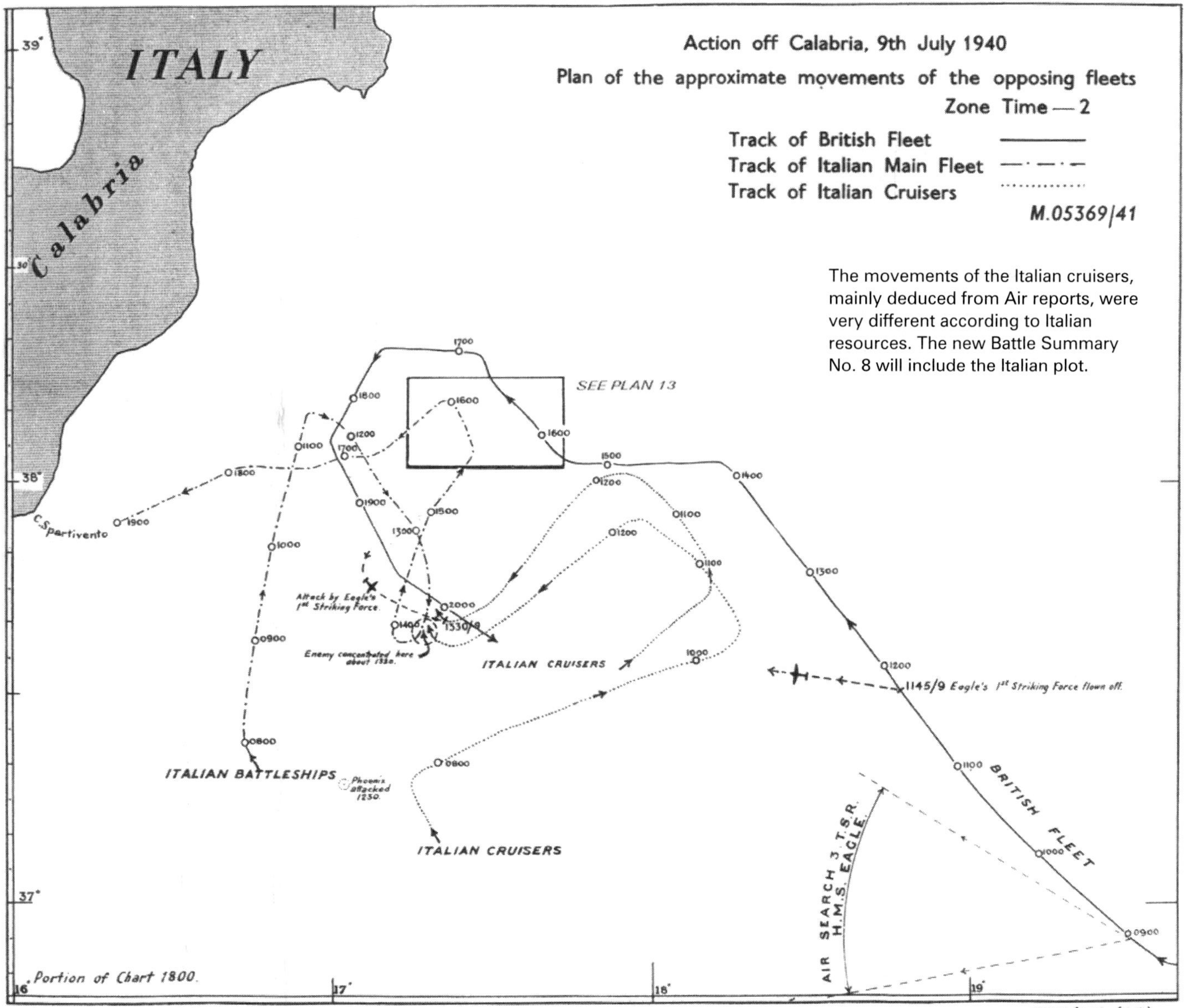

PLAN 11

Action off Calabria, 9th July 1940
Plan of the approximate movements of the opposing fleets
Zone Time — 2

Track of British Fleet	————
Track of Italian Main Fleet	—·—·—
Track of Italian Cruisers	··········

M.05369/41

The movements of the Italian cruisers, mainly deduced from Air reports, were very different according to Italian resources. The new Battle Summary No. 8 will include the Italian plot.

Battle Summary (8).   TSD/HS. (95.)

PLAN 12

"Owing to the occasional glimpses of the enemy obtained through smoke screens, etc., the number of Italian cruisers was considerably over-estimated. At 1500, there were six 8-inch cruisers roughly half-way between groups A and B, and four 6-inch cruisers roughly half-way between C and D. Four other 6-inch cruisers were over-hauling the Battle fleet from the south-west,—still some way off, i.e., altogether 10 cruisers 'present' plus 4 on the way instead of 15 'present' as shown."

Force C
Malaya / Royal Sovereign
Royal
Eagle
Stuart (10th D.F.)
Hyperion (2nd D.F.)

Destroyer Screen

Force B
Warspite
Nubian (14th DF)
Destroyer Screen
Gloucester

Force A
Liverpool
Neptune
Orion (7th C.S.)
Sydney

A ◁ 8in. CRUISERS
B
C ◁ 6in. CRUISERS
D ◁ 6in. CRUISERS
X, Y, Z, R

Action off Calabria, 9th July 1940
Approximate positions of the opposing fleets at 1500
(Zone Time −2)
Italian Battleships, Cruisers △, Destroyers

0 2 4 6 8 10 Miles

M.05369/41

38°N
17°30′   45′   18°E

TSD/HS.(137)

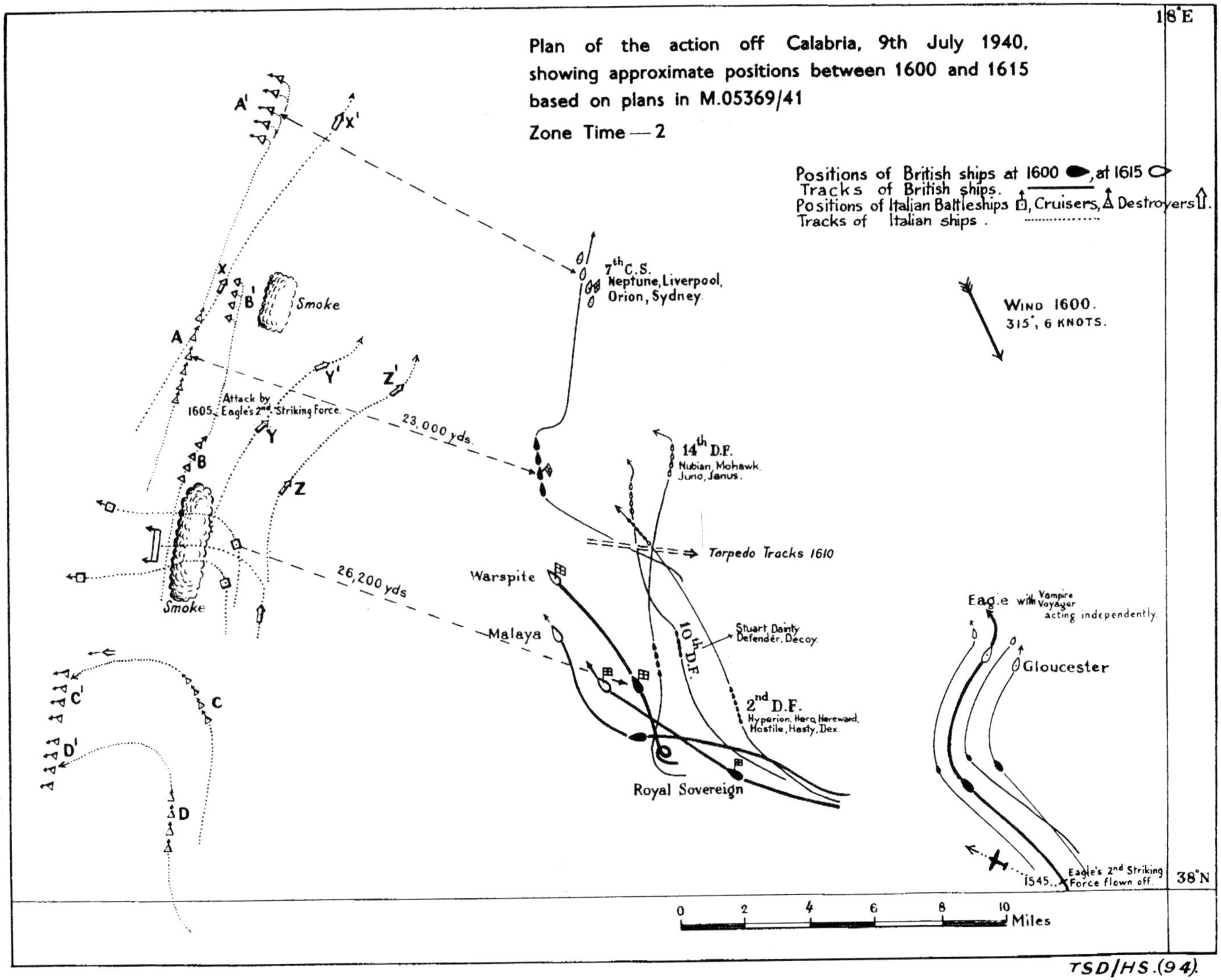

PLAN 13

Plan of the action off Calabria, 9th July 1940, showing approximate positions between 1600 and 1615 based on plans in M.05369/41

Zone Time — 2

Positions of British ships at 1600 ●, at 1615 ○
Tracks of British ships.
Positions of Italian Battleships ▣, Cruisers, △ Destroyers.
Tracks of Italian ships.

WIND 1600.
315°, 6 KNOTS.

Gloucester
Eagle with Vampire, Voyager acting independently.
Eagle's 2nd Striking Force Flown off
1545.

7th C.S.
Neptune, Liverpool, Orion, Sydney

14th D.F.
Nubian, Mohawk, Juno, Janus.

Torpedo Tracks 1610

2nd D.F.
Hyperion, Hero, Hereward, Hostile, Hasty, Ilex.

Stuart, Dainty, Defender, Decoy
10th D.F.

Royal Sovereign

Warspite
Malaya

23,000 yds
26,200 yds

Smoke

Attack by 1605 Eagle's Striking Force

Smoke

Miles 0 2 4 6 8 10

38°N

TSD/HS.(94)

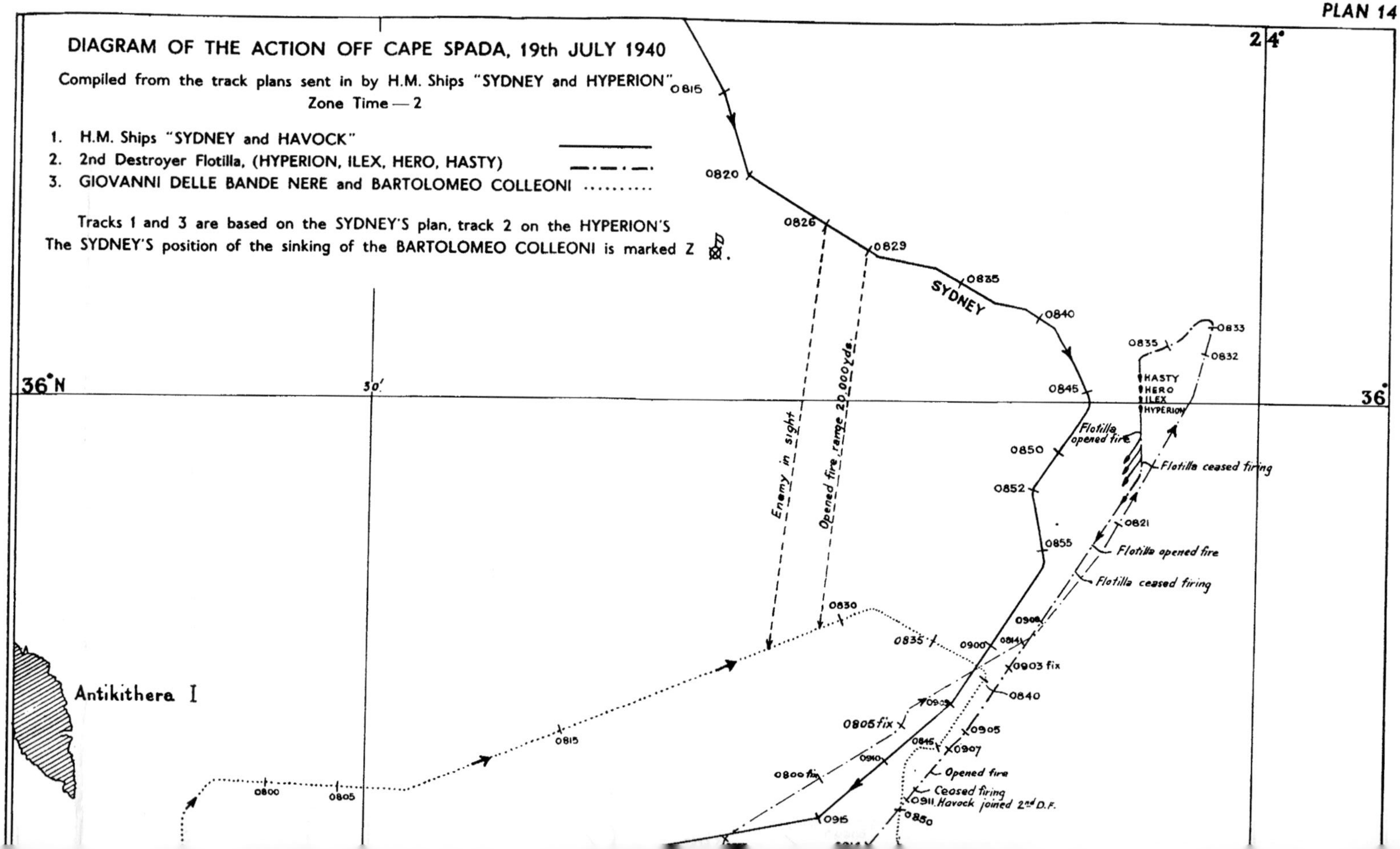
DIAGRAM OF THE ACTION OFF CAPE SPADA, 19th JULY 1940
Compiled from the track plans sent in by H.M. Ships "SYDNEY and HYPERION"
Zone Time — 2
1. H.M. Ships "SYDNEY and HAVOCK"
2. 2nd Destroyer Flotilla, (HYPERION, ILEX, HERO, HASTY)
3. GIOVANNI DELLE BANDE NERE and BARTOLOMEO COLLEONI
Tracks 1 and 3 are based on the SYDNEY'S plan, track 2 on the HYPERION'S
The SYDNEY'S position of the sinking of the BARTOLOMEO COLLEONI is marked Z
24°
36°N
36°
30'
Antikithera I
SYDNEY
0815
0820
0826
0829
0835
0840
0845
0850
0852
0855
0900
0915
HASTY
HERO
ILEX
HYPERION
0832
0833
0821
Flotilla opened fire
Flotilla ceased firing
Enemy in sight
Opened fire range 20,000yds.
0800
0805
0830
0903 fix
0905
0907
0805 fix
0800 fix
Opened fire
Ceased firing
0911 Havock joined 2nd D.F.
0850

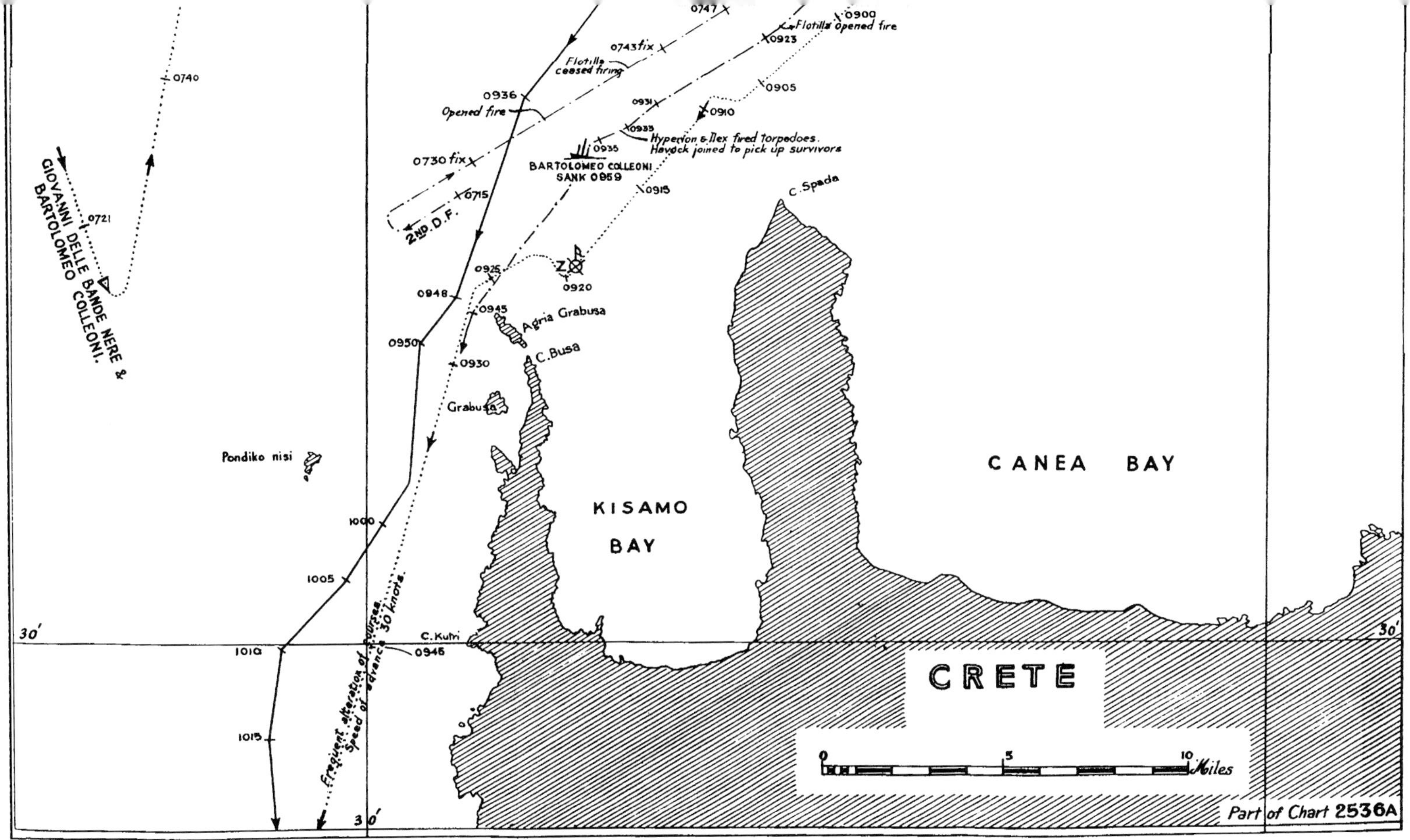
GIOVANNI DELLE BANDE NERE & BARTOLOMEO COLLEONI.
0721
0740
0747
0743 fix
Flotilla ceased firing
0900
Flotilla opened fire
0923
0905
0910
0931
0933
Hyperion & Ilex fired torpedoes.
Havock joined to pick up survivors
0935
BARTOLOMEO COLLEONI SANK 0959
0915
0936
Opened fire
0730 fix
0715
2ND D.F.
0925
0920
0948
0945
Agria Grabusa
C. Busa
0950
0930
Grabusa
C. Spada
Pondiko nisi
KISAMO BAY
CANEA BAY
1000
1005
Frequent alteration of courses.
Speed of advance 30 knots.
30′
C. Kutri
0946
1010
1015
CRETE
0
5
10
Miles
Part of Chart 2536A

PLAN 15

The Swordfish Strike in Bomba Bay — 22-8-40
FROM ADMIRALTY ACCOUNT OF NAVAL AIR OPERATIONS, "THE FLEET AIR ARM," CHAP. 1

KEY

Capt. Patch ——— Lt. Wellham —·—·— Lt. Cheeseman ··········

TSO/HS(585)

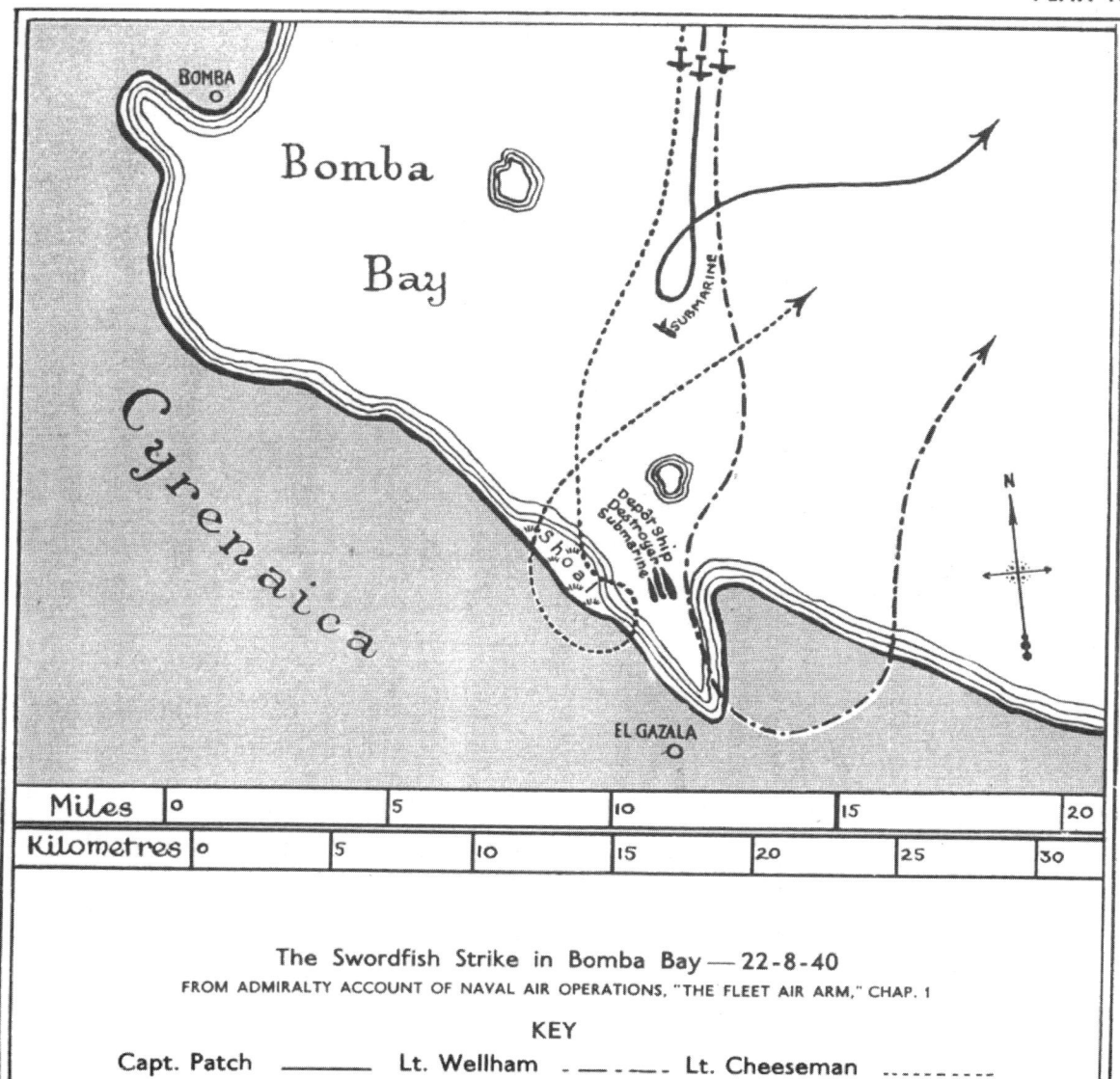

PLAN 16

Operations in Cyrenaica — June–Dec. 1940

FROM "CAMPAIGNS IN THE MIDDLE EAST" (Sec'n. 1) HISTORICAL SECTION OF THE WAR CABINET

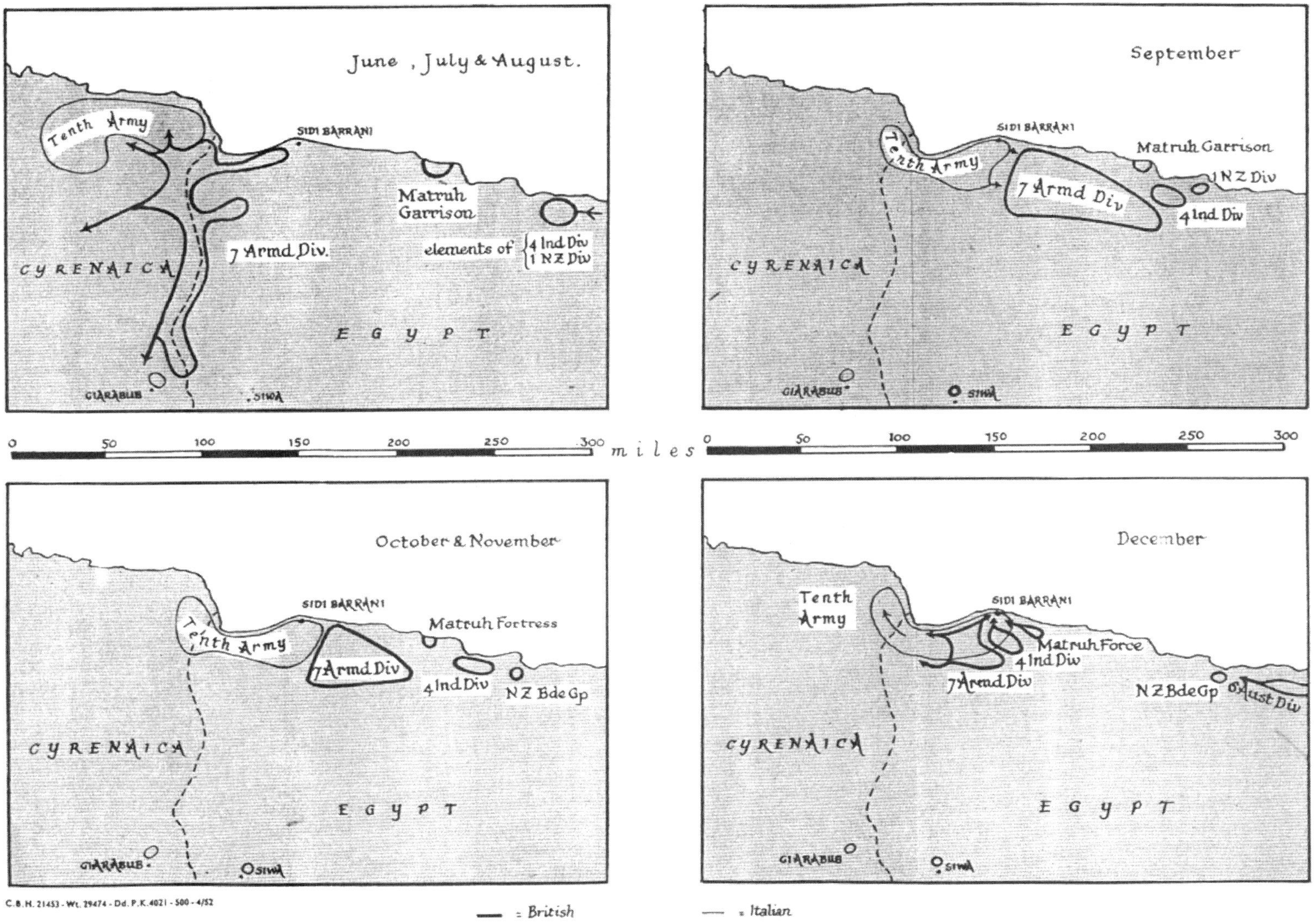